# Caving in Derbyshire
## – 17th Century style

– as described in this extract from *"Journal of Edward and Thomas Browne's Tour into Derbyshire in 1662"*, written by Sir Thomas Browne (1605-1682).

'And so wee led our horses downe a steep mountain to Castleton, so called from the castle situated upon the left buttock of the peak hill. As soon as wee were got to the town, wee prepar'd our selves to see this place so much talk'd of, called, save your presence, the devill's arse, which in my judgement is no unfit appellation considering its figure, whose picture I could wish were here inserted, but for want of it you must bee content with this barren description.

At the bottome of the backside of a high rocky mountain, bipartite at the top and perpendicularly steep from thence to the leavell of the ground, wee beheld a vast hole or den which was presently understood by us to bee the anus, into which by the helpe of light and guides wee did not onely enter, but travailed some space up the intestinum rectum, and had made further discovery of the intralls had the way been good, and the passage void of excrement; but the monster having drunke hard the day before, did vent as fast now, and wee, thinking it not good sayling up Styx against the tide; after some inspection, with no small admiration of these infernall territories, wee returned again to the upper world.

The next place wee saw, two miles distance from hence, was Elden hole, a pit such vast depth, that the greatest ingines and the boldest fellows that could bee found to goe down could never find any bottome. Several have descended eight score fathom, and have neither found water nor can perceive any bottom, it struck some terror in us to hear the noise of the stones which wee threw downe, so long after they were out of our hand. This hole is a fitter place for cleanly conveyance then I know, and any thing once thrown in is as safe as if it were in the moon. One wretched villain confessed upon a time at the gallows that hee rob'd a gentleman and threw him in together with his horse.'

The following poem was written by participants of a Derbyshire Poet Laureate workshop led by Cathy Grindrod held at Poole's Cavern on 8 July 2006.

## Cave

Captured and held, a coral sea,
warm slowing water
replaced by cool still air.
Darting fish long turned to stone,
now evolved into bats
that flit this upturned world.
Whirlpool stone funnel chamber
projecting sense of up out to sky,
down into core, moving,
spinning dance in rock
with a curtained audience
of crustacean memory.

If a man looks up and sees beauty,
he follows it in his spirit.
Here is the one green gift –
a fern arrowing the way to light.
Somehow, life finds a way.

Here are the antennae of the cave,
the snails' eyes, listening and watching
as the water tank of the old house fills.

The wishing stone, a giant mammary,
nipple inverted, a thousand wishes
drip feeding in to nourish it,
reversing nature.
A dropped breast, hard blancmange,
shot with wishes.

In the final end chamber
almost an altar,
coated glistening calcite brain.
A sugar coated boulder,
a glacier, snow-frosted winterscape
in miniature, cauliflower-cheese shaped,
twinkling crystals encrusted.

The pilgrimage to the shrine,
arrival at the sanctuary.
The holy of holies.
Here she lies in her crystal splendour,
always forming,

holding memory in her bones.

© Cathy Grindrod and participants. Reproduced by kind permission of Derbyshire County Council.

# Caves of the Peak District

Compiled by
Iain Barker & John S. Beck
on behalf of the
Derbyshire Caving Association

Entrance to Peak Cavern – from a late 19th Century print

**2010 Edition**

First published 1964
as "Caves of Derbyshire"
5th edition 1984
6th edition 1991
This edition 2010

ISBN: 978-0-9563473-2-9

©

**DERBYSHIRE CAVING ASSOCIATION**

All rights reserved. No part of this publication may be reproduced, stored in a retrieval system, or transmitted, in any form or by any means, electronic, mechanical, photocopying, recording or otherwise, without the prior permission of the Derbyshire Caving Association.

This book is sold subject to the condition that it shall not, by way of trade or otherwise, be lent, re-sold, hired out or otherwise circulated without the prior consent of the Derbyshire Caving Association in any form or binding or cover other than that in which it is published and without a similar condition including this condition being imposed on the subsequent purchaser.

Designed and Published for and on behalf of the
Derbyshire Caving Association
by
Hucklow Publishing

Printed by Northend Creative Print Solutions
Sheffield

# CONTENTS

|  | Page |
|---|---|
| Acknowledgements | 7 |
| Area Map | 8 |
| Introduction | 9 |
| The British Caving Association | 10 |
| The Derbyshire Caving Association | 10 |
| The Cave Diving Group | 11 |
| Plan to be Safe | 12 |
| Cave Rescue | 13 |
| Radon in Derbyshire Caves | 15 |
| Weather forecasts and other information | 15 |
| Cave Conservation in Derbyshire | 16 |
| Geological Cave and Mine SSSI areas | 19 |
| Bats in Underground sites | 20 |
| Cave and Mine Archaeology | 22 |
| Abbreviations | 26 |
| The Grading System | 26 |
| Further Reading | 27 |
| The Caves | |
|     *Alderley Edge* | *29* |
|     *Ashover and Crich* | *33* |
|     *Bradbourne Brook* | *37* |
|     *Bradford* | *41* |
|     *Bradwell* | *45* |
|     *Buxton* | *65* |
|     *Castleton* | *76* |
|     *Derwent South (Matlock etc)* | *139* |
|     *Dove* | *167* |
|     *Gritstone Caves* | *188* |
|     *Hamps and Manifold* | *191* |
|     *Lathkill* | *225* |
|     *Magnesian Limestone* | *247* |
|     *Stoney Middleton* | *253* |
|     *Wormhill* | *291* |
|     *Wye* | *297* |
| Glossary | 312 |

## MAPS AND SURVEYS

Page
| | |
|---|---|
| 8 | Location of areas covered in the book |
| 19 | Cave and Mine SSSI areas |
| 28 | The Main Workings at Alderley Edge |
| 32 | Caves of the Ashover Inlier |
| 36 | Caves of the River Bradford and Bradbourne Brook Catchment Areas |
| 46 | Caves of the Bradwell Catchment Area |
| 48 | *Bagshawe Cavern* |
| 57 | *Hazlebadge Cave* |
| 59 | *Long Rake Mine* |
| 60 | *Moorfurlong Mine* |
| 64 | Caves of the Buxton Catchment Area |
| 72 | *Poole's Cavern* |
| 77 | Caves of the Castleton Catchment Area |
| 79 | *Blue John Cavern* |
| 83 | *Christmas Swallet* |
| 86 | *Dr Jackson's and Perryfoot Caves* |
| 89 | *Eldon Hole* |
| 90 | *Gautries Hole and Car Pot* |
| 92 | *Giants Hole* |
| 103 | *Nettle Pot* |
| 106 | *Odin Mine* |
| 112 | *P8 – Jackpot* |
| 116 | *Peak and Speedwell Caverns key plan* |
| 118 | *Peak and Speedwell Caverns eastern area* |
| 119 | *Peak and Speedwell Caverns western area* |
| 135 | *Winnats Head Cave* |
| 138 | Caves of the Derwent South (Matlock) Catchment Area |
| 143 | *Brightgate Cave* |
| 146 | *Cumberland Cavern and Wapping Mine* |
| 147 | *Devonshire Cavern* |
| 155 | *Jug Holes Mine and Cave* |
| 159 | *Old Ash Mine and Cavern* |
| 168 | Caves of the Dove Catchment (South) |
| 169 | Caves of the Dove Catchment (North) |
| 179 | *Owl Hole* |
| 183 | *Robin's Shaft Mine* |
| 189 | Gritstone Caves |

| Page | |
|---|---|
| 192 | Caves of the Hamps and Manifold Catchment Areas |
| 193 | Caves of the Wettonmill Area |
| 197 | *Darfar Crag Swallet, Darfar Pot, Moonmilk Pot and Riverside Swallet* |
| 208 | *Ladyside Pot* |
| 214 | *Redhurst Swallet* |
| 220 | *Waterways Swallet* |
| 226 | Caves of the River Lathkill Catchment area |
| 227 | Caves of the Upper Lathkill |
| 229 | *Lower Cales Dale Cave* |
| 235 | *Knotlow Cavern and Hillocks Mine* |
| 238 | *Lathkill Head Cave* |
| 244 | *Water Icicle Close Cavern* |
| 246 | Caves of the Magnesian Limestone between Maltby and Mansfield |
| 248 | Caves of Creswell Gorge |
| 254 | Caves of the Stoney Middleton Catchment Area |
| 255 | Caves of Stoney Middleton Dale |
| 259 | *Carlswark Cavern and Merlin Mine* |
| 265 | *Eyam Dale House Cave* |
| 267 | *Fatigue Pot* |
| 270 | *Hungerhill Swallet* |
| 273 | *Lay-by Pot* |
| 279 | *Nickergrove Mine* |
| 284 | *Streaks Pot and Yoga Cave* |
| 286 | *Waterfall Hole* |
| 290 | Caves of the Wormhill Springs Catchment Area |
| 293 | *Cowlow Pot* |
| 296 | Caves of the Central River Wye Catchment Area |
| 303 | *Holme Bank Chert Mine* |

## Acknowledgements

The authors would like to thank the following for their assistance in the revisions for this edition:

D. Arveschoug, J. Barnatt, M. Bennett, I. Bishop, S. Brooks, P. Bush, P. Chandler, A. Chamberlain, J. Cordingley, R. Dearman, R. Eavis, A. Foster, J. Gunn, C. Knox, R. Lockyer, P. Lydon, M. Milner, D. Nixon, J.E. Potts, R. Shone, W. Sheldon, J. Taylor, P. Vale, D. Webb, R.H. Whitehouse, J. Wilmot.

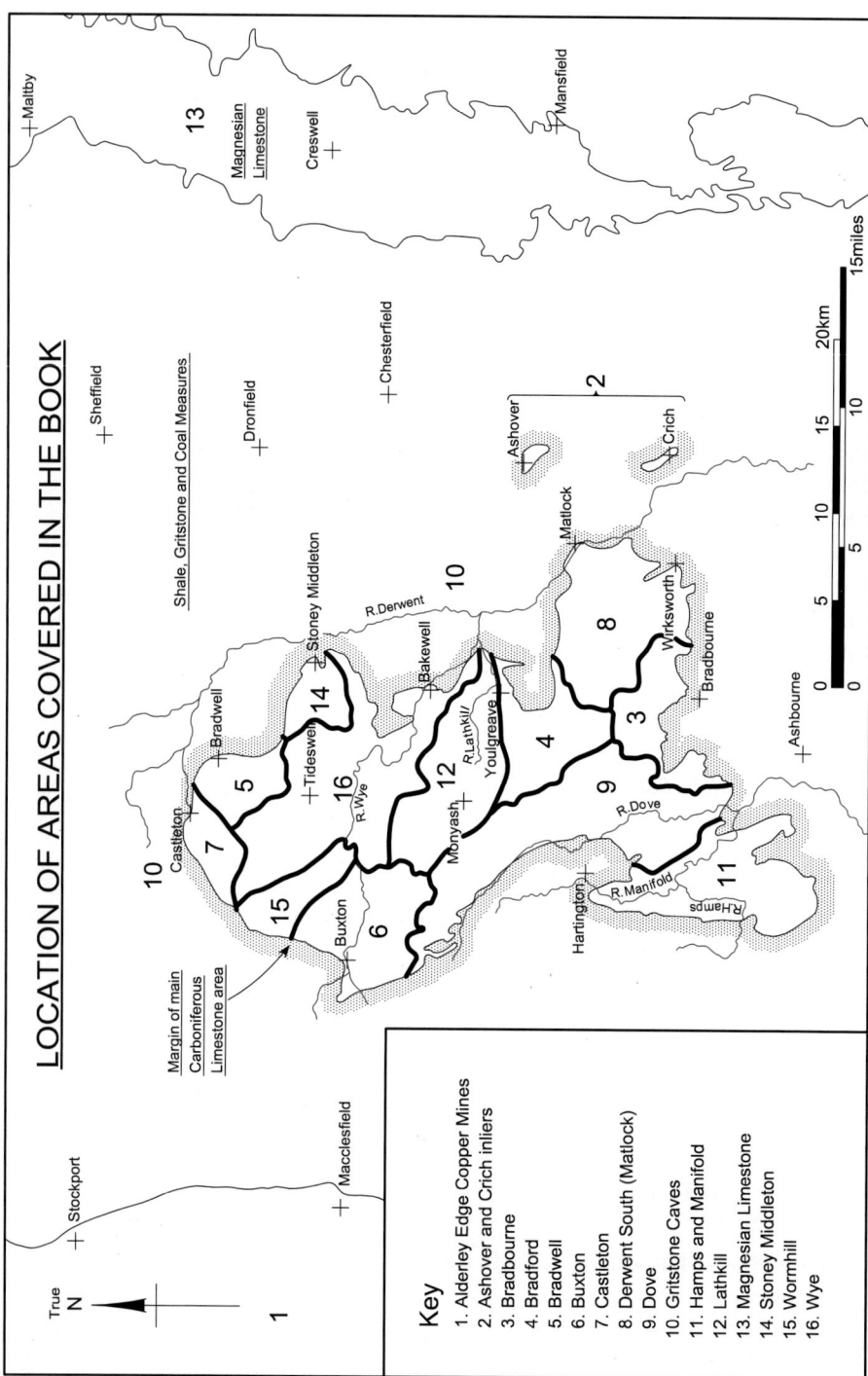

# INTRODUCTION

This edition is based largely on the previous editions compiled by T.D. Ford, D. Allsop, T. Travis, D.W. Gill, J.S. Beck and many other cavers who have supplied their information.

As in the 1991 edition, the caves are listed in alphabetical order within the catchment areas of the major resurgences or rivers. The actual catchment areas depend on the underlying geological structure and are therefore complex and not yet completely defined, so the areas in the book are drawn according to the surface topography. The caves of the central River Wye are grouped in one area, as there are few known caves and many small risings. Some caves in the south of the area drain to the River Churnet, and they are included in the Hamps / Manifold area.

The references are intended to give an overview of the caves, and particularly of discoveries or extensions made since the last edition. It is essential that cavers publish the results of new digs and discoveries in widely circulated journals, for it is from these that a lot of the information is derived.

Some unnamed sites are listed at the end of the relevant sections. Some of these may be rock shelters with no speleological interest, but they are listed for completeness.

Only basic tackle information is given, ie. rope lengths, or ladder and lifeline requirements where appropriate. Pitch lengths are given, and rigging guides are now available for popular caves. Rigging is very much a matter of opinion, and Single Rope Techniques are now used almost exclusively on big pitches in preference to ladders and lifelines. Only cavers proficient in SRT should attempt such descents. The authors consider that such cavers will have the knowledge and expertise to use their own initiative in deciding on rigging techniques, and the safety and position of the belays used in order to carry out a safe descent. It should be borne in mind that artificial belays deteriorate with age, and they should be assessed carefully by those using them.

Basic access details are given. However, more detailed access and rigging descriptions are to be found the Caves of the Peak District Access and Rigging Guide. Access arrangements should be strictly adhered to as failure to do so could well lead to access being denied to cavers in the future. Where no access details are available this does not mean there is a public right of way. Permission should be politely requested from the tenant or landowner. If in doubt contact the Derbyshire Caving Association Access Officer.

The authors, the Derbyshire Caving Association, and the publishers cannot accept any responsibility for errors or inaccuracies in this guide, although every effort has been made to make the guide as accurate as possible. It will help if any errors or omissions could be notified to Iain Barker (56 Thornbridge Crescent, Birley, Sheffield S12 3AE) or John Beck (Glebe Cottage, The Hillock, Eyam, Hope Valley S32 5RB: e-mail john.beck6@btinternet.com).

## The British Caving Association

The British Caving Association (BCA) is the official national governing body for the sport of caving. It co-ordinates regional and club activities through the work of various committees, including access and conservation, training, equipment, legal and insurance. It also publishes a journal, "Speleology", and various other useful guides and pamphlets. It is open to club and individual members and all cavers are encouraged to join to support the work it does on their behalf. Full details can be found on its web site at www.british-caving.org.uk, or by writing to its headquarters at The Old Methodist Chapel, Great Hucklow, Buxton, Derbyshire, SK17 8RG.

The British Cave Research Association (BCRA) is a constituent body of BCA and focuses more closely on the scientific side of caving, including research into geology, geomorphology, biology, archaeology and the technical aspects of caving. It publishes a peer-reviewed scientific journal, "Cave and Karst Science", as well as a series of occasional publications. It also organises regular symposia and meetings. Further details can be found on the web site at: www.bcra.org.uk, or by writing to the address above.

## The Derbyshire Caving Association

The Derbyshire Caving Association (DCA) was formed in 1960, and membership is open to any caving club, non-club group or individual interested in caves and caving in the Peak District and adjoining areas.

DCA's main function is to maintain access to the caves and mines, promote conservation, and provide a united negotiating body to deal with the ever increasing pressure on our caves. It is directly responsible on behalf of the national body for caving, the British Caving Association (BCA), for all access and conservation matters on a regional basis.

DCA also disseminates information to its members by means of a regular newsletter, information circulars, its website and through its meetings. It produces an updated "Peak District Access and Rigging Guide" (free to members) at intervals to complement the book: "Caves of the Peak District".

Current addresses for all caving clubs active in the Peak District and adjoining areas can be obtained from the DCA Secretary. For current information on contacting DCA see our website at www.theDCA.org.uk or write to the British Caving Association at: The Old Methodist Chapel, Great Hucklow, Buxton, Derbyshire. SK17 8RG.

## The Derbyshire Cave Registry

The Cave Registry was set up in order to collect all available data on Derbyshire caves. It is constantly updated, and provides a source of up to date information for both sporting cavers and researchers.

The Registry is, of course, only kept up to date by cavers reporting their discoveries. The current Cave Registry Secretary is John Beck, Glebe Cottage, Eyam, Hope Valley. S32 5RB, who will be pleased to receive any amendments or additions.

## Cave Diving

The Peak District cave systems have many sections which are totally flooded. A few can conveniently be baled or siphoned but most are permanent and require cavers to submerge themselves in order to pass or explore these "sumps". Short flooded sections may sometimes be negotiated by holding ones breath as a "free dive". This is potentially hazardous and should only be attempted by very experienced cavers. In many cases prior knowledge about the sump (and line situation) and extra equipment (other than that normally taken caving) are essential to reduce the risk.

Most sumps are too long, awkward or deep to be free dived and so full diving equipment is needed. This requires extensive training and anyone remotely interested in this aspect of caving should get in touch with the Cave Diving Group. Full information is available on the CDG website at www.cavedivinggroup.org.uk together with further contact details. The CDG exists to "educate and support cavers for recreational and exploratory operations in British sump conditions". It publishes indexes of sumps for each caving region, training literature and a quarterly newsletter. The most recent information on sumps in caves within this guide book may be found in the CDG's Peak District Sump Index 1994 and the Peak District Sump Index Update 1997, together with CDG Newsletters published since 1997. At the time of writing there is a new sump index in preparation.

Anyone wishing to learn cave diving is normally expected to be an experienced caver first. Certain other diving organisations teach some cave diving skills to people who are already divers; in general such training is not considered appropriate for the often difficult conditions encountered in British sumps. Cavers join the CDG via one of four regional Sections; those interested in the Peak District's sumps should make contact with the Derbyshire Section. Anyone diving in caves should submit dive logs to the CDG newsletter editor so that a complete record of exploratory work is maintained.

Modern cave diving often involves considerable depth and long submersions, which increase the risk of a serious condition (after diving) known as decompression illness or "the bends". Symptoms and signs include pain in joints, nervous system problems (such as tingling, paralysis, visual disturbance, becoming withdrawn), skin rashes or breathing difficulties. If a diver is suffering from any of the above then help must be sought urgently. Call 999 and ask for cave rescue in the normal way. Explain that this is a diving emergency; all British cave rescue teams have the necessary information to deal with this effectively. First aid treatment involves the casualty breathing oxygen (if available), drinking fluids (but not those containing caffeine) and being despatched to a recompression chamber. These three measures, which can be remembered as OFD, are needed as fast as possible. Any cavers helping on a diving project should be aware of this information and be ready to take the above action if necessary.

John Cordingley

# A Plan to be Safe

All parties should be properly organised, equipped, and supervised by a responsible and experienced leader.

Pick a cave or mine well known to the leader and within everyone's capabilities.

Let others know where you are going.

Ask for permission to enter sites on private land, and securely replace gates, grills, and shaft cappings.

No less than 3 in the party, and no more than 3 novices for each experienced leader makes sense.

Take notice of the weather forecast before going down caves where water flows.

One helmet and reliable cap lamp for each person.

Beware of disturbing stacked rock, loose boulders or props, especially in mines.

Ensure that ladders, belays, ropes are rigged properly before hanging your life on them.

Someone should carry emergency lights, food and first aid.

Act sensibly – do not drop stones down mine shafts or cave pitches.

Falls, loose boulders, flood water, exhaustion and being cold and wet cause most accidents – take care.

Exit takes more effort than entry, especially on long trips-plan with the return in mind.

## In the Event of an Accident Underground

1. Decide whether outside help is needed or not.
2. To summon help, send competent persons to the surface with reliable information for passing to the authorities (see paragraph 5 below).
3. Administer First Aid. Bearing in mind the inevitable delay before rescuers arrive, encourage injured persons who are still mobile to start moving towards the surface. At all events, reassure and keep injured persons warm.
4. To call out the D.C.R.O. telephone 999 and ask for Cave Rescue.
5. Useful initial information for passing to the Police:-
    i. Identity of person telephoning and where calling from.
    ii. Name of cave or mine and its location.
    iii. Wheareabouts in the cave or mine the accident occurred.
    iv. Time and nature of accident and injuries sustained.
    v. Number of persons still underground at the scene.
6. The caller should be prepared to stay within reach of a phone to give any further information required.

## Cave Rescue in the Peak District

Underground searches and rescues in the places described in this book are carried out by the Derbyshire Cave Rescue Organisation (DCRO) acting on behalf of the police. DCRO is one of currently fifteen similar voluntary organisations who collectively provide rescue cover to the whole of the British Isles. All are members of the British Cave Rescue Council (see http://caverescue.org.uk).

DCRO was founded in 1952 by the major caving clubs then operating in the Peak District primarily as a sort of practical self help insurance for their own members following the logic that cavers are the best people to be going into caves and rescuing cavers! This reasoning is still valid and current team members are therefore experienced and active local cavers.

Since its formation DCRO teams have been out on hundreds of occasions, not only to rescue cavers but also to search for missing persons, recover animals from mineshafts and support the other emergency services when our skills are needed. There are hundreds of people (thousands when families and friends are taken into account) who have cause to be grateful that DCRO exists.

Today the team is around 150 strong and is made up of a number of components with different levels of commitment. The core of the team is some 40 to 50 members who volunteer to undertake training in rescue techniques, casualty care, the use of specialist equipment, search and rescue management and so on. Backing up this core are a further 100 plus cavers some of whom are specialists (e.g. cave divers) and some are probationary members undergoing their initial training.

Anybody who is a competent caver or who has specialist skills needed by the team may apply to become a probationary member by writing to the secretary. If accepted, they then have to undertake some initial training in search and rescue skills before becoming eligible for full team membership.

DCRO maintains a comprehensive stock of access, rescue, first aid, communications and underground engineering equipment which it keeps together with its rescue vehicle at Buxton fire station, courtesy of the Derbyshire Fire and Rescue Service.

The Organisation is run by a committee of officers and members who are elected annually by the team members. Operations are managed and led by controllers and leaders appointed (and assessed annually) by the committee. There are no paid officials and everybody involved at every level is an unpaid volunteer.

The organisation has to raise all the money it needs for its vehicle, equipment, training and running costs itself. This involves a lot of effort on the part of volunteer team members and a lot of generosity from members of the general public (most of whom are not cavers!). We are a registered charity (no. 1017362).

There are a number of ways for you or your club to help to maintain DCRO's service to the Peak District and its cavers. You can be a rescue team member (and if you are an active local caver why aren't you already?) or you can help once in a while with fund raising. Your club can become a member body of the Organisation paying an annual subscription and it can also help to raise money by running or supporting fund raising events. What about it?

If you do want to help or even if you only want to find more information about DCRO please visit our website at http://derbyshirecro.org.uk.

Photos of the Derbyshire Cave Rescue team in action. On the left is from an actual rescue at Giants in 2004 when a casualty with serious back injuries was being brought out after falling down Garlands Pot. The one below was taken in the Peak streamway during an excercise when a 'casualty' was evacuated from Main Stream to Victoria Aven. Photos by Bill Whitehouse

## Radon in Peak District Caves

When the last edition of COPD was published in 1991 the potential risks from exposure to radon in caves had only recently been recognised and it was felt necessary to provide some general background information. Since then, the National Cave Association (NCA) Radon Working Party prepared a very useful publication, "Radon Underground" which was updated in 2005 and is now available from the British Caving Association (http://british-caving.org.uk). A summary was published in "Cave and Karst Science" 23(2), 1996, p.49-56. General information on radon is available on the Health Protection Agency website (http://www.hpa.org.uk/radiation/radon/index.htm). As these sources provide all relevant background material this is not repeated here but two points need to be emphasised :

(1) by law anyone providing instructed caving needs to have their radiation dose monitored even if they are self-employed. PICA (Peak Instructed Caving Affiliation; http://www.thedca.org.uk/PICA.htm) can provide more information. (2) Recreational caving lies outside of the Ionising Radiations Regulations (1999) but the predecessor of the HPA, the National Radiation Protection Board (NRPB) have suggested a time integrated radiation dose limit of 106 Bq m-3 h in any year.

In terms of radon measurements in Peak District caves, Rob Hyland completed his PhD on cave radon in 1995 and this included a full year of radon measurements in selected Peak District caves. Further measurements have been made by PICA working with the Limestone Research Group. They show that some Peak District caves, especially those in the Castleton area, have very high concentrations of radon (and radon decay products), particularly in those months when the outside air temperature is greater than 9°C. Individuals spending long hours in these caves need to be aware that they are likely to accrue a high radiation dose and that, in the words of the HPA web site : "There is a great deal of evidence that exposure to radon, or rather its decay products, leads to lung cancer in miners."

John Gunn

## Weather Information

Some Peak District Caves are susceptible to flooding in wet weather. A few can become impassable or even flood to the roof. Nowadays the easiest source of local weather forecasts is the Met. Office website, at www.metoffice.gov.uk/weather/ and follow links to the nearest listed town to your area. Alternatively you can dial Weathercall on 09014 722 062 then when connected enter 1202 for Bakewell or 1203 for Buxton. In 2010 this cost 60p per minute (at date of publication).

# Cave Conservation in Derbyshire

Caves form a unique and vulnerable part of our natural heritage. It takes tens to hundreds of thousands of years for cave passages to form, along with beautiful and delicate cave formations, and for life to colonise and develop within a cave. It takes only a moment for irreparable damage to occur. We have a duty to conserve caves for the benefit and enjoyment of future generations.

Cave conservation is important for several reasons:

- Caves are an integral part of our natural heritage and are worthy of conservation in their own right.
- Caves provide a valuable scientific and educational resource.
- Caves are important habitats for bats and other specialised life forms, which have evolved to live underground.
- Caves and cave formations are aesthetically important, providing some of the most amazing natural spectacles on Earth.
- Caves provide a valuable recreational resource.

Caves are at risk from both external and internal activities. Quarrying, landfill and some land management practices are examples of external activities which can be damaging. Potentially damaging internal activities include irresponsible caving.

## External Threats

Quarrying can be a serious threat to cave conservation and, in extreme cases, can result in complete destruction of cave passages. Landfilling of disused quarries can lead to loss of access to caves and can cause serious pollution of cave systems. Processes which affect the water table level or cause water pollution can damage or destroy cave systems. These include water extraction, inappropriate use of fertilisers, distribution of certain types of waste material on farmland and dumping of effluent.

## Internal pressures

From the moment a cave is discovered, deterioration begins. Damage inevitably occurs as a result of the passage of cavers. Conservation is about limiting or avoiding this damage. It is important that cavers are aware of the importance of cave conservation. If cavers follow a number of simple guidelines as part of normal caving, then much of this damage can be minimised.

- Observe taped routes.
- Treat calcite formations with great care – avoid breakage.
- Do not leave litter or dump carbide
- Take care not to disturb cave life, especially bats.
- Cave sediments are vulnerable. Do not trample needlessly on undisturbed deposits.
- Archaeological and palaeontological features should be left undisturbed. This is especially important in and around the entrance to the cave.
- Digging should take place in a responsible manner. Notify Natural England if dig

site is within an SSSI (see below).
- Artificial aids should be kept to a minimum.
- Supervise novice cavers carefully and follow any recommendations to limit numbers in group.
- Respect mining artefacts and structures.

## SSSIs and Cave Conservation Monitoring

Approximately 75% of known cave passage in the UK is located within designated Sites of Special Scientific Interest (SSSIs). In England, Natural England is the government agency which has responsibilty for the designation and conservation of SSSIs. Regular underground monitoring is an important part of cave conservation.

A very effective method of monitoring caves is for cavers to record their observations about condition of underground features and provide reports to Natural England. In 2002, a national strategy for cave monitoring by cavers was agreed between Natural England, the NCA (now BCA) and the BCRA. For legal reasons, Natural England cannot request cavers to visit specific caves or parts thereof, but is requesting information on cave condition obtained by cavers in the course of their normal caving activities.

The project was carried to Derbyshire with enthusiasm. Since 2002, the DCA and local caving clubs have been working in partnership with Natural England on monitoring cave SSSIs in the county. Designated SSSI area coordinators take responsibility for each SSSI to coordinate the field work in their area. Cavers report on the condition of each cave and its special features as part of a normal caving trip. Local divers even provide information on the condition of cave passage and features in sumped sections. This information is entered onto a site-specific monitoring form and passed to the DCA Conservation Officer to ensure consistent reporting. The forms are then submitted to Natural England.

The system as operated in Derbyshire has been in use for three years and is uniquely successful. It continues to provide valuable information to Natural England, who in return have provided funding through DCA to enable the caving community to complete much-needed clean-ups and other work in and around cave entrances. The SSSI area coordinators and Natural England meet twice-yearly to provide feedback, discuss and prioritise conservation issues in their "patch".

It is important to understand that the features of interest in cave SSSIs have been selected primarily for their scientific value and not necessarily their aesthetic appearance. Hence, a much-abused muddy speleothem on a tourist route may not look important but can still provide evidence of ancient climatic conditions and the timing of cave development. Cave sediments generally warrant little more than a passing glance from the average caver. We happily wallow though mud and sand with little thought as to how they got there, but cave sediments are an essential part of the evolutionary history of the cave system, and, if undisturbed, can provide valuable geological information.

## Statutory Protection

It is estimated that up to 75% of all known cave passage in England has a Site of Special Scientific Interest (SSSI) designation, affording a high degree of statutory protection for these caves systems. Natural England is a statutory consultee on any development requiring planning permission, that may directly or indirectly impact on a cave system. When a site is designated as a SSSI, the owners and occupiers are notified of the importance of sites and provided with a list of operations likely to damage the site. Owners and occupiers are required to obtain formal consent from Natural England before undertaking any activities on this list. The list of potentially damaging operations also applies to third party users of a site. For most cave SSSIs, consent is required from Natural England before disturbing or removing any geological materials, such as cave sediments or speleothems. Consent can be granted for sediment disturbance for cave exploration purposes and for removal of specimens for scientific study.

## Some Conservation Measures

**Taped Pathways.** Several of our more vulnerable caves, such as Dreamtime, Lathkill Upper Entrance, Darfar Ridge Cave, The Kingdom and others, have taped pathways to minimise damage to sediments and formations. The DCA Conservation Team hold equipment and quantities of plastic tape and stainless wire pegs to enable threatened sections of existing cave and new discoveries to be similarly treated. This system, whereby the narrow orange tape can be pegged clear of the floor and the pegs fixed in rock or sediment, is gaining acceptance as it is both visible and sympathetic to the cave environment at the same time. By pointing the end of the wire loop of the pegs into the "no-go" area, it is also apparent which side of the tape you should be on.

**Clothing.** Delicate formations have been protected from becoming smeared with mud in at least one new discovery in Bagshawe Cavern, where lightweight coveralls were made available to change into on entering and leaving the more vulnerable areas.

**Digging.** The discovery of new cave passage is the holy grail of cave exploration but brings with it a responsibility to protect important scientific features for future generations to enjoy and study. Digging activity within an SSSI, whilst not discouraged, needs prior consultation with Natural England in order to confirm that important features will not be damaged or removed during the dig and to obtain consent for the dig. In most cases this is a formality.

**Removal of material.** Consent from Natural England is also required before removing any material, such as mineral specimens or speleothems from a cave SSSI.

Attitudes towards conservation are changing but only slowly, and the topic still remains a "conversation killer" round the bar in the pub. Natural England have entrusted us with the responsibility for our own environment and, like it or not, we must show that this trust is not misplaced.

David Webb, DCA Conservation Officer in conjunction with Natural England, Peak District & Derbyshire Team

# Geological Cave and Mine SSSI areas within the boundary of the Derbyshire White Peak Natural Area

Notes: The Upper Lathkilldale SSSI contains only the Knotlow/Hillocks Complex and is generally counted as one area with Lathkilldale.

Masson Hill SSSI contains seven separate areas, Brightgate, Oxclose, Jugholes, Tearbreeches, the Cumberland/Wapping Complex, the larger area of Masson Hill itself, and Youd's Level.

## SSSI Areas and Caves / Mines

Note: Not all of these sites are currently accessible due to collapse or other reasons.

**Masson Hill:** Masson Hill complex, Devonshire Cavern, Tear Breeches complex, Brightgate Cave, Oxclose Cavern, Jugholes Upper, Jugholes Lower, Cumberland / Wapping complex.

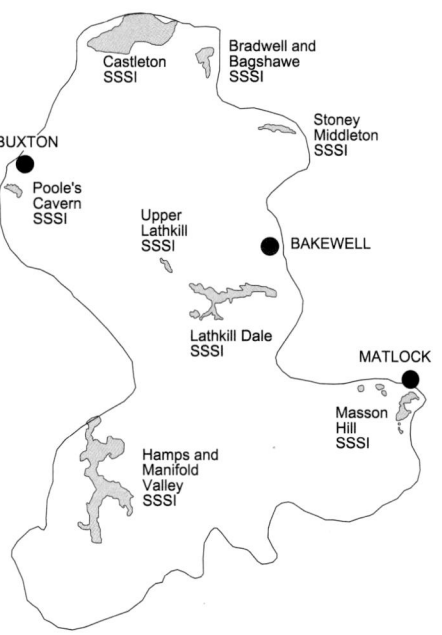

**Bradwell and Bagshawe Cavern:** Bagshawe Cavern, Bradwell Parish Cave, Dowse Hole, Durham Edge Swallet, Hazelbadge Cave, Outlands Head Cave, Walkers Grotto.

**The Hamps and Manifold Valleys:** Darfar Pot, Darfar Ridge Cave, Elderbush Cave, Ladyside Pot, Redhurst Swallet Waterways Swallet.

**Lathkill Dale / Upper Lathkill:** Hillocks/Knotlow Cavern and Mine, Lathkill Head Cave, Lower Cales Dale Cave, Mandale Mine, Water Icicle Close Cavern.

**Pooles Cavern**

**Stoney Middleton Dale:** Bossen Hole, Carlswark Cavern, Cucklet Church Cave, Delph Hole, Eyam Dale House Cave, Hole in the Wall, Hungerhill Swallet, Ivy Green and Keyhole Caves,Lay-by Pot, Nickergrove Mine, Streaks Pot, Waterfall Swallet, Yoga Cave.

**Castleton:** Alsops Cave, Blue John Cavern, Christmas Swallet, Dr Jacksons/Perryfoot/Yoga, Eldon Hole, Eldon Quarry cave, Giants Hole/Oxlow/Maskhill, Gautries Hole/Car Pot, Longcliffe Mine, Nettle Pot, Odin Cave, Odin Mine, Old Tor Mine, Peak and Speedwell Caverns, P5 Swallet, P7 Swallet, P8 (Jackpot), Rowter Hole, Russet Well, Sheepwash Cave, Suicide Cave, Treak Cliff Cavern, Windy Knoll Cave, Winnats Head Cave.

## Bats in Underground Sites

The Peak District is home to at least ten species of bat, half of which regularly make use of underground sites, such as caves, mines, ice houses and railway tunnels at various times of the year. As bat populations have severely declined over the last century all species of bat that occur in the UK have been afforded protection by law making it an offence to damage any place in which they roost or deliberately or recklessly disturb bats.

In recent years there has been a significant increase in cooperation between bat conservationists and members of cave and mine exploration communities within the Peak District. This has led to a better understanding of the issues on both sides and has helped to ensure that cavers and bats co-exist in underground sites quite happily.

In the past, many published caving guides have highlighted caves that have a history of use by bats. It is now considered that most caves and mines in the Peak District are used by bats at some point during the year either as winter hibernation sites, autumn mating sites or throughout the spring and summer as feeding or roosting sites.

Bats are most vulnerable to disturbance whilst breeding (mid-summer) and hibernating (winter). They will return to favoured breeding and hibernation sites and tend to use less disturbed sites.

By following a few simple guidelines we can avoid disturbing bats and still go about our underground activities.

If you find bats:

- Do not be tempted to touch or handle them. The law requires all handlers to possess a licence and you could do significant harm to the bat without the proper training.
- Do not linger. By all means have a brief look – it is only by doing this that we begin to appreciate what it is that we are trying to conserve, but bear in mind that your body heat could arouse the bat from its torpid state which may be harmful to the bat, so keep any observation brief. Each time a bat is woken up during hibernation, it uses up vital energy that has been stored in its body as fat to enable it to sleep through the winter. Arousal uses enough energy for possibly as much as ten day's hibernation.
- Do not shine bright lights directly on bats or use flashguns near bats. Doing so may result in the bats being disturbed (a licence is required to photograph bats).
- Be careful not to dislodge bats. Whilst many bats will tuck themselves into crevices often well out of our way, sometimes they will hang in the open so look ahead and check the walls and ceiling particularly in narrow passages before proceeding.
- Smoking and use of carbide will disturb bats and may even cause them to

move roost sites.
- Avoid congregating in large groups where bats are known to roost.
- The importance of digging as a means of discovering a new cave or mine passage is recognised and can even lead to the creation of new hibernation or roost sites. However it should be borne in mind that the use of some of the more extreme methods employed when enlarging passageways can impact upon any existing bat population and co-operation between cavers and the local bat group will ensure a mutually acceptable solution.

There are still many more people using caves and mines for recreation in the Peak District than there are bat conservationists, so please help in increasing our knowledge of these fascinating creatures by passing your sightings on to the local Bat Group. Contrary to popular belief, bat conservationists have more to gain by working with the caving community than against it.

## Useful contacts:

### Derbyshire Bat Conservation Group
www.derbyshirebats.org.uk,
email: derbybcgos@hotmail.com

c/o Derbyshire Wildlife Trust,
East Mill, Bridge Foot,
Belper,
Derbyshire, DE56 1XH

### Staffordshire Bat Group
c/o Staffordshire Wildlife Trust,
The Wolseley Centre,
Wolseley Bridge,
Stafford, ST17 0WT.
Tel: 01889 880 100

### Natural England
Endcliffe,
Deepdale Business Park,
Ashford Road,
Bakewell,
DE45 1GT.
Tel 01629 816640

Peter Bush

Hibernating bat. Photo Dennis Jump

# Cave and Mine Archaeology

Archaeology is the study of all that has been left by people from the past. In the case of natural caves, people have left artefacts and bones, while in mines, by definition, it is not just miners' artefacts but the cavities and structures created that are of interest. Archaeological remains can tell us much about how caves have been used and about how and when miners delved for lead and other minerals. Thus, it is important to respect this evidence for the benefit of researchers and for underground explorers to see, both now and in the future. For many, going underground is far more that a sporting experience, but a visit to an environment that is full of interest.

The distinction between caves and mines in the Peak District is often blurred in the sense that many caves have been explored and modified by miners where mineral deposits have been found, while mines have just as frequently broken into cave passages. In some cases the minerals were deposited in ancient caves that existed before the mineralising fluids passed through about 300 million years ago. Much more recent cave streams often carved their way through mineralised deposits and laid down sediments further into the cave that were lead-rich, which were worked by miners.

## Caves

Natural caves in the Peak District, particularly in the passages near their entrance, have been used by people for thousands of years. Sometimes they lived here, often on a temporary basis while hunting in the vicinity, or used them as temporary refuges in times of trouble. In other cases caves were used for human burial or for other ritual activity, or to store valuables for safekeeping. Evidence for past cave explorations over the last 200 years is archaeology in its own right.

The remains of past activity, from distant prehistory through the Roman and medieval periods, can take on a variety of forms. These are usually buried in floor deposits and hard to spot even when digging. They include human and animal bones (often the remains of meals, or other occupants of the cave), potsherds, and metal, wooden and bone objects. In ancient cave deposits, bones of exotic animals such a reindeer, bison, elephants and rhinoceros can be present. These, and more commonly evidence from small mammals, birds, snails and pollen, can tell us much about past environments. Sometimes human remains may have been brought into the cave by predators such as hyenas. In other cases remains have been washed in by once-active streams. It is often the exact stratigraphic relationships of finds and soil layers that allow such matters to be answered.

## Mines

All mines are inherently important for the study of their history and archaeology. While many accessible mines date from the 17th century onwards, there has been lead mining in the Peak District since at least Roman times and copper mining at Ecton was started in the Bronze Age nearly 4000 years ago. Occasionally evidence for early mining survives and has been found for example by careful study of the types of pickwork present and the physical evidence for mining techniques such as firesetting (burnt surfaces, sooting, cinders, etc).

Archaeological evidence can take a wide variety of forms and only the more common are noted here. There are worked-out stopes (vein cavities), mineralised caverns, shafts, adits, drainage soughs and engine chambers. The walls can have shotholes from gunpowder work and notches for ladderways, platforms and roof supports. The 'stemples' used for these are often of wood but sometimes of stone. There are stacks of waste rock (deads) and crushed minerals from underground ore processing. The floors of levels often have timber sleepers (or their impressions where removed) and sometimes the wooden or iron tramway rails survive, as do drainage channels. Occasionally miners' artefacts survive, although all too often these have been removed by past explorers. They include ore tubs, tools, powder horns and sharpening stones. Some archaeological evidence is delicate, as with wooden stemples, clay-lined water channels, artefacts, charcoal (that can be used for radio-carbon dating), and now rare examples where miners' clog prints can be found in clay on the floor. In mines, as with archaeological evidence in caves, retaining context is vital.

## Disturbing the Archaeology

For the most part visiting caves and mines does no harm to archaeological evidence as long as you take care not to step on delicate features or, for example, pull down mine deads or wooden stemples. The real problem for many underground explorers comes when they do not recognise the evidence for what it is, and therefore don't know when to treat it with respect. The answer is to seek advice, or better still to explore in the company of people who can explain. Similarly, if artefacts are moved or taken from the cave or mine without adequate recording, then much of their meaning for the researcher is lost. Out of context, an interesting artefact is only that, much of what it can tell us about what people were doing in the cave or mine, and how this relates to previous and subsequent activity, is lost.

Digging in the hope of finding new passages is potentially the major cause of archaeological damage. While this a worthwhile activity in its own right, advice should be sought at the outset about how to proceed while minimising damage. If built-structures, artefacts or bones are found, then digging should be halted until advice has been given upon how to record the finds. Similarly, discussion can take place as to how further digging can be carried out so that as much as possible is left undisturbed, while what is dug through is documented in an appropriate way. Don't forget, it is often not the obvious features such as human skulls or pots full of coins that tell us the most about past human activity, but rather small and insignificant-looking fragments of metal, pottery and bone that are the most informative. Similarly, stratified layers of gravel, sand and clay can hold important evidence invisible to the naked eye about changes in environment through time. It should also be remembered that some caves and mines are designated as Scheduled Monuments or Sites of Special Scientific Interest and it is a prosecutable offence to disturb them without first seeking permission via English Heritage or Natural England.

## Seeking Advice

For designated sites contact the local/regional offices of English Heritage (Northampton/Birmingham) or Natural England (Bakewell). Don't forget, Natural England does not employ archaeologists, and thus separate archaeological advice should be sought for SSSIs. For advice about the archaeology at other sites (or informal advice at designated sites) contact the archaeologists in the Cultural Heritage Team at the Peak District National Park Authority (Bakewell) or the Conservation Officer at Peak District Mines Historical Society (c/o The Mining Museum, Matlock Bath). Advice can also be sought from Archaeology Departments at universities, but not all have specialists in underground archaeology. As contact details for personnel and their addresses can go out of date, these are not given here – it is a simple matter to make contact after first using a web search or telephone directory.

John Barnatt – PDMHS Conservation Officer

Some archaeological features are obvious, such as this very rare ore-chute in Clayton Mine at Ecton. But how many people have noticed the delicate easily damaged soot deposits on the walls from smoke produced in the early 19th century steam engine boiler that once was installed nearby, or the remains of a timber wall that stopped the smoke entering the rest of the working part of the mine, just out of the photograph peeking through the mud behind the figure? One careless footfall would destroy this.

The main chamber in Clayton Mine at Ecton is dominated by the massive chimney base at the end, built in association with nearby steam engines, probably in the 1880s. There are good reasons for not standing in the water, not least the flooded shaft that goes down into the workings that are about 300m deep. However, how many people notice that just beyond are the only two remaining fastening bolts for one of the steam engines set in rotten timbers hidden in the mud; one careless trip would do irreparable damage.

These fastening bolts in Clayton Mine at Ecton, may well be for an air compressor and steam engine installed in the 1880s. While people always walk around these during visits, what is more problematic is the associated timberwork under the water, which after the first of a party has passed becomes obscured as the water clouds with mud. People are not aware there are delicate features unless forewarned by the first to pass.

Many thousands of people have visited the main chamber in Devonshire Cavern at Matlock Bath. Ironically many cavers have assumed this old lead mine has little of interest, whereas careful study has shown that the extensive workings are one of the most important medieval and possibly earlier mines in Britain. Much of the evidence is provided by the character of the walls themselves, which in parts have distinctive smooth surfaces that could only be formed by firesetting, and extensive but delicate soot coatings. There are also layered backfill deposits with buried charcoal that is invaluable for radiocarbon dating.

Photos by Paul Deakin ©

## Abbreviations

| | | | |
|---|---|---|---|
| BCRA | British Cave Research Association | OMMRE | Operation Mole Mines Research and Exploration |
| BCA | British Caving Association | PAS | Peakland Archaeological Society |
| CCPC | Crewe Climbing and Potholing Club | PDHMS | Peak District Mines Historical Society |
| CDG | Cave Diving Group | | |
| CRG | Cave Research Group | RIGS | Regionally Important Geological Site |
| DCC | Derbyshire Caving Club | | |
| DCA | Derbyshire Caving Association | SSSI | Site of Special Scientific Interest |
| DSG | Derbyshire Speleological Group | STPC | Stoke on Trent Pothole Club |
| DUG | Disley Underground Group | SUSS | Sheffield University Speleological Society |
| EEG | Eyam Exploration Group | SYCC | South Yorkshire Caving Club |
| EPC | Eldon Pothole Club | TSG | Technical Speleological Group |
| LRG | Limestone Research Group | TVCG | Trent Valley Cave Exploration Group |
| MSG | Moldywarps Speleological Group | | |
| OCC | Orpheus Caving Club | | |

## The Cave Grading System

These grades should be applied by fit and properly equipped cavers, and can only be regarded as an approximate indication of severity. Novices should bear these facts in mind when undertaking a caving trip. What is to them a Grade 5 will only be a Grade 3 to an expert.

Grade I: Easy caves. No pitches or other difficulties.

Grade II: Moderate caves and small potholes.

Grade III: Caves and potholes without any hazardous, difficult, or dangerous sections.

Grade IV: Caves and potholes which present some hazard or difficulty such as a long underground pitch or a long wet crawl.

Grade V: Caves and potholes which include very strenuous sections, wet underground pitches, or tight and long wet crawls.

Arch: Caves that have been or could be archaeologically excavated.

Dig: Any site of speleological interest which has been or could be dug.

Dive: Accessible only to fully equipped divers.

Lost: Site destroyed or entrance buried.

Mine: Mines or caves that have been modified by mining.

Show: Show caves open to the public.

Spring: A rising with no associated cave passage.

# Further Reading

## Archaeology
Bramwell, D. 1977. *The Archaeology of the Peak*. Moorland, Ashbourne.

Campbell, J. 1978. *The Upper Palaeolithic of Britain*. Oxford University Press.

## Caves
Barker, I. 1997. *Classic Caves of the Peak District*. Crowood Press Ltd.

Cordingley, J.N. & Carter, R.L. 1994. *Peak District Sump Index*. Cave Diving Group.

Cordingley, J.N. & Carter, R.L. 1997. *Peak District Sump Index Update*. Cave Diving Group.

Flindall, R. & Hayes, A. 1976. *Caverns and Mines of Matlock Bath*. Moorland, Ashbourne.

Ford, T.D. (ed) 1977. *Limestones and Caves of the Peak District*. Geo Abstracts Ltd., University of East Anglia, Norwich.

## Lead Mining
Ford, T.D. & Rieuwerts. 2000. *Lead Mining in the Peak District*. Landmark Publishing, Ashbourne.

Rieuwerts, J.H. 2007. *Lead Mining in Derbyshire: History, Development and Drainage. 1.Castleton to the River Wye*. Landmark Publishing, Ashbourne.

## Conservation
Gibbs, T. (ed) 1997. *A Cave Conservation Plan for Jugholes*. BCA.

Hardwick, P. (ed) 1994. *The White River Series, Peak-Speedwell System*. LRG.

Hardwick, P. (ed) 1995. *A Cave Conservation Plan for James Hall's Over Engine Mine & Cave*. Natural England.

Hardwick, P. (ed) 1995. *A Cave Conservation Plan for Darfar Ridge Cave*. Natural England.

Milner, M. 2007. *A Cave & Mine Conservation Audit for the Manifold & Hamps Valleys*. DCA.

Mycroft, D. & Bentham, K. (Ed. Page, K.N.) 1997. *A Management Plan for the Caves of Lathkill Dale*. Natural England.

Webb, D. 2001. *A Cave and Mine Conservation Audit for the Masson Hill Area*. DCA.

In addition to the above general works there are many articles in the journals and newsletters of caving clubs. Many descriptions have appeared in the Derbyshire Caving Association newsletter (now the "Derbyshire Caver"), and in "Descent" magazine. The journals of the British Speleological Association and Cave Research Group, and their successor the British Cave Research Association also contain many detailed descriptions and surveys. Derbyshire's lead mines and their history are extensively covered by the journal of the Peak District Mines Historical Society. Many surveys of popular caves are available through caving shops.

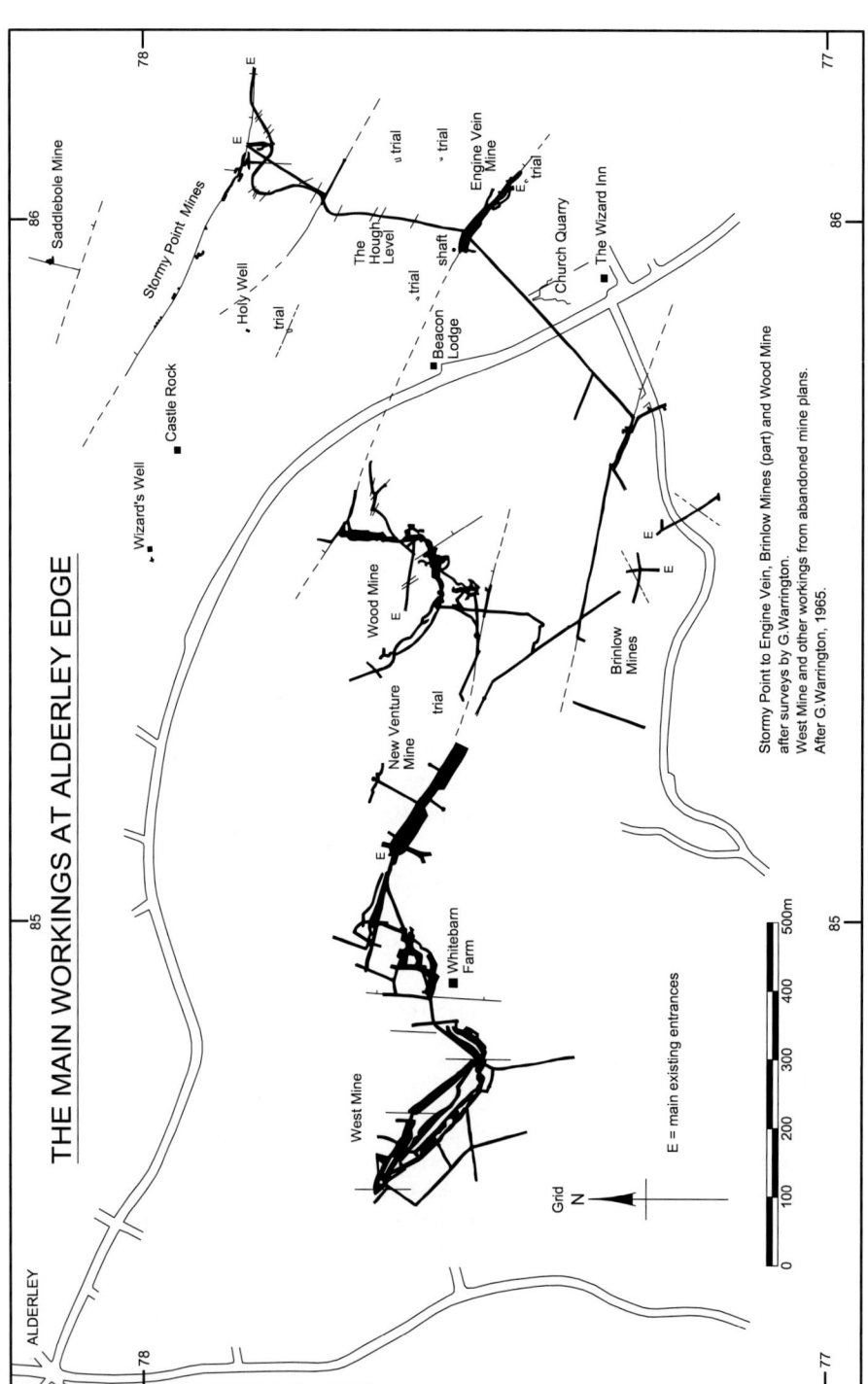

# ALDERLY EDGE

The mines at Alderley Edge are not unique, as there are several similar sites around the Cheshire/Staffordshire basin. Nevertheless, Alderley has long proved of interest because of the extent of the mines and the variety of minerals found there. Geologically, Alderley Edge is a horst of Triassic sandstone, capped with the base of the harder Helsby (Keuper) Sandstone series, but formed mainly of softer Wilmslow (Bunter) Sandstone. The minerals are mainly carbonates of copper and lead, although a considerable amount of galena is also present. Cobalt was mined at times. The history of mining is unknown before 1700, although there is evidence of probable Bronze Age origins. After 1700, the mines were worked sporadically until 1919 with the most productive period being between 1857 and 1877. The mines were blocked off in the 1960's, and have been reopened from 1970 onwards by the Derbyshire Caving Club.

Access. Except for West Mine, all the mines are on National Trust property and have been reopened by the D.C.C. According to the terms of the lease of the mines to D.C.C., all entrances are securely locked. Please contact D.C.C. to arrange access.

### BRINLOW MINE
NGR SJ 8555 7723
Grade: 2 (Mine)
Altitude: 510ft (155m)
Length: 980ft (300m)
Depth: 80ft (25m)

A hand picked level leading from Brinlow Dell.

Entrance level leads to a small 18th century mine cut through at depth by the later Hough Level. After 330ft (100m) take the right branch (straight on is dead end) to ledge over 35ft (10m) drop and further workings. Fixed ladders lead up to three levels above and shaft entrance (covered). Fixed ladder leads down 35ft (10m) to partial blockage on Hough Level (qv). Passage is accessible in both directions.

### COBALT MINE
NGR SJ 8594 7727 & 8594 7733
Grade: 2 (Mine)
Altitude: 625ft (190m)
Length: 1000ft (300m)
Depth: 52ft (16m)

There are four entrances: shaft at N end of Wizard Restaurant car park, an old well adjacent to the car park, shaft inside the mining museum and shaft in trees S of Wizard Restaurant. All four are connected underground by a compact mine formed on a N-S fault at several shallow levels.

There are signs of there having been several shaft entrances at 10-20m intervals. The mine forms part of a series of unconnected shallow workings from Saddlebole in the N to Finlow Wood in the S, all believed to have been worked for cobalt in the early 19th century.

### ENGINE VEIN
NGR SJ 8605 7747
Grade: 2 (Mine)
Altitude: 640ft (195m)
Length: 2500ft (750m) approx
Depth: 148ft (45m)

Exposed workings in woods near the Edge.

Entrance is hinged door on side passage to S side. Walking passage leads onto main passage after 165ft (50m). Climb down of 10ft (3m). Turn right (east) to short drop into chamber that was once in open air, now covered with concrete slab. Vein can be seen in roof at end and in following chamber. Steep descent leads to ore chute (now blocked) that connects to Hough Level. Return past climb for steep slope down below old timbering in roof to drop to floor of main chamber, bridged and with staircase down. At bottom follow curve of main chamber round past hole in roof and down slope to end of mine at this level. Just before the end, a low passage on the right leads to Blue Shaft. Quick way to Blue Shaft is to turn opposite way at bottom of staircase and follow a stooping passage down a slope. Bear Pit (148ft/45m) is seen on left, leading from surface to the bottom of the mine where access can be gained to Hough

Level. Just beyond is the top of the inclined Blue Shaft, which also leads to Hough Level. There is a climbing route that avoids the top section of Blue Shaft. Returning to the main chamber and across the bridge is a continuation with further access to Bear Pit. Near the end are some small coffin levels and a run-in from surface. A crawl leads to a section of smaller passages near surface on fault heading West. Most of Engine Vein is either excavated on the fault (Bronze Age to 18th C) or to the S of the fault (19th C).

| **HOUGH LEVEL** |
| --- |
| NGR SJ 8622 7781 |
| Grade: 3 (Mine) |
| Altitude: 443ft (135m |
| Length: 5000ft (1500m) approx. |

In the 19th century all the mines were connected at depth by the Hough Level. The blocked entrance was near West Mine. It can be entered from Wood Mine, Stump Shaft, Field Shaft, Brinlow, Engine Vein, Square Shaft, and Stormy Point. The section in Wood Mine is a branch tunnel meeting the main Hough Level near its W limit. Heading SE, waist deep water is met which ends at a blockage at Field Shaft. This can be passed to another section of deep water, which becomes shallower until Brinlow is reached. There, the water becomes deeper again and shortly after the passage turns NE and heads straight towards Engine Vein for 1300ft (400m). Under Engine Vein a short branch leads to a well preserved ore chute. After the bottom of Bear Pit, Blue Shaft is passed. Another 820ft (250m) on is Square Shaft, and 18th century shaft to surface (165ft/50m). The passage then takes a number of turns before emerging on the surface below Stormy Point.

| **MOTTRAM ST. ANDREWS MINES** |
| --- |
| NGR SJ 872 783 |
| Grade: 1 (Mine) |
| Altitude: 361ft (110m) |
| Length: 165ft (50m) |
| Depth: 66ft (20m) |

Access is not currently possible.

Two shafts in private gardens straddle the Alderley-Prestbury road.

Most of the Mottram Mines are flooded but one section was opened by the DCC in 1982 and again in 1996 from a second shaft. At 10m below surface, the shafts are connected by a level which has been cleared and shored up by the DCC. There is little of interest except the rare vanadium mineral Mottramite which is found in the mine.

| **WEST MINE** |
| --- |
| NGR SJ 8519 7760 |
| Grade: 3 (Mine) |
| Altitude: 480ft (146m) |
| Length: 6.25 miles (10000m) app. |
| Depth: 165ft (50m) |

Access is by arrangement with the owner of the old entrance, Mr P.V.R. Sorensen, or through the DCC on behalf of the National Trust who own the new entrance.

West Mine consists of a series of large tunnels on three levels following the dip down towards the WSW and then turning NW on the strike towards the end of the mine. The description is of the main route only. The original entrance is buried. The entrance is a hinged steel cover. Fixed ladders lead to the Main Chamber. This can be followed to an end after 460ft (140m). The main branch (The Canyon) leads off on the south side after about 300ft (90m). Above and to the north are a series of older, smaller passages known as the Roman Galleries where the new route into the mine enters. These can be reached from the N side by a climb after 330ft (100m) or by a climb on the opposite side and cross-over passage. Following on down the Canyon leads past a junction (E side) at 165ft (50m) where the Railway Tunnel enters. This is a short cut back to the entrance. At this junction a passage leads S into Twisted Pillar Cavern, while the main passage continues SW to Sphinx Chamber. The Sphinx was a prominent rock that was vandalised in the 1950's. Above this route is another large stope reached from the Cavern of the Twisted Pillar and ending in a covered shaft to surface above Sphinx Chamber. The mine is cut in two after Sphinx Chamber by a major N-S fault. At Sphinx Chamber a short climb (fixed ladder and chain) leads to a steep incline up to the bridge across the infamous Plank Shaft. From here two routes can be followed that converge on the Great Arroyo, the first large stope after Plank Shaft. At the end of the Great Arroyo, which runs NE-SW, a second fault is met, and the mine turns NW again. At this point is Chain Shaft, an inclined shaft on a fault, connecting all levels. When the mine was working, a railway level led from the Sphinx Chamber, through the bottom of Plank Shaft and Chain Shaft to the end of the mine. This level is partly flooded, and accessible from Chain Shaft and the Bottom Level (see below). A bypass to Chain Shaft leads round the W side of it. Chain Shaft can be climbed upwards with the use of a fixed chain to the top level, and downwards (10m ladder needed) to the railway level. From the top of Chain Shaft, the Top Level can be followed to the NW limit of the mine. Below this and connected to the Top Level at Chain Shaft and 650ft (200m) further along is the Middle Level route to the end of the mine, including a traverse over Springboard Caverns. The next level down is straight across Chain Shaft, and joins the old railway level after a gentle slope down. Just after joining the railway level is a prominent rock known as The Dog or The Lion. From here, access is possible by some easy climbs and devious routes to the Middle and Top Levels. The Bottom Level can also be followed to the stopes at the NW end of the mine. 330ft (100m) before the end, a branch leads W. below Doctor's Shaft to a steep incline up to the Top Level. There are a number of branch tunnels on the NE side of the three main levels in the further part of the mine.

## WOOD MINE
**NGR SJ 8544 7760**
**Grade: 3 (Mine)**
**Altitude: 525ft (160m)**
**Length: 1.5 miles (2400m)**
**Depth: 100ft (30m)**

Entrance is a hinged steel lid in Windmill Wood. An alternative entrance door on the adit can only be opened from inside.

Entrance drops into the roof of the adit that leads E. to a T-junction. N. (left) leads 360ft (110m) to the N. Boundary fault and North End Chambers. Ladderway leads to surface at Timber Shaft (50ft/15m). S (right) leads across a bridge to Sand Cavern. From here three routes lead off. To the SW is a passage heading to Rabbit Caverns, and then turning W to meet the lower hauling level. This level leaves the mine in a S direction to join the Hough Level (qv). W and down dip from the junction with the hauling level leads to a flooded stope, the Blue Lake. N from this junction leads to the deepest point in the mine, where trial passages and workings head off on two levels to the NW. Turning E, the Railway Level can be followed through Key Chamber and the Stream Passage for about 650 ft (200m) walking and crawling through the bottom of the mine to re-emerge in North End Chambers. Leaving Sand Cavern on the S side leads to Junction Shaft (fixed 8m ladder) which drops into a complex of passages under Sand Cavern. These can be followed SW to join the Railway Level at Key Chamber, or NE via the Green Waterfalls to rejoin the main top level on the way to North End Chambers. A third route from Sand Cavern (13ft/4m fixed ladder) leads to the Green Waterfalls by a shorter route.

## OTHER MINES
**NGR SJ 85 77**

Apart from the mines described above, there are three accessible mines in Brinlow Dell, one in Church Quarry, one at Scout Hole, and four at Stormy Point.

*References:*
*Carlon, C.J. 1979 The Alderley Edge Mines, J. Sherratt & Son*
*Paxton, S.R.A. 1951 B.S.A. Cave Science Vol. 3. No.4. pp. 71-82. Survey.*
*Prag A.J.N.W. & Timberlake S. (eds) 2005. Archaeological Report on Alderley Edge (in prep.)*
*Warrington, G. 1965. The Metalliferous Mining District of Alderley Edge, Cheshire. Mercian Geologist Vol.1. No.2. pp.111-129*
*Warrington, G. 1980. Amateur Geologist Vol.3. No.2.*
*Warrington, G. 1981. Jour. Chester Archaeological Soc. Vol.64.*

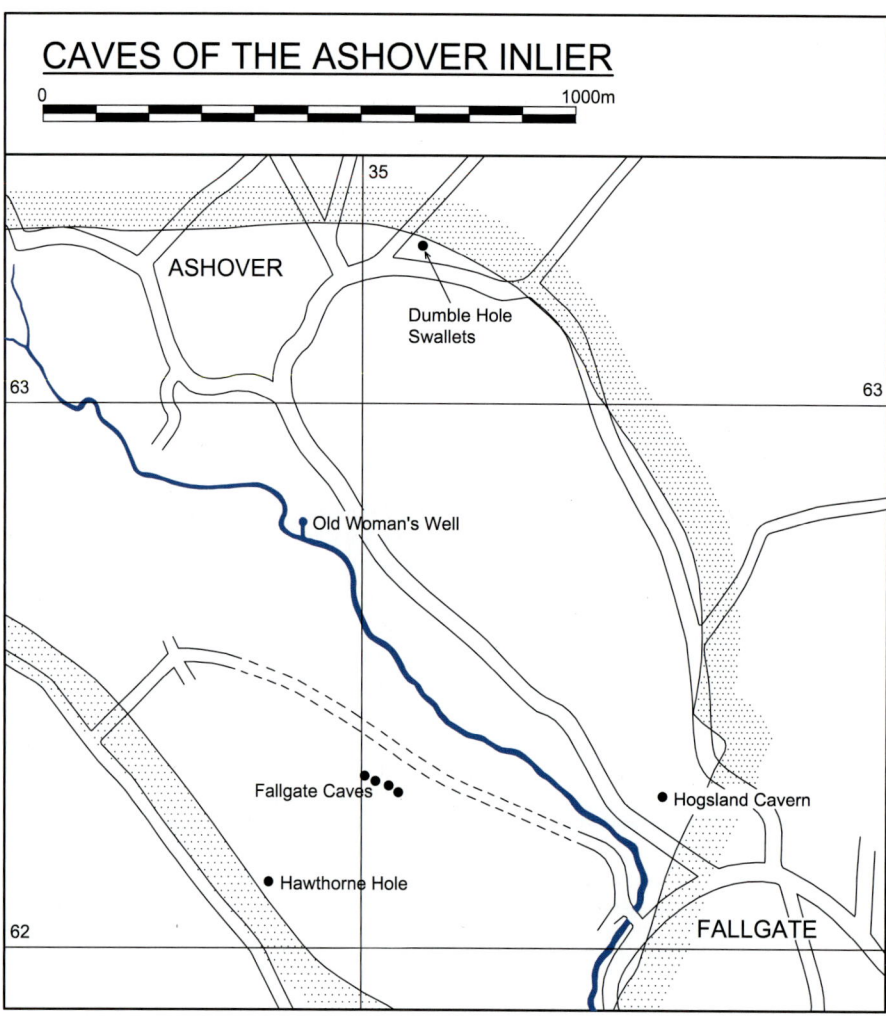

# THE ASHOVER AND CRICH INLIERS

These small isolated imestone outcrops lie to the east of the main White Peak area. They are completely surrounded by the later Namurian rocks. There are a number of old mines, but accessible caves are few.

Near Crich, Wakebridge Cavern was documented in lead mining records, and was re-entered recently by cavers. This is the only listed cave in the Crich Inlier.

The Ashover Inlier, a little further to the north, boasts a group of small swallets, which feed water to a rising 150ft (46m) lower. Digging in the 1990s led to a short section of cave, and there is the possibility of a system of limited size here. The Fallgate Caves, in the cliff on the east side of the River Amber, are of no great extent, but here again digging may be repaid.

---

**DUMBLE HOLE SWALLETS**
(Spout Swallow Hole, Bull Hole, and Tunnel Hole)

**NGR 3502 6325**  **Digs**
**Alt. 650ft (198m)**
**Length: 160ft (50m)**
**Depth: 50ft (15m) approx.**

Owner is Mr C. Chapple, Grange Farm, Ashover.

History: Dye test 1968. Positive at Old Woman's Well, Demonsdale, Ashover. 150ft (46m) lower and 0.8km away. Excavated by T.S.G. 1996-7.

Three small shakeholes take a small amount of water. Tunnel Hole is the shakehole behind the Black Swan pub. To the east opposite the village hall is a tree-lined shakehole containing Dumble Hole Swallet.

Oil-drum entrance drops into a short excavated passage to the head of an 8m deep pot. Below leads via two squeezes to a rift leading down to Smith's Chamber. Below second drop is a crawl to the head of a pitch into Main Chamber. Climb down to where rift crosses passage. Left over large block follows cross rifts to end near surface. Right leads through squeeze and either drops down hole in floor to a stretch of small streamway, or over the hole and through another squeeze. Climb up and traverse at roof level to drop back into Smith's Chamber.

**Tackle: 8m ladder + lifeline.**
*References: Westwood, R. 1998. T.S.G. Jour. No.16. pp.4-6. Survey.*

---

**FALLGATE CAVES**
**Archaeological**
**Altitude: 600ft (180m)**

Land owner is Mr Wilmot, Hilltop Farm, Hilltop Road, Ashover. Prior permission not needed.

Cave No.2. was briefly excavated archaeologically by Sheffield University in 2001. No significant finds were recorded.

Four entrances in the cliff face across the river from Fall Hill. Caves are numbered from left to right facing the cliff.

---

**Cave No. 1**
**NGR 3507 6228**
**Grade: 1 / Arch**
**Length: 60ft (18.2m)**

Large entrance leads directly into a chamber with one crawl leading off 5ft (1.5m) off the ground. Crawl leads to small chamber and exit between boulders close to entrance No.2.

Fallgate Cave No.1.

**Cave No. 2**
NGR 3505 6229
Grade: 1 / Arch
Length: 57ft (17.3m)

Large entrance leads into walking sized passage which turns sharply right. Passage soon lowers to crawl over earth fill. Can be seen to continue, but requires removal of earth fill to proceed. An attempt at archaeological excavation in 2001 revealed bedrock at a depth of only 1m.

**Cave No. 3**
NGR 3504 6230
Grade: 2 / Arch
Length: 100ft (30m)

Climb 12ft (3.6m) up cliff face leads to a tight meandering rift cave with formations. It ends in a small decorated chamber near the surface, which was being dug by persons unknown in 1988.

**Cave No. 4**
NGR 3503 6230
Grade: 1 / Arch
Length: 36ft+ (11m+)

Low crawl under fractured rock (care needed) leads directly into small chamber with two ways off. Small passage straight ahead soon ends, and contains an animal sett. Other passage is small and narrow but can be seen to enlarge slightly. Not explored.

## HAWTHORNE HOLE
**NGR 3484 6211**     **Grade: 1**
**Altitude: 650ft (195m)**
**Length: 51ft (15.5m)**

Land owner is Biwater Pipes and Castings (ex Clay Cross Company), Clay Cross.

Difficult to find. Behind a bush in a field south east of Overton Hall.

Short level nearby with fence round entrance. A single chamber with a crawl leading off. The nearby mine level is best avoided as it is rather unstable.

## HOGSLAND CAVERN & MINE
**NGR 3558 6227**
**Lost**

No access. Owner lives at "Spath Fluor" house, Milltown.

Shaft capped with concrete.

A cavern struck in the workings down the Hogsland lead mine shaft and now under water. Exact position not known but believed to lie in a series of pipe-vein workings some 200ft (61m) below the surface under the east side of Fall Hill. The grid reference given is for Hogsland Mine Shaft.

## OLD WOMAN'S WELL
**NGR 3488 6278**     **Spring**
**Altitude: 510ft (155m)**

A rising on the north east bank of the River Amber.

The resurgence of water which sinks at the Dumble Hole Swallets.

## WAKEBRIDGE CAVERN
(Bacchus Pipe)
**NGR 339 558**
**Grade: 2 (Mine)**

No access at present.

Rediscovered by Wirksworth Mines Research Group.

In the workings of Wakebridge Mine.

A large cavern struck in the workings of the Wakebridge Mine, and once drained by a sough.

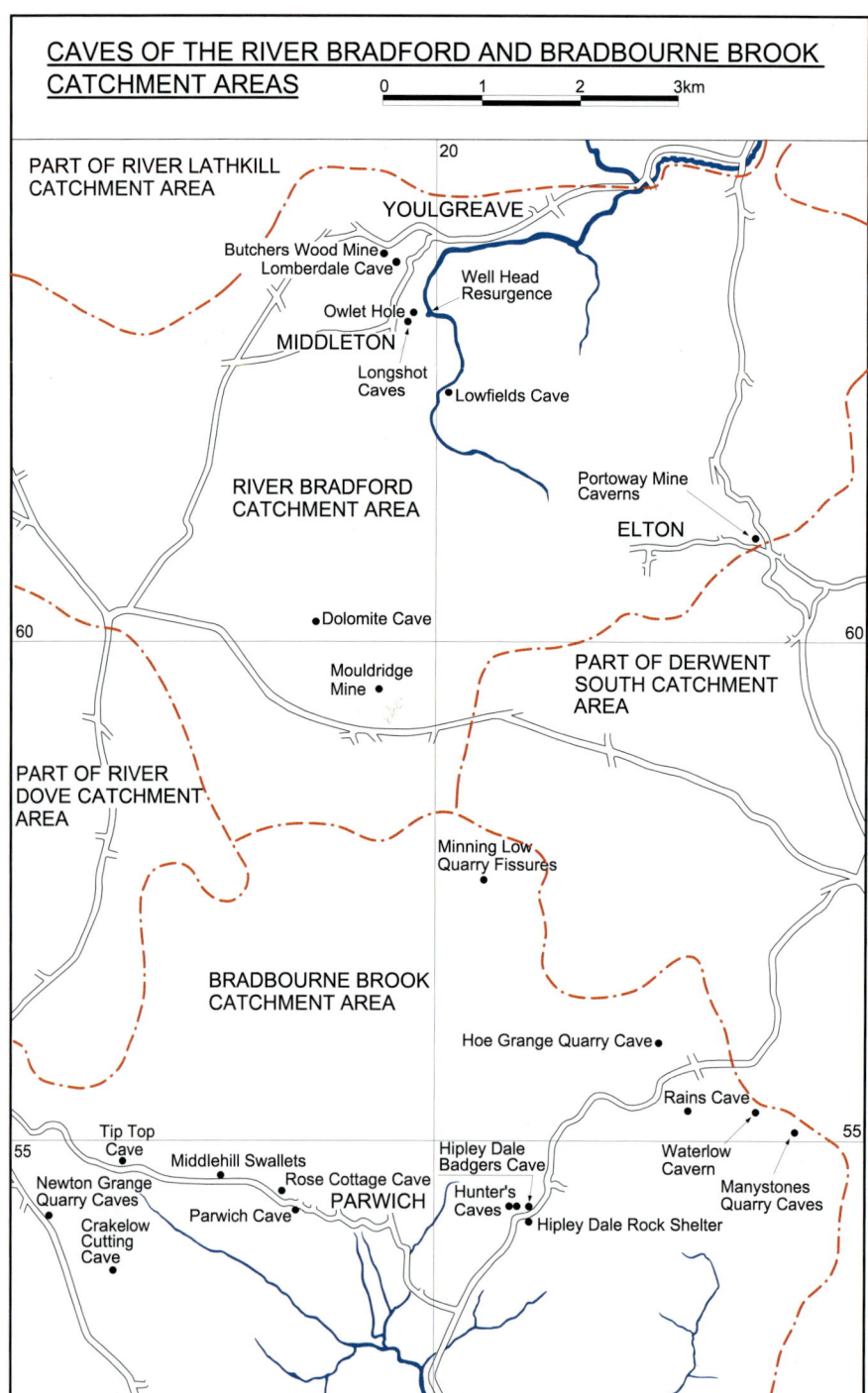

# THE BRADBOURNE BROOK CATCHMENT AREA

Hipley Dale

At the southern extremity of the White Peak lies the seldom visited area which, topographically, drains to the Bradbourne Brook. It is dominated by reef limestones, with distinctive dolomites to the west which can be seen as the periglacial weathered tors of Rainster and Harborough Rocks. To the south lies the small isolated Kniveton - Bradbourne limestone inlier.

Of geological interest is the Tertiary Brassington Formation, preserved as silica sand pockets up to 43m thick in large solution collapse hollows scattered over a 4km wide area from Parsley Hay to Brassington.

Along the limestone margin small sinks lie to the west of Parwich, but their risings are unknown. Small springs feed the Bletch and Havenhill Dale Brooks, as at Parwich, Ballidon, and Brassington, but some drainage from the area may go westwards to rise in the Dove. Also of interest are the dry valleys and gorges at Hipley Dale and Ballidon.

It seems unlikely that large penetrable caves exist, but digging at the sinks, coupled with a dye testing programme, may yield interesting results.

### CRAKELOW CUTTING CAVE
**NGR 167 537**
**Grade: 1**
**Length: 13ft (4m)**

On the north side of Crakelow Cutting on the Tissington Trail 80ft (25m) before a bridge. On a small ledge 10ft (3m) above the trail.

A small tube 2.6-3ft (0.8-0.9m) diameter. Blocked with rocks after 13ft (4m).

*Reference: Brooks. S, 2005. OCC N/L. Vol.41. No. 7-9. p.33.*

### HIPLEY DALE BADGERS CAVE
**NGR 2096 5429**
**Grade: 1**
**Altitude: 650ft (195m) approx**
**Length: 5ft (1.5m)**

Approx. 100ft (30m) west of a small trial adit on the north side of the B5056 at the base of a small outcrop.

A 3ft (0.8m) x 2ft (0.5m) entrance that can be entered for 5ft (1.5m) before it becomes too tight. Site lived in by badgers – could be dug.

*Reference: Orpheus Caving Club log book. Jan 2006.*

### HIPLEY DALE ROCK SHELTER
**NGR 2097 5424**
**Grade: 1**
**Altitude: 650ft (195m)**
**Length: 90ft (27m)**

On south side of B5056 where road cuts through Hipley Hill. Large double entrance at base of cliff.

Large arched entrance 37ft (11.5m) x 16ft (5m) high divides after only 13ft (4m) into two parallel passages. Left is passage 12ft (3.8m) wide x 10ft (3m) high that runs into hill on bearing of 150º for 26ft (8m) to blank wall. Right hand passage is 18ft (5.5m) wide x 13ft (4m) high and runs into hill also on bearing of 150º for 36ft (11.1m) to where it pinches out. Fine anastomosis can be seen in roof of the right hand passage. Both passages appear to have been modified/enlarged. A further smaller rock shelter lies approx. 100ft (30m) to the east.

*Reference: Orpheus Caving Club log book. Jan 2006.*

### HOE GRANGE QUARRY CAVE
**NGR 223 560**
**Grade: 1 (Arch)**
**Altitude: 1100ft (335m)**
**Length: 20ft (6m)**

Entrance 25ft (8m) up in lower quarry face.

Yielded Pleistocene mammal remains, now almost all quarried away. Only a 20ft (6m) crawl remains. Quarry exhibits a variety of solution features along joints and bedding.

*Reference: Bemrose, H.A. and Newton, E. 1905. Quart. Jour. Geol. Soc. Vol.61. pp.43-62. Survey.*

### HUNTERS BEDDING CAVE
**NGR 2080 5435          Dig**
**Altitude: 690ft (210m) approx.**
**Length: 5ft (2m)**

North side of valley overlooking the Fenny Bentley – Grange Mill road in a limestone bluff.

Low arch entrance 8ft (2.5m) x 10ins (25cms) high. Rubble and earth-floored bedding passage for 7ft (2m). Possible dig but with limited prospects.

*Reference: Brooks. S, 2006. OCC N/L. Vol.42. No. 3/4. p.16.*

### HUNTERS CAVE
**NGR 2076 5435**
**Grade: 1**
**Altitude: 690ft (210m) approx.**
**Length: 27ft (8.2m)**

North side of valley overlooking the Fenny Bentley - Grange Mill road.

Impressive entrance 16ft (4.8m) x 7ft (2.2m) faces down the Bradbourne Valley. Quickly tapers to 3ft (1m) x 3ft (0.95m) and enters small chamber. Cave closes after a further 13ft (4m).

*Reference: Brooks. S, 2006. OCC N/L. Vol.42. No. 3/4. p.16. Survey.*

Hunters Cave. Photo by Simon Brooks

### MANYSTONES QUARRY CAVES
NGR 237 551　　　Lost
Altitude: 1050ft (320m)

In a large disused limestone quarry. Small solution caves. All now buried under industrial waste. One small blind solution tube and small tubes high up.

### MIDDLEHILL SWALLETS
(Parwich Sink)
NGR 178 546　　　Digs
Altitude: 660ft (201m)

In hollows beside the Parwich-Alsop road.

Two active sinks. The more northerly sink was forced in 1971 to a small muddy chamber, but the entrance has since collapsed and dumped farm rubbish obscures much of the site. The swallet nearest the road is choked with masonry from collapsed former barn (shown on earlier maps as "Tithe Barn"). Resurgences not known.

*References: Mellors, P.T. 1971. D.C.A. N/L No.11. pp.3-4.*
*Potts, J. 1976. D.C.A. N/L No.27. p.6.*

### MINNING LOW QUARRY FISSURES
NGR 205 576
Grade: 1
Depth: 3ft (1m)

In the rear wall of Minning Low Quarry, at the south end.

A fissure 2ft (0.6m) x 4ft (1.2m) drops for 3ft (1m) to a fill of football-sized boulders. A possible dig. An entrance 26ft (8m) to the right of the fissure opens into an earth-filled cavity on the same vein as the fissure. 66ft (20m) to the right again is an arch 3ft (0.8m) x 18in (0.4m) leads to a 7ft (2.1m) long earth-filled tube.

*Reference: Brooks, S, 2005. OCC N/L. Vol.41. No.10. p.43*

### NEWTON GRANGE QUARRY CAVES
NGR 1605 5425
Grade: 1
Depth: 7ft (2m)

In quarry immediately west of the A515 south of New Inns.
Entrance 4ft (1.2m) x 4ft (1.2m) enters a solution cavity approx. 7ft (2m) deep. To the left is a second fissure approx. 7ft (2m) long. To the right again is a third fissure, earth filled. Little prospect of extension.
*Reference: Brooks. S, 2005. OCC N/L. Vol.41. No. 7-9. p.34.*

### PARWICH CAVE
NGR 1860 5435
Grade: 2
Altitude: 625ft (190m)
Length: 50ft (15m)

Obvious entrance in a bluff of limestone 33ft (10m) south/west of the bend on the Parwich to Alsop-en-le-Dale road, west of the village.
Main entrance opens into a large chamber. To the right a short length of passage leads to another, smaller entrance. To the left a short climb leads to a tube which can be followed for 5ft (1.5m) to a 3ft (1m) dia. pot. This is 3ft (1m) deep to enter a low, boulder-floored chamber which draughts well.
**Reference: 2003. OCC N/L, Vol. 39, No. 7-10. P.38**

### RAINS CAVE
(Longcliffe Fissure)
NGR 226 553
Grade: 1 (Arch)
Altitude: 1100ft (330m)
Length: 30ft (9m)

Behind large boulders at the east end of Longcliffe Crags, about 100 yards (91m) west of Observer Corps Box.
A sloping chamber with crawls off. Incompletely excavated. Numerous animal remains and some prehistoric pottery found.
*References: Ward, J. 1889. Derbys. Arch. Jour. No.11. pp.31-45. Plan.*
*Ward, J. 1892. Derbys. Arch. Jour. No.14. pp.228-250. Section.*
*Ward, J. 1893. Derbys. Arch. Jour. No.15. pp.161-176.*

### ROSE COTTAGE CAVE
NGR 1855 5460
Grade: 1
Altitude: 605ft (185m)
Length: 33ft (10.2m)

There is normally no access to this cave.
Entrance in the cottage garden on Smithy Lane, Parwich.
A 13ft (4m) entrance passage leads to a chamber some 13ft (4m) by 10ft (3m) high. To the left a second entrance leads to the rear of the cottage. Minimal prospects for extension.
*Reference: 2003. OCC N/L, Vol. 39, No. 7-10, p.38*

### TIP TOP CAVE
NGR 168 548
Grade: 1 (Dig)
Altitude: 720ft (220m)
Length: 20ft (6m)

At the top of a small quarry adjacent to the road some ¾ km east of Alsop-en-le-dale.
High in quarry a small hole leads to a 20ft (6m) bedding cave. Left leads to a smaller second entrance, right leads down-slope to an earthy blockage.
*Reference: 1998. OCC N/L, Vol.34, No.3/4. p.18*

### WATER LOW CAVERN
NGR 233 553 approx.
Lost

Explored by the Derbyshire Pennine Club in May 1907. The hill between Manystones Quarry and Longcliffe is unnamed on the 6 inch map, but was once known as Waterlow. It is presumed to be the site of the cavern explored by the Derbyshire Pennine Club.

A 6ft (1.8m) by 4ft (1.2m) mineshaft 30ft (9m) deep led to a natural chamber 10ft (3m) wide, 30ft (9m) high and 30ft (9m) long. A further climb down of 16ft (5m) led to a small continuation to the south east which became too tight. At the north end, a climb up led into a passage 18ft (5.5m) high by 3ft (1m) wide. A climb down a narrow slot for 10ft (3m) entered a passage which ended at a small chamber. The continuation from here was dug, but soon choked. Would be an interesting dig if the site could be located. *Reference: Smithard, W. 1st June 1907. Nottinghamshire Guardian.*

# THE RIVER BRADFORD CATCHMENT AREA

The River Bradford at Youlgreave

The main catchment for the River Bradford is the shale and sandstone upland to the east, but a small proportion of its flow emerges from active risings in its left banks. No known swallets feed these risings: the nearest swallets are the small ones at Duckett Wall and Astonhill, in the Derwent South Catchment. These could be associated with the Bradford risings, but dye testing has not confirmed this.

Gratton Dale has a wet-weather rising, but for the most part the dale has no surface flow. There has been some suggestion that the flow of the River Bradford has declined since the driving of the Hillcar Sough.

Speleologically, very little is known, and there is a very large blank area on the map containing no known caves. However, a dip slope of limestone rises gently westwards from the river, and it is possible that an integrated underground drainage system lurks beneath it awaiting the lucky explorer. Determined digging in the vicinity of the risings, or at the Longshot Caves, may well bring some worthwhile discoveries.

### ALPORT QUARRY FISSURE
Lost

A fissure which yielded red deer remains according to Bemrose.
*Reference: Bemrose, H.H.Arnold. Victoria County History of Derbyshire. p.36.*

### BUTCHER'S WOOD MINE
NGR 195 639
Grade: 2 (Mine)
Altitude: 825ft (251m)
Length: 70ft (21m)
Depth: 40ft (12m) approx.

On hillside opposite Needleseye Corner on the B5056 road.
Stooping adit entrance. Walking for 30ft (9m) to lip of first pitch in natural pot. 20ft (6m) sloping descent to sloping boulder floor of small chamber which forms the northern end of an enlarged rift running at right angles to the entrance passage. 2nd Pitch of 12ft (3.2m) is off perched boulders in the rift which then drops steeply to terminal silt choke in floor. Good active formations in the lower section of the mine.

*Tackle:*
*1st pitch: 6m ladder + lifeline.*
*2nd pitch: 4m ladder + lifeline.*

### DOLOMITE CAVE
NGR 188 602
Grade: 1
Altitude: 900ft (270m)
Length: 15ft (5m)

In branch of Long Dale near the dolomite/limestone junction.
A small cave exposed by collapse, with an outer and an inner chamber connected by a squeeze.

### LOMBERDALE CAVE
NGR 196 638
Grade: 1
Altitude: 770ft (235m)
Length: 15ft (5m)

Entrance in south side of dale, 100 yards (91m) or so west of Youlgrave road.
A scramble down into a wide low bedding plane with roof pendants and a channel in the floor. Becomes too tight for progress without excavating the floor.

### LONGSHOT CAVES
(Rusden Caves)
NGR 1980 6325
Grade: 2
Altitude: 580ft (176m)
Length: 200ft (61m) total
Status: R.I.G.S. (Alport Dale)

Two slot entrances one above the other at the foot of the cliff, behind excavated material visible from the footpath in Middleton Dale.
Low bedding crawls ending in chokes. The upper passage trends south, becoming too tight after 70ft (21m) in gour pools and flowstone. This passage is thought to be an old outlet for water rising at Well Head nearby in the main valley. The lower passage lies parallel to the dale side. Right hand branch ends at blocked hole in the floor close to the cliff face. The left branch develops into a vadose modified tube soon becoming too tight in partial fill of mud and rock. A strong draught at times.
*References: Brooks, S. 1992. D.C.A. N/L No.77. p.10. Location plan.*
*Christopher, N.S.J. & Mellors, P.T. 1977. Bull. B.C.R.A. No.17. pp.16-19.*
*Mellors, P.T. 1972. D.C.A. N/L No.13. pp.2-3.*

### LOWFIELDS CAVE
(Badger Hole)
NGR 201 625   Grade: 1
Altitude: 600ft (180m)
Length: 30ft (9m)

On the east bank of Rowlow Brook, well hidden.

A low bedding cave. May be a former outlet for sinks higher up the scarp. It soon becomes too tight.

### MOULDRIDGE MINE
NGR 1943 5952   Grade: 2 (Mine).
Altitude: 900ft (274m)
Length: 1800ft (550m)

The adit entrance is fitted with a grill, and spanner for shaft entrance obtainable from Mr Walker, Keeper's Cottage, Astonhill.

The site was last worked for ore in the 1950s.

Obvious adit entrance by tips in the south branch of upper Gratton Dale. Other shafts close by have been sealed.

A complex maze of worked out pipe veins and scrins, with links to surface via a number of partially blocked shafts. The shaft entrance is blocked at 90ft (27m) but has workings opening off it at 30ft (9m) and 50ft (15m).

*Reference: Pearce, A. et al, 1984. Bull. P.D.M.H.S. Vol.9. No.2. pp.108-122.*

### OWLET HOLE
(Owlet Hole Cave)
NGR 198 633
Grade: 1 (Arch)
Altitude: 600ft (183m)
Length: 10ft (3m)
Status: R.I.G.S. (Alport Dale)

High in the cliff face seen from the footpath down Middleton Dale.

A prominent entrance. The roomy threshold closes down to a vadose slot too tight for entry. Archaeologically excavated. Animal remains found.

*Reference: Bramwell, D. & Wood, C. 1947. Northwestern Naturalist Vol.22. pp.235-239.*

### PORTAWAY MINE CAVERNS
NGR 232 610 to 234 607 Mines
Altitude: c.800ft (244m)
Depth: over 300ft (91m)

Permission rarely given.

Between Winster and Elton.

Access via deep shafts. A very extensive series of pipe vein caverns and workings last worked in the 1950s.

### WELL HEAD RESURGENCE
NGR 1995 6325   Spring
Altitude: 550ft (168m)

The largest of a series of risings on the west bank of Rowlow Brook between Smerrill Grange and Youlgrave.

The outlet is a wide low impenetrable bedding plane beside the footpath through the dale. Flow is held back by a small concrete dam which diverts some of the water along an iron pipe to a ruined pumping station at the foot of Middleton Dale. The spring dries up in mid to late summer, and Rowlow Brook has been seen to sink into its bed close by.

*Reference: Christopher, N.S.J. & Mellors, P.T. 1977. B.C.R.A. Bull. No.17. pp.16-20.*

## Features listed as potential archaeological sites

1: NGR 1998 6229  Alt: 175m   A low narrow rock shelter on the west side of Rowlow Brook.
2: NGR 2025 6187  Alt: 199m   A partly quarried away cave on the west side of Rowlow Brook.
3: NGR 2021 6183  Alt: 205m   A fissure cave high above Rowlow Brook.
4: NGR 2020 6185  Alt: 196m   A collapsed rock shelter below 3.
5: NGR 1990 6247  Alt: 175m   A very long rock shelter in Peak Park woodland.
6: NGR 1992 6245  Alt: 194m   A shallow, low rock shelter.
7: NGR 1992 6247  Alt: 195m   A low, deep rock shelter.
8: NGR 1988 6246  Alt: 192m   A long moderate rock shelter at the top of a cliff.
9: NGR 1990 6244  Alt: 192m   A low deep rock shelter/cave.
10: NGR 1988 6244  Alt: 186m   A single square chamber with an open mouth.
11: NGR 1976 6237 Alt: 205m   A collapsed cave.
12: NGR 1981 6241 Alt: 221m   A small, low rock shelter.
13: NGR 1981 6239 Alt: 210m   An open fissure.
15: NGR 1987 6335 Alt: 197m   Rock cut chamber formed by falling blocks.

## THE BRADWELL CATCHMENT AREA

Bradwell Lumb in drought

Bradwell Lumb in flood

Bradwell Dale contains many small caves, but none is of any great extent. Running sub-parallel to the dale on the west side, however, is Bagshawe Cavern, a system of mature passages consisting mainly of a flood overflow route. The large stream is only briefly seen in a short stretch of streamway at the southern end of the system, close to the level of the resurgence cave in Bradwell village. The cave ends at deep sumps, but there are still some digging prospects.

A look at the map soon reveals that there is a very large cave system waiting to be found upstream of Bagshawe Cavern. The size of the stream itself suggests an extensive system, and the geography of the catchment area confirms it. In a similar manner to the Stoney Middleton and Castleton areas, there is a line of sinks along the shale margin from which water must follow the strike of the beds to the resurgence.

The farthest swallet is Dowse (or "Duce") Hole at Grindlow, 400ft (122m) above the rising, and over 2 miles (3.5km) distant. There is a very large unexplored area in between. In addition to the route from swallet to resurgence, there must be a number of large tributaries from the west, where the limestone rises gently onto the summit of Bradwell Moor. Digs in the swallets at Grindlow and Hucklow have so far proved inconclusive. Dowse Hole was extensively dug by a number of clubs from as early as 1936 until 1991.

The Bradwell area is thus one of the best areas of future potential, probably second only to the Wormhill area. It may take years to find it, but the cave is there waiting.

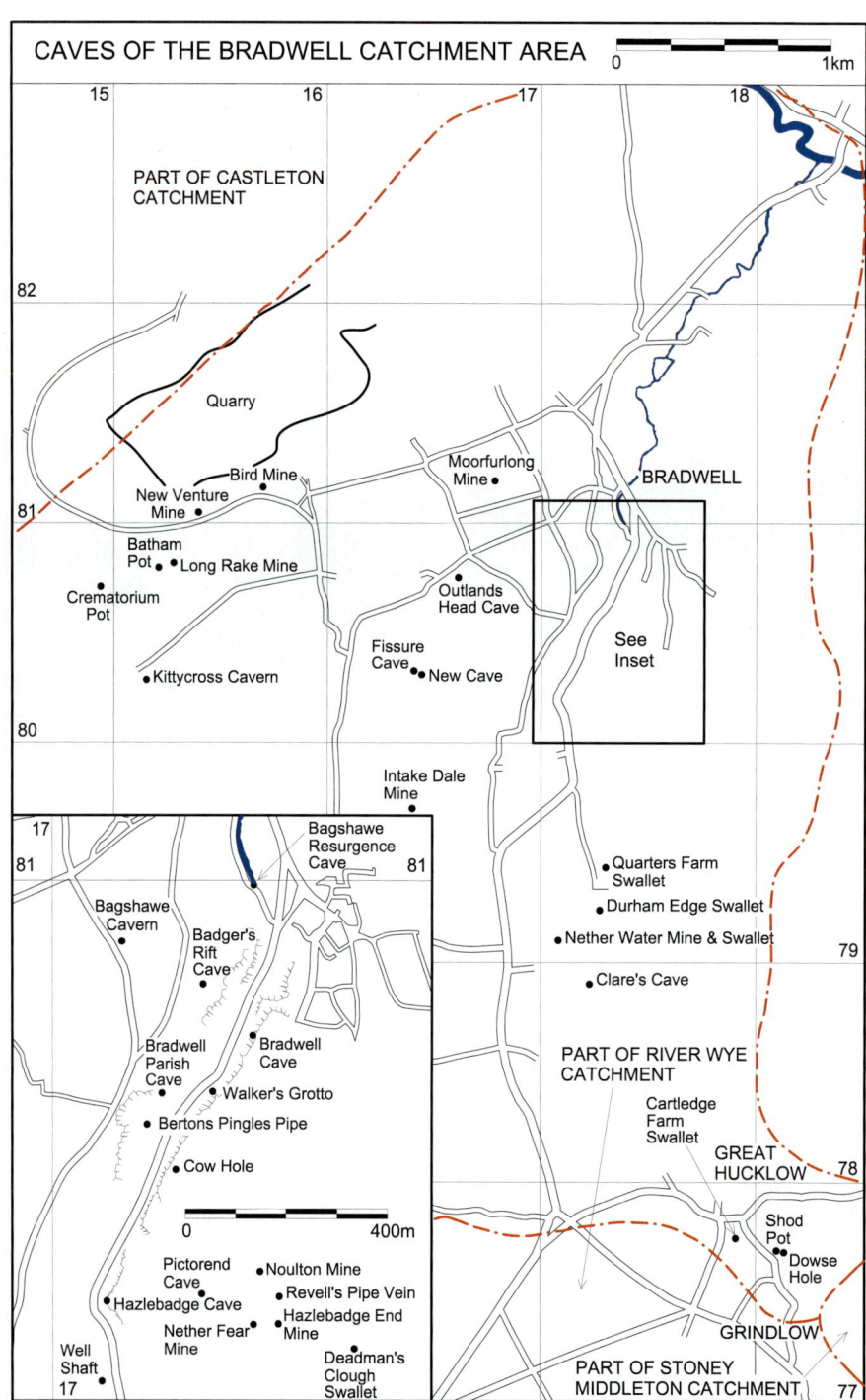

## BADGER'S RIFT

**NGR 173 808  Grade: 1**
**Alt. 630ft (192m) Length: 60ft (18m)**

In field above Bagshawe Resurgence Cave.

Extended in1995. A sloping passage becomes a 3 inch wide rift on the left. Looking through the rift it appears wider beyond. Entrance may be blocked with rubbish from time to time.

*Reference: Orpheus Caving Club Hut Log. 1978.*

## BAGSHAWE CAVERN
(Mulespinner Mine)

**NGR 1714 8088 Grade: 3 (Part Show)**
**Alt. 770ft (235m)**
**Length: 3.15 miles (5.07km)**
**Depth: 209ft (63.8m)**

*Tackle for Pitches:*
*Dungeon: 6m ladder + lifeline*
*Glory Hole: 20m rope*
*Madame Guillotine    25m rope*
Status: S.S.S.I.

Contact Amanda Revell beforehand: amandarevell@hotmail.com

Old show cave on southern outskirts of Bradwell village. Limited access at present. See Eldon Pothole Club website for current information.

### Upper Levels

Old workings at and below entrance formerly known as Mulespinner Mine. Entrance covered by a small stone building. Descend steps in vein, then turn left along obvious passage following tourist path for 540ft (165m) to the junction with Calypso's Cave, 180ft (55m) long to a choke. Tourist path turns left, passing the wide low Agony Crawl on the left.

Just beyond, steps lead down to the top of the Dungeon, an 18ft (5.5m) pitch. The main passage continues beyond the Dungeon for 295ft (90m), and lowers to a crawl. To the right is the Cave of Worms, where a climb down boulders rejoins the main route, which continues as a large passage for 460ft (140m) to the Hippodrome, a wide boulder-strewn chamber. Turning left at the Hippodrome, a sloping muddy passage leads to the streamway.

Left (downstream) is sump, obstructed by chert nodules some 122ft (37m) in. Right (upstream) can be followed to where, in low water, the stream emerges from a culvert on the right and sinks on the left, 50ft (15m) beyond is the start of Sump 1, now drained and passable as a wet crawl for 220ft (67m). It is not advisable to progress beyond this sump in wet weather unless diving, as it will sump completely and the airspace beyond fills to the roof. Beyond sump one is a low chamber with a dig on the right, Sam's Dig, leading via a vertical boulder-choke to the large Paternity's Fault. The passage continues as Sump 2, 30ft (9m) long, followed by a 70ft (21m) crawl, Valve Wrecker Crawl, leading to Sump 3, 15ft (4.5m) quickly followed by Sump 4, 25ft (8m) long. 50ft (15m) of canal passage leads to Sump 5, which has been dived to a gravel choke 500ft (150m) from base at a depth of 100ft (30m). 70ft (20m) into Sump 5 a low arch in the left hand wall leads to air and a small chamber with a blind aven, Joe's Garage.

An oxbow on the west side of the Hippodrome leads to a short climb down into Glory Hole Passage, a phreatic joint-controlled inlet which descends to a duck, then rises again to the head of an impressive pothole, 45ft (14m) deep to water, the Glory Hole. The water level in the Glory Hole falls considerably in dry weather. It has been dived for 30ft (9m) to a constricted route through boulders into a 10ft (3m) x 3ft (1m) westward trending passage with a strong flow. Just to the right of Glory Hole Passage is a crawl, the Snake's Pyjamas, excavated to connect with Taylor's Way in the Full Moon Series.

### Lower Series

From the bottom of The Dungeon 330ft (100m) of crawling and walking leads to a chamber where the Agony Crawl enters at roof level. Shortly beyond is The Lake, a waist deep pool. A further 1000ft (305m) of varied passage leads to a sump, which becomes a duck in dry weather. 300ft (91m) of passage follows, mostly crawling, to a permanent sump. Just before the sump, a passage on the right is the entrance to the Far Drought Series, first entered in 1989, consisting of 395ft (120m) of stooping and crawling to a sump.

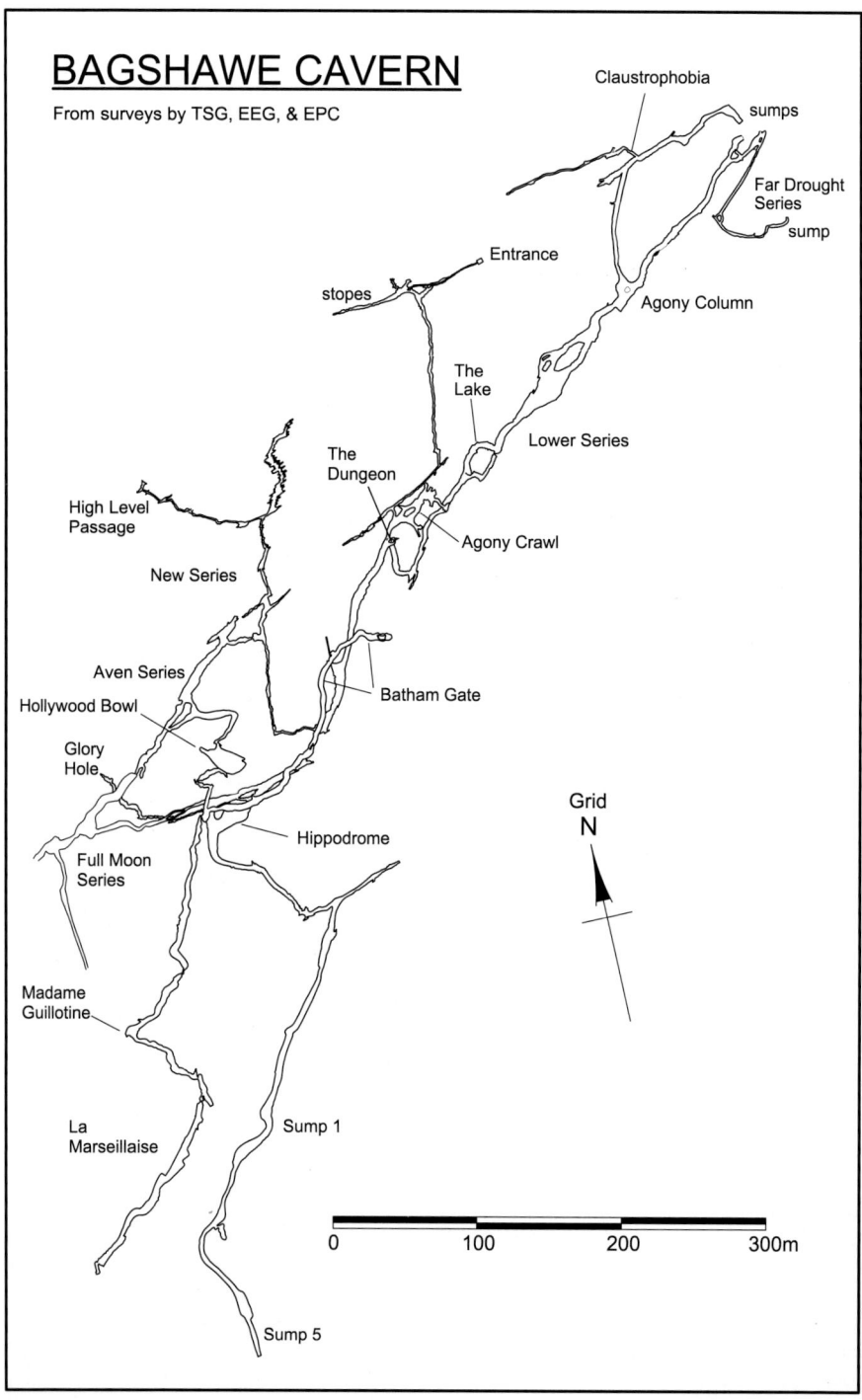

The Full Moon Series. Photo by Rob Eavis

The Hollywood Bowl, Bagshawe Cavern. Photo by Robbie Shone

Shortly before the duck, a left hand branch can be followed to a T junction. The draughting crawl to the left leads to a series of chambers and crawls, and a series of mine workings in Moss Rake, which end close to the shaft just downhill of the entrance buildings. To the right, a hole in the floor is Claustrophobia, a very tight crawl to a mine level in the shale. The main route continues beyond Claustrophobia to a further sump. All the sumps are close to the level of the resurgence at the head of Bradwell Brook.

**The New Series**

On the right of the Upper Series between the Cave of Worms and the Hippodrome, a gate leads to an ascending hands and knees crawl. After a tight squeeze the passage enlarges, in places to walking size, and leads to a junction at Pool Chamber.

To the left a crawl (flooded in winter) leads to the Aven Series, a series of passages with high avens including Green and Pleasant Land, dug into in 1995, and the Great Aven. A squeeze below the Great Aven at the end of the Aven Series was passed in 1998 to a continuation. The passage, Taylor's Way, leads westwards, well decorated, up to 4 metres wide, sometimes stooping sized and often up to 2 metres high, with the occasional larger breakdown chamber. After about 200 metres a passage on the left is the main way on, and ahead is Dead Ahead Dig. The branch begins as a vadose passage before the trench dies and a phreatic tube ends at a pot in the floor. The bottom of the pot is choked with gravel, but represents a good dig. Shortly before the junction the Snakes Pyjamas enters on the left.

To the right the route soon lowers to an unpleasant restricted muddy duck. Beyond the duck the passage soon becomes larger, and further branches lead up-dip to the left. The main route continues until it lowers and ends at clay chokes close to the entrance vein. Just before the muddy duck a dig on the right leads to a chamber, The Real Thing.

In the Aven Series, Namread Aven was climbed to an arduous crawl leading to a sump. This was passed in drought in 1992 to a very large and impressive chamber, the Hollywood Bowl. A passage in the roof led via more tight squeezes to emerge in a large fossil trunk passage, Batham Gate, followed back over the main cave to a silt choke after nearly 700ft (213m). The passage also runs southwards as La Marseillaise, and beyond a further tight squeeze as Frogs Legs and Cognac, for nearly 1000ft (300m) to a very remote dig close to Earl Rake. Madame Guillotine, a 70ft (21m) pitch was descended to a series of chokes, where a connection was made with Moose's Revenge in the Full Moon Series in 2010 after a long dig by Eldon P.C., allowing easier access to the remote high level passages.

*References: Arveschoug, D. 1994. BCRA Caves & Caving No.66. p.2.*
*Baker, E.A. c.1910. Moors, Crags and Caves of the High Peak. Chapter XXV. Survey.*
*Farr, M. 1977. CDG N/L No.45. pp.18-19.*
*Ford, T.D., Burek, C., and Beck, J.S. 1975. The Evolution of Bradwell Dale and its Caves. Trans B.C.R.A. Vol.2. No.3. pp.133-140. Survey.*
*Revell, A.C. 1999. BCRA Caves & Caving No.83. pp.13-14. Survey (Full Moon Series).*
*Taylor, J. 2000. DCA N/L No.106. pp.5-8.*

### BAGSHAWE RESURGENCE CAVE
(The Yeld, The Lumb)

**NGR 1739 8100**

**Grade: 1 & Dive**

**Alt. 600ft (183m)**

**Length: 130ft (40m)**

Entrance is in masonry once supporting a water wheel for the lead smelter, at the head of Bradwell Brook.

The rising for a large catchment to the west and south which includes Bagshawe Cavern. More water resurges per annum than the combined flow from the nearby Peak Cavern and Russet Well.

Main entrance is normally a 20ft (6m) sump above 6.5ft (2m) high waterfall. In drought this may be reduced to an almost dry crawl but in flood the current prevents entry. Alternative entrance is low culvert 3ft (1m) to north, which is normally dry. Both routes soon join at partly natural chamber with two ways on.

To right is tight bedding plane ending at Sump 3 which soon becomes too low. Straight on from chamber is bouldery passage leading to Sump 2 on left and 8m long adit straight ahead (now backfilled with debris dug out from Sump 2). Sump is excavated flooded pot 15ft (4.5m) deep to tight bend followed by spacious bedding. In 1995 CDG members Andy Morrison, Tim Hallam and Bill Griffith dug out sump 2. A connection was later made to Bagshawe Cavern, and work continues to find the source of the main flow.

*References: Carter, R.L. & Cordingley, J.N. 1994. Peak District Sump Index.p.9. Survey.*
*Carter, R.L. & Cordingley, J.N. 1997. Peak District Sump Index Update. pp.6-7.*
*Cordingley, J.N. 1987. D.C.A. N/L. No.64. p.12. Survey.*
*CDG N/L No.124 pp.23-24. Survey.*

### BATHAM POT
(Pigeon Hole, Moss Pot)

**NGR 152 808**

**Alt. 1250ft (375m)**

100ft (30m) west of Long Rake Mine on Bradwell Moor.

A large open pot 100ft (30m) long and 50ft (15m) deep, now largely filled in. Easy scramble down the east end. Old mine workings to the west and abortive dig in floor. Probably communicated with natural caverns in Long Rake Mine (q.v.). 700ft (210m) to the north east a mine shaft 30ft (9m) deep led to a large natural cavern 60ft (18m) high and 40ft (12m) wide. (NGR 153 808). It has now been obliterated by fluorspar working. 100ft (30m) further east-north-east is a group of shafts and natural pots some 30ft (9m) deep (NGR 154 810).

*Reference: Tottle, P. 1957. The Lyre Vol.1. No.2. pp.38-41. Survey.*

### BERTONS PINGLES PIPE
(Shawley Cave)

**NGR 1719 8053 Grade: 2**

**Alt. 700ft (213m)**

**Length: 525ft (160m)**

On the west side of Bradwell Dale, a short distance up the dale from Bradwell Parish Cave. A narrow entrance at the base of the cliff in the quarry floor.

The short narrow entrance turns almost immediately sharp right into 250ft (76m) of dry passage. A 30ft (9m) shaft descends to lower flooded workings. The shaft drops straight into the sump pool with two ways on. C.D.G.divers have explored 140ft (42m) of sump to three run-in chambers where the air is suspected to be bad. At right angles to this sump another sumped passage continues to a junction. Left has been dived for approx 120ft (36m) with no end in sight, right terminates in boulders after 15ft (4.5m).

To the left at the base of the entrance, a dig in 1999 revealed a further 130ft (40m) of passage, with a small stream entering through a too-tight squeeze at the end.

**Tackle:** *Internal shaft:10m ladder + lifeline.*

*References: Buckley, A.L. 1974. DCA N/L No.21.*
*Drakeley, K. 1978. DCA N/L No.37.*
*Taylor, J. 2000. Descent No. 155. p.8.*

### BIRD MINE
**NGR 157 811 Grade: 3**
**Alt. 1130ft (339m)**
**Depth: 328ft (100m)**

A mine shaft some 200ft (60m) west of the top Castleton-Tideswell road south west of Earle's Quarry.

**Now in a dangerous condition due to quarry workings nearby.**

The shaft is 328ft (100m) deep with levels off at 110, 193, and 263ft (33, 58 and 79m). The first level extends into a rift now blocked. The second extends into a short series of flat workings and a natural rift chamber 70ft (21m) high. The third level is short and goes into workings only, whilst at the bottom there is only a short trial level. The shaft can be descended directly, or the levels can be entered and interconnecting winzes can be descended to the bottom.

*Tackle: 107m rope.*

Reference: Lord, P.J. & Thompson, S.J. 1969. Jour. S.U.S.S. Vol.1. No.4. pp.166-169. Survey.

### BRADWELL CAVE
**NGR 174 807 Grade: 1**
**Alt. 663ft (200m) Length: 106ft (32m)**

On east side of Bradwell Dale, 130ft (40m) north of the lay-by north of Walker's Grotto.

Scramble up a series of ledges to an obscure cave entrance in the cliff some 50ft (15m) above the road. A low crawl descends down dip, becoming larger before ending at a mud choke. A few small side passages all quickly become too low. There is another small cave entrance high in the buttress on the east side of the dale near the village tip immediately south of Bradwell. This is said to extend for 30ft (9m) although access is not allowed.

### BRADWELL PARISH CAVE
(Old Brook Cave)
**NGR 172 805 Grade: 1**
**Alt. 640ft (195m)**
**Length: 130ft (40m)**

In the abandoned quarry to the west of the track up from the road opposite layby near Bradwell Cave.

Large truncated phreatic tube. Obvious entrance continues as an easy passage up dip to a low section over calcited rocks and gravel. Beyond the squeeze the cave ends at a complete choke.

References: Crabtree, P.W. 1964. Cave Science Vol.5. No.36. Survey.

Turner, D. 1950. British Caver Vol.21. p.22.

Bradwell Parish Cave.
Photo by John Beck

## CARTLEDGE FARM SWALLET

**NGR 1791 7774 Grade: 1**
**Alt. 1010ft (308m)**
**Length: 55ft (17m)**
**Depth: 45ft (14m)**

Access not normally granted.

In garden of Cartledge Farmhouse, in the centre of the lawn.

A collapse close to the house took a considerable stream from an ancient land drain. Excavated for 25ft (8m) to bedrock by Eyam Exploration Group in 1988. Paving slab covers short drop into concrete culvert, leading to 23ft (7m) concrete shaft. Short descending passage with shale roof leads to 15ft (5m) climb down narrow rift to a very tight continuation.

*Reference: Beck, J.S. 1993. Jour. T.S.G. No.14. p.46.*

## CLARE'S CAVE

**NGR 1722 7890 Grade: 3**
**Alt. 835ft (255m)**
**Length: 150ft (45m) approx**
**Depth: 60ft (18m)**

Access from Mr S. Sidebottom, Nether Water Farm.

Discovered during site clearance and investigated by Derek Stables in 1995.

Behind the new buildings of Nether Water Environmental Services.

Entrance shaft of 25ft (8m) formed by collapse of shale into a cavity in the limestone. A narrow rift passage leads southwards to a series of further short descents to reach the bottom of the cave. A climb in the roof led to a small chamber and a further blocked pot. A stream could be heard at the lowest point, and a draught was reported.

**Tackle:**
**8m ladder + lifeline. Scaffold bar for belay.**

*References: Arveschoug, D. 1995. Caves & Caving No.70. pp.5 & 7. Survey.*
*Beck, J.S. 1995. Descent No. 127. p.17. Survey (part).*

## COW HOLE

**NGR 1725 8044 Grade: 1**
**Alt. 780ft (238m)**
**Length: 130ft (40m)**

Large entrance overlooking Bradwell Dale from the east.

A large mined out chamber, partly natural, leads to a short passage.

*Reference: Crabtree, P.W. 1964. B.S.A. Cave Science Vol.5. No.36. pp.188 & 190. Survey.*

## CREMATORIUM POT

**NGR 150 808 Dig**
**Alt. 1250ft (380m)**
**Depth: 40ft (12m)**

In field north west of Batham Pot (Pigeon Hole).

A natural pothole which has been dug for 40ft (12m) to a descending mud-filled passage. A resistivity survey suggested the presence of a large chamber 50ft (15m) below the surface. Digging by SUSS in the 1990s revealed a chamber, and a further short shaft was sunk. A draught was noted.

*References: Anon. 1979. Jour. S.U.S.S. Vol.3. No.1. p.59.*
*Lord, P.J. 1970. Jour. S.U.S.S. Vol.1. No.6. p.229.*
*Smith, G. 2001. Descent No. 160. p.11. Survey.*

## DEADMAN'S CLOUGH SWALLET

**NGR 176 801 Dig**
**Alt. c.800ft (244m)**

About 1/4 mile (400m) east of Hazlebadge Hall, near Old Pig Tor End Lead Mine.

A choked swallet which takes little water now owing to reservoirs higher up.

## DOWSE HOLE
(Duce Hole)

**NGR** 1812 7767 **Grade:** 3
**Alt.** 1000ft (305m)
**Length:** 370ft (113m)
**Depth:** 40ft (12m)
**Status:** S.S.S.I.

Permission from Duce Farm.

There is some confusion over the name. Farey (1811, p.295) noted Dowse Hole, Grindlow, near Eyam, a deep open hole. He also refers (p.293) to "Duss Pit, in Eyam". Duss Pit is likely to be Hungerhill Swallet, near Dustypit Mine. There is evidence to suggest that the hole known as "Duce" or "Dowse" was blown in early last century, and local people refer to it as "The Dowse". It is called "Dowse Hole" on the earliest Ordnance Maps, but the name seems to have changed to "Duce Hole" on maps of the late 1800's.

First investigated by cavers in 1942 (Rotherham Cave Club). Stream sink dug by British Speleological Association in 1959. Tight rifts followed to streamway. Dug by Pegasus Caving Club in early 1970's. Dug by Orpheus Caving Club to impenetrable fissure in late 1970s/early 1980s. Fissure enlarged by Eyam Exploration Group in 1989. Continuation dug 1989 - and sump by-pass driven. Streamway beyond enlarged to present limit at tight sump.

Please park in a manner that does not obstruct roads or entrances. Immediately north of Grindlow, near Great Hucklow. Two streams sink. Shod Pot is a 20ft (8m) timbered shaft in the field nearest to the road, taking a stream. Dowse Hole lies in the fir plantation near to the track.

A sizeable stream which includes farm sewage flows down over boulders into a chamber, and on down a short stretch of roomy stream passage. The original entrance lies above the stream sink, and led through very tight squeezes to drop into the roof of the streamway. Stream drops down impenetrable hole in second chamber, now cleared of three generations of old digging gear. Passage lowers to a crawl, and becomes narrow beyond a short incline. Enlarged joint passage continues to a sharp right hand bend 230ft (70m) from entrance, followed by a crawl through boulders. Impenetrable sump can be bypassed by climbing above pool into chamber, now largely backfilled from the dig. Way on from chamber was a very awkward and loose squeeze into flat out crawl in stream, which flows into low bedding, but this is backfilled and by-passed by an artificial level which rejoins the stream. Enlarged stream passage ends at a sump which has so far proved too tight for divers.

References: Batey, A. & Lord, P.J. 1970. Jour. S.U.S.S. Vol.1. No.6. p.246-247. Survey.
Beck, J.S. 1993. Jour. T.S.G. No.14. pp.46-47.
British Speleological Association Records. 1959-1960.
Farey, J. 1811. A General View of the Agriculture and Minerals of Derbyshire.pp.293 & 295.

Area around the Dowse Hole swallet. Swallet in foreground is Shod Pot.

## DURHAM EDGE SWALLET

NGR 1727 7924  Grade: 3
Alt. 785ft (239m)
Length: 200ft (61m)
Depth: 80ft (24.5m)
Status: S.S.S.I.

Permission from Mr.R Mycock at the Buxo-plas factory at Quarters Farm.

Entrance excavated November 2000 by E.E.G.

Stream sink in plantation adjacent to plastics extrusion factory at Quarters Farm.

### Warning: The entrance climb is impassable after heavy rain

A stream sinks over a short fall and flows into a passage leading to the top of a rift. A wet climb down lands on a floor at 20ft (6m) depth, and a further very wet climb down under the full force of the stream is in two steps, for a total of another 20ft (6m). The stream flows into a tight continuation, but a parallel rift can be followed. A climb down on the right leads to short series of inlets, becoming too tight. The main rift has been enlarged to gain access to the continuation of the rift, but all leads have so far become too tight. There is a draught, inwards in cold weather.

*Reference: Beck, J.S. 2001. Descent No. 158.p.17. Survey.*

## HARTLE DALE CAVES
### (Gelly Dale Caves)
Permission from Hartlemoor Farm.

### New Cave
(Upper Hartle Dale Cave, Upper Gelly Dale Cave)

NGR 1644 8031  Grade: 1 (Arch)
Alt. 980ft (299m)
Length: 50ft (15m)

On the south side of the valley on a bench a short distance above the valley floor. Entrance 6ft (1.8m) high and 6ft (1.8m) wide, diminishing to a crawl. There is little doubt that this is the "New Cave" referred to by Pennington in 1877.

### Fissure Cave
(Lower Hartle Dale Cave, Lower Gelly Dale Cave)

NGR 1642 8033  Grade: 1 (Arch).
Alt. 975ft (297m)
Length: 10ft (3m)

30 yards (27m) north west of New Cave. An obvious fissure with a tiny bedding plane passage directly above. The fissure is about 13ft (4m) high, dwindling from several feet wide at the top to a few inches at the bottom. There is no doubt that this is the "Fissure Cave" referred to by Pill (1963) and Turk (1966).

### Top Cave

A very small feature. It may lie on the same terrace as New Cave, just west of Fissure Cave.

*References: Gilks, J.A. 1990. Derbys. Arch. Jour. Vol.CX. pp.6-23.*
*Pennington, R. 1877. Quart. Jour. Geol Soc. pp.240-241.*
*Pill, A.L. 1963. B.S.A. Cave Science Vol.V. No.33. pp.25-35.*
*Turk, S.M. 1966. B.S.A. Cave Science Vol.V. No.40. pp.426-439.*

### HAZLEBADGE CAVE

NGR 1711 8019  Grade: 2
Alt. 700ft (213m)
Length: 391ft (119m)
Depth: 54ft (106m)
Status: S.S.S.I.

Gated. Limited access. Contact D.C.A. for up to date information. Situated on hill spur 600ft (182m) north of Hazlebadge Hall and 180ft (55m) east of the road.

A short mine level ends at the base of a run in shaft which lies beneath a blocked depression on the surface. Near the end of the level is a shaft 24ft (7m) deep. 12ft (4m) down this shaft a short level can be entered which gives access to the top of the main chamber. From the bottom of the shaft an upward level ends after 20ft (6m) while down the slope a series of short climbs (rope useful for novices), gives access to the main chamber which is natural. The passage to the left ends after 10ft (3m) while a low muddy tube on the right can be followed southward for 50ft (15m) into a high tight rift passage terminating in a small chamber. From a ledge above the chamber a small tube becomes too tight, and a bedding plane to the west can be followed for a short distance. The way on from the main chamber is straight ahead through a muddy crawl, or climb above which drops to the same point. A couple of sporting climbs follow (rope useful). The cave terminates at the top of a steeply ascending rift in a chamber with a flowstone cascade. A short distance before this a climb in the roof gives access to a narrowing decorated crawl.

Tackle:   Entrance Pitch: 8m ladder + lifeline.
          Climbs: 20ft (6m) handline useful.

References: Crabtree, P.W. 1964. B.S.A. Cave Science Vol.5. No.36. pp.180,183, & 185.
Survey. Farey, 1811. A general view of the agriculture and minerals of Derbyshire. p.296.

### HAZLEBADGE END MINE

NGR 1745 8015  Grade: 1 (Mine)
Alt. 780ft (238m)
Length: 100ft (30m)

Permission from Hazlebadge Hall. Unlikely.

At extreme south end of limestone hill behind Hazlebadge Hall, a few yards north east of Pictor End Mine.

Entrance from mined trench, by sliding down among boulders. Single natural but mined out chamber, with a crawl through boulders at the end.

Reference: Crabtree, P.W. 1964. B.S.A. Cave Science Vol.5. No.36. pp.183,184, & 186. Survey.

### INTAKE DALE MINE

NGR 164 797  Grade: 5 (Mine)
Alt. 965ft (295m)
Length: 300ft (91m) app.
Depth: 280ft (85m) app.

On a bluff on the south side of Intake Dale.

**Warning: The mine is very loose and dangerous almost throughout.**

100ft (30m) entrance shaft is very loose and dangerous with stacked deads on timbers. Loose stope provides a route down for a further 65ft (20m) through stacked deads. A sideways traverse to the head of another 20ft (6m) shaft, leading to workings in the vein, with four natural chambers and passages. The strong draught present at the entrance has not been located in any of the chokes.

References: Arveschoug, D. 1994. Caves & Caving No.66. p.2.
Bentham, K. 1994. Descent No. 121. p.12.

### KITTYCROSS CAVERN

NGR 151 803  Grade: 3 (Mine)
Alt. 1275ft (388m)
Depth: 450ft (137m)

Mine shaft east of Moss Rake spar-washing plant.

At bottom of main shaft a short passage leads into narrow natural fissure with a 10ft (3m) drop into a single chamber in the top of a decomposed lava.

Reference: Ford, T.D. 1951. British Caver. Vol.22. pp.45-48. Survey.

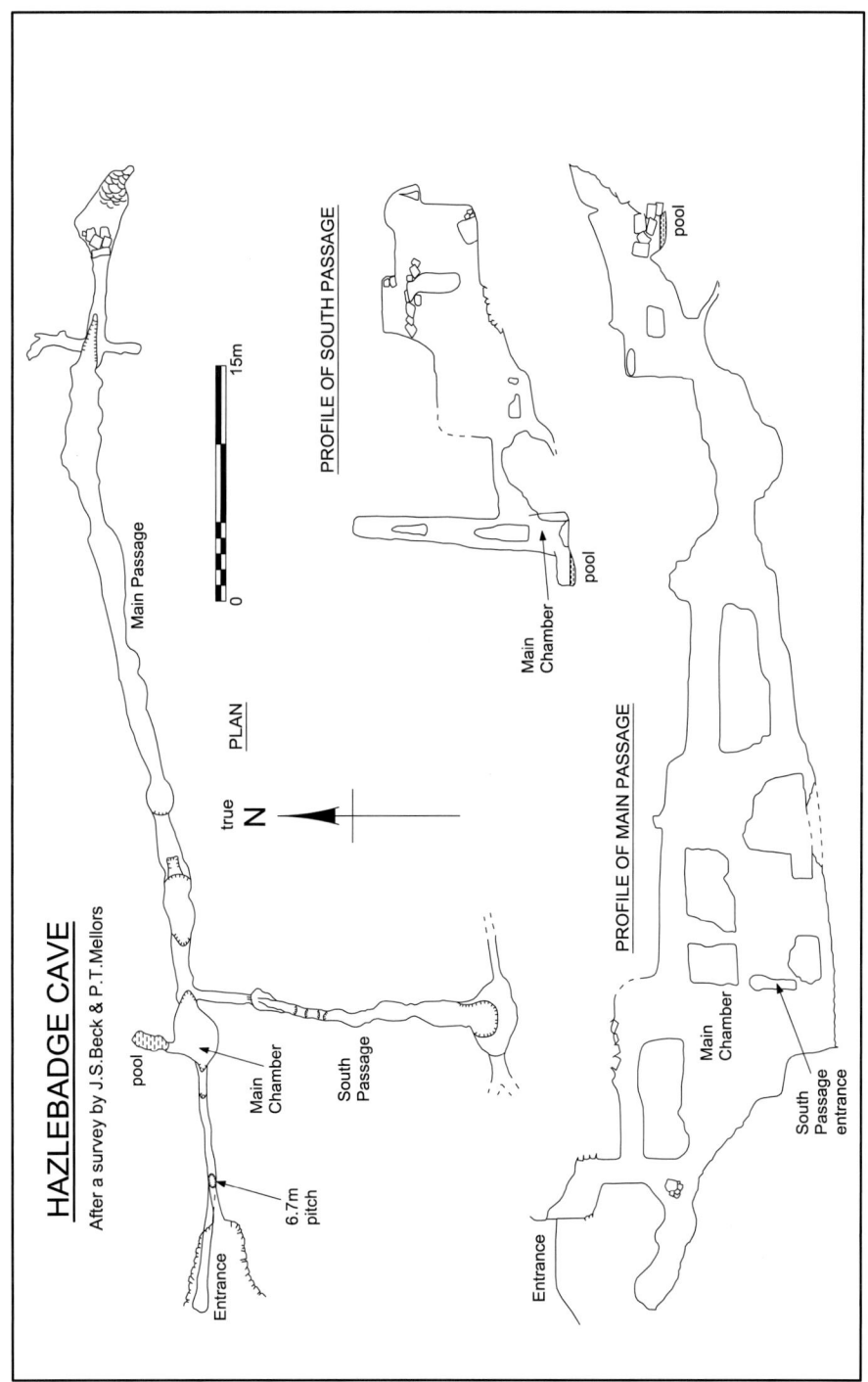

> **LONG RAKE MINE**
> (Long Rake Founder Shaft)
> NGR 153 808 Grade: 5 (Mine)
> Alt. 1235ft (310m)
> Depth: 500ft (150m)

No access at present. Contact DCA for updated information.

An obvious mine shaft about 100ft (30m) east of Batham Pot.

**Warning: Mine contains many unstable stacked deads. Treat with extreme caution.**

First pitch of 130ft (40m), partly a ginged mine shaft, partly a worked out vein. Levels off at 30, 69, and 92ft (9, 21, and 28m) into natural cavities and stopes. Second pitch follows soon, 170ft (50m), in a vein cavity with a ledge and short level at 120ft (37m) down. Main level runs east-west at 300ft (92m) depth, with short pitches downwards. Climbing at the western end leads into a large stope with a steeply sloping floor to the head of the third pitch, 48ft (15m) into a large oval chamber with stemples opposite. A short climb down below these leads into another large cavern 50 x 90ft (15 x 27m) with short stalactites. A stream can be heard and digging has reached a short pitch to a chamber with a washed out lava bed and no way on. The stopes can be climbed for 120ft (37m) to a level which enters another chamber 40ft (12m) long and 130ft (40m) deep. A ledge round this leads to another chamber and a series of climbs down to lower levels.

Tackle:   First and second pitches: 130m rope. 6 possible rebelays.
          Third pitch: 20m rope.

References: Lord, P.J. & Thompson, S.J. 1968. Jour. S.U.S.S. Vol.1. No.3. pp.104-111.
Lord, P.J. & Worthington, S.R.H. 1969. Jour. S.U.S.S. Vol.1. No.5. pp.181-185. Survey.

> **MILL DAM CAVERN**
> Lost

In the vicinity of Great Hucklow, on the Hucklow Edge Vein. A large cavern found during mining operations said to be "as big as Tideswell Church". The infilled Hilltop Mine shaft is thought to be about 35m deep, and the most likely shaft to give access to the cavern.

Reference: Kirkham, N. 1963. Bull. P.D.M.H.S. Vol.2. No.1. p.32.

> **MOORFURLONG MINE & CAVERNS**
> NGR 1678 8119
> Grade: 2 (Mine)
> Alt. 943ft (287m)
> Length: 700ft (210m)
> Depth: 70ft (21m)

Permission from Within Farm, above the road.

In corner of field almost opposite the entrance to Within Farm.

Entrance shaft 44ft (13m) with ancient metal ladder. A short passage leads to the second pitch of 12ft (4m). At the bottom a series of pipe workings and natural caverns extends to the south east and north west. The longer series is to the south east, running for some 600ft (180m) and bending round to the east, via old buddle pools and "The Vice" crawl. Passages beyond The Vice consist of a network of crawls. To the north west of the entrance is about 100ft (30m) of large bedding cave.

Tackle:   Entrance pitch: 17m rope
          Second pitch: 4m ladder and lifeline

References: Marsh, A.L. 1953. The Speleologist. Vol.1. pp.3-8. Survey.
Beck, J.S. & Worley, N.E. 1976. Trans. B.C.R.A. Vol.3. No.1. pp.49-53. Survey.

> **NETHER FEAR MINE**
> NGR 1740 8015 Grade: 2 (Mine)
> Alt. 800ft (240m)
> Length: 120ft (36m)
> Depth: 110ft (34m)

280 yards (256m) north east of Hazlebadge Hall.

A 100 ft (30m) shaft leads to a ledge with a scramble down to worked out pipe vein with some natural chambers leading eastwards to a muddy crawl into rifts. Probably no longer accessible.

Reference: Crabtree, P.W. 1964. B.S.A. Cave Science Vol.5. No.36. pp.184 & 186. Survey.

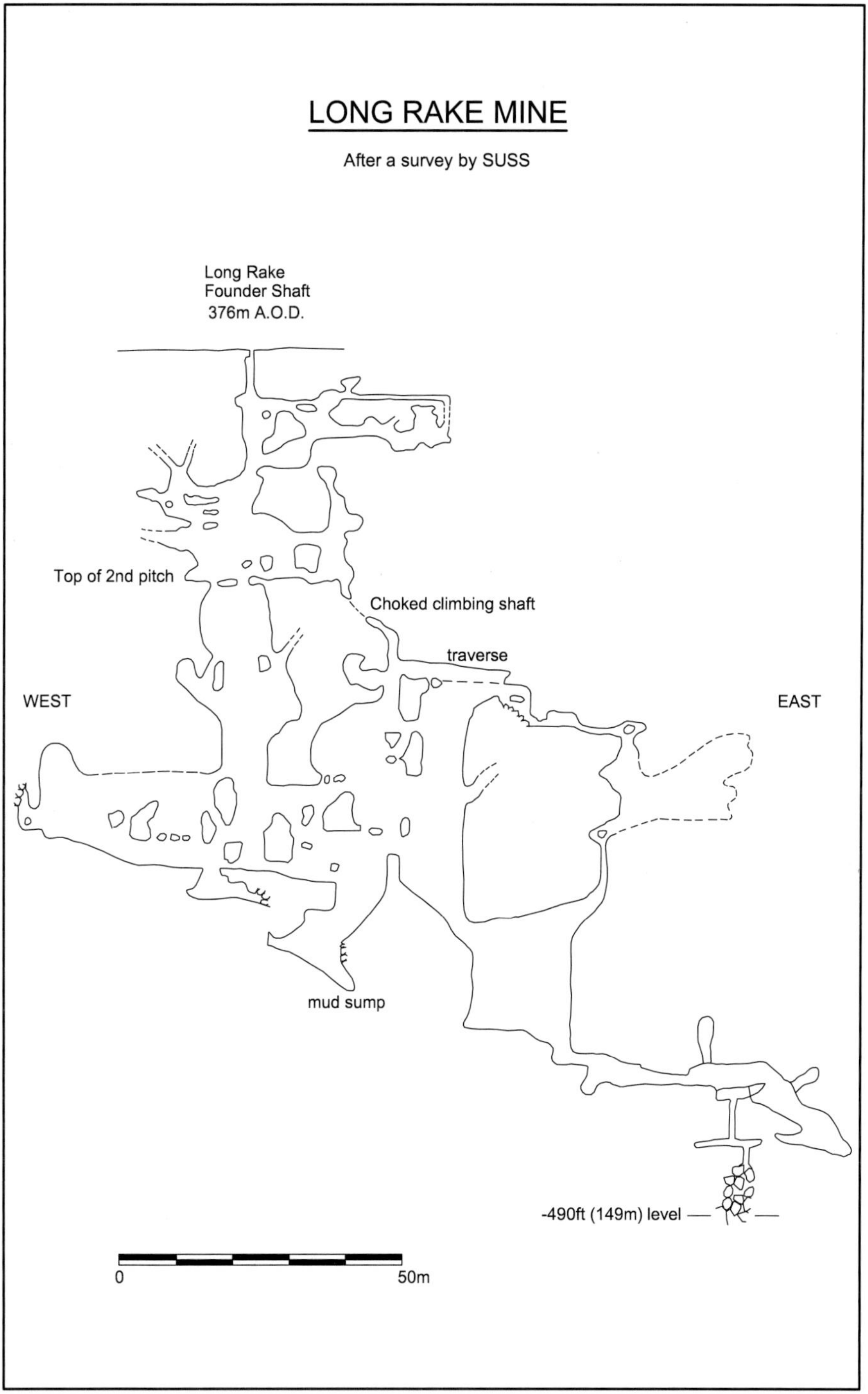

## LONG RAKE MINE

After a survey by SUSS

Long Rake Founder Shaft 376m A.O.D.

Top of 2nd pitch

Choked climbing shaft

traverse

WEST

EAST

mud sump

−490ft (149m) level

0    50m

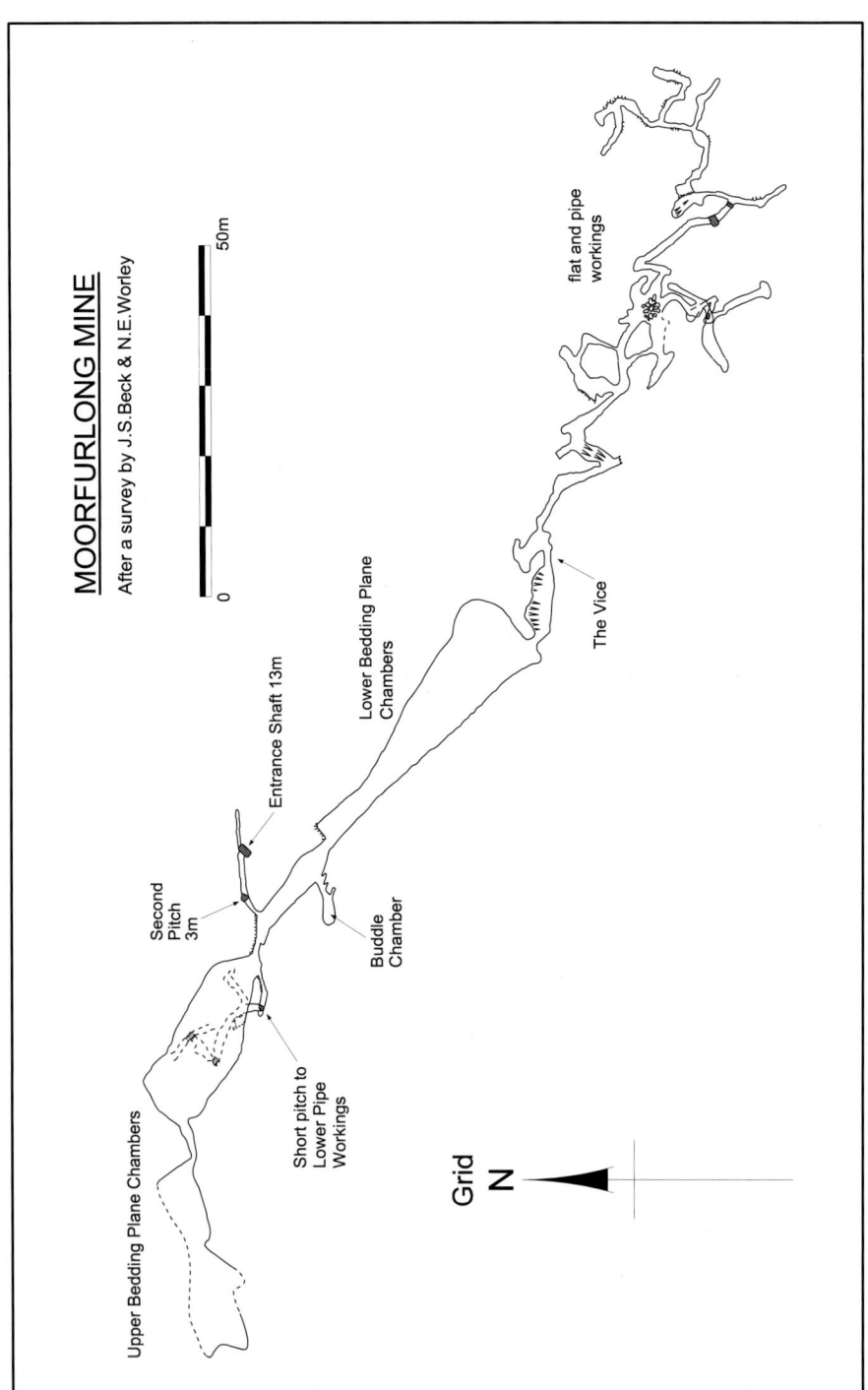

## NETHER WATER MINE
NGR 1708 7910   Grade: 4
Alt. 835ft (255m)
Length: 1000ft (305m) approx.   Depth: 120ft (37m) app.

Access from Mr S.Sidebottom, Nether Water Farm.

On the shoulder of the hill above Stanlow Dale, north of Nether Water Farm.

### Warning: The cartgate sumps in wet weather

The climbing shaft entrance lies in a small vein trench a short distance below the fence. Short scramble down leads to the head of the stopes. An old iron ladder drops 12ft (4m) to the top of the first pitch (60ft/18m), and a second pitch of 30ft (9m) leads down to the cartgate. Crawling and walking eastwards in deep silt leads to deep water after approx. 100ft (30m). To the west it is possible to traverse over the second pitch, or descend the pitch and crawl in the mud and climb to the higher level beyond. Further traversing leads to a climb down into a chamber where the old timbered shaft enters in the roof, and the continuation of the cartgate. The route is now thought to be blocked here. A forefield was reached 720ft (220m) from the bottom of the climbing way. Near the forefield a series of natural rifts with small inlet streams cross the cartgate. The most easterly rift can be free-climbed to a large natural rift on the north side of the cartgate, with a phreatic tube leading off which eventually becomes too tight. To the south of the cartgate a series of rifts can be followed to inconclusive leads which have so far proved too tight.

*Tackle:*   First pitch: 25m rope
            Second pitch: 15m rope

*Reference:* Beck, J.S. 2003. Descent No. 171. p.10.

## NETHER WATER SWALLET
NGR 171 791   Dig
Alt. 790ft (237m)

100 yards (91m) below Nether Water Farm, immediately below the fluorspar mine. The precise location of the swallet is unclear: surface water flows into an excavated pit in the floor of the valley.

A choked swallet. Has been used in attempts to dispose of water pumped from the mine, though it is also thought that it leads flood water into the mine. Water probably reappears at Bagshawe Cavern.

## NEW VENTURE MINE AND CAVERN
NGR 1540 8104   Grade: 4 (Mine)
Alt. 1250ft (381m)
Depth: 220ft (67m)

Permission needed in writing from PDMHS due to insurance issues - close to expanding quarry and may well become more unstable once active face comes nearer.

### Now in a dangerous condition due to quarry workings nearby.

Shaft No.6. on New Venture Vein, 100 yards (91m) north of and parallel to Long Rake.

First pitch, a ginged shaft, is 80ft (24m) deep to a level, which leads east to link with a single cavern reached from the adjacent Shaft No.5. A shaft in the floor leads to further pitches to the lower workings. The second pitch is almost under the first, and at a depth of 50ft (15m) it reaches a four way junction. Here miners levels run east and west, and a natural cave trends from north to south. To the north a single chamber is nearly full of miners' debris, but to the south a well decorated fissure can be climbed for 80ft (24m). Whole system rather unstable.

*Tackle:*   First Pitch: 30m rope        Second Pitch: 20m rope
            Lower stopes: 30m rope

*Reference:* Wright, A. and Worthington, S. 1971. S.U.S.S. Jour. Vol.2. No.1. pp.21-23. Survey.
Heathcote, C. 1997. Mining History Vol.13. No.3. pp.53-56, No.4. pp.51-54, No.6. pp.23-24. Sketch surveys.

## NOULTON MINE

NGR 1742 8025  
Grade: 2 (Mine)  
Alt. 790ft (241m)  
Length: 207ft (63m)  
Depth: 41ft (12m)

Approximately 400 yards (366m) north east of Hazlebadge Hall. A 41ft (12m) shaft leads to worked out pipe vein caverns, leading north north west. Partly removed by opencast mining.

*Tackle: 15m rope*

Reference: Crabtree, P.W. 1964. B.S.A. Cave Science Vol.5. No.36. p.187. Survey.

## OUTLANDS HEAD CAVE

NGR 166 808          Lost  
Alt. 1150ft (350m)  
Length: 1215ft (370m)  
Depth: 86ft (26m)  
Status: S.S.S.I.

No access at present. May no longer be accessible. Explored and surveyed by E.P.C. 1973. In floor of Outlands Head Quarry.

Two entrances in quarry floor, each needing 20ft (6m) handline. Original entrance drops into small unstable chamber, leading to stooping sized phreatic passage. Eventually passage breaks into large high cross rift with passage continuing on the far side to end at a clay blockage after about 400ft (122m). Climb up left wall of cross rift leads to large passage which after a short distance becomes a hands and knees crawl, eventually becoming too low. There are seven other small caves in the quarry, one of which, the Frantastic Way, has a strong draught. These may be lost to land-filling.

References: Bentham, K. 1989. Descent No.91. p.14.

Gill, D.W. 1973. D.C.A. N/L No.17. p.2.; Gill, D.W. 1976. E.P.C. Jour. Vol.9. No.1. pp.13-14. Survey.

Gill, D.W. 1989. Descent No.88. p.16. Survey.; S.U.S.S. N/L No.21. May 1973.

## PICTOREND CAVE

NGR 173 802  Grade: 2 (Mine)  
Alt. 800ft (244m)  
Length: 200ft (61m)  
Depth: 45ft (14m)

Entrance in old surface lead workings 70ft (21m) south of walled Pictorend Mine Shaft (200ft/61m deep).

15ft (4.5m) climb leads into a large chamber 30 x 60ft (9 x 18m) with crawls beyond. Right leads into partly collapsed old workings. Left to window into mine shaft 40ft (12m) below surface. Partly removed by opencast mining.

Reference: Ryder, P.F. 1973. S.U.S.S. Jour. Vol.2. No.2. pp.25-27. Survey.

## PIPPIN HOLE

The Pippin at Hazlebadge is referred to only in passing by Farey. It is likely to have been Quarters Farm Swallet. He certainly wasn't referring to Little Waterfall Swallet, or the swallow near Glebe Mine, Eyam, which was rediscovered in 2006 and is the "Pippin Swallow" (qv) mentioned by William Wood in his "History of Eyam".

Reference: Farey, J. 1811. A general view of the agriculture and minerals of Derbyshire Vol.1. p.296.

## QUARTERS FARM SWALLET

(Hazlebadge Swallow)  
NGR 1730 7943         Dig  
Alt. 750ft (229m)

Was dug in 1937, again in 1949 by Eccles Grotto Group (Turner, 1950), and by M.Noble and others from 2001-2004. May have been Farey's "Pippins Hole" or "Hazlebadge".

In trees some 200 yards (183m) north of Quarters Farm. A sink in a tree-lined shakehole.

Only narrow fissures were found when the sink was excavated in the 1940s, but the dig was only opened to a depth of 15ft (5m) before being abandoned. A slight draught was reported. In 2001 a short overflow cave was opened up on the east side of the shakehole, reaching a total depth of around 20ft (6m), and various exploratory shafts were sunk. A collapse in shale on the north rim was excavated to a depth of 24ft (7m) in 2002. A new sink was opened near the south end of the shakehole in 2004, and now takes the entire stream.

References: Beck, J.S. 2001. Descent No.161.

Farey, J. 1815. View of the Agriculture and Minerals of Derbyshire Vol.1. p.290 & 296.

Turner, D. 1950. B.S.A. Cave Science No.14. p.250.

### REVELL'S PIPE VEIN
**NGR 1745 8020  Grade: 1**
(Mine)
Alt. 780ft (238m)
Length: 386ft (118m)

Permission rarely granted.

A few yards north of Hazlebadge End Mine.

Two low entrances at the base of a small scar. The more southerly may have been a trial, but the other entrance leads into the pipe, trending south east. Several crawls lead to mined out caverns with a short climbing shaft to lower levels and another to the surface.

*Reference: Crabtree, P.W. 1964. B.S.A. Cave Science Vol.5. No.36. pp.184,187, & 189.*

### SHOD POT
**NGR 1809 7767  Dig**
Alt. 1000ft (305m)

Permission from Mrs Ollerenshaw at Duce Farm.

Excavated by Stockport Caving Group in the 1970s.

A small swallet in a prominent hollow close to Dowse Hole.

A timbered shaft was sunk through what appears to be road widening debris. It must therefore have been a large open hole and may have been part of the original "Dowse Hole" referred to by Farey. Voice contact was established with Dowse Hole in 1992.

*References: Beck, J.S. 1978. Bull. P.D.M.H.S. Vol.7. No. 2. pp.106-115.*
*Farey, J. 1811. A general view of the agriculture and minerals of Derbyshire. p.293.*

### WALKER'S GROTTO
(Bradwell Dale Cave. Nickerlow Cave)
**NGR 173 806  Grade: 1**
Alt. 630ft (189m)
Length: 130ft (40m)
Status: S.S.S.I.

Obvious entrance at foot of cliff, across the valley from Bradwell Parish Cave, and south of the first lay-by coming from Bradwell village.

Immediately inside, a tight crawl to the right is blocked after 16ft (5m). The main passage follows a calcite vein to a large and muddy chamber with flowstone deposits, now sadly vandalised. A hole in the floor of the chamber is choked, as is the continuation of the chamber in the roof at the end. In wet conditions a temporary lake forms at the base of the chamber. 50ft (15m) to the south of Walker's Grotto is a low tube choked with mud after 14ft (4m).

*References: Crabtree, P.W. 1964. B.S.A. Cave Science Vol.5. No.36. Survey.*
*Turner, D. 1950. British Caver Vol.21. p.22.*

### WELL SHAFT
**NGR 1710 8032      Grade: 2**
(Mine)
Alt. 650ft (198m)
Length: 200ft (61m) approx.
Depth: 50ft (15m)

Concrete capped shaft a few yards west of the road in Bradwell Dale.

Crawl under the south side of the lid into the shaft. Shaft is 50ft (15m) deep, usually to water. Natural passage off at 30ft (9m) to the west, ending at a gravel and rock choke, dug unsuccessfully. Opposite this is a passage leading under the road to a further run-in. Base of shaft usually flooded but in drought very unstable workings can be followed for 24m to chokes.

**Tackle     20m rope**

*Reference: Whitehouse, R.H. 1966. E.P.C. Jour. Vol.7. No.1. pp.23-24.*

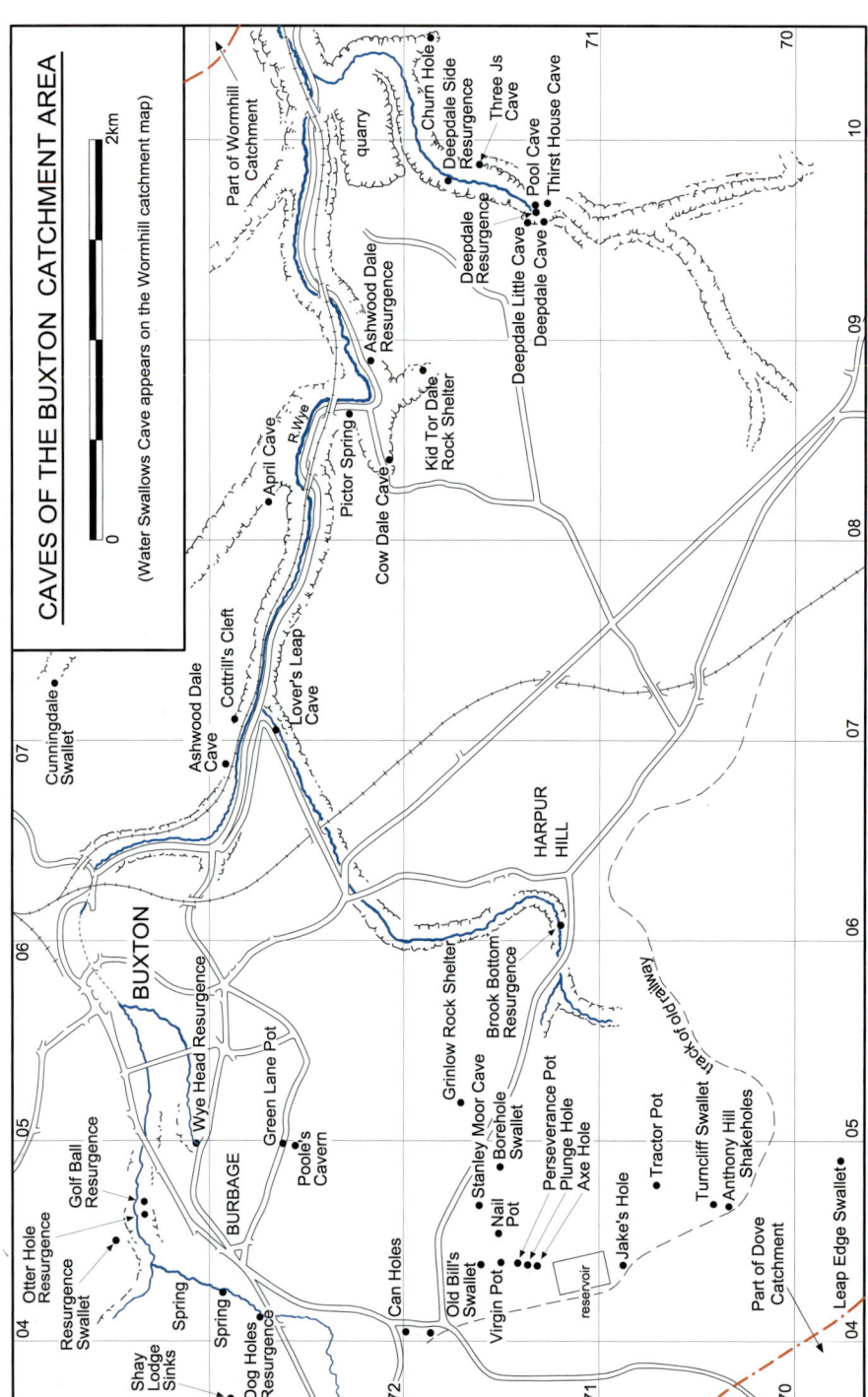

# THE BUXTON CATCHMENT AREA

Stanley Moor and Axe Edge

The River Wye rises on the shales and sandstones of Axe Edge Moor, and first encounters the limestone just west of Buxton. It does not sink, but flows on the surface through the town. It is augmented by numerous springs before continuing eastwards down Ashwood Dale. Further springs swell the river here. Some appear to be in the river bed itself, and may be fed from the Water Swallows area to the north, where digging only revealed a narrow fissure. It seems unlikely that a penetrable cave system exists to the north of the river although little serious work has been done.

The majority of the risings in the Buxton area lie on the south bank, and are fed from the swallets of Stanley Moor. The hydrology is complex, but most of the drainage goes to Wye Head Resurgence via Poole's Cavern. Dye tests have also revealed connections to Brook Bottom and Otter Hole Resurgences.

Prior to deepening of the Wye Valley, Poole's Cavern may have been the main outlet, but today the water rises at Wye Head, 46m lower. The drainage route between the two is immature, and it is doubtful if it would be penetrable.

The swallets have been dug over the years, but a large vadose system has not been entered. This may be due to the existence of the north-south Grin Low Anticline, leading to adverse dips in the Stanley Moor Region. The swallets lie to the south west of the anticline, and the upstream end of Poole's Cavern is only 20m below the lowest points reached in the swallets. The chances of entering an extensive vadose system do not seem hopeful, but there is scope for further work.

The other drainage system of interest is the Shay Lodge - Dog Holes Resurgence system, which seems to run down dip, and may well repay further work.

The large Ashwood Dale Resurgence appears to be fed by percolation water from a large area of limestone to the south, as are smaller risings issuing from the valley floor in Deep Dale. Little work has been attempted in Deep Dale, and a protracted dig at Thirst House Cave, above the risings, may bring results.

### ANTHONY HILL SHAKEHOLES
NGR 047 703  Dig
Alt. 1250ft (375m)

South of Stanley Moor Reservoir, a few yards east of the railway line and near Turncliffe Swallet.
Two small wet weather swallets close together. Possible dig?

### APRIL CAVE
NGR 082 727  Grade: 1
Alt. 980ft (299m)
Length: 36ft (11m)

Discovered by EPC in 1969.
A short distance up Cunning Dale from the River Wye in disused quarry.
Enlarged entrance to 10ft (3m) high passage with large mud bank up to roof. At roof level two passages diverge. Right hand passage closes down after 7ft (2.1m) and left hand passage curves round to where daylight can be seen, too tight to exit.
*Reference: Bridger, R. 1976. D.C.A. N/L No.30.*

### ASHWOOD DALE CAVE
NGR 0688 7291  Grade: 1
Alt. 1000ft (300m)

On north side of dale, immediately east of sewage works. Go up path under bridge and cave is high up on right.
15ft (4.5m) passage, squeeze past boulder into small chamber. Might repay archaeological digging as it is probably the cave which yielded a few Romano - British remains to Salt in 1895.
*References: Eldon Pothole Club Newsletter Vol.4. No.1.*
*Eldon Pothole Club Newsletter Vol.5. No.10. Survey.*
*Haverfield, F. in Victoria County History of Derbyshire. p.238.*
*Turner, W. 1899. Ancient Remains Near Buxton. p.75.*

### ASHWOOD DALE RESURGENCE
NGR 0895 7222  Dig
Alt. 820ft (246m)

Was used for a water supply.
A large volume of water rises immediately south of the A6 from a cave entrance and lower fissures.
The source is unknown. In dry weather can be forced in a very tight passage for approx. 20ft (6m) to where it becomes too tight. It emits a very strong draught when dry.
*References: Needham, J. 1966. Eldon Pothole Club Journal Vol.7. No.1. pp.9-12.*
*Gregson, P. 1996. O.C.C. NL 32 (6).*

### AXE HOLE
NGR 044 713  Grade: 2
Alt. 1250ft (375m)
Length: 200ft (60m)

In first shakehole north of Stanley Moor Reservoir.
Squeeze down for 12ft (4m), then tight rift 8ft (2m). Further sideways squeeze for 10ft (3m). Left turn into walking passage for 20ft (6m), terminating in muddy sump. Crawl beyond in muddy 3ft (1m) high passage round several bends and undulating to final chamber. There is a shaft from final chamber down to water. Climbing into roof leads to small chambers with straw stalactites. Turning right at entrance rift it is possible to squeeze into sandy crawl for 60ft (18m). Tight connection with Plunge Hole. Dye tested to Brook Bottom, Otter Hole, Wye Head via Pooles Cavern.

**Tackle: 50ft (15m) rope is useful at the entrance and down the rift.**

## BOREHOLE SWALLET
**NGR 049 715**     Dig
Alt. 1160ft (384m)

50 yards upstream from the Borehole pump house. Stream sinks under a wall.

Dug out (assisted by collapse) to 15ft (5m) to uncover a tight passage blocked after a few feet, but later filled in. Active dig by C.C.P.C. in 2004 (Johnson, 2004). Dye tested to Wye Head via Pooles Cavern.

*References: Eldon Pothole Club N/L Vol.5. No.7.*
*Johnson J.R. 2004. C.C.P.C. N/L No.82. p. 2.*

## BROOK BOTTOM RESURGENCE
**NGR 056 710, 0575 7115, 057 713**    Digs
Alt. 1025ft (312m)

Three risings to the west of the road.

The two southerly risings have been dye tested from the Stanley Moor Swallets. The third is probably local drainage above a lava bed.

## CAN HOLES
**NGR 041 721 & 040 718** Digs
Alt. 1200ft (366m)

Small sink near the Macclesfield-Buxton and Leek-Buxton road junction, and another at 040 718 which takes more water in wet weather.

At the first swallet water can be seen falling through boulders for 5ft (1.5m).

*References: Gilman, J. 1985. Karst Hydrology of the Buxton area, Derbys. Unpublished BSc. Thesis. Manchester Polytechnic.*
*Gunn, J. & Edmans, A. 1989. The Wye Head systems - some hydrological observations.*
*Caves & Caving No.45. p.35.*

## CHURN HOLES
**NGR 1054 7186**     Grade: 1
Alt. 880ft (264m)
Length: 200ft (60m)

At head of Marl Dale, the southern branch of Deepdale near Topley Pike.

Two pothole entrances drop into a chamber, with 200ft (60m) of partly excavated low passage, passing a number of cross joints. A large joint entrance opposite is blind.

*References: Drakeley, K. 1981. Churn Holes. The Lyre No.5. pp.23-26.*
*Turner, W. 1899. Ancient Remains near Buxton. p.78.*

## COTTRILL'S CLEFT
**NGR 072 728**   Grade: 1 (Dig)
Alt. 807ft (246m)

300m to the east of Ashwood Dale Cave. An obvious entrance in the rock face to the north of the railway line.

A small fissure cave which could be dug.

*References: Brooks, S. 2003. OCC N/L Vol.39, No. 1-6, p.13*

## COW DALE CAVE
**NGR 084 721**     Grade: 1
Alt. 855ft (260m
Length: 6ft (2m)

On the south side of the dale, just before the road steepens at the first bend.

A small fissure.

*References: 2002, OCC N/L, Vol.38, No.1-2, p.8*

### CUNNINGDALE SWALLET
NGR 073 738     Dig
Alt. 1000ft (305m)

At head of Cunningdale, just past allotments in middle of waste ground.
The sink takes a small stream largely composed of sewage from a pig farm.

### DEEPDALE CAVE
(Nettle Cave)
NGR 0962 7129     Grade: 1
Alt. 975ft (292m)
Length: 70ft (21m)

The name strictly applies to a cave opposite and higher than Thirst House Cave (q.v) but the name has often been applied to the latter.
A bedding plane crawl, extensively dug by Orpheus Caving Club in the 1950's. Above Deepdale Cave is a rift in the wood once dug.
*Reference: Smith, P. 1956. Lyre No.1. pp 13-14.*

### DEEPDALE LITTLE CAVE
NGR 0958 7133 Grade: 1 (Dig)
Alt. 820ft (250m)
Length: 10ft (3m)

High on the west side of Deepdale, opposite Pool Cave. A small tube.

### DEEPDALE RESURGENCE
NGR 097 713     Dig
Alt. 875ft (267m)

In the floor of Deepdale, a short distance downstream of Thirst House Cave.
A large volume of water rises from an indeterminate source among the boulders in the valley floor in wet weather.

### DEEPDALE SIDE RESURGENCE
NGR 098 718     Dig
Alt. 860ft (262m)

Resurgence in the floor of Deepdale.

### DOG HOLES RESURGENCE
NGR 041 727     Dig
Alt. 1000ft (300m)

First entered by Tim Hallam (TSG & UASS) in 1996.
A large resurgence behind two small cottages at Dog Holes.
A small entrance gives access to a slope down to a pool in a small chamber (Mhairi's Chamber), dived to 5m depth to a possible underwater dig. Excavated using diving gear to a depth of 2 metres. It consists of a 2m diameter chamber, open to day light, with a very low bedding under the back wall heading back up the valley - this was not entered. Dye tested from Shay Lodge Sinks.
*References: Gunn, J. & Edmans, A. 1989. BCRA Caves & Caving No.45 p.35.*
*Hallam, T. 1996. Descent No. 132. p.9. Survey.*

### GOLF BALL RESURGENCE
NGR 047 733     Dig
Alt. 1000ft (305m)

A small rising at river level which sometimes acts as a sink. The source is unknown.

### GREEN LANE POT

NGR 050 726  Grade: 2
Alt. 1000ft (305m)
Length: 80ft (24m)
Depth: 70ft (21m)

Permission required from the Borough Surveyor.

Entrance through manhole in road a few yards uphill from Poole's Cavern.

An unsafe wooden ladder leads to a platform 30ft (9m) down. (Use a 70ft (21m) ladder belayed to car or lamp post). The bottom of the pot is usually flooded to a depth of several feet. In drought a tube can be entered, 30inches (0.8m) high and two thirds full of liquid mud. Apparently part of the Poole's Cavern to Wye Head system.

*Reference: Eldon Pothole Club Newsletter Vol.5. No.10. Survey.*

### GRINLOW ROCK SHELTER

NGR 052 717  Grade: 1
Alt. 1150ft (345m)
Length: 10ft (3m)

In crags halfway between Solomon's Temple and the road, to the south west of the Temple.

A tight passage for 10ft (3m) between boulders leads into a breakdown chamber and a possible continuation dig.

### JAKES HOLE

NGR 0445 7080  Grade: 3
Alt. 1250ft (380m)
Length: 80ft (24m)
Depth: 35ft (11m)

In deep shakehole near the south wall of Stanley Moor Reservoir. Shakehole has large limestone slab at one side.

Tight 6ft (2m) crawl down slope. Squeeze over boulder to top of 25ft (8m) pitch. Very tight. Belay to iron bar in floor. 10ft (3m) square chamber at the bottom is very muddy. Tight squeeze into 20ft (6m) silted passage on left. Cave is difficult to get out of. Only for thin agile cavers!

**Tackle: 25ft (8m) ladder + 30ft (9m) lifeline**

### JAKES HOLE (LOWER)

NGR 0445 7080  Dig
Alt. 1250ft (380m)

In same shakehole as Jakes Hole.

A small stream sinks among boulders. This has been dug and penetrated for 20ft (6m) but was considered to be impossible for further work. Dye tested to Otter Hole, & Wye Head via Pooles Cavern.

*Reference: Eldon Pothole Club N/L Vol.5. No.10.*

### KID TOR DALE ROCK SHELTER

NGR 088 718  Grade: 1
Alt. 855ft (260m)
Length: 10ft (3m)

On the North-East side of the dale, 500ft (150m) down from the gate at the top.

A small rock shelter.

*Reference: 2002, OCC N/L, Vol. 38, No.1-2, p.8*

### LEAP EDGE SWALLET
(Dale Head Swallet)

NGR 0490 6975  Dig
Alt. 1275ft (389m)

South of Stanley Moor.

Active swallet taking a fair sized stream down an impenetrable hole. Dye tested to Brook Bottom.

### LOVERS LEAP CAVE
NGR 071 726    Grade: 1 (Dig)
Alt. 853ft (260m)
Length: 8ft (2.5m)

On the North-West side of the Lovers Leap Gorge, 80m from the road.
A small solution cave situated in an alcove.
*Reference: 2002, OCC N/L, Vol.38, No.1-2, p.9*

### LOVERS LEAP FISSURE CAVE
NGR 072 727   Grade: 1 (Dig)
Alt. 885ft (270m)
Length: 5ft (1.5m)

40m along the cliff from the Lovers Leap Gorge, towards Buxton
An obvious fissure. 33ft (10m) up the right-hand wall is a small cave entrance. 33ft (10m) climb is required to reach the cave; rope useful.
*Reference: 2002, OCC N/L, Vol.38, No.2. p.9*

### NAIL POT
NGR 045 715    Lost
Alt. 1250ft (375m)
Length: 50ft (15m) approx.
Depth: 50ft (15m)

50 yards (46m) south of Stanley Moor Cave. Contained about 50ft (15m) of passage. Partly collapsed in 1962, and now filled in for safety.
*Reference: Anon. 1963. The Caves of Stanley Moor. E.P.C. N/L. Vol.5. No.10/11 p.63. Survey.*

### OLD BILL'S SWALLET
NGR 044 716   Grade: 1 / Dig
Alt. 1300ft (390m)
Length: 10ft (3m)

At base of rock outcrop on Stanley Moor.
A small cave 10ft (3m) long. A small stream sinks among boulders in wet weather. An impenetrable crack to the right.

### OTTER HOLE RESURGENCE
NGR 046 733    Grade: 2
Alt. 1025ft (312m)
Length: 120ft (37m)

On site of housing development. Access unknown.
Dug by Eldon Pothole Club 1962/3.
In field by Otter Hole Farm. A powerful resurgence.
Crawl in the stream for 35ft (11m) to a flake dividing the passage. Pass on left, then squeeze lying on side in water. Follow stream crawling to duck which can be passed, and 5ft (1.5m) on is crawl into chamber with tin bath jammed in hole in roof! Stream flows out of silted up bedding plane and is known to come from Resurgence Swallet 120ft (37m) away. Dye tests were positive from the Stanley Moor Swallets. Solution cavities were found during the nearby housing development.
*Reference: Eldon P.C. N/L Vol.5. No.2. & Vol.5. No.10. Survey.*

### PERSEVERANCE POT
NGR 044 714    Grade: 3
Alt. 1250ft (381m)
Length: 120ft (37m)
Depth: 90ft (27m)

Dug by Eldon Pothole Club in 1962.
In third shakehole north of Stanley Moor Reservoir.
6ft (1.8m) drop between boulders to 20ft (6m) slope, then further 6ft (1.8m) drop into passage at right angles. Turn left and cross two holes in the floor (care - 40ft/12m deep). Continue to hole on left which is 25ft (8m) pitch. Pitch tight and ends on muddy slope of 15ft (4.5m). Then short iron ladder to short muddy passage and three muddy chambers. Has been dug in vain.
*References: Downhill, C. 1964. Eldon P.C. N/L Vol.5. No.10/11. p.64. Survey.*
*Dunn, J.A. & Hockenhull, C. 1963. Eldon P.C. N/L Vol.5 No.4. pp.11-12.*
**Tackle: 25ft (8m) ladder. 40ft (12m) lifeline.**

## PIGTOR SPRING
(Pictor Spring, Cowdale Spring)
**NGR 0867 7230**    **Dig**
**Alt. 840ft (256m)**

On the south west side of the A6 just north of the Cowdale turning.

A small pumphouse lies on the spring, which was used as a domestic water supply. The flow does not vary greatly in floods, and rarely (if ever) dries up.

*Reference: Beck, J.S. 1980. Speleogenesis in the Carboniferous Limestone of North Derbyshire. Unpublished PhD Thesis. Univ. Leicester. p.243.*

## PLUNGE HOLE
(Ladmanlow Cavern?)
**NGR 044 713**    **Grade: 2**
**Alt. 1220ft (372m)**
**Length: 30ft (9m)**
**Depth: 50ft (15m)**

Second shakehole from the north wall of the Stanley Moor Reservoir, where the stream runs into boulders.

Crawl under large boulder into a small chamber with a large boulder apparently blocking the way on. Route is under this (care) into 40ft (12m) deep rift (rope or ladder useful) which it is possible to climb down. Stream at bottom. Downstream after 20ft (6m) is too narrow. Upstream for 10ft (3m) to boulders through which the stream enters. Low crawl leads to small chamber, then tight squeeze into 5ft (1.5m) deep hole with choked bedding plane. Tight connection made with Axe Hole. Dye tested to Brook Bottom, Otter Hole, and Wye Head via Pooles Cavern.

*Reference: Anon. 1950. British Caver No.20. p.83. Reprinted Manchester Evening News 17-1-50.*

## POOL CAVE
**NGR 0968 7133**    **Grade: 1**
**Alt. 850ft (259m)**
**Length: 30ft (12m)**

Mine level below Thirst House Cave which was pumped dry and found to be blind.

## POOLE'S CAVERN
**NGR 050 725**    **Grade: Show**
**Alt. 1100ft (335m)**
**Length: 800ft (244m)**
**Status: S.S.S.I.**

In Green Lane, Buxton.

Show Cave, most of which is seen on normal tourist trip. An archaeological show cave. Romano-British animals and artefacts on show in museum attached. Roman Chamber a short distance from the entrance. Stream is seen sinking in large passage with fine stalactites and stalagmites. One of the chambers is 100ft (30m) high. Once lit by gas, now electric. After leaving the public section it is possible to crawl upstream into a boulder choke.

Above the choke are two further chambers, roots from surface being seen in upper one. Stream originates from the Stanley Moor Swallets, and sinks in the cave to reappear at Wye Head. Stalagmites three inches long grew on the victorian gas pipes.

Surveys using ground penetrating radar beyond the terminal choke in 1998 suggested further voids, and a subsequent borehole entered a cavity with large stalactites. Digging in the final choke has so far been unsuccessful, and small loose crawls above the choke have been followed for about 30ft (10m).

*References: Adam, W. 1838. Gem of the Peak. pp.307-309 in 1973 reprint by Moorland Publishing, Hartington.*
*Dawkins, W.B. 1874. Cave Hunting. pp.126-127. MacMillan, London.*
*Ford, T.D. & Allsop, D. 1975. Pooles Cavern Guide Book. Survey.*
*Glennie, E.A. 1953. C.R.G. N/L No.48. pp.12-13.*
*Glennie, E.A. 1953. C.R.G. N/L No.45. pp.5-10.*
*Johnson R.J. 1999. C.C.P.C. N/L No. 61. p.1.*
*McIntosh, J. 1972. E.P.C. Jour. Vol.8. No.1. p.13. Survey. Pitty, A. 1969. Proc. B.S.A. No.7. pp.7-15.*

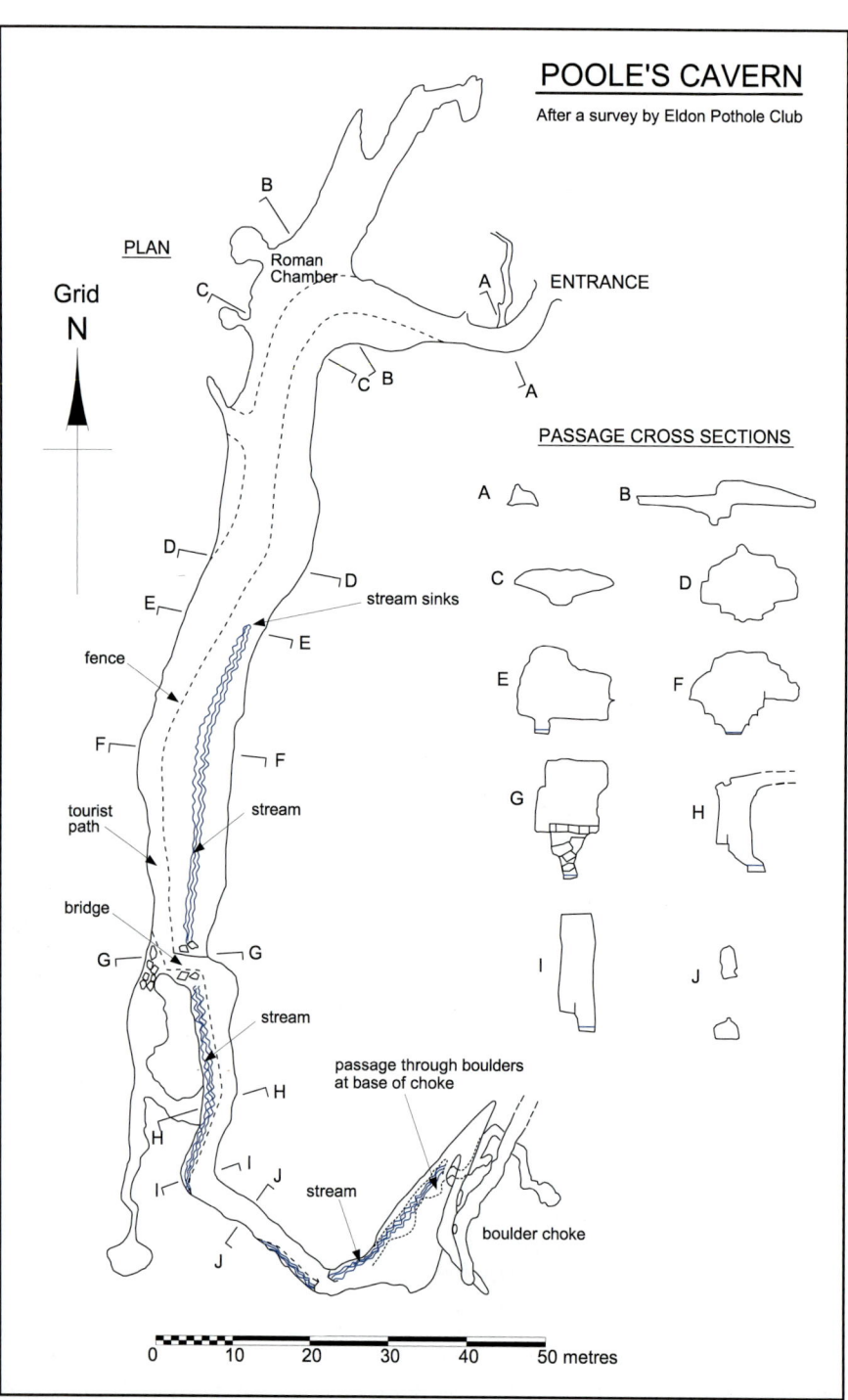

## RESURGENCE SWALLET

NGR 045 734  Grade: 2
Alt. 1200ft (366m)
Length: 120ft (37m)

Dug by Eldon Pothole Club in 1963.

In centre of fairway on Cavendish Golf Course.

Stream runs across floor of shakehole. Possible to squeeze into bedding in sink in passage 2.5ft (76cms) high. Possible to crawl and swim for 120ft (37m) when water is low. Has been dived but became too low. Water reappears at Otter Hole.

*Reference: Anon. 1963. E.P.C. N/L Vol.5. No.2. pp.23-24. & No.10, p.48. Survey*

## SHAY LODGE SINKS

NGR 035 729  Grade: 3
Alt. 1300ft (396m)
Length: 150ft (46m).
Depth: 90ft (27m).

The area around Shay Lodge Farm above Burbage, Buxton has 3 sinks. One cave can be entered by a series of squeezes to a free-climbable pitch of 33ft (10m). A crawl follows after a further awkward squeeze which has been dug, but is still blocked by boulders. Dye testing has shown that the water rises at Dog Holes.

*References: Needham, J. 1963. E.P.C. N/L Vol.5. No.4. pp.9-10.*
*Dickinson, S. 1983. E.P.C. Jour. Vol.9. No.3. p.11.*

## STANLEY MOOR CAVE

NGR 047 716  Grade: 1
Alt. 1220ft (372m)
Length: 70ft (21m)

Discovered by Eldon Pothole Club in 1958.

In large shakehole on Stanley Moor.

Slope of 10ft (3m) into entrance chamber. Tight passage on left slopes down into two small chambers with boulder chokes. 6ft (2m) hole on right of entrance chamber leads into fine grotto with curtains and straw stalactites. Further sloping passage for 20ft (6m) to choke.

*Reference: Anon. E.P.C. N/L No.10. p.67. Survey.*

## SWALLOW HOLES

Lost

An unknown cave near Buxton referred to by Cox, 1878.

*Reference: Cox, J.C. 1878. The Tourist Guide to Derbyshire. p.43.*

## THIRST HOUSE CAVE

NGR 0970 7127 Grade: 1. (Arch)
Alt. 890ft (271m)
Length: 190ft (58m)
Status:  R.I.G.S. (Deepdale)

An obvious entrance on the east side of Deepdale well above the dry bed.

Opposite is Deepdale Cave, and Thirst House has often been incorrectly called Deepdale Cave. A large entrance 15ft (4.5m) high and 20ft (6m) wide. Height soon drops to 6ft (2m) and after 72ft (22m) the floor descends to a second chamber. Hole in floor among boulders descends to a short crawl and a rift with a pool below. Both chambers have been archaeologically excavated.

*References: Cox, Rev. J.C. 1890. Arch. Jour. Vol.12. pp.228-230.*
*Cox, Rev. J.C. 1891. Arch. Jour. Vol.13. pp.194-199.*
*Turner, W. 1899. Ancient Remains near Buxton. pp.7-71. Survey. (Largely reprinted from Derbys. Arch. Jour.).*
*Ward. J. 1894. Arch. Jour. Vol.16. pp.185-189.*
*Ward. J. 1895. Arch. Jour. Vol.17. pp.60-81. Survey.*

### THREE Js CAVE
(Deep Dale Trial Level)
NGR 109 717     Grade: 1
Alt. 920ft (280m)
Length: 160ft (49m)

A mine level high on the east side of Deep Dale, on a steeply hading vein. Little evidence of natural solution.

*Reference: Gunn, J. 1985. D.C.A. N/L No.57. pp.3-4. Survey.*

### TRACTOR POT
NGR 048 707     Lost
Alt. 1300ft (396m)

A hole which appeared under a tractor and refilled for safety.

### TURNCLIFF SWALLET
NGR 0472 7034     Dig
Alt. 1200ft (366m)
Length: 10ft (3m)

Stream comes from under embankment and sinks. Not to be confused with large pool fed from a leat just off the limestone at 0460 7005. A 6ft (2m) drop between boulders into a bedding cave blocked by a boulder. Could be a productive dig. Dye tested to Brook Bottom, Otter Hole, and Wye head via Pooles Cavern.

### VIRGIN POT
NGR 044 715     Dig
Alt. 1250ft (381m)
Depth: 45ft (14m)

Dug in 1962 by Eldon Pothole Club.
In fourth shakehole north of Stanley Moor Reservoir.
A short drop between boulders to a tight oval hole in the floor for 25ft (8m), followed by a 20ft (6m) drop. Then too narrow. Entrance now blocked with large boulders.

*Reference: Anon. Undated. Eldon P.C. N/L Vol.5. No.10/11. Survey.*

### WATERSWALLOWS CAVE
NGR 079 749     Grade: 1
Alt. 1100ft (335m)
Length: 25ft (8m)

In middle of field south of the Buxton - Wormhill Road.
A stream sink, now capped and culverted. The stream flows into a tight bedding plane, opened by blasting for 25ft (8m) into a narrow rift which closes up. The stream was dye tested, and reappeared in the bed of the River Wye (exact location unknown).

*Reference: Woodall, B. 1972. E.P.C. Jour. Vol.8. No.1. pp.42-43.*

### WYE HEAD RESURGENCE
NGR 0499 7304     Digs
Alt. 1000ft (305m)

On the north side of Macclesfield Road, Buxton. The River Wye appears from several places among rocks.
Eldon Pothole Club penetrated 15ft (5m) by clearing boulders but were stopped by unstable roof under the road. Now blocked again. Water sinks at Stanley Moor Swallets and flows via Pooles Cavern.

*Reference: E.P.C. N/L. Vol.5. No.10.*

## Feature listed as potential archaeological site

1: NGR 1058 7187 Obvious joint entrance at the head of Marl Dale.

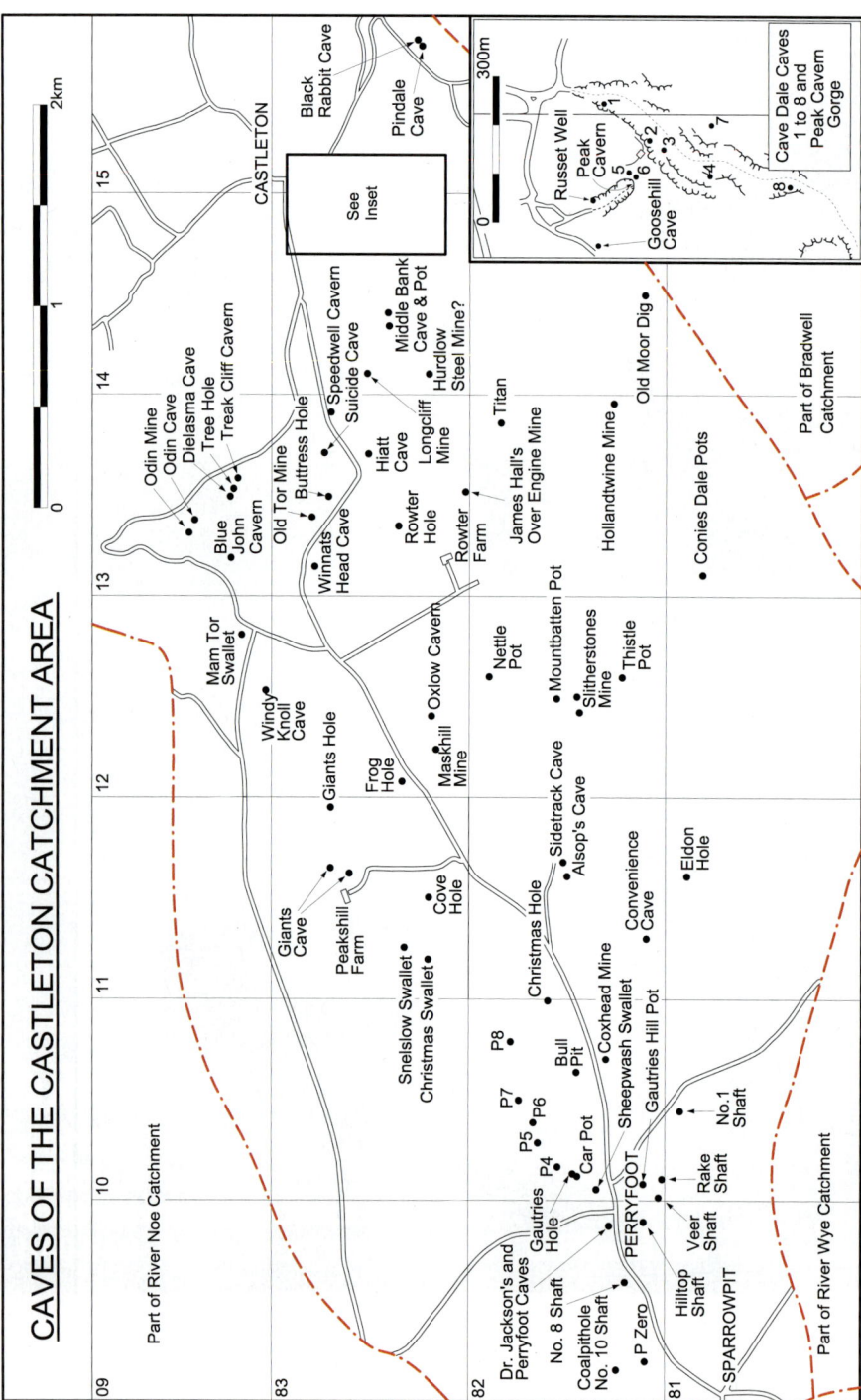

# THE CASTLETON CATCHMENT AREA

Cave Dale

The Castleton area is the best known caving area in Derbyshire. It was first noted by Charles Leigh in 1700 that the water from the Rushup Edge Swallets was that which emerged in the Peak Cavern gorge, and Lloyd and King's survey of Eldon Hole in 1772 was one of the first detailed cave surveys to be published.

Many streams enter swallet caves on the shale / limestone junction to the west of Castleton, and all this water drains to the Peakshole Water by way of either Peak or Speedwell Cavern. Topographically, the Rushup Vale should drain down Perry Dale, Dam Dale, Monks Dale etc. to the River Wye, but the underground drainage is diverted eastwards by the underlying structure to cross the surface watershed.

Water flows eastwards, its path determined by the large east-west mineral veins, which happen to line up quite nicely with the maximum hydraulic gradient. It surfaces at the low point on the shale margin at Castleton where the reef belt is thin, and where a series of joints have provided an easy passage.

The Peak - Speedwell Cave System consists of two major stream passages, with a complex network of tributaries and high level fossil passages. Most of the swallet water flows via the Speedwell Streamway, while the Peak Streamway carries percolation water from the limestone area to the south.

Exploration of the main Speedwell route ends upstream at a very deep and spectacular sump, Main Rising. This lies at roughly the same elevation as the East Canal in Giants Hole, and there may be a very large flooded area in between. However, many of the swallet caves are still unexplored because the swallets themselves are choked with debris from the gritstone escarpment to the north, so that there may be many inlets to explore on the way.

The 1991 edition of "Caves of the Peak District" stated that "the best prospects for extensions lie in some very remote digs at the western limits of the Peak - Speedwell system". One such dig led into the base of Titan, the biggest natural shaft in Britain. There is also potential in the excavation of some of the unexplored swallets, and possibly in digging some of the smaller dry caves and dolines which abound in the area. Exploration of the Castleton area is far from finished, and although many of the most promising sites are only available to experienced divers, the inquisitive explorer may still stumble upon interesting leads to follow.

### ALSOP'S CAVE
NGR 1161 8150
Dig/Lost
Status: S.S.S.I.

Discovered during quarrying operations in December 1994. The accessible part of the cave was removed during 1995.

On the upper bench east of the Northern Knoll. The present entrance lies in the north face below the Slitherstones Road.

The cave consisted of a large passage some 3m in diameter, restricted by a fill of clay and pebbles. It was very well decorated. A northward branch approximately 25 metres from the original entrance led through a low crawl to a well decorated aven. Crawling over large gours led to more walking sized passage, extended by digging to a point under the Slitherstones track. The exposed entrance lies close to the original limit of exploration, high in the north face of the eastern section of the quarry. The right hand branch lies further along the face, and was dug and pushed in 2002 (see Sidetrack Cave).

*References: Arveschoug, D. 1995. Caves & Caving No.68. p.5. Surface related survey.*

*Bentham, K. 1995. Descent No. 124. p.10. Survey.*

### BLACK RABBIT CAVE
NGR 157 823
Grade: 3
Alt. 800ft (244m)
Length: 500ft (152m)

Opposite Pindale Cave at the north west end of the quarry.

**Warning: The lower chokes are VERY UNSTABLE and it is inadvisable to enter them.**

Trends south east. SYCC dig through entrance boulder choke leads after 60ft (18m) to a tight squeeze. Wide low bedding cave beyond leads after 20ft (6m) to a further tight squeeze into a further low area with the main passage to the left and a choked passage to the right. Main passage is a wide crawl over boulders to a junction where the passage enlarges to walking size, but soon ends in a huge boulder choke. Right hand passage about 60ft (18m) long. A way down through the choke was found in 1985. A small stream and a short and very unstable extension were found.

*References: Noble, M. 1983. T.S.G. N/L No.10. p.10. Survey.*

*Cordingley, J.N. 1985. T.S.G. Members newsletter p.2.*

### BLUE JOHN CAVERN
NGR 1319 8320
Grade: 2 (Show)
Alt. 1250ft (375m)
Length: 4180ft (1274m)
Depth: 296ft (90m)
Status: S.S.S.I.

Generally no access beyond the show cave.

A mile west of Castleton on the Mam Tor Road.

Most of the cave is seen on a tourist trip. Artificial entrance for 18ft (5m) then descent of steps to Ladies Walk, sloping passage to 90ft (27m) high Crystallised Cavern. Second stairway leads to Stalactite Cavern and Lord Mulgrave's Dining Room, 140ft (43m) high and 30ft (9m) wide, where water is met in a fissure. These caverns make a very large and impressive vadose canyon. Several passages lead off, one to Fairy Grotto and Stemple Cavern, also reached from Stalactite Cavern. Show route ends in Variegated Cavern, over 100ft (30m) high and 30ft (9m) wide, seen from ledge 20ft (6m) up. Large passage continues beyond with rock barrier passable by muddy Rabbit Burrow into final chamber. Descent to final sump requires a 30ft (9m) ladder. Climbs of 48ft (15m) and 26ft (8m) reach to Superior Gallery. Branch passage

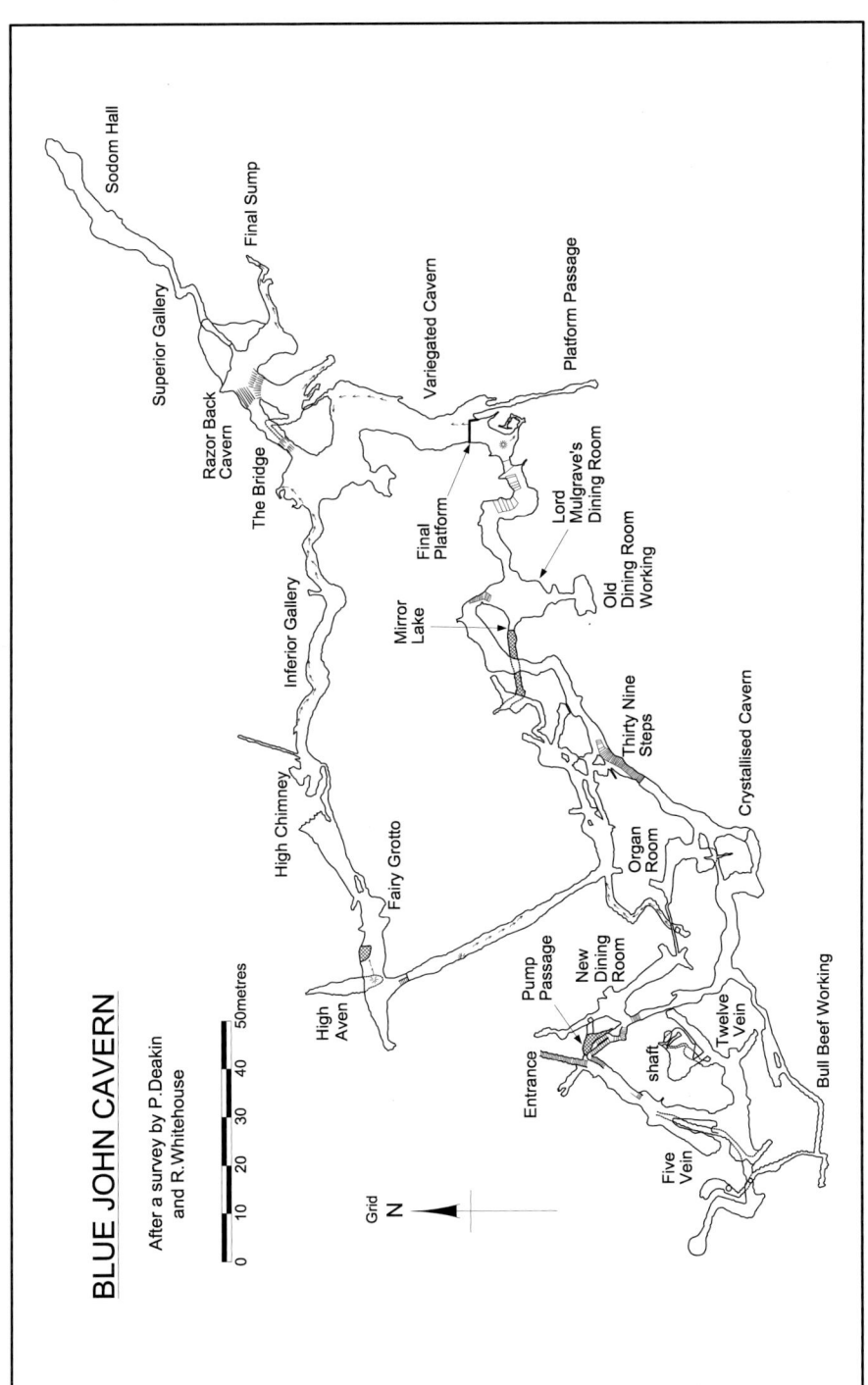

leads up to choke where one can communicate with Fairy Grotto.
*References: Barnes & Holroyd, 1896. Trans. Manch. Geol. Soc. Vol.XXIV.*
*Ford, T.D. 1955. Proc. Yorks. Geol. Soc. Vol.30. Survey.*
*Ford, T.D. 2000. Derbyshire Blue John. Landmark Publishing.*
*Martel, E.A. (transl. Winder, F.) The Caverns of Castleton. Survey.*
*Royse, J. 1943. Ancient Castleton Caves. Survey.*
*Westlake, C.D. 1979. Eldon P.C. Jour. Vol.9. No.2. pp.3-6. Survey.*
*Whitehouse, R.H. 1970. Eldon P.C. Jour. Vol.7. No.3. pp.33-42. Survey.*

### BULL PIT
NGR 1064 8143   Grade: 1
Alt. 1185ft (361m)
Depth: 80ft (24m)

600 yards (546m) east of Perryfoot, north of the road.
A deep open pothole choked at the bottom with large boulders. Easy scramble down south east side. Various digs in the bottom. Shaft No.1. is 20ft (6m) deep, then 30ft (9m) crawl in side passage to chamber. Downward passage and 20ft (6m) pitch leads to second chamber. Passage over leads to T-junction and left is over jagged rocks to a third chamber containing a stream. Other passage leads back to entrance pitch through natural and mined passages. Digging now abandoned and shaft hidden.
*Reference: Elliot, D. 1975. Caves of Northern Derbyshire. Part 4. p.22. Survey.*

### BUTTRESS HOLE
NGR 135 827   Grade: 1
Alt. 1072ft (326m)
Length: 30ft (9m)
Status: National Trust. S.S.S.I.

High on prominent buttress on north side of Winnats Pass. Obvious round hole leads to single chamber with muddy crawl to the left.
*Reference: Elliot, D. 1975. Caves of Northern Derbyshire. Part 5. p.12. Survey.*

### CAR POT
NGR 101 814   Grade: 1
Alt. 1040ft (317m)
Length: 50ft (15m)
Status: S.S.S.I.

Permission from Perryfoot Farm.
In the Gautries Hole shakehole, just west of Gautries entrance. A hands and knees crawl to the east, choked with silt. A short crawl on the left ends close to Gautries Hole.
*References:*
*Salmon, L.B. and Boldock, G. 1948. B.S.A. Cave Science Vol.1. No.6.*
*Elliot, D. 1975. Caves of Northern Derbyshire Part 4. p.4. Survey.*

### CAVE DALE CAVE No.1
NGR 1502 8264   Grade: 1
Alt. 730ft (219m)
Length: 20ft (6m)

Immediately on the right on entering the dale, under an overhanging rock. A short mine level with evidence of solutional activity.

### CAVE DALE CAVE No.2
NGR 1495 8254   Grade: 1 (Arch)
Alt. 875ft (262m)
Length: 15ft (4.5m)

At top of slope under south side of Castle Keep.
A bedding cave 8ft (2.5m) wide and 18 inches (0.5m) high. Crawling on rubbish for 15ft (4.5m). Archaeologically excavated.
*References: Pennington, R. 1875. Quart. Journ. Geol. Soc. 31, p.238.*
*Pennington, R. 1877. Barrows and Bone Caves of Derbyshire. p.53.*

## CAVE DALE CAVE NO.3
(Creep Hole?)

NGR 1493 8251   Grade: 1 (Arch?)
Alt. 850ft (255m)
Length: 6ft (2m)

Below and to the west of cave No.2. Halfway down the slope, close to old water pipe.

Small rock shelter ending in collapsed boulders. Reputed to have extended further at one time, and to have been dug archaeologically. This may be the Creep Hole noted by Pennington as connecting with a cave in the top of the Peak Cavern Gorge, probably Peveril Castle Cave.

*Reference: Pennington, R. 1877. Barrows and Bone Caves of Derbyshire. p.57.*

## CAVE DALE CAVE NO.4

NGR 1488 8240   Grade: 1
Alt. 850ft (255m)
Depth: 100ft (30m)

In cleft to west of footpath up dale, where the dale narrows and steepens. Narrow fissure descended by Puttrell into the roof of the Orchestra Chamber of Peak Cavern. Fitted with steel gate.

## CAVE DALE CAVE NO.5
(Peveril Castle Cave)

NGR 1488 8259   Grade: 1
Alt. 900ft (274m)
Length: 20ft (6m)

20ft (6m) higher and to left of caves 2 & 3. Below the west wall of the Castle Keep in the top of the Peak Cavern Gorge.

Low chamber sloping down to the north east for 20ft (6m) mostly 2ft 6in (0.8m) high. Reputed to connect with cave No.3.

## CAVE DALE CAVE NO.6
(Gorge Top Cave)

NGR 1487 8257
Grade: 1
Alt. 900ft (274m)

By Peveril Castle Keep directly above Peak Cavern entrance. A rock shelter in the trees.

## CAVE DALE CAVE NO.7
(Cave Dale Pipe)

NGR 1498 8231
Grade: 1
Alt. 1000ft (305m)
Length: 200ft (60m)

High on the east side of Cave Dale. A dig entered a pipe cavern enlarged by the miners.

*Reference: Penney, D. 1974. Bull. B.C.R.A. No.3. Survey.*

## CAVE DALE CAVE NO.8
(Path Cave)

NGR 1485 8225   Grade: 1
Alt. 925ft (282m)

Gated. Ventilation for Peak Cavern. No access. On the right of the path just below the gate.

Excavated in 1997 to reveal open passage leading to 230ft (70m) of pitches into the Five Arches of Peak Cavern. Now gated and used for Peak Cavern ventilation.

*Reference: Descent No. 143. 1998.*

## CHRISTMAS HOLE

NGR 110 816
Dig. Lost
Alt. 1180ft (360m)
Depth: 100ft (30m)

No access allowed. Dug by B.S.A. in Dec. 1947.

In shallow dry valley 656 yards (600m) approx. south east of P8 and nearer the Sparrowpit-Castleton road. Now covered and exact location uncertain.

A fissure cave dug to an impenetrable choke about 60ft (18m) down.

*Reference: Salmon, L.B. & Boldock, G. 1950. B.S.A. Cave Science Vol.2. No.11. pp. 122-123.*

## CHRISTMAS SWALLET
(Swallet P9)

**NGR** 112 822  **Grade:** 3
**Alt.** 1112ft (339m)
**Length:** 230ft (70m)
**Depth:** 230ft (70m)
**Status:** S.S.S.I.

Access controlled by Peakshill Farm. No access at present.
On the shale margin between Jackpot P8 and Snelslow Swallet.

**Warning: The stream is present throughout the cave, and does not have to be very high to cause problems. The catchment area is as large as P8 and Giants together. All the pitches become impassable very easily, and the entrance section sumps in flood. Rescue of an injured caver from the bottom would be almost impossible.**

A sporting little stream cave with four pitches after the capped artificial entrance shaft (23ft/7m). Climbable, but bolt belay available on left wall. Enlarged rift passage leads via two small drops to a low crawl with a pool (the old sump). The crawl is 20ft (6m) long, and must not be attempted in high water or threatening weather. Beyond the pool is short drop into 10ft (3m) high chamber, then stooping narrow passage for 90ft (27m) to First Pitch. The passage becomes walking height, but still narrow and awkward. First Pitch (26ft (8m) deep with bolt belay) is constricted at the top. Leads immediately to Second Pitch (33ft/10m). The two can be rigged as one 62ft (19m) pitch. Natural eyehole belay on second pitch, or bolt. A short obvious traverse 10ft (3m) down this pitch avoids a wet descent. The passage is now the largest in the cave, and swings to the right. Third Pitch is quickly reached (30ft (9m) deep with bolt belays). Passage at bottom descends with a 6ft (2m) climb back under the pitch, and meets a rift turning 90 degrees to the right. This is the narrow blasted Ochre Rift, 13ft (4m) long, with a small ochre-coloured inlet, and is a crawl in the stream, emerging at a steeply descending and slightly larger passage. This leads to a pool in a low passage, and drains out over the Fourth Pitch (25ft/8m) with a bolt belay. The pitch has been enlarged, but is still constricted, and dangerous in high water. A 10ft (3m) climb at the bottom reaches a sump which was dived to a blockage at -30ft (-9m).

**Tackle**

| | | |
|---|---|---|
| Entrance Shaft: | 35ft (11m) rope. | Bolt. |
| First Pitch: | 50ft (15m) rope. | Bolt. |
| Second Pitch: | 60ft (18m) rope. | Eyehole or bolt. |
| Second Pitch (dry traverse): | 65ft (20m) rope. Eyehole or bolt. | |
| Third Pitch: | 50ft (15m) rope. | Bolt. |
| Fourth Pitch: | 50ft (15m) rope. | Bolt. |

References: Arveschoug, D. 1987. B.C.R.A. Caves & Caving No.35. pp.10-12. Survey.
Salmon, L.B. & Boldock, G. 1950. B.S.A. Cave Science No.11.p.121.
Whitehouse, R.H. 1967. Eldon P.C. Jour. Vol.7. No.2. pp.41-42

## COALPITHOLE RAKE

### No. 1 Shaft
**NGR** 104 809
**Grade:** 2-3 (Mines)
**Alt.** 1060ft (323m)
**Length:** 200ft (60m) approx.
**Depth:** 220ft (67m)

Permission from Mine Cottage.

Three shafts in Perry Dale close to Mine Cottage, all now blocked.

Most westerly shaft is the hauling shaft, probably blocked for most of its depth. The other two, blocked at surface, were 100ft (30m) deep, connected at the bottom by a short level where a 35ft (11m) shaft led to a second level ending in a boulder choke close to the hauling shaft. From this level a 40ft (12m) shaft led to bottom level blocked to east and west, close to bottom of hauling shaft. The 'lost' swallow which drained the rake was at 870ft (265.2m) A.O.D., 100 yards (91m) west of No.1. shaft. Water reappears at Russet Well, taking 3-4 days to flow through.

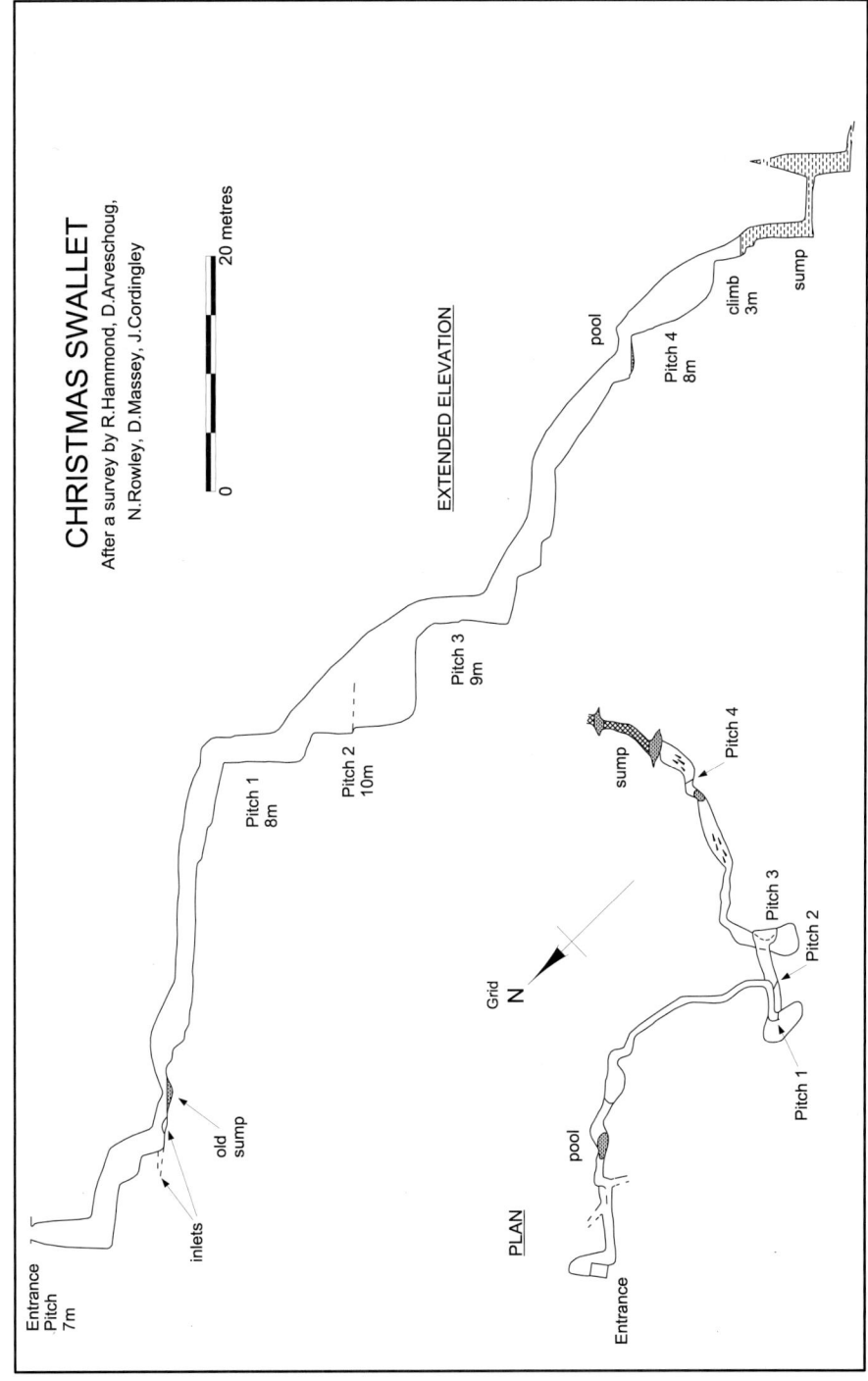

### Rake Shaft
**NGR 101 810  Grade: 3 (Mine)**
**Alt. 1225ft (373m)**
**Length: 500ft (152m)**
**Depth: 320ft (97m)**

Permission from Gautries Side Farm.

On Gautries Hill, south of Perryfoot Farm. Covered with concrete slabs.

Entrance shaft 310ft (94m) deep. Beware of loose ginging for the first 50ft (15.2m). Blocked at the bottom, but with five cross cuts connecting to the vein and probable old climbing shaft. The lowest cross cut at about 285ft (87m) enters level to west blocked after 150ft (45m), and to east is 35ft (11m) shaft to bottom level. Across shaft a level can be entered, blocked after 50ft (15m). At bottom of shaft stream flows from west to east. Immediately west of foot of shaft, water rises from a sump which has been dived for 40ft (12m) to air space with level continuing. To east (downstream), narrow level ends after 150ft (45m) at a boulder choke where the stream sinks. Stream has been dye tested from No.8, shaft and might also be the water from Perryfoot Swallets, although this has not been confirmed. Stream probably goes to "Lost Swallow" in no 1 shaft, and from there to Russet Well.

*Tackle     107m rope. Scaffold bar needed for belay.*

### Veer Shaft
**NGR 100 810  Grade: 3**
**Alt. 1060ft (323m)**
**Length: 200ft (61m) approx.**
**Depth: 220ft (67m)**

Permission from Gautries Side Farm.

On Gautries Hill above Gautries Hill Pot.

Shaft is 120ft (36m) deep (beware of stacked deads). 10ft (3m) above bottom an unstable slope to the west leads to the 2nd pitch 25ft (8m) deep. At bottom steeply descending passage with false floor soon leads to 40ft (12m) pitch. Traverse over pitch and rig hand line on 3rd pitch of 20ft (6m) with large chamber at the bottom. The 40ft shaft is visible in the roof. At end of chamber 10ft (3m) climb down with short blocked crawl. Awkward 20ft (6m) traverse across the climb leads to 4th pitch of 30ft (9m) with minor workings at the bottom, well above the presumed natural water course.

*Tackle*
*Main Shaft: 46m rope    Scaffold bar needed for belay*
*2nd Pitch:  10m rope*
*3rd Pitch:  handline 9m*
*4th Pitch:  12m rope*

### Hilltop Shaft
**NGR 099 811  Grade: 2 (Mine)**
**Alt. 1225ft (373m)**
**Length: 100ft (30m)**
**Depth: 100ft (30m)**

Permission from Gautries Side Farm.

On the north side of Gautries Hill.

Three minor levels at 50ft (15m), 60ft (18m) and 90ft (27m). Shaft blocked at bottom, well short of natural water course.

*Tackle    37m rope  Scaffold bar needed for belay*

### No. 8 Shaft
**NGR 096 812**
**Grade: 2**
**Alt. 1100ft (335m)**
**Depth: 185ft (56m)**

Permission from Gautries Side Farm.

100 yards (91m) north of the road.

Large shaft 12ft (4m) across through the shales. 185ft (56m) to water with no levels going off. Water has been dye tested to Rake Shaft, taking two days.

*Tackle    61m rope  Scaffold bar needed for belay*

## No. 10 Shaft
NGR 092 812
Grade: 2
Alt. 1200ft (366m)
Depth: 250ft (76m)

Permission from Rushup Edge Farm. Close to Rushup Edge Farm.

12ft (4m) diameter shaft through shales. 250ft (76m) to water. Only one level known at 20ft (6m) depth. Water enters through the brick lining, and can be heard at surface.

**Tackle**          85m rope   Scaffold bar needed for belay

References.
Crabtree, P.W. 1966. Jour. B.S.A. Vol.6. No.42. pp.43-61.
Elliot, D. 1975. Caves of Northern Derbyshire. Part 3.
Ford, T.D. 1966. B.S.A. Cave Science Vol.5. No.39. p.379.
Salmon, L.B. 1963. B.S.A. Cave Science Vol.5. No.33. pp.36-52. Survey.
Salmon, L.B. & Boldock, G. 1949. B.S.A. Cave Science Vol.2. No.9. pp.15-20.
Salmon, L.B. & Boldock, G. 1956. Trans. C.R.G. Vol.4. No.2.

## COCKSHEAD MINE
(S-P Hole)
NGR 107 813
Grade: 3 (Mine. Lost)
Alt. 1230ft (375m)
Depth: 165ft (50m)

Through gate on right coming up hill from Perryfoot.

Second shaft to the east, 50ft (15m) from the wall. The first shaft from the road also led into the mine. Both entrances now blocked. Narrow entrance shaft. East from the base led to cavern and passages. Westwards from the shaft bottom led to 30ft (9m) pitch with loose boulders. Small passage led off, across second shaft to join up in lower levels by 35ft (11m) shaft. Lower levels flooded in wet weather. Water was believed to come from swallets to the north.

References: Chandler, B. 1953. British Caver Vol.24. pp.73-75. Survey.
Elliot, D. 1975. Caves of Northern Derbyshire. Part 1, Eldon Hill. pp.1-3.

## CONIES DALE POT
NGR 131 808 to 131 811
Grade: 1 (Digs)
Alt. 1300ft (390m)
Depth: 50ft (15m)

On the slopes north of the head of Conies Dale.

A series of choked fissures and potholes. Most have been dug at some time or other, but were abandoned before reaching rock bottom. Still a promising site.

Reference: Workman, G. 1954. C.R.G. N/L No.49/50. pp. 7-8.

## CONVENIENCE CAVE
NGR 113 811
Grade: 2
Alt: 1246ft (380m)
Length: 425ft (130m)
Status: S.S.S.I.

Discovered 26 June 2010 by 'Big Jim' Alder, Richard Tooley, Mike Soulby, Ali Mortizavi, Henry Rockcliffe and others during the 2010 Credit Crunch Expedition.

Entrance situated at quarry floor level at south west end of Eldon Hill Quarry. Contact DCA for current access conditions.

**Warning: Scree slope above can be 'mobile' in wet conditions. Fine formations. Keep to taped pathway and stay low at all times.**

Muddy entrance crawl to face of dig after 25m leads to 5m of tight crawl breaking into well decorated phreatic passage which ends in sizeable rift chamber. Possible way on is choked. Digging continues….

# DR. JACKSON'S AND PERRYFOOT CAVES (SWALLET P1)

Dr. Jackson's Cave after a survey by C.Poole & K.Barnard.
Perryfoot Cave after a survey by L.B.Salmon & G.Boldock.

## Perryfoot Cave

- inlet
- Super Mousehole
- Mousehole
- Boulder Pot
- Iron Maiden
- Low Road
- The Rack
- First Chamber
- climb
- Entrance
- stream sinks
- Tight Street
- High Road
- Sump
- Flood Passage
- Backwater Chamber
- Terminal Sump

## Dr Jackson's Cave

- Entrance
- Anvil Sump
- stream sinks
- sumps in flood
- Yoga Hole
- muddy stals
- Rift Chamber
- Sump
- Mud Bowl
- 8m climb down
- 2nd Chamber
- 2nd Pitch
- 3rd Pitch
- Bridge
- Traverse
- 5th Pitch (Chasm)
- Terminal Sump
- Sump
- 4th Pitch
- Traverse
- 6th Chamber
- 2.5m pitch
- aven
- 6m climb down

Grid N

0    30m

### COVE HOLE
(Snelslow Dry Valley Cave)
NGR 115 822
Grade: 2 (Dig)
Alt. 1215ft (370m)
Length: 75ft (23m)
Depth: 92ft (28m)

Owned by Peakshill Farm. Access not normally granted.

In dry valley on left of track down to Peakshill Farm between Middle Hill and Snelslow.

Originally referred to as a short tight rift cave about 10ft (3m) deep. Dug to reveal a narrow twisting vertical tube, which has been enlarged. 15ft (5m) down leads to a small chamber excavated through in 1986 to a tight crawl. This reaches a pitch of 20ft (8m), which is broken and climbable with care. This is followed by a slope of calcited boulders to a tight choked rift. Blasting in this rift revealed a hole on the left wall, which has led to a tight pitch of 25ft (8m) into a choked calcited chamber.

*Reference: Kitchen, G. 1965. B.S.A. digging report.*

### DIELASMA CAVE
NGR 135 832
Grade: 1
Alt. 1000ft (305m)
Length: 50ft (15m)

On Treak Cliff, north west of the show cave, near the crest of the ridge.

A small cave enlarged by mining, and easily explored by stooping. Named after the fossil abundant in the adjacent rocks.

*Reference: Elliot, D. 1975. Caves of Northern Derbyshire. Part 5. p.12. Survey.*

### DR. JACKSON'S CAVE
NGR 0989 8127
Grade: 5
Alt. 1033ft (310m)
Length: 1000 ft (300m) approx.
Status: S.S.S.I.

Permission from Mr. Bagshawe, Torr Top Farm, Perryfoot.

Dug into and explored by D.C.C. in 1969/70. Extended by E.P.C. 1972.

A few yards west of Perryfoot Cave and the stream sink.

Warning: Passage beyond Yoga Hole sumps in wet weather, and rescue from beyond would be exceptionally difficult.

20ft (6m) entrance climb to small stream passage, left blocked with boulders where stream enters in wet weather. Right through short squeeze eventually leads to Yoga Hole after passing a few small inlets on the left, all blocked after a few feet.

Stream sinks down 1 inch wide cracks where water backs up, forming a short canal, duck, or sump depending on weather. Through canal, an upward crawl leads to Yoga Hole, which must be entered feet first. Narrow slippery tube descends 10ft (3m) (difficult to reverse) to small chamber. Upward crawl on left leads to large inclined rift passage to first pitch (25ft / 8m). Short crawl on right of rift passage ends in a small static sump. From first pitch large passage leads to short traverse and second pitch (25ft / 8m). At the bottom the chamber appears to be a dead end but the far wall is a rock bridge which can be climbed by a good climber. One alternative is a very dangerous and greasy traverse over from the top of the second pitch to Rock Bridge. Other side of Rock Bridge can be descended for 25ft (8m) to a static sump. From top of Rock Bridge a very dangerous traverse out over the top of the final chamber leads to a passage in the right wall. Short walking sized passage leads to hole in floor to 25ft (8m) pitch into The Chasm. Right to static sump, left to high passage which soon descends to low crawl blocked with boulders and very narrow.

At top of hole leading to The Chasm the passage continues, breaking into The Chasm at a higher level. Very greasy and dangerous traverse across The Chasm to the continuation of the passage. After a few feet, very narrow passage on left leads to 25ft (8m) climb down rift. At bottom, left is too narrow while right soon ends in a static sump, dived for 10ft (3m) but then silted up. Back in the main passage, straight on leads to an interesting series of muddy crawls and chambers.

**Tackle**
1st Pitch    10m rope
2nd Pitch   10m rope
or Pitch to Bridge  18m rope
Rock Bridge 15m fixed line

*Traverse Chasm Pitch (lower) 9m rope*
*Chasm Pitch (upper)  15m rope*
*Chasm Traverse  9m fixed line*
*Terminal Rift  9m hand line.*

*References: Elliot, D. 1975. Caves of Northern Derbyshire. Part 3. pp.8-12. Survey.*
*Gill, D.W. 1973. D.C.A. N/L No.16.*
*Poole, C., Darroch, C., and Borthwick, P. 1970. D.C.A. N/L No.8. pp.3-4.*

### ELDON HOLE
NGR 1161 8089
Grade: 3
Alt. 1383ft (415m)
Depth: 245ft (82m)
Status: S.S.S.I.

At the time of writing (2010) no prior permission is required.

Approach from Perry Dale up Eldon Lane and park at top end, just beyond Sweetknowle House. Recognisable footpath from here. On southern slopes of Eldon Hill.

The largest open pothole in Derbyshire, 110ft (34m) long and 20ft (6m) wide at the surface. Upper end of hole is most used for descent. Avoid using fence posts as belays. Rope assisted scramble for 70ft (21m) ends at an outward sloping ledge. Pitch from here is 120ft (37m). From south end of the hole a free hang of 200ft (61m) can be obtained. From bottom of shaft, cavern is reached through timbered shaft and crawl. Wide cavern 90ft (27m) high with good formations. Good light required! Climb on left leads to crawl passage, a possible dig. Fissure on right has been dug out for 60ft (18m) but has run in since. Lloyd (1780) reports a lower shaft with a stream in the bottom, but this has not been seen since. New Eldon Series has been reached by Eldon Pothole Club climbing 80ft (24m) up the north wall of the Main Chamber. A series of well decorated rifts lead upwards to Millers Chamber, where a further 42ft (13m) climb leads to Damocles Rift, choked with flowstone at the top. This section is generally rigged, but contact Eldon Pothole Club to make sure.

**Tackle**
| | | | | |
|---|---|---|---|---|
| N. End 1st Pitch: | 30m rope  Bolts | | *South End:* | 73m rope  Bolts |
| Main Pitch: | 46m rope  Bolts | | *East Side:* | 73m rope  Bolts |
| *New Eldon Series:* | *Contact Eldon Pothole Club before attempting this section.* | | | |

*References: Adam, W. 1840. The Gem of the Peak.*
*Atkinson, F. 1949. B.S.A. Cave Science No.8. Survey.*
*Kinsman, J, & Westlake, C.D. 1966. B.S.A. Cave Science No.38. pp.298-303. Survey.*
*Lloyd, J. & King, E. 1780. Phil. Trans. Roy. Soc. Vol.61. pp,250-265. Survey.*
*Simpson, E. 1949. B.S.A. Cave Science Nos. 7 & 8.*
*Workman, G. 1953. The Speleologist Vol.1. Nos.2 & 3.*
*Wright, A. 1971. Jour. S.U.S.S. Vol.2. No.1. pp.8-11.*

### ELDON QUARRY CAVE 1
NGR 114 814
Lost
Alt. 1350ft (405m)
Status: S.S.S.I.

Thought to have lain in the "Northern Knoll" of Eldon Hill Quarry, largely removed in 1996.

An enlarged joint type of cave some 50ft (15m) deep intersected by quarrying during the War and since removed. Its blocked continuation may be represented by Alsop's Cave (qv). It was well decorated with stalactites. There were rumours in the past about blasting smoke appearing in Eldon Hole, 1/4 mile (400m) to the south.

*Reference: British Speleological Association Records.*

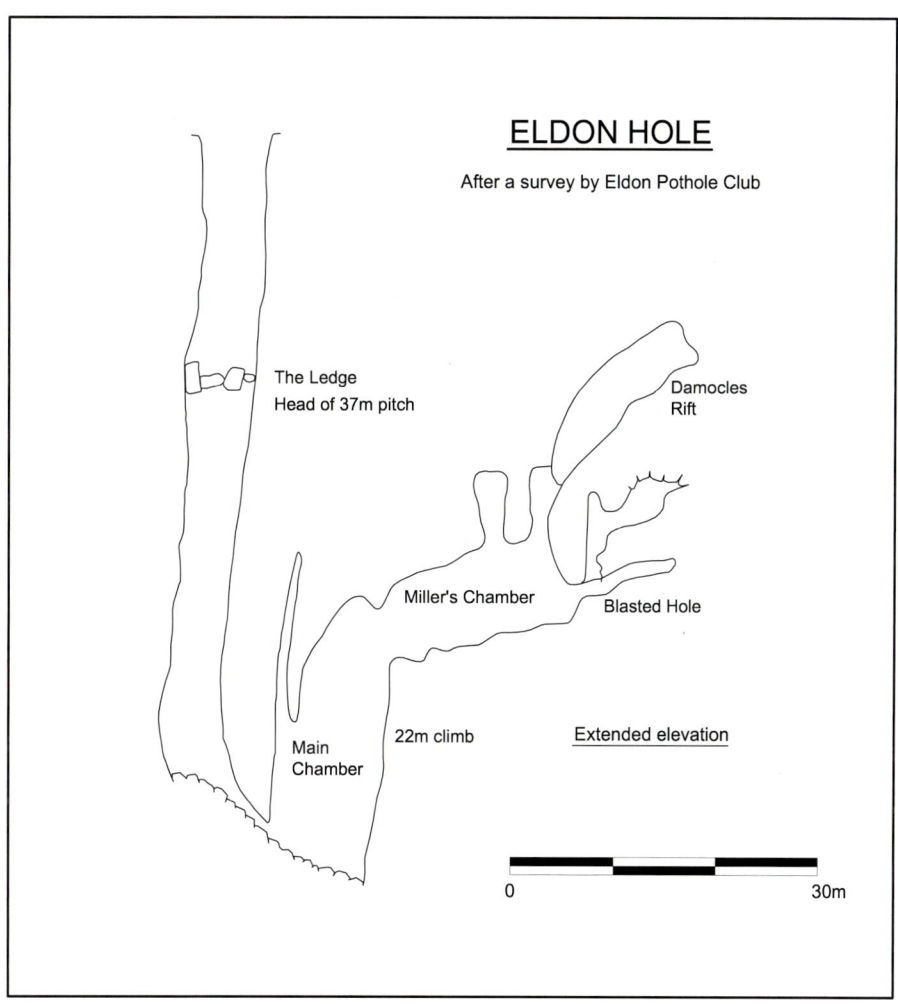

**FROG HOLE**
NGR 121 823
Dig
Alt. 1380ft (420m)

No access normally allowed.

In old quarry north of the road from Castleton to Perryfoot, west of Oxlow Farm.

Digging over several years revealed a narrow fissure dropping 6ft (1.8m) into a passage at the head of a mud-filled pot. Now filled almost to the surface with rubbish, but was dug to a depth of 27ft (8m).

*Reference: Elliot, D. 1975. Caves of Northern Derbyshire. Part 4. p.23*

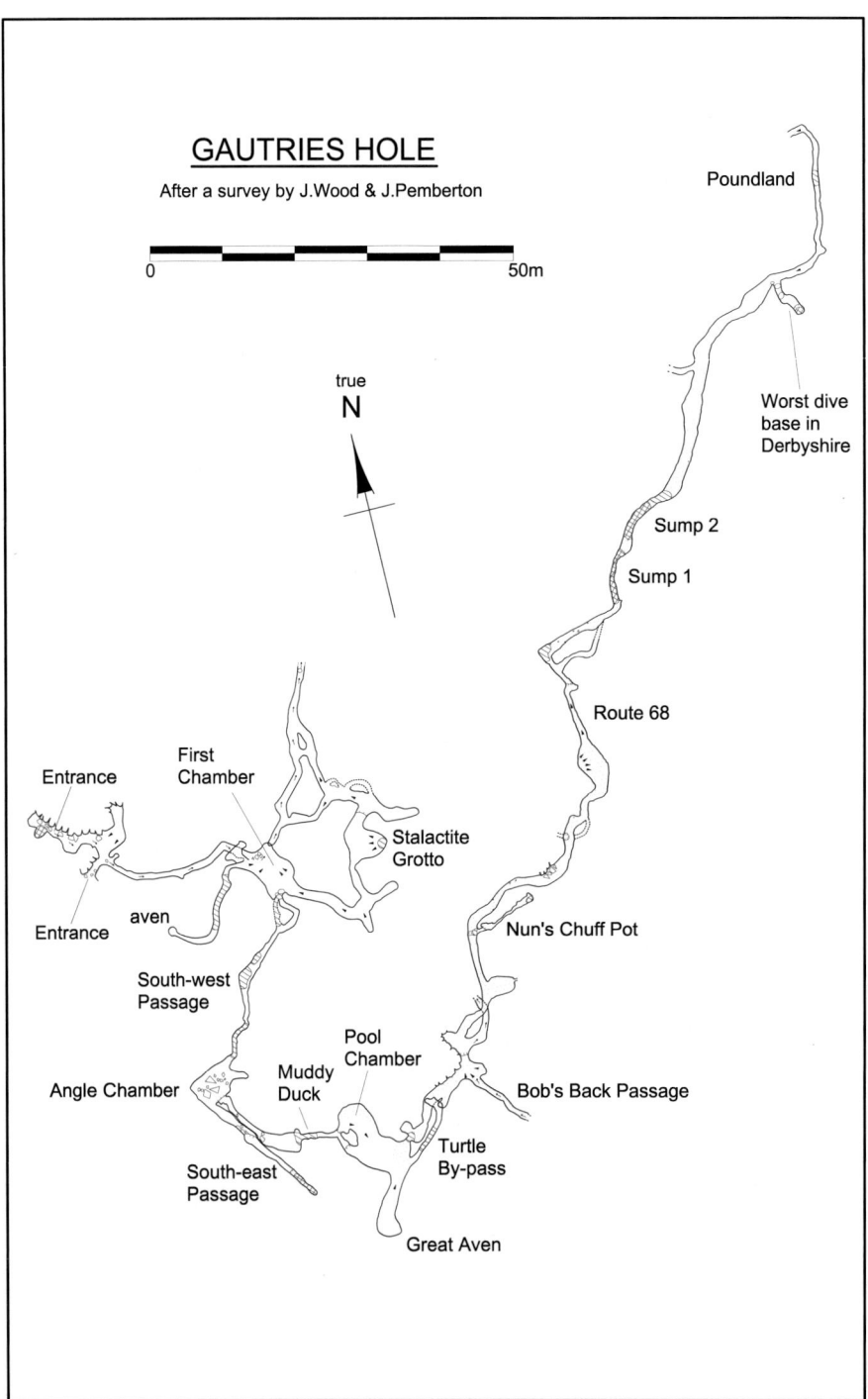

## GAUTRIES HILL POT
(Coalpithole Pot)

**NGR** 101 811
**Grade:** 1
**Alt.** 1150ft (350m)
**Depth:** 80ft (24m)

Permission from Perryfoot Farm.

Shaft in the bottom dug by Rubber Duck Caving Club.

Fenced open pot on the north east slope of Gautries Hill.

A steep slippery scramble leads down a slope of collapsed boulders and clay which runs into the undercut at the base of the opposite wall. The way on to the west is blocked immediately. At the east end a shaft was sunk through boulders and flowstone to end at a small pool roughly 80ft (24m) below the surface.

*References: Elliot, D. 1975. Caves of Northern Derbyshire. Part 3. p.13. Survey.*
*Beck, J.S. 1991. Descent No.98. p.12.*

## GAUTRIES HOLE
(Jackdaw Pit, Swallet P.3)

**NGR** 1015 8145   **Grade:** 3
**Alt.** 1040ft (312m)
**Length:** 800ft (240m)
**Status:** S.S.S.I.

Permission from Perryfoot Farm.

Entrance in tree-lined shakehole 200 yards north of the road at Perryfoot.

Right entrance to short dry passage only. Left entrance is to stream passage. Upstream it can be followed for only a few yards. Downstream crawl through water until it disappears down an eye-hole supported with concrete. Turn right up into chamber. Climbing a muddy chute leads into partly flooded muddy rift and back to stream and terminal sump. Nearby tube ends at silt choke and a narrow joint where the sound of water has been reported beyond. Back at the chamber, two holes in the middle lead to small passage which increases in size after a few feet. Continue along passage to Angle Chamber and syphon with concrete dam. Return and climb up muddy slope on right (care - rope useful). After climb and muddy duck, passage leads to twin eyeholes and 30ft (9m) pitch into Pool Chamber.

From Pool chamber two ways can reach the chamber starting the Eldon series. Either a steep descent with hand-line leading to a flat out muddy crawl through the old sump passing a constriction or a small tube at the far end of Pool Chamber leads for 33ft (10m) to a short pot followed by a crawl, Turtle Bypass which bypasses the sump. At the chamber an inlet flows in from the right (Bob's Back Passage) leading for 30ft (9m) to a clay blockage. Follow the stream down a 5ft (1.5m) climb into chamber. The stream can be followed for 23ft (7m) in a squalid crawl to a sink against a solid wall. A climb up at the far end of the chamber with a crawl leads to an aven 23ft (7m) high. A constriction at the top leads to a silt choke. Beyond the aven after a squeeze at floor level a water-washed pot Nun's Chuff pot can be descended on the right (very tight and awkward) for 20ft (6m) with a crawl going back on itself for 23ft (7m) in water leading to a small chamber with a mud sump. The main passage ascends as a gravelly crawl where a boulder choke is met on the left. Just after the choke a small silted tube in the floor draughts well but is too small to enter. The passage continues passing silt filled tubes on both sides leading to the top of 41ft (12.5m) muddy slope (Route 68) with hand-line. At the bottom siphoned water sinks in a boulder choke. A short climb above the sink leads as a hands and knees crawl up a gravel slope to meet Sump 1, a 21ft (6.5m) crawl which can be siphoned or bailed. A dry bank is met followed by a 23ft (7m) duck, Sump 2. The passage slowly descends as a muddy crawl passing a draughty silted tube on the left. A crawl underneath a false roof leads to large, wider section of passage. A short crawl over boulders on the right reaches the top of a 20ft (6m) pot which leads to a sump, The Worse Dive Base in Derbyshire. The sump has been dived (50ft/15m of line laid) in a body-sized tube to a depth of -16ft (-5m) rising to -12.5ft (-3.8m) in a rift reaching silty bedding with no natural line belays in zero visibility. At the main passage a steep ascending mud slope reaches a small chamber. A Flat out muddy crawl starts Poundland. This eventually enlarges slightly followed by a short constriction to hands and knees crawl for a few feet.

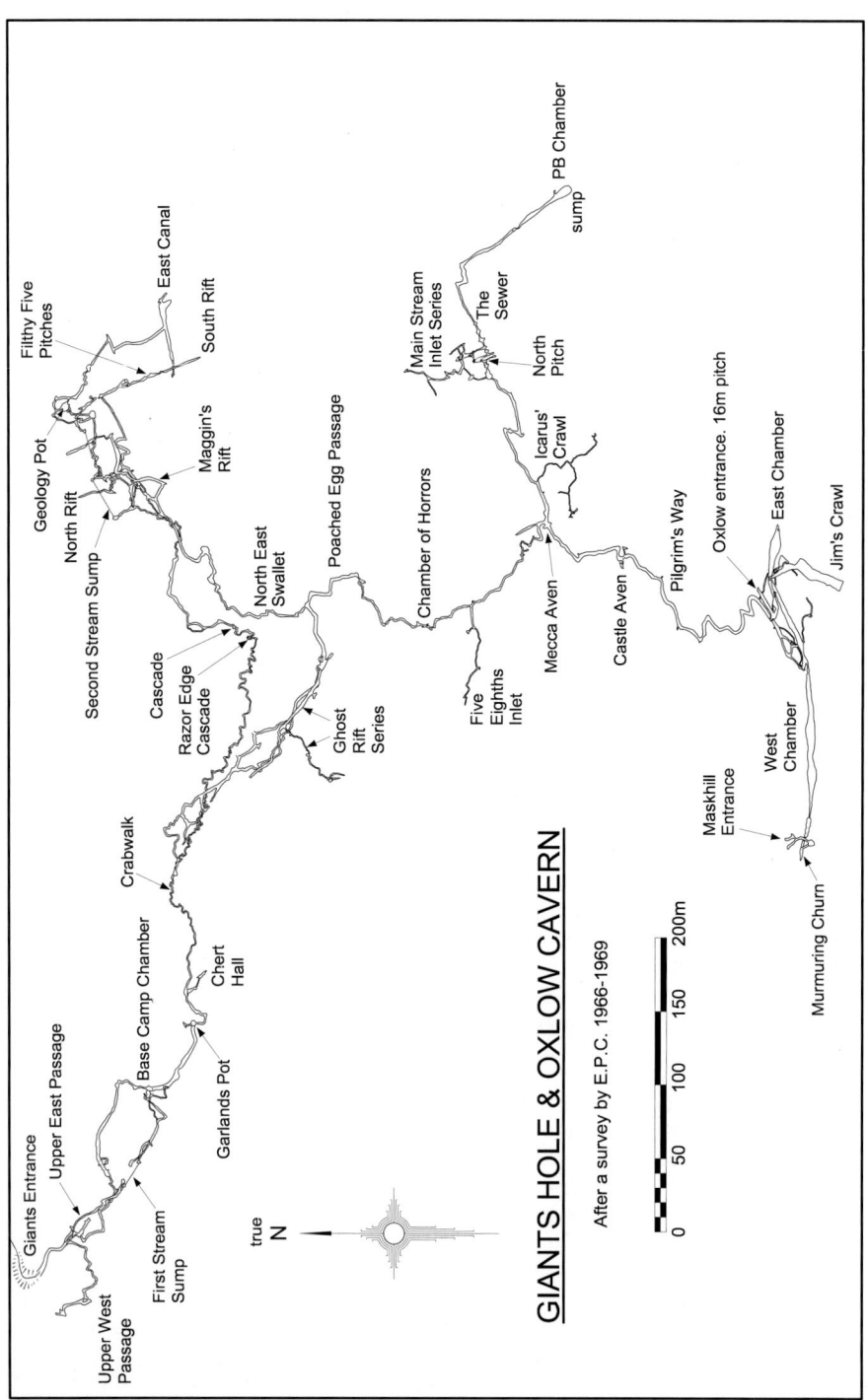

It enters a large heavily silted passage which terminates at a steep descending mud slope which eventually becomes too tight but draughts strongly.

**Tackle**     12m rope

*References: Anon. Undated. E.P.C.Jour. Vol.6. No.1. p.19.*
*Martin, J. 2000. C.C.P.C. N/L 67. p.6.*
*Salmon, L. and Boldock, G. 1948. B.S.A. Cave Science Vol.1. No.6. pp.186-190. Survey.*

### GIANTS CAVE
(Peakshill Cave, P.11 & P.13)
NGR 116 826.
Upper Cave: 118 827
Grade: 2
Alt. 1215ft (370m)
Upper Cave: 1245ft (380m)
Length: 295ft (90m)
Depth: 33ft (10m)

Permission from Peakshill Farm.

The resurgence cave is situated approximately halfway between the farm track and Giant's Hole, on the north flank of Peakshill.

The Upper Cave is a small swallet, but with another entrance as a concealed sloping rift close by, and the only way in. This is an awkward muddy drop of 15ft (5m) into a small streamway that can be followed westwards, mainly crawling, to an impenetrable sump after about 100ft (30m). The water re-emerges about 50ft (15m) west at the start of Giant's Cave, to go immediately underground again into this small system, which consists of 110ft (24m) crawl downstream to a sump (not free-diveable). The stream re-emerges from the upstream sump in the Giant's Cave resurgence, which consists of an 80ft (24m) flat out crawl to the sump. The stream flows past the Giant's Hole car park, and sinks again at P9 - P10.

*References: Elliot, D. 1975. Caves of Northern Derbyshire. Part 4. p.21.*
*Salmon, L.B. & Boldock, G. 1950. B.S.A. Cave Science No.11.p.121.*

### GIANTS HOLE
(Swallet P.12)
NGR 1194 8268
Grade: 2-5
Alt. 1224ft (373m).
Length: 10,231ft (3.13km).
Total length incl. Oxlow / Maskhill: 15,513ft (4.8km)
Depth: 420ft (128m).
Depth from Maskhill: 693ft (211m).
Status: S.S.S.I.

Owned by Peakshill Farm. A charge is made at the parking area. Extended by B.S.A. 1953 - 1957. Connected to Oxlow Caverns in 1966 by Eldon Pothole Club.

Large swallet cave entrance in valley between Middle Hill and Peakshill. Reached from the Peakshill Farm track.

**Warning: Stream passages below Garlands Pot may become impassable in flood conditions. The cave should not be descended by novices during heavy rain.**

The Giants Hole - Oxlow Caverns - Maskhill Mine system was the deepest in Derbyshire until the connection was made from James Hall's Over Engine Mine to Peak Cavern.. A fine system with everything for the sporting caver. The through trip from either Maskhill or Oxlow Caverns into Giants Hole is one of Britain's classics but is quite a serious undertaking.

Cavers making through trips from Oxlow or Maskhill must leave the same way. The connection between Oxlow and Giants is very tight, and the ducks in the Chamber of Horrors may become impassable. Also the owner of Giants does not allow through trips using Giants as exit.
Interesting trips are:

**Giants Hole to Oxlow Caverns (Pool Chamber). Depth 224ft (68m).**
**Giants Hole to New Oxlow (Terminal Sump). Depth 256ft (78m).**
**Oxlow Caverns to Giants Hole (East Canal). Depth 640ft (195m).**
**Maskhill Mine to Giants Hole (East Canal). Depth 693ft (211m).**

## A. Entrance to Eating House and Upper Series
## Grade 3  Length 8524ft (2.6km)

Large stream passage leads after 100ft (30m) to a short climb into the roof where Upper West Passage can be followed to the right, walking and crawling for 329ft (100m) blocked at the end. Also to left Upper East Passage is a crawl for 310ft (94m) to blockage, a grade 2 sporting trip for beginners. Back in stream, artificially enlarged walking passage, passing the former obstacle of "The Curtain", can be followed for a further 300ft (91m) to First Stream Sump. Large blasted tunnel on left leads past other former obstacles, "Pillar Crawl" and "Backwash Pool". An awkward climb on the right leads to a tight passage (Ralph's Bit) up to a small aven with a tight rift passage to a small chamber at the top. The main route continues to Base Camp Chamber, with the stream entering from the right. Stream can be followed upstream in a high narrow passage to the outlet of the First Stream Sump. Climb in roof leads to decorated passage leading back above streamway to small chamber above Base Camp Chamber. Ahead is passage to High Level Sump, which has been baled but is blocked with flowstone.

From Base Camp Chamber a fine high passage leads downstream past Boss Aven to Garlands Pot, a 15ft (4.5m) pitch. A crawl on the left at the pitch top leads to October Aven, climbed for 30ft (9m) to a short choked passage. At bottom of Garlands Pot, high and narrow Crabwalk can be followed for just over 2000ft (610m) to Second Stream Sump. After first 120ft (37m) Chert Hall can be reached by a crawl at roof level on the right. After a further 380ft (116m) the 46ft (14m) climb to the Upper Series is reached. Crabwalk continues high and narrow for further 842ft (257m) to a squeeze, The Vice, followed after 25ft (8m) by the aptly named free-climbable Razor Edge Cascade. A further 110ft (34m) leads to Comic Act Cascade, 10ft (3m) deep. Great Relief passage which follows is larger, and leads to the Second Stream Sump after a further 575ft (175m).

50ft (15m) before the Second Stream Sump a passage on the right leads to the Eating House, where a small inlet stream enters from above. Left leads to St. Valentine's Sump and the Lower Syphon Complex, while a 10ft (3m) climb up by the inlet leads to Maggin's Rift and the Upper Series. A short crawl enters Maggin's Rift, actually a large vadose inlet passage rising steeply over boulders for 464 ft

Garlands Pot.  Photo by Paul Deakin

Razor Edge Cascade. Photo by Rob Eavis

(141m). At the top the passage has been dug and can be followed past two squeezes to a 30ft (9m) aven. Beware of loose rubble. At bottom of Maggin's Rift just beyond the entrance crawl muddy passage on the right leads to North East Swallet containing a small stream. A fine high passage can be followed upstream for 611ft (166m), free-climbing a 26ft (8m) cascade. A high level tube, Jubilee Passage, above the cascade oxbows back into North East Swallet downstream after about 200ft (60m), with a low bedding continuation. At end of North East Swallet is a junction. Left is Poached Egg Passage, 144ft (44m) long to Sardine Chamber, choked at the end. Just before the end a low opening on the right is the Chamber of Horrors (connection to Oxlow), a 728ft (222m) long flat out crawl with ducks, passing Five Eighths Inlet on the right. This is 250ft (76m) long, too tight for further progress. Stream sink on left (also too tight) dye tested to Main Stream Inlet in Oxlow Caverns. At end of Chamber of Horrors, just before the really tight section (original EPC dig) is Oxlow Aven on the right emitting a small stream. Back at junction with Poached Egg Passage, on the right is Letter Box Passage leading to Ghost Rift, a 46ft (14m) scaling pole climb to the Ghost Rift Series, 816ft (214m) long. Main passage leads to a choke, but a tight awkward passage on the left can be followed to pitches of 26ft (8m), 7ft (2m), 10ft (3m) where the way on is too tight but takes a small stream which probably goes to Five Eighths Inlet. Digging in the choke in 1990 led to a very dangerous route up through boulders (The Earth Leakage Trip) to a chamber and an upward continuation of the choke. A passage continues westwards to a further choke and short blocked pitch. At the east end of Ghost Rift, a traverse and two short climbs on flowstone lead to the base of an aven (Knox Aven), about 33ft (10m) high. At the top, a hands and knees crawl leads to a draughting, calcite choke, which discharges a small stream in wet weather. From Ghost Rift at far end is a small hole in hollow which is Giant's Windpipe, a wet low crawl with ducks to a junction. Left is Handshake Crawl which oxbows back into the passage after 176ft (54m) but is too tight in one place. To the right a larger passage continues, passing the other end of Handshake Crawl on the left and No Way Passage which is a high level passage blocked with calcite to right and left. Passage eventually breaks into the roof of Crabwalk. From here 46ft (14m) careful traverse/climb down into Crabwalk (rope or ladder useful for novices). Alternatively high level traverse in roof of Crabwalk, descending near Chert Hall.

## B. East Canal via Geology Pot

**Grade 4 Length (from entrance) 4513ft (1.38km) Depth 420ft (128m) to normal East Canal surface level**

From Eating House small hole in the floor is a crawl to Lower Syphon Complex, but best way is forward under small waterfall to junction with climb up to Maggin's Rift, and left to a further junction. Right is East Overflow Passage to St. Valentine's Sump while left is a crawl to a further junction. Left leads back to Eating House, straight on to North Rift (100ft/30m) long to a tight sump leading to an ascending passage and choke), and right to the roof of the streamway between the Second and Third Stream Sumps. Obvious roof traverse downstream to gain a high level passage above the Third Stream Sump. Walking passage to The Plughole, an awkward 13ft (4m) climb down (hand line useful) into chamber with 2ft of water. In roof is Cork Screw Shaft, a steep climb for about 200ft (61m) to a choke. Inlet also enters from St. Valentines Sump. A short passage leads to the head of Geology Pot, 40ft (12m) deep. Climb and traverse above Geology Pot to alternative route via Carnival Aven, which enters stream passage just before Far Curtain. Short crawl from bottom of Geology Pot to the stream. Upstream for 117ft (36m) to 18ft (5.5m) cascade, with outlet of Third Stream Sump at the top. Downstream to a 13ft (4m) cascade, soon followed by Far Curtain, a wet crawl or duck. Spout Hall, a wet 8ft (2.5m) climb down into a deep pool, follows shortly. The route continues with short climbs, or a swim depending on water levels, to the deep East Canal. The Filthy Five pitches enter on the right, and the sump is to the left. It has been dived for 450ft (137m) to a depth of 100ft (30m) passing two air bells, first of which can be reached by non-divers in low water. In high water East Canal has been known to back up to bottom of Geology Pot. Far end of East Canal has been climbed for 50ft (15m) to 40ft (12m) of passage ending in blind avens, one of which has been climbed for 120ft (37m). Water has been dye tested to Russet Well via Speedwell Caverns.

## C. East Canal via Filthy Five

**Grade 4 Length (from entrance) 4011ft (1.2km) Depth 420ft (128m) to normal East Canal surface level**

**Warning: St. Valentine's Sump rapidly fills, and is difficult to bale from the other side. Baling outlet frequently blocked now. Make sure Far Curtain is accessible before abseiling Filthy Five for a round trip via Geology Pot!**

Turn left at junction after Eating House and right to East Overflow Passage, a hands and knees crawl to St. Valentine's Sump. Small concrete dams enable sump to be baled into hole in floor until air space appears. Right turn after sump leads to Filthy Five Pitches of 13ft (4m), 8ft (2.5m), 16ft (5m), 8ft (2.5m), and 15ft (4.5m), one after the other, and very muddy. Dog Kennel follows, a crawl in glutinous mud which can require excavating. Junction follows. Straight on is South Rift, 100ft (30m) long, and right leads to a 25ft (8m) pitch to water, the 4m deep blind Salmon's Sump. Left is a short passage to the final pitch of 26ft (8m) into East Canal.

Tackle:
| | |
|---|---|
| Garlands Pot: | 20m rope |
| Comic Act Cascade: | 5m rope |
| Descent to Crabwalk from Upper Series: | 25m rope (Can be free climbed, but novices should be lifelined). |
| Geology Pot: | 25m rope |
| Cascade: | 10m rope |
| Filthy Five Pitches: | 8m rope; 6m rope; 8m rope; 6m rope; 8m rope |
| Dog Kennel Pitch: | 10m rope |

References: Atkinson, F. 1948. B.S.A. Cave Science Vol.1. No.5. pp.132-140. Survey.
Deakin, P.R. 1966. E.P.C. Jour. Vol.7. No.1. pp.60-62.
Salmon, L.B. 1956. B.S.A. Cave Science Vol.4. No.25. pp.1-33. Survey.
No.29. pp.230-241. Survey.
Salmon, L.B. 1965. B.S.A. Cave Science Vol.5. No.38. pp.287-297. Survey.
Westlake, C.D. 1967. Proc. B.S.A. No.5. pp.1-11.
Westlake, C.D. 1972. E.P.C. Jour. Vol.8. No.1. pp.39-42.
Whitehouse, R.H. 1966. E.P.C. Jour. Vol.7 No.1. pp.58-59.
Yonge, C. Undated. Jour. S.U.S.S. Vol.2. p.31.

Above, a group of Chesterfield cavers emerging from Giants Hole, Sunday 3rd September 1939, to find that war with Germany had been declared. Left to right, back row – Stan Miles, Ted Orris, Jack Smith and Merve Martin (name of man holding torch unknown).

Below, some of the same group from Chesterfield about to enter Giants Hole in September 1948. Adults left to right – Stan Miles, Jack Miles, Jim Neil, Jack Smith, (Ginger?), Doug Martin and Ernie Hill. The boys are Peter Miles (designer of this book) and Tony Smith. During this expedition Jack Miles fell and broke his leg when the party were a considerable way into the system and had to be 'cave rescued' by the other members of the group.

### GOOSEHILL CAVE
NGR 1475 8273   Grade: 1
Alt. 701ft (213.7m)
Length: 15ft (5m)

In the last garden on the left on the footpath behind Goosehill Hall towards Cowlow and the Winnats. Entrance now concealed behind a garage.

A low arch 4ft (1.2m) wide, and 3ft (0.9m) high. Soon ends in a silt choke. Could have been an old resurgence.

### HIATT CAVE
NGR 137 825   Grade: 1
Alt. 1200ft (360m)
Length: 50ft (15m)

In Shining Tor cliff high on the south side of the Winnats Pass.

A tube extending for approx. 50ft (15m), entered by digging. Several other small holes nearby.

### HOLLANDTWINE MINE
NGR 1396 8125
Grade: 4 (Mine. Lost)
Alt. 1410ft (430m)
Length: 1500ft (457m)
Depth: 420ft (128m)

On Dirtlow Rake. Shaft recently obliterated by opencast mining. Attempts to re-locate the shaft were unsuccessful as it was too deeply buried.

Recorded as intersecting a "great swallow" at a depth of 600ft (183m). Hauling shaft was 375ft (114m) entrance pitch. The entrance shaft could also be descended for 150ft (46m) to a side level which allowed descent to be continued through a series of climbing shafts with fixed ladders to the bottom level. After 200ft (61m) a dug out rift on the left leads to the natural series. Upstream leads to 40ft (12m) aven with 250ft (76m) of tight passage at the top. Downstream water can be followed to a 70ft (21m) pitch. At the bottom water sinks down an impenetrable fissure, and has been positively dye tested to Ink Sump in Peak Cavern. At the top of the pitch 400ft of dry passage can be followed to a bedding plane collapse. A small hole, Dysentry Crawl, leads after 40ft (12m) of very tight and muddy passage to a further 350ft (107m) of passage terminating in a collapse.

*References: Anon. 1972. Descent No.22. p.13.*
*Jarratt, A & Sulonen, S. 1972. D.C.A. N/L No.14. pp.2-3.*
*Kinsman, J. 1966. Jour. E.P.C. Vol.7. No.1. p.12.*

### HURDLOW STILE PIPE
(Hourdllo Steel Pipe)
NGR c. 141 822
Mine. Lost

In the vicinity of Hurdlow Barn.

Three mine shafts on an old plan and section lead to a natural swallow passage. The shafts are approximately 110ft (34m) deep.

*Reference: Ford, T.D. 1965. Bull. P.D.M.H.S. Vol.2. No.4. pp.230-233.*

### JAMES HALL'S OVER ENGINE MINE
NGR 1350 8201
Grade: 4
Alt. 1408.5ft (429.3m)
Depth: 560ft (171m) (Through trip to Peak Cavern entrance 804ft (245m))

Permission from Rowter Farm. Fee to be paid.

For through trips, access to Peak Cavern (qv) must also be booked.

Explored and surveyed by B.S.A. 1964. Excavated 1993-1995 by D.Nixon to connect with Boulder Piles in Speedwell Cavern.

Walk down the track from the farmyard to join the footpath, the follow this to the left along the rake until the shaft lid is seen to the left.

A fine descent of 158ft (48m) lands on a pile of debris. The level can be followed to the west for a short distance, but eastwards leads beneath a number of collapses and over a series of flooded shafts (dry in summer) to a blind shaft in which the accumulated stream sinks. Traverse over, pass under more unstable deads, and traverse over a further shaft. A scramble through more boulders, and level divides. Upper route is crawling then walking to a short climb down, then a dry stone ramp and traverse over a blind hole, under more loose boulders, and forward to the head of a deep open stope. Awkward descent (Bitch Pitch) of 130ft (40m) leads to the Workshop, with stone benches and mining relics. A short scramble down a natural passage leads to a bridge over Leviathan, a massive natural shaft. A descent in two steps totalling 262ft (80m) lands on a boulder floor, and an iron-laddered descent leads to the Boulder Piles dig in Speedwell Cavern. The connection is gated. The outlet sump at the bottom of Leviathan was drained and excavated to give a connection (also now gated) to Stemple Highway in the Far Sump Extension of Peak Cavern, but may not always be accessible.

*Tackle:*
*Entrance Shaft:* 60m rope
*Bitch Pitch:* 60m rope. Eco hangers + 1 rebelay.
*Leviathan :* 120m rope. Eco hangers + 2 rebelays + 1 deviation.
Reference: Beck, J.S. 1994. Descent No.116. p.19.

### LITTLE BULL PIT
(Swallet P6)
**NGR 1038 8167**
**Grade: 1. Dig**
**Alt. 1100ft (330m)**
**Length: 40ft (12m)**
**Depth: 25ft (8m)**

Permission from Perryfoot Farm. Small fee to be paid.
Pit adjacent to swallet P6.

The pit itself is an open pot (10m handline useful) floored with boulders and mud. Leads to chamber 15ft (5m) high. Several old digs under the walls. The swallet nearby is a walking sized passage which has been dug, silted up, and redug several times. Some 10m of passage have been gained, with avens rising upwards. Mine shaft in field to west reaches a narrow vein. Crawl under stacked deads leads to silted natural passage which takes a small stream in wet weather.

References: Elliot, D. 1975. Caves of Northern Derbyshire. Part 4. pp.10-12. Survey.
Hatherley, P. 1978. Jour. S.U.S.S. Vol.2. No.6. pp.34-37. Survey.
Hatherley, P. 1980. Jour. S.U.S.S. Vol.3. No.1. p.60.
Salmon, L.B. & Boldock, G. 1950. B.S.A. Cave Science Vol.2. No.11. p.120.
Worsencroft, K. 1963. E.P.C. Jour. Vol.5. No.4. pp.14-16.

### LONGCLIFF MINE AND POT
**NGR 141 825**
**Grade: 2 (Mine)**
**Alt. 1000ft (305m)**
**Depth: 150ft (45m)**
Status: S.S.S.I.

Shaft on highest prominent hillock behind Speedwell Cavern. A mineshaft leads through the roof of a natural pot. Workings and a short second pitch extend some 200ft (61m) eastwards. Main shaft at present blocked by collapse of the hillock, and the ginging is unstable at the top.

*Tackle:*
*Entrance Pitch:* 45m rope  Beam for belay.
*2nd Pitch & traverse:* 12m rope

Reference: Ford, T.D. 1962. Bull. P.D.M.H.S. Vol.1. No.7. pp.1-4. Survey.

### MAM TOR SWALLET
**NGR 1284 8313**
**Grade: 2**
**Alt. 1250ft (381m)**
**Length: 80ft (24m)**
**Depth: 30ft (9m)**

Large entrance in shakehole by the roadside at the junction of the Chapel-en-le-Frith to Castleton and Sparrowpit roads where a small stream sinks.

Small chamber and low passage lead to the head of a 10ft (3m) pitch with a tight take-off. The chamber at the bottom contains much rubbish and bones, a choked aven in the roof, and the small surface stream which sinks in the floor. From the chamber a dug out crawl leads to a further 10ft (3m) drop where a tight crawl can be followed which takes a trickle of water, intersecting a small passage at right angles. Left is choked, and right becomes too low. The final 10ft drop has been buried by collapse. It has been said that the water reappears in Blue John Caverns, but this is unlikely. At the time of writing the roof-arch has collapsed, blocking the entrance.

*Reference: Elliot, D. 1975. Caves of Northern Derbyshire. Part 4. pp.27-29. Survey.*
*Saville, B. 1959. The Lyre No.3. pp.56-58. Survey.*

### MASKHILL MINE
NGR 1224 8216
Grade: 5 (Mine)
Alt. 1497ft (456m)
Length: 650ft (198m)
Depth: 500ft (152m). To East Canal of Giants Hole: 693ft/211m
Status: S.S.S.I.

Permission must be gained from Oxlow House Farm before descending.

Follow the access route as for Oxlow Caverns. A plate on Oxlow Entrance indicates the direction of Maskhill, 200 yards (183m) west of Oxlow Entrance, and 52ft (16m) higher, near a dry stone wall.

Parts of the mine are in a dangerous state of collapse, and great care is needed.

A narrow mineshaft capped with concrete and covered with a steel lid. Entrance pitch 100ft (30m) deep. Second pitch follows immediately to a large natural passage. A 7ft (2m) climb down leads to a steep slope arriving at the head of the third pitch, 36ft (11m) deep. A further steep slope follows to the head of the fourth pitch, Murmuring Churn. To the east is a 180ft (55m) drop which should not be descended due to loose deads. Descend in stages. The 82ft (25m) fourth pitch lands on a steep unstable slope, which drops for 13ft (4m) to the fifth pitch, 26ft (8m) deep. At the bottom is a further pitch. Do not approach the edge as it is very loose. Descend via a walled shaft in the floor which can be descended in stages for about 50ft (15m). The bottom is the base of Murmuring Churn, where an impenetrable stream inlet enters and water flows down the pitch into Waterfall Chamber of Oxlow Caverns. Traverse over pitch to a bridge of debris. An in-situ tyrolean gives access to a rock bridge from where a descent can be made into West Chamber of Oxlow Caverns. Maskhill sixth pitch is 141ft (43m) deep. At the bottom is Pearl Chamber, and the fifth pitch of Oxlow Caverns (not free-climbable) enters at the east end. The final wet pitch, the sixth of Oxlow or seventh of Maskhill, can be descended for 13ft (4m) to Pool Chamber and the terminal sump. The sump has been dived but is blocked with rubble after a short distance. Tackle should be left in situ as through trips using Giants Hole as exit are not permitted.

**Tackle:**

**First and Second pitches:**
70m rope. Belay to rings in lid + backup stake. 5 rebelays. 2 deviations.

**Third pitch and slopes below:**
55m rope. 4 rebelays. 2 deviations.

**Murmuring Churn, slopes, fifth pitch and traverse to bridge:**
95m rope. 1 deviation. 4 rebelays +eco hangers on traverse.

**Sixth pitch:** 50m rope.

**Seventh pitch:** 10m rope.

**Tyrolean and pitch into Oxlow West Chamber:**
50m rope. 1 rebelay.

*References:*
*Salmon, L.B. and Boldock, G. 1951. B.S.A. Cave Science Vol.3. No.17. pp.13-20. Survey.*
*Westlake, C.D. 1972. E.P.C. Jour. Vol.8. No.1. pp.39-42. Survey.*

### MIDDLE BANK CAVE
NGR 144 824   Grade: 1
Alt. 1050ft (320m)
Length: 50ft (15m)

Completely excavated by the Technical Projects Unit of the B.S.A. in 1971.

Above and to the east of Middle Bank Pot. A small bedding cave, found by digging to end in a small chamber with no way on.

## MIDDLE BANK POT
**NGR 143 824**
Dig
Alt. 1000ft (305m)
Depth: 50ft (15m) (now run-in)

On the east side of Middle Bank Gully on the hillside west of Peak Cavern. A large open pothole, which was excavated to a depth of 50ft (15m). The shaft started to run back under the choke, and further excavation would have been too dangerous. The shaft has since run in.

## MOUNTBATTEN POT
(Nettle Shaft Pot)
**NGR 125 816**
Grade: 2
Alt. 1480ft (451m)
Depth: 137ft (42m)

Permission from Oxlow House Farm. 1/4 mile south of Nettle Pot. A narrow natural fissure with a metal lid on top. Has been dug out to a small calcited chamber. Very tight.

## NERVOUS BREAKDOWN
**NGR 113 811** Grade: Lost
Alt. 1250ft (381m)

Entered in 1977 by Orpheus Caving Club.

In the south west end of Eldon Hill Quarry. Contact DCA for current access conditions.

A phreatic passage 4ft (1.2m) high and wide petered out after 70ft (21m) to an unstable bedding crawl. At the start of this crawl, a squeeze to the south was excavated, leading to a fine free-climbable pitch of 60ft (18m) choked at the bottom. The whole cave was well decorated, but has either been destroyed or buried by further quarrying.

*Reference: Phipps, M. 1981. The Lyre No.5. p.8. Survey. O.C.C. N/L Vol.13. No.6.*

## NETTLE POT
**NGR 126 819**
Grade: 3-5
Alt. 1515 ft (461m)
Length: 2100ft (640m) approx
Depth: 590ft (180m)
Status: S.S.S.I.

Permission must be gained from Oxlow House Farm before descending.

Dug out by D.P.C. 1934. Extended D.C.C. 1987.

Cavers must approach exactly as for Oxlow Caverns, then follow the direction marker on Oxlow entrance uphill to a gate. One gatepost has a fluorescent marker. Another marker can be seen on a distant post beyond Nettle entrance, or use the waymarker as a pointer and pace out 75 yards. The shaft is fitted with a steel lid.

### Entrance & Stalactite Passage
### Grade 3

Entrance pitch (160ft/49m) is tight in parts for the first 60ft (18m) through The Narrows. Rig rope from the rings on the lid. Rebelay just below, then use a bolt at The Narrows and a Y-hang 30ft (10m) below the Sentry Box. On ladders best lifelined as two pitches as communication is difficult. At bottom of pitch is The Flats, a washed out lava bed. There are short choked shafts in the floor, but to the east is the Gulley and Grand Canyon Pitch, 20ft (6m) deep. Traverse past the top of Elizabeth Shaft with care (handline or lifeline needed). The area around the top of Elizabeth Shaft collapsed in 1995, and requires great care. Stalactite Passage is reached by crossing Elizabeth Shaft to a short climb down into a boulder strewn chamber. Small hole beyond is the top of Crumble Pot, while straight on is Stalactite Passage, becoming low, and floored with flowstone. Passage ends at 20ft (6m) aven with various digging possibilities heading for Jim's Crawl in Oxlow Caverns, separated by 197ft (60m) horizontally and 56ft (17m) vertically.

Derbyshire Hall.
Photo by Rob Eavis

## Elizabeth Shaft
### Grade 4

From the bottom of the Grand Canyon, Elizabeth Shaft can be descended via the first large hole in two pitches of 70ft (21m) and 100ft (30m). Not recommended due to loose boulders. Best descent is via a small hole at the far end, which is a 170ft (52m) fine direct descent. The pitch lands on a rubble floor. A climb up a slope leads to a short free-climbable pitch with a small stream entering from Firbeck Hall and sinking into an impenetrable crack. From the foot of Elizabeth to the east a further 40ft (12m) pitch in two sections can be descended. Same stream enters and can be followed through EPC dig, The Sting, 30ft (9m) of crawling through a tight duck and a boulder choke, entering the bottom of Beza Pot at The Shakes.

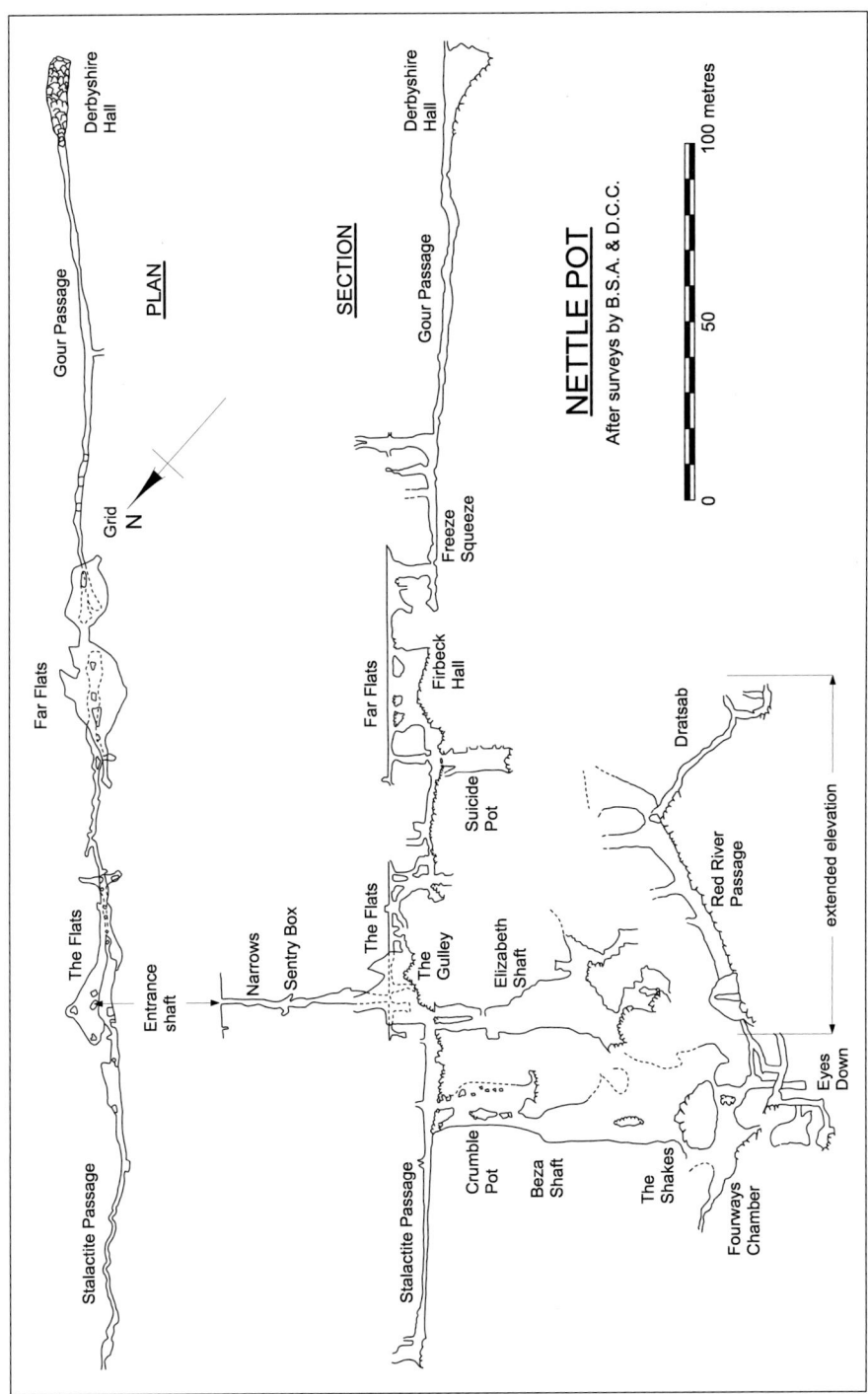

## Crumble and Beza Pots

Crumble Pot is 95ft (29m) deep. Belay to boulders at head of pitch. At bottom a climb up of 20ft (6m) leads to a small hole where a 12ft (4m) pitch can be descended to the head of Beza Pot, 150ft (46m) deep. Belay to calcited boulders. From the bottom a steep boulder slope (50ft/15m handline useful) leads to The Shakes, where the crawl enters from the bottom of Elizabeth Shaft. At the far end of The Shakes a 20ft (6m) deep pot is blind. From the foot of the Beza Pot ladder, to the left facing the ladder, a crawl leads to a tight 50ft (15m) rope pitch into a very unstable area.

Digging here revealed a further 30ft (9m) climbable pitch (Fin Pot), but the way on is too tight for further progress. Digging in the area of Fin Pot in 1987 led to two extensions. One crawl was followed to Bingo Pot, and a further crawl to another climb, Eyes Down, to the lowest point 580ft (177m) below the entrance. Further digging at Fin Pot revealed another crawl into a chamber, Easy Pickings. The ascending Red River Passage continues, leading away from the main joint, passing beneath avens to the base of a further aven. An awkward descending crawl (Dratsab) ends at another climb, choked at the bottom.

## Far Flats

The Flats at the bottom of the entrance pitch can be followed to the southeast alongside the Gulley. 100ft (30m) of flat out crawling passes two choked shafts in the floor, but the third can be descended for 35ft (11m) to a landing on boulders opposite the entrance to Boulder Passage. This pitch can be descended for a further 70ft (21m) where a small stream appears briefly on its way from Firbeck Hall to Elizabeth. 100ft (30m) along Boulder Passage is Suicide Pot, choked at the bottom after 60ft (18m). Ahead is Firbeck Hall where an obvious aven was climbed with the aid of a scaling pole (pull through in place) to Far Flats. Far Flats extends to the south east along the same washed out lava bed as The Flats. After 150ft (46m) a 40ft (12m) pitch leads to the very tight Freeze Squeeze, leading in turn to Gour Passage, generally walking size, and leading after approximately 400ft (122m) to Derbyshire Hall. This chamber is 70ft (21m) long, 20ft (6m) wide, with a flat roof and a floor consisting of a funnel of boulders from which a draught issues. Three avens near the start of Gour Passage were climbed, but were blind. A small inlet passage was pushed for 10ft (3m).

*Tackle:*

*Entrance Pitch:*
70m rope. 2 rebelays + 1 deviation + eco hangers.

*Gully Pitch and traverse:*
20m rope

*Elizabeth Shaft and lower pitches:*
75m rope. Eco hangers on lower pitches.

*Crumble and Beza Shafts:*
70m rope. Scaffold bar backup at top. Eco hangers at sidetep. Rebelay + 2 deviations in Beza Shaft and natural belay for lower slope.

*Flats southeast pitch:*
20m rope.

*Traverse over Suicide Pot:*
5m rope.

*Pull through to Far Flats:*
15m and 25m ropes.

*Pitch to Freeze Squeeze:*
20m rope.

*References: Chantry, M.H. 1937. Caves and Caving (pre-war series) No.1. pp.34-37. Survey.*
*Gill, D.W. 1970. E.P.C. Jour. Vol.7. No.3. pp.43-47. Survey.*
*O'Neill, P. 1987. D.C.A. N/L No.65. pp.2-4. Survey.*
*Salmon, L.B. and Boldock, G. 1951. B.S.A. Cave Science Vol.2. No.16. pp.331-338.*

### ODIN CAVE
**NGR 135 834**
**Grade: 1**
**Alt. 850ft (255m)**
**Length: 140ft (42m)**
Status: National Trust. S.S.S.I.

No known access restrictions. On the west side of the Mam Tor road close to Odin Mine.

Large cave entrance left of Odin Gorge. Very muddy. One chamber. 40ft (12m) shaft on hillside above leads into mud-filled continuation.

*Elliot, D. 1975. Caves of Northern Derbyshire. Part 5. pp.13-14. Survey.*

### ODIN MINE
**NGR 133 834   Grade: 3-4**
**(Mine)**
**Alt. 950ft (290m)**
**Depth: 450ft (137m)**
Status: National Trust. S.S.S.I.

Approach from west side of Mam Tor road to top of impressive fissure.

**Warning: Much of this old mine is highly unstable.**

Belay handline round tree on north side and descend into first crack. Along passage 25ft (8m) chimney is climbed (rope handy) and leads to second shaft 35ft (11m) deep to lower workings. At bottom away from the entrance is 125ft (38m) pitch into a series of levels and stopes (great care - lower levels very unstable). To the right down steep slope, along a level containing dressed stone stemples in roof, to a climb down into the impressive Cartgate Chamber with stone arching in the roof. The chamber ends in a major collapse. Obvious arched passage entered by a short climb leads to two further pitches (tackle required).

*Tackle:*
*Entrance climb:*              20m rope.
*Handline climb:*              20m rope.
*Internal shaft and slope below:*   30m rope.
*Cartgate Chamber pitches:*    2 x 20m ropes.

*References: Adam, W. 1838. Gem of the Peak. (Moorland Publishing reprint 1973 p.355).*
*Anon. 1975. S.U.S.S. Jour. Vol.2. No.4. p.9.*
*Bartrop, R. Undated. S.U.S.S. Jour. Vol.3. No.2. pp.16-17.*
*Drury, D. 1980. Descent No.46. p.20.*
*Ford, T.D. and Rieuwerts, J.H. 1976. P.D.M.H.S. Vol.6. No.4. Special publication. Survey.*
*Smith, M.E. 1962. Bull. P.D.M.H.S. Vol.1. No.6. pp.18-23.*

### OLD MOOR DIG
**NGR 145 811**
**Grade: Dig**
**Alt. 1350ft (411m)**

An abortive dig in a shakehole, which was afterwards filled in.
*Reference: Drakeley, K. 1981. The Lyre No.5. p.1.*

### OLD TOR MINE
(Triangle Cave)
**NGR 134 828**
**Grade: 2 (Mine)**
**Alt. 1246ft (380m)**
**Length: 300ft (91m)**
**Depth: 70ft (21m)**
Status: National Trust. S.S.S.I.

Gated. Permission required from National Trust.

Adit entrance high on the north side of the Winnats Pass at the end of the path.

Short adit leads into main chamber with a blocked exit to surface. Pipe vein workings for Blue John stone extend north westwards to a 10ft (3m) pitch into lower passage. Muddy sump at end leads only to short passage.

*References: Elliot, D. 1975. Caves of Northern Derbyshire. Part 5. pp.22-24. Survey.*

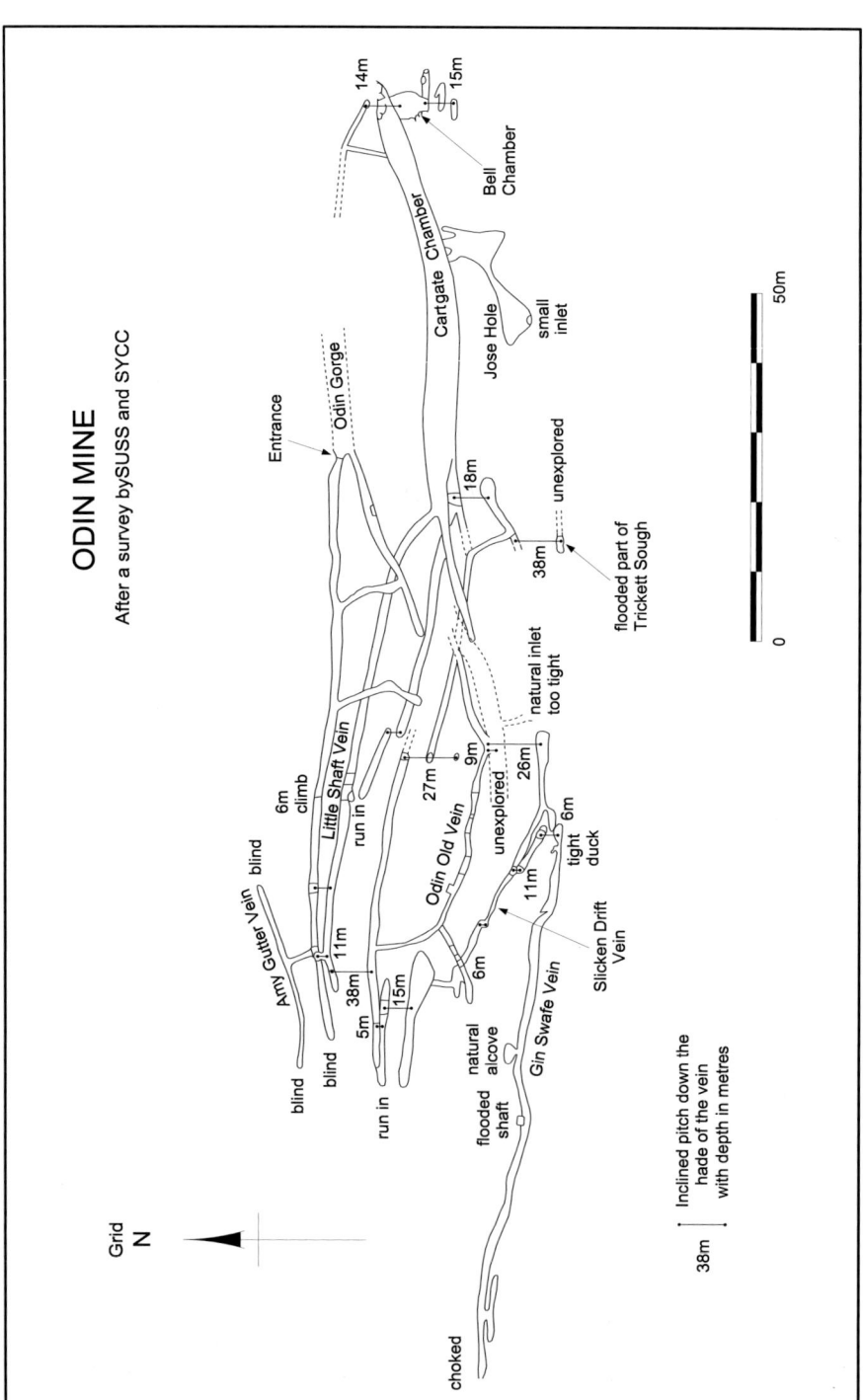

## OXLOW CAVERNS
(Rackety Mine, Rickety Mine, Opens Mine)

**NGR 1241 8218**
**Grade: 3-5 (Mine)**
**Alt. 1445ft (440m)**
**Length: 4632ft (1.4km) (Including Maskhill 5282ft/1.6km)**
**Depth: 477ft (145m) (To East Canal in Giants Hole 640ft/195m)**
**Status: S.S.S.I.**

Permission must be sought from Oxlow House Farm, and an access fee paid.

Extended 1964 by B.S.A. and connected to Giants Hole by E.P.C. in 1966.

Access is via the lowered section of wall and wooden stile just before the third gate towards Perryfoot. Follow the wall uphill, and cross into the Oxlow Field by a stone stile in the wall. Proceed round the hillside, climbing up over the brow to Oxlow entrance.

Note: Cavers undertaking a trip from Oxlow to Giants must leave tackle in situ as exit is not allowed via Giants.

### Oxlow to bottom of Maskhill
**Grade 4    Length: 1502ft (458m)    Depth: 445ft (135m)**

Entrance is mine shaft capped with concrete and fitted with an iron lid. First pitch is 53ft (16m) deep. Belay to bolts in concrete. Rebelay to eco hanger at bottom of shaft and descend steep slope and step of miners deads. At bottom straight on is choked, but low passage to left leads to head of Second Pitch, 36ft (11m) deep. At bottom, a slope and a short climb down where stream enters on right leads to Third Pitch, 46ft (14m) deep. This is a good vantage point, with a fine view of East Chamber. At the bottom, a slope to the east and a short climb down lead to East Chamber, of impressive dimensions. At the far end is a short choked shaft in the floor. The north wall has been climbed by E.P.C. for 180ft (55m) to a 30ft (9m) passage ending at a tight aven, and a large rock bridge. From the bottom of the Third Pitch to the west, West Swirl Passage can be followed down a steep slope over deads to the head of the Fourth Pitch, 40ft (12m). From the foot of the Fourth Pitch a steep slope leads down into West Antechamber. To the right (north) a pull-through is in place for the 30ft (9m) pitch to Pilgrim's Way and New Oxlow Series. Straight on is a low arch. An inlet enters on the right, and can be followed for 115ft (35m) to a sump which has been dived for 140ft (43m). Stream has been tested from Black's Folly, the Rocky Tube before Castle Aven in New Oxlow Series. The low arch leads into West Chamber, of impressive proportions. At the far end a climb up a boulder slope leads to a short mined passage to the head of the Fifth Pitch, 46m (14m) deep. At the bottom is Pearl Chamber, the base of Maskhill Mine's Sixth Pitch. A small waterfall enters. The Sixth Pitch of Oxlow immediately follows, 13ft (4m) deep to Pool Chamber and the terminal sump, which has been dived but is blocked with rubble.

### Oxford Aven and Coconut Airways
**Grade 5**

Explored 1976 by E.P.C. Oxford Aven can be reached by turning left at the first junction in Pilgrim's Way. The passage leads via a tight squeeze to The Flue, dug in 1976 by T.S.G., which oxbows back into the wall of West Chamber at an aven. This has been climbed up 8 pitches to a height of 300ft (91m), choked at the top. The roof of West Chamber was traversed by bolting starting from the top of the Sixth Pitch in Maskhill. The three Coconut Avens were found, and the Great Aven was climbed to a height of 270ft (82m). Passage opposite Pilgrim's Way. Reached with scaling poles, this tube can be followed as a crawl for 96ft (29m) to a voice connection with a similar tube off Suicide Chamber in the New Oxlow Series.

## Jim's Crawl  Grade 4
Discovered 1968 by E.P.C. Above the Third Pitch is a 30ft (9m) bolt climb up to a crumbling rock bridge. A further 30ft (9m) exposed climb leads to the top of East Chamber where 166ft (51m) of very low but wide washed out lava bed can be followed to a too-low section where water can be heard ahead. Four pitches in the floor, all blocked at the bottom. Three can be free climbed. The fourth requires 36ft (11m) of ladder. The passage is formed on the same bedding plane as The Flats of Nettle Pot. Digging has reached a point 60m away from the aven in Stalactite Passage in Nettle.

## New Oxlow Series
**Grade 4     Length: 3034ft (925m)                 Depth: 477ft (145m)**
Discovered by the B.S.A. in 1964. Entered by climbing the 30ft (9m) pitch from West Antechamber to a high level phreatic tube leading after a short distance to a junction. Left leads to The Flue and an eyehole into the roof of West Antechamber. Right is Pilgrim's Way, 1010ft (308m) of hands and knees crawling. A short distance along, two crawls on the right unite and lead to Suicide Chamber, very unstable, and situated almost below East Chamber. The tube continues to voice connection with the tube opposite Pilgrim's Way.

Further along Pilgrim's Way on the left is the low arch to Castle Aven, climbed for 50ft (15m) to a passage which is soon too tight. Castle Aven emits a small stream which crosses Pilgrim's Way and enters Rocky Tube on the right, which can be followed for 51ft (15m) to Black's Folly, a pitch of 26ft (8m). The stream has been dye tested to the inlet in West Antechamber. Pilgrim's Way continues to Mecca Aven, climbed for 130ft (40m) to a 6ft (2m) long tube too tight for further progress. Just beyond Mecca Aven a passage on the left leads to the Water Rift, 65ft (20m) high with no passages at the top. Crawl on the left can be followed to small stream which sinks and has been dye tested to Main Stream Inlet. Upstream is a low crawl and very tight section to Oxlow Aven and the connection with Giant's Hole via the Chamber of Horrors, 728ft (222m) of flat out crawling with ducks.

Back in Pilgrim's Way, the hands and knees crawl continues beyond Mecca aven to Rainbow Aven. Walking size passage beyond passes low tube on right after short distance. This is Icarus's Crawl, flat out for 225ft (69m) to a small stream inlet. Downstream is too tight after a short distance. Halfway along Icarus's Crawl is Henry Mares' Crawl on the right, 133ft (41m) of tight crawling to a 20ft (6m) pitch with 5ft (1.5m) of water at the bottom. Passage just before the pitch can be followed for about 20ft (6m), very tight. Another low passage about halfway along can be followed for about 30ft (9m) before becoming too low.

The main passage continues at walking size to Jacob's Ladder, where a small stream enters from an aven. Beyond is North Chamber leading to North Pitch, 17ft (5m). At the bottom a low crawl, the Portcullis, can be followed to Main Stream Inlet entering on the left from a fissure. This tight fissure can be followed upstream to a 26ft (8m) cascade which can be free climbed up two different routes. At the top is the Main Stream Inlet Series, consisting of 300ft (91m) of hands and knees crawling. Main stream comes from small crack, while side passages are either too tight or break into avens. One passage branches back into roof of North Chamber and another into the top of North Pitch. Downstream from the Portcullis a low wet crawl, The Sewer, leads to Boulder Chamber, where a high stream passage can be followed down to a sump and concrete dams. Originally passed by baling, and more recently by digging and diving through a very tight passage, the sump leads to P.B. Chamber and the terminal sump, which backs up and does not look hopeful. Three avens in the roof of PB Chamber (the largest 26m (85ft)high) are blind.

**Tackle:**
**Oxlow to Bottom of Maskhill:**
| | |
|---|---|
| Entrance Pitch to bottom of step: | 40m rope. Belay to rings + eco hangers + rebelay |
| Second Pitch and slope to Third Pitch: | 40m rope. 1 deviation + eco hangers |
| Third Pitch and slope to Fourth Pitch: | 60m rope. 1 deviation + eco hangers |

| | |
|---|---|
| Fourth Pitch: | 20m rope. 1 deviation |
| Fifth Pitch: | 20m rope. |
| Sixth Pitch: | 10m rope. |
| East Chamber climb: | 25m rope. Eco hangers + rebelay |

**New Oxlow.**
**Rope for pull-through on 30ft (10m) up pitch**

| | |
|---|---|
| North Pitch: | 10m rope |

References: Banner, C. 1972. E.P.C. Jour. Vol.8. No.1. pp.11-12.
Bentham, K. 1978. D.C.A. N/L No.35. pp.1-2.
Chantry, M.H. 1937. Oxlow Caverns survey.
Crabtree, P.W. 1965. B.S.A. Cave Science Vol.5. No.37. pp.229-238. Survey.
Deakin, P.R. 1966. E.P.C. Jour. Vol.7. No.1. pp.60-62.
Gill, D.W. 1970. E.P.C. Jour. Vol.7. No.3. pp.43-47.
Mort, J. (Barmaster). B.S.A. Records.
Pill, A.L. B.S.A. Cave Science Vol.1. No.5. pp.152-155.
Salmon, L.B. & Boldock, G. 1951. B.S.A. Cave Science Vol.3. No.17. pp.13-20. Survey.
Smith, P.B. 1966. B.S.A. Bull. No.72. pp.12-13.
Westlake, C.D. 1966. B.S.A. Bull. No.71. pp.10-13.
Westlake, C.D. 1967. Proc. B.S.A. No.5. pp.1-11.
Westlake, C.D. 1972. E.P.C. Jour. Vol.8. No.1. pp.39-42. Survey.
Westlake, C.D. 1967. E.P.C. Jour. Vol.7. No.2. pp.1-4.
Winder, F.A. 1938. Unconventional Guide to the Caverns of Castleton. pp.48-56.

## P0 SWALLET
(P Zero)
**NGR 092 811**
Grade: 2. (Dig)
Alt. 1150ft (350m)
Length: 120ft (36m)
Depth: 60ft (18m)

A swallet taking a small stream. Loose descent using handline (80ft/24m needed) to 40ft (12m) of walking passage to a diminutive sump. Care needed.

Reference: Bentham, K. 1988. T.S.G. Jour. No.13. pp.19-20.

## P1 SWALLET
**NGR 0989 8127**
Dig
Alt. 1033ft (315)

Permission from Torr Top Farm.
At foot of blind valley between Dr. Jackson's and Perryfoot Caves.
Dangerous in all but dry weather.
A large stream sinks into a rift passage. This was forced in 1986 down some short cascades to a very wet duck to enter Perryfoot Cave. In wet weather the stream overflows to flood both Dr. Jackson's and Perryfoot Caves. Some of the water enters Dr. Jackson's Cave through tight inlets.

References: Gibson, R. 1986. Caves & Caving No.32. pp.22-23.
Salmon, L.B. 1963. B.S.A. Cave Science Vol.5. No.33. pp.36-52.
Salmon, L.B. & Boldock, G. 1949. B.S.A. Cave Science Vol.2. No.9. pp.15-20. Survey.

### P4 SWALLET
(Sludge Pit)
NGR 1016 8154
Dig
Alt. 1050ft (320m)

Permission from Perryfoot Farm.
Wet weather stream sinking in small blind valley 100 yards (91m) north east of Gautries Hole. Attempts at excavation foiled by black mud.
*References: D.C.C. Bulletin 1969.*
*Descent No.145, 1998. p.11.*
*Elliot, D. 1975. Caves of Northern Derbyshire. Part 4. p.9.*

### P5 SWALLET
NGR 1029 8163
Grade: 1 (Dig)
Alt. 1050ft (320m)
Length: 150ft (46m)
Depth: 70ft (21m)
Status: S.S.S.I.

Permission from Perryfoot Farm.
Excavated D.C.C. 1969 and E.P.C. 1980-83.
Small stream sinks in shakehole 240 yds (219m) north east of Gautries Hole.
A short passage leads to hauling shaft 43ft (13m) deep, best descended by a free-climbable pitch just beyond into Kaiser 1, a chamber now filled with excavated material. Rope Passage on left ends after 30ft (9m) and is formed in mud and boulders. Straight on is Dark Lane leading to Kaiser II and III and Fingers Choke with no possibility of further extension. Majority of cave has been excavated.
*References: Bentham, K. 1983. D.C.A. N/L No.52. pp.1-8. Survey.*
*D.C.C. Bulletin 1969.*
*Elliot, D. 1975. Caves of Northern Derbyshire. Part 4. p.9.*
*Salmon, L.B. & Boldock, G. 1950. B.S.A. Cave Science Vol.2. No.11. pp.118-122.*

### P7 SWALLET
NGR 1051 8173
Grade: 4
Alt. 1020ft (311m)
Length: 240ft (73m)
Depth: 118ft (36m)
Status: S.S.S.I.

Permission from Perryfoot Farm.
Excavated 2000-2001 by the Technical Speleological Group.
Stream sinking in large shakehole approximately 450ft (137m) north east of Little Bull Pit.
A 50ft (15m) entrance shaft was excavated through the shakehole fill to give access to a 12ft (3.5m) pitch into a rift chamber, descending through a series of rifts and crawls to a depth of 120ft (36m). A small hole, The Wormhole, was enlarged to 8m of stooping passage to a sump. Water has been dye tested to the upstream inlet sump in the Lower Streamway of P8. Downstream sump was dived to 23ft (7m) depth, with a side rift to a blind airbell.

**Tackle: 5m ladder + lifeline. Belay to boulders.**

*References: Beck, J.S. 2001. Descent No. 163. p.11. Survey.*
*CDG N/L 152. p.24, and 153. pp.8-9.*
*Westwood, R. 2001. Descent No. 162. p.15.*

P7 Swallet. Photo by John Beck

**P8**
(Jack Pot)
NGR 1079 8179
Grade: 3
Alt. 1068ft (326m)
Length: 3340ft (1018m (+2000ft/600m of passage approx. beyond the sumps
Depth: 230ft (70m)
Status: S.S.S.I.

Approach from Perryfoot Farm where permission must be sought and a small fee paid.

Explored B.S.A. 1964. Extended C.D.G. and E.P.C.

Entrances are in an irregular depression where a small stream sinks, 1000 yards (915m) north east of the farm, beyond Little Bull Pit. Please follow the way-markers.

**Warning: This cave is not suitable for novices in wet weather when the First Pitch becomes very wet.**

Old entrance leads to a muddy chamber with short crawls, a rift, and tight crawl to Cascade Chamber. 8ft (2.5m) concrete shaft down which the stream sinks leads quickly to the same place. Crawl over boulders to a clean-washed streamway. Above the first chute is a high level route along a mineral vein. The stream can be rejoined beyond Idiot's Leap by descending a 30ft (9m) pitch.

The streamway can be followed down several small cascades to Idiot's Leap, an 8ft (2.5m) climb. Narrow streamway with chutes and pools to the wet First Pitch of 25ft (8m), 270ft (82m) from entrance. Climbing into the roof just before the pitch allows a drop of 50ft (15m) clear of the water. Two routes below the pitch. Streamway continues for 100ft (30m) to the Second Pitch, 25ft (8m) into spectacular little chamber. The other route is a 10ft (3m) climb to the Upper Series, opposite the First Pitch. Short hands and knees crawl and easy traverse above the stream to a sharp left hand

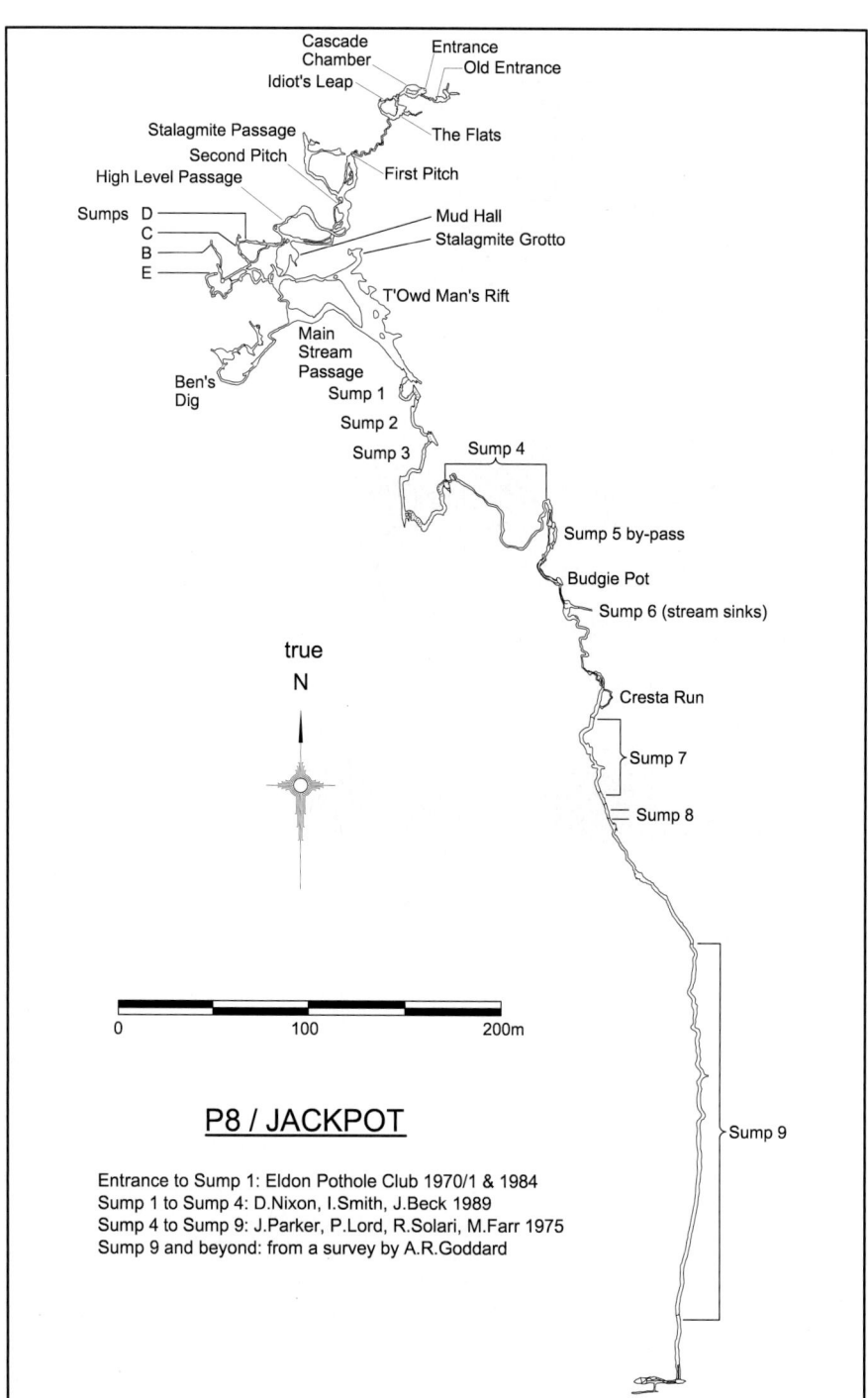

The First Pitch in wet conditions.
Photo by Rob Eavis

bend. Step over to the right leads to Stalactite Passage, 194ft (59m) long with a small stream, ending in a calcite choke. 20ft (6m) above the entrance to Stalactite Passage on the right is Steve's Passage leading back to a point high above the First Pitch.

Main route is round left hand bend, and traverse over holes above the Second Pitch. Eyehole through flowstone leads to Upper Series Pitch. A further climb down leads to the foot of the Second Pitch. From the bottom of the Second Pitch, a series of wet crawls lead via Overflow Passage to Sump D. Left just before Sump D leads to the Main Stream Passage, passing Sump C on the right. Possible to leave Second Pitch partway down, and climb round to bottom of Upper Series Pitch. The route contracts to the smaller Gour Passage on the left. 75ft (23m) on is Mud Hall with High Level Passage on right, 200ft (61m) of roomy passage to a point opposite the top of the Upper Series Pitch. Across Mud Hall a dirty passage leads to the Main Stream Passage, which usually takes more water than the P8 stream. Upstream is 100ft (30m) to the inlet sump, where the combined streams from P2 to P7 reappear. On the left are two openings to Sand Passage, mostly crawling with a tight duck and sump which must be bailed. Ends in static sump at the bottom of a slope. It is said that bad air has been met here. Just beyond Sand Passage on the right is the opening of Overflow Passage.

Downstream the passage is 30ft (9m) high with chutes and pools. A bouldery region follows, then a fine flowstone cascade and a final 100ft (30m) in a big hading rift (T'Owd Man's Rift) to Sump 1. A slippery climb up to the left leads to the vandalised Stalagmite Grotto and a low crawl to Christmas Aven. A handline climb up the right wall of the Main Streamway before T'Owd Man's Rift leads into Ben's Dig, 600ft (180m) of walking passage leading to four chambers. The upstream sump has been dived for 150ft (46m) to a depth of 90ft (27m) too tight for further progress. Only one air filled chamber below a boulder choke has been found. Sand Passage has been dived in static water to a dead end after 15ft (4.5m).

Downstream Sump 1 is 105ft (32m) long and 15ft (4.6m) deep to an air bell. Sump 2 (12ft/4m deep and 100ft/30m long) leads to a further air bell 30ft (9m) across. Sump 3 (75ft/23m long) enters 130ft (40m) of stream passage to Sump 4. 300ft (91m) of constricted sump leads to a short stretch of streamway to Sump 5, 50ft (15m) long, and bypassed via an aven. A short stream passage leads to Budgie Pot, 15ft (4.5m) deep. After a further 100ft (30m) a small inlet enters, and the combined streams flow into Sump 6 which is blocked with pebbles and backs up. A rising phreatic tube, the Cresta Run, can be followed to Sump 7, which emits a trickle of water flowing to Sump 6. A passage continues to a 50ft (15m) pitch leading back into the Cresta Run. Sump 7 is 200ft (60m) long with a 20ft (6m) vertical pot. A short canal leads to the shallow Sump 8. 350ft (107m) of passage leads to Sump 9, passed in 1987 after a dive of 600ft (183m) to 85m of passage leading to two pitches. These unite into one large shaft, and a total descent of 55ft (16m) leads Sump 10, choked at 20ft (6m) depth. Estimates place this approximately 60ft (18m) above Main Rising in Speedwell.

**Tackle:**
**Idiot's Leap: 5m rope.**         Handline may be in place.
**First Pitch: 20m rope.**
    Alternative Pitch (from roof): 25m rope.     Natural and bolt belays.
**High Level Pitch: 15m rope.**     Natural and bolt belays.
    Alternative wet Second Pitch:     15m rope.          Bolt belays.
    Traverse to High Level Passage:    15m rope.          Natural and bolt belays.
    High Level pitch above Idiots Leap: 15m rope.        Natural and bolt belays.

*References:* Bentham, K. 1984. E.P.C. Jour. Vol.9. No.4. pp.4-8. Survey.
Bentham, K. 1986. E.P.C. Jour. Vol.9. No.5. pp.6-18.
C.D.G. N/L No.113. pp.32-33 & No.121. pp.24-25.
Smith, P.B. & Waltham, A.C. 1973. B.S.A. Cave Science No.50. pp.21-28. Survey.
Westlake, C.D. & Cobbett, J.S. 1972. E.P.C. Jour. Vol.8. No.1. pp.15-31. Survey.

## PEAK CAVERN
(The Devil's Arse)
**NGR 1486 8259**
**Grade: 1-5 (Part Show)**
**Alt. 625ft (188m)**
**Length: 5.5 miles (8.9km) (Incl. Speedwell: 10.3 miles/16.5 km**
**Depth: 560ft (170m) approx. (from James Hall's Over Engine Mine: 770ft (234.7m))**
**Status: S.S.S.I.**

Run by Peak Cavern Ltd. Visiting clubs must carry B.C..A. insurance or equivalent. Individuals must sign an indemnity form, and must be at least 18 years of age. Access (Sundays only, November to March) controlled by B.C.R.A. Send S.A.E. with suggested date to J.S.Beck, Glebe Cottage, The Hillock, Eyam, Derbys. or (preferably) E-mail john.beck6@btinternet.com. Note that exit via Speedwell Cavern is not allowed.

Immense entrance at the head of the Peak Cavern Gorge below Peveril Castle.

**Warning: Frequent flooding occurs during the winter months, resulting in long stretches of the show cave being sumped, sometimes for several days.**

A fine cave which with Speedwell Cavern forms a major system of considerable sporting and scientific interest. The following description should be regarded as a brief summary.

### The Show Cave
Entrance chamber is 330ft x 102ft x 60ft high (101m x 31m x 18m). The terraces were used for rope making. Low down in the left wall is the Swine Hole, a large passage leading to a series of crawls, and to a 330ft (100m) sump which connects with the Outer Styx, the resurgence below the main entrance. Several avens in the Vestibule roof have been climbed to reveal high level passages. Most extensive is the Krypton Series, above the Swine Hole, a series of joint-oriented passages almost reaching the surface in Cave Dale. The large aven above the bend in the top rope walk was climbed for 100ft (30m) to a large well decorated ascending passage (The Mendip Beer Monster's Secret Tap Room), ending at a calcite choke after 200ft (60m). The visitors path descends to the inner gate, and via Lumbago Walk to the Inner Styx, a shallow pool. Then through a short low passage to two more large chambers, the Great Cave and Roger Rains House. The former is 150ft x 90ft x 60ft high (46m x 27m x 18m), and has several high level digs, a 150ft (45m) aven (with blocked connection to Cave Dale Cave No.4) and the high level Orchestra Passage, which leads to the Balcony overlooking Roger Rains House. Roger Rains Aven here is 130ft (40m) high, with a waterfall entering from the Cave Dale sink. The route continues through Pluto's Dining Room, with inlet passages to right and left. That on the left is the Devil's Cellar, and is 395ft (120m) long. The show cave now ends at the top of the Devil's Staircase. Down the steps is the Peak Cavern stream, flowing into Halfway House, which can be followed downstream for 120ft (37m) to a sump, whence it flows to the Swine Hole and Outer Styx. (Sump dived to a slot after 170ft (52m)). Nearby Styx Inlet Sump was dived for 150ft (45m). The large main passage continues along the Five Arches for 500ft (152m), passing several avens, one of which supplies ventilation via a connection to Cave Dale Cave No.8. The show cave used to end here at the junction of Buxton and Speedwell Water passages.

### The Far Reaches
The Buxton Water can be followed upstream to the left to Buxton Water Sump, a 330ft (100m) dive via a high aven (climbed to a total height of 187ft (57m)) into the Main Stream Passage. The right hand passage, or Speedwell Water, leads under the 250ft (76m) high Victoria Aven, with high level passages at both ends of the shaft still in the course of exploration. A series of pools and canals leads past a narrow muddy passage on the right (eventually leading via an awkward climb and crawl to the high choked aven of Perseverance Pot) to a short stretch of large passage. A right hand branch leads to Speedwell Pot (capped with concrete) where floodwater used to enter the cave. A crawl to the huge choke in the bottom of Perseverance Pot follows, and one descends into Mucky Ducks, first passed by the B.S.A. in 1949 after a long dig. The large Upper Gallery follows. After about 390ft (119m) a hands and knees crawl on the right is B-Cubed, a short dig. After a further 100ft (30m) a

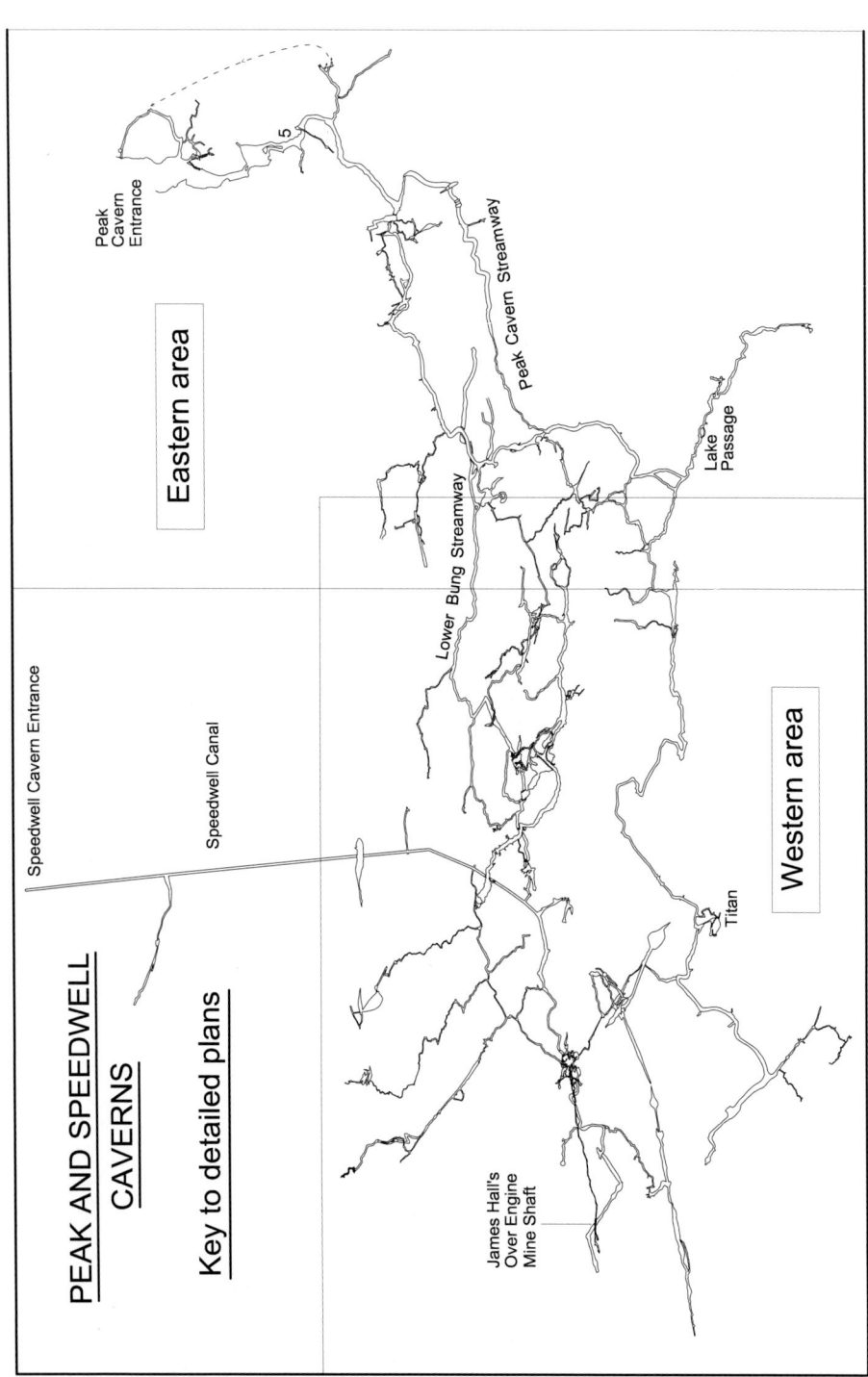

similar passage emitting a small stream is Pickering's Passage (see below).
Upper Gallery continues for 230ft (70m) to the junction with Treasury Passage on the right. The next right hand branch leads directly into Watershed Aven, where a second emergency food dump was created in 2006. Upper Gallery continues, developing a narrow vadose trench originating at a tight sump reached by a squeeze, to the head of Surprise View. A 20ft (6m) climb with a fixed iron ladder descends into the lofty Main Stream Passage. At the top of Surprise View a passage on the right leads into the Main Stream Inlet Series.

Below Surprise View the Main Stream Passage can be followed downstream for 1080ft (329m). The last 500ft (152m) is a fine large phreatic tube, which gradually degenerates towards the upstream end of Buxton Water Sump, passing the 75ft (23m) long Buxton Water Inlet Sump on the right, which ends too low. Upstream one reaches the waterfall at Squaw's Junction after 560ft (171m). Climbing this again leads into the Main Stream Inlet Series.

The next inlet on the left is Lake Passage with Lake Sump (free-dive or by-pass via a muddy crawl) to Ink Sump. A 630ft (192m) dive surfaces beneath a 75ft (23m) aven at the top of which is Doom's Retreat, and a dig amongst huge boulders close to Dirtlow Rake. Above the near end of Ink Sump, a slippery climb up a large phreatic ramp leads to two possible digs.

Beyond Lake Passage the main cave assumes very impressive proportions and passes a high level tube on the right connecting once again with the Main Stream Inlet Series, with the flat out Window Dig on the left. The next feature is Maypole Inlet, an ambitious dig in a large phreatic roof tunnel 40ft (13m) above the stream. Shortly after this, the main route ascends a boulder pile, with the Picnic Dig (and old emergency food dump) higher still on the left. The large main passage continues, and the stream is regained just after the 250ft (75m) approx. of avens (not normally rigged) leading up on the left into Crystal Inlet. Easy walking, broken by one final boulder pile, soon leads to Far Sump, the limit of the cave for non-divers.

## Far Sump Extension

Far Sump is a serious dive of 1265ft (385m) into Far Sump Extension. At 1150ft (350m) is the 40ft (12m) high White Feather Aven. Near upstream end is difficult submerged side passage to left, from which main Peak stream flows. Crawl through boulders from the end of the sump into AJ Passage, the main way on. A series of climbs and squeezes up through the choke emerges, 115ft (35m) above the sump, into the base of Titan, the largest natural shaft in Britain, 492ft (150m) high. AJ Passage enlarges into a pleasant stroll for 1500ft (460m) to the large static Major Sump, choked at 25ft (7.5m) depth. A passage to the left approx. 500ft (150m) before Major Sump leads to Minor Sump, and a difficult crawl to a small stream passage, The Rasp. Two upstream sumps have been drained here by baling to reach a third sump, not yet passed.

A low inlet crawl on the right of AJ Passage 300ft (90m) beyond Far Sump enters Stemple Highway, a large complex phreatic rift. To the right, pitches up and down enter Salmon's Cavern, with steep muddy tube at far end to short crawl and tight sump. To the left are 40ft (12m) and 20ft (6m) pitches up into 400ft (122m) of easy going to a junction. Straight ahead is the connection to the bottom of Leviathan in James Hall's Over Engine Mine, while 60ft (18m) to the right is the 150ft (46m) high Calcite Aven. At the top of Calcite Aven is a large passage, Western Highway. A short distance along here is the 100ft (30m) high Cascade Aven on the left. At the top is Donatella's Aven, with various crawls leading off its base. The aven is 50ft (15m) high and leads to 100ft (30m) of passage via a final 13ft (4m) aven ending at a mud sump. This is 425ft (130m) above Far Sump level, about 200ft (60m) below surface. Below the base of Cascade Aven, a dry passage leads to a scramble up into Fingernail Chamber. Here a 40ft (12m) pitch in the floor enters the impressive Balcombe's Way. Descending a loose boulder climb leads to the brink of a spectacular 200ft (60m) pitch back down into the roof of Salmon's Cavern, The Ride of the Valkyries. Partway along Balcombe's Way is a loose boulder slope up to the 100ft (30m) high Balcombe's Way Aven, entering an extensive bedding complex, The Total Perspective Vortex. To the right a crawl becomes too tight close to Donatella's Aven. To the left

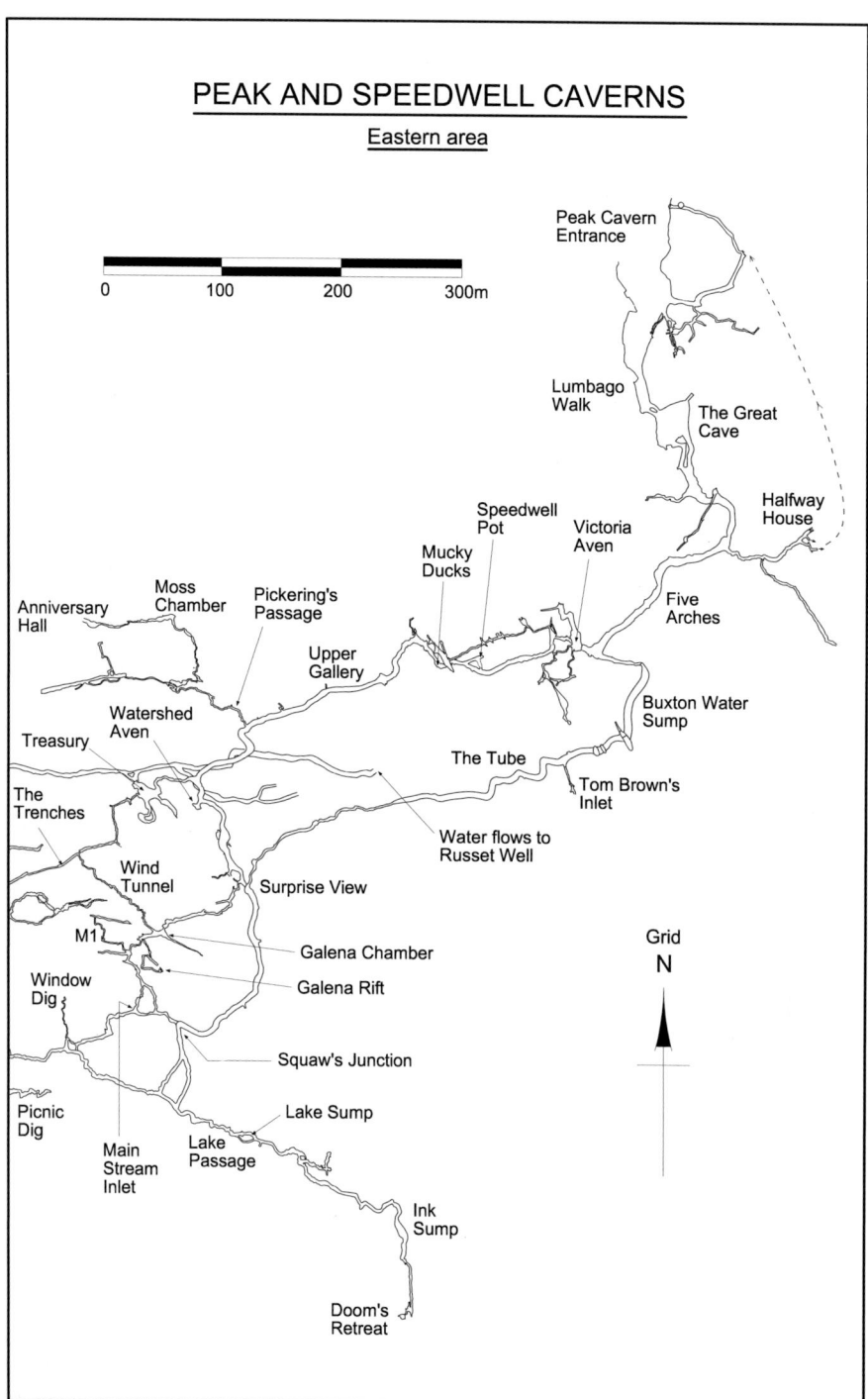

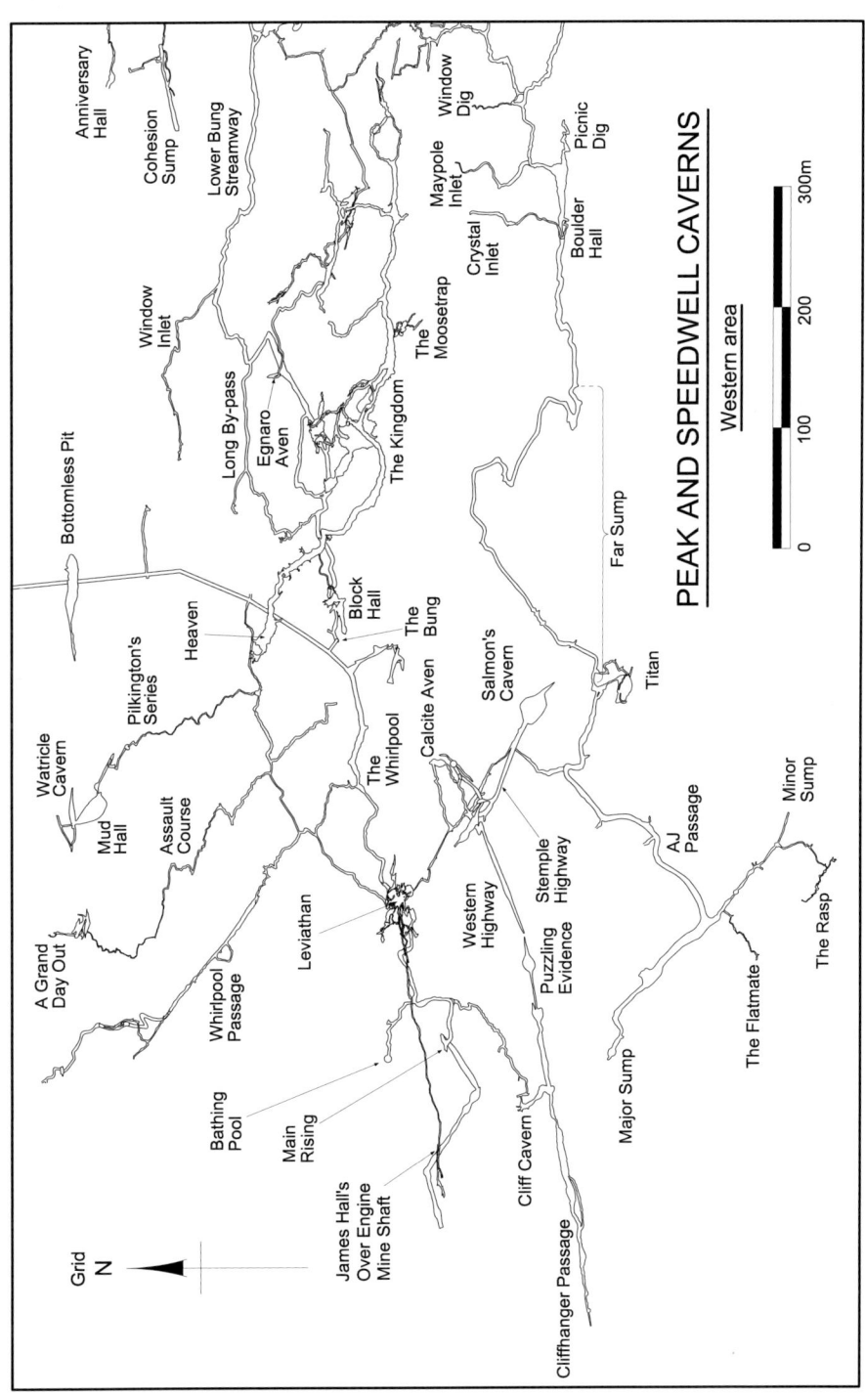

another crawl leads to three separate big shafts down. Vortex 1 is a 150ft (45m) pitch connecting with an aven in Balcombe's Way. Vortex 2 is a 33ft (10m) pitch, reached by a 50ft (15m) traverse, dropping into the roof of Western Highway. Vortex 3 is a loose wet shaft choked at 100ft (30m) depth.

## The Main Stream Inlet Series

A short distance downstream from the Maypole Inlet ladder, a climb up (dubious rope often in place) leads to a tube which immediately forks. Left is Window Dig, and to the right a slippery crawl leads to a further junction. To the right is a dangerous window into the roof of the Main Stream Passage, while ahead, crawling and stooping leads to the Main Stream Inlet, where the stream emerges from the bedding slot in the left wall. This is now largely concreted, and pipes led the water away for use in various digs. A right turn leads downstream to the top of the Squaw's Junction waterfalls, while straight on leads to a T-junction. Right leads to Squaw's Junction again, while left leads to Wigwam Aven, 90ft (27m) high with a tight passage at the top to the large Disappointment Rift, and connecting with the NCC Shafts. Emerging in the bottom of Wigwam Aven, to the left and 10ft (3m) up is Cadbury Crawl, a 130ft (40m) long dig, and opposite is the main route. The crawl soon enlarges at a junction. Left is a dig. A cross rift gives access to Galena Rift, a series of pitches which ascends to a dig at the level of the White River Series. Beyond, the passage soon develops a vadose trench and emerges into Galena Chamber. Climb down via the floor trench. Above the climb down into Galena Chamber is the entrance to Wind Tunnel, 1250ft (381m) of arduous crawling to the top of Egnaro Aven in Speedwell Cavern. From Galena Chamber, an obvious rather muddy passage leads back to the top of Surprise View.

## NCC Shafts

A small opening at the top of Wigwam Aven is the M1, an awkward 100ft (30m) crawl via Z bends into easier passage. A further awkward squeeze enters Disappointment Rift, 100ft (30m) long and up to 23ft (7m) high. To the left is choked rift while to the right two short climbs lead to an ascending passage. A slippery mud slope can be traversed for 50ft (15m) to an eyehole overlooking the NCC shafts. A 20ft (6m) pitch drops onto the floor of the NCC shafts. Down to the NW leads to a short 6ft (2m) climb then three pitches of 56ft (17m), 43ft (13m) and 32ft (10m) in a large shaft to a chamber with a small sump pool in the SE corner, and a sight/voice connection with the base of the aven at the end of the Rocky Tube. About 30ft (10m) above is a small window into a 13ft (4m) crawl (connection 3), while in the north-west corner, a 10ft (3m) pitch drops into a smaller chamber, sloping down to a mud floor. 56ft (17m) above the 43ft (13m) pitch is the entrance to the Traverse of the Spods (approached by traversing from the head of the 56ft (17m) pitch). 65ft (20m) of well decorated passage leads to a squeeze into the base of an aven, climbed for 33ft (10m) to a rock blocking the way, passed to a short extension. From the head of the 43ft (13m) pitch, a traverse to the NW upwards at 45 degrees leads to Mummy Inlet, a very slippery squeeze for 6ft (2m) into a 13ft (4m) high rift. The rift closes up downwards while back over the squeeze calcited boulders block the way. Ahead after five metres, a 2ft (60cm) diameter tube rises for 26ft (8m) until it closes. From the floor below the eyehole, heading north is a series of up pitches of 20ft (6m), 26ft (8m) to a rebelay and a choice of three routes. Stepping off the rope onto the ledge, 20ft (6m) pitch upwards, then a 6ft (2m) climb into a bedding, soon choked. A 46ft (14m) pitch up from the rebelay leads to a roomy sandy passage heading NNW and reducing to hands and knees after 33ft (10m), passing a bat skeleton in the floor before a terminal choke after a further 26ft (8m). This passage has been voice connected with the one below. Reaching over to the east wall, a 33ft (10m) pitch precedes a short gully into a chamber with a climb at the back to a calcite choke. A low crawl from floor under the eyehole (base of pitch from Disappointment Rift) leads to a 23ft (7m) pitch landing in a rift, and some short climbs to Robbie's Gloom Room, a tight sloping crawl for 16ft (5m) to a further pitch. A 20ft (6m) pitch lands you in Galena Rift (connection one). Up the slope to the SE (from the base of the pitch from Disappointment Rift), a 5ft (1.5m) climb up, then pitches of 21ft (6.5m) and 10ft (3m) lead to a steeply descending narrow rift to a flat out crawl and a rising rocky slope to an opening in the side of EMT aven (connection two).

## EMT Aven
A small climb up into a high narrow rift quickly leads to a short 20ft (6m) fixed rope (take care) to Galena Rift, a short section of passage to a chamber with an aven rising above. A small opening at the top leads to the M2 and the NCC shafts (connection one). Beyond the aven, a crawl leads after about 33ft (10m) to a boulder choke. A route up through the choke, keeping left brings you to a squeeze passing a boulder into the base of EMT Aven. A very muddy slope rises 13ft (4m) to a vertical pitch of 16ft (5m), stepping off the pitch onto a loose boulder slope for 3m to a rebelay. Easy slope from here for 23ft (7m) leads you to a further pitch of 50ft (15m), then a large steeply ascending passage to a calcite choke. Just before the choke, a 33ft (10m) pitch up a narrow tube leads to a bedding plane full of clay. This point is at a similar level to the White River Series. From the rebelay a traverse line takes you across the slope into a 10ft (3m) high rift, a boulder slope reduces to a flat out crawl. Squeezing through leads you into a steeply ascending rift passage to the NCC shafts (connection two).

## The Rocky Tube
The Rocky Tube is a tight, wet crawl for 65ft (20m) to the base of an aven. The aven rises vertically for 33ft (10m), then it slopes upwards at 45 degrees for a few metres into a small horizontal passage for 13ft (4m) to an opening into the bottom pitch of the NCC Shafts about 33ft (10m) above the floor (connection three).

## Pickering's Series
An obvious hands and knees crawl on the north side of Upper Gallery, discharging a small stream, is Pickering's Passage. After 300ft (91m) a letter-box squeeze is followed by a left turn. A hole on the right is the way to Moss Chamber (see below) while straight on is Cohesion Crawl, leading to a large sump, 100ft (30m) deep which overflows down the crawl. A small draughting passage lies just above water level. Climbing the boulder slope above the sump leads to Toadstool Aven, and a short side passage blocked with flowstone. The hole on the right of Pickering's Passage leads to the base of a long slippery mud slope. At the top a narrow canyon passage leads via The Eyehole, a squeeze at roof level, to the top of a flowstone slope in a large chamber. Climb down to a pool, and up the far side (fixed rope usually in place). A short crawl and canal lead to the bottom of Moss Chamber, with its fine beehive slope of flowstone. On the right is the vertical tube in which Neil Moss died in 1959. At the top of the slope the passage continues through crawls and squeezes to the Balcony in Anniversary Hall. The boulder choke beyond here is extremely dangerous and should not be entered.

## Treasury
From the junction in Upper Gallery, a keyhole shaped passage leads after 215ft (66m) to Treasury Chamber. On the far side of the chamber a gated crawl leads to Fawlty Tower, where an iron ladder leads to a stooping passage which joins the long and tedious Wind Tunnel route to Egnaro Aven in Speedwell Cavern. On the left in Treasury Chamber is a low bouldery crawl to S.E.P. Sump. The main route out of the chamber is a boulder slope which leads down to a short pitch (fixed handline) and down a gravel slope to Treasury Sump, 80ft (24m) long and connecting (when it is not choked) with the Lower Bung Hole Series in Speedwell Cavern. In extreme floods, water rises up the slopes until it flows out to Upper Gallery, and on to join the main Peak Stream at the end of the Show Cave. Halfway House then backs right up the Devil's Staircase, and water flows out through the rest of the show cave to the Vestibule.

## The White River Series

Beyond the gated dig from Treasury, the route soon becomes flat crawling in mud. A squeeze leads to a fork. Right is Liam's Way, leading to Colostomy Crawl and Egnaro Aven. Left is a slippery climb of 10ft (3m) and a steeply ascending crawl to a large chamber, The Ventilator. A pitch of 52ft (16m) leads up to the base of a loose boulder slope, The Terminator. A short pitch of 12ft (3.5m) and a short climb lead to Fever Pitch (50ft / 15m), which emerges at the base of two flowstone ramps. To the right is the Fourth Pitch of 50ft (15m) to a small chamber. A dangerous traverse round the rim of the Fourth Pitch leads to a flowstone ramp up to the base of a well decorated aven, The Source of Perfection. To the left a large passage leads to White River Passage, very well decorated, and with an almost continuous flow of white calcite. All leads in this area end at complete flowstone chokes.

From the top of the Fourth Pitch a roomy crawl, Monday the Thirteenth Passage, leads to a T-junction with a large trunk passage, The Kingdom. Breakdown soon gives way to exceptional formations, including a "white river" of calcite. A short pitch in the floor leads to the Moosetrap Series, five spectacular wet pitches to a sump, 10ft (3m) deep and becoming too tight, roughly 300ft (91m) below The Kingdom. An inlet sump in the roof of the largest pitch has been siphoned and two short sumps passed to a third sump.

The White River Series. Photo by Paul Deakin

Beyond the Moosetrap The Kingdom continues, varied and impressive. A deep shaft (The Nameless Pitch) is by-passed by an oxbow. A crawl on the left connects with the top of Block Hall in Speedwell Cavern. The Kingdom ends at a blank flowstone wall, and a crawl at the top rejoins the vadose trench, which ends at a chamber (Heaven) 2010ft (613m) from the Ventilator. The Nameless Pitch, a fine free hang, leads down to a complex series of large chambers and mine workings.

## The Titan Entrance

The 150ft (45m) entrance shaft was sunk in a shakehole above the choke in the West Passage, near the top of Titan. An artificial tunnel leads eastwards for 72ft (22m) to a window into the main Titan shaft, 33ft (10m) above the entrance to West Passage, and 395ft (120m) above the floor. Opposite the window, its base nearly 200ft (60m) below, is Horne's Gully, an unstable boulder slope whose top is very close to the surface. The stream enters from a vadose streamway at the base of Horne's Gully, at the Event Horizon, 200ft (60m) above the floor. Digging at the choke at the upstream end of the streamway led to approx. 650ft (200m) of very well decorated passage. Digging down into the choke to the west of the entrance shaft continues.

*Tackle:*
**No tackle is needed for a tourist trip of the main cave. Iron ladders are in place on Surprise View, Fawlty Tower, and Egnaro Aven.**
**Many other pitches and climbs may be rigged, but you should check on the current status before the trip.**

*References: Adam, W. 1838. Gem of the Peak. Reprinted Moorland Publishing 1973. pp.343-346. Anon. 1981. The Lyre No.5. pp.14-15.*
*Arveschoug, D. 1999. B.C.R.A. Caves and Caving. No.83.*
*Brown, T. 1970. B.S.A. Bull. No.85. pp.1-4. Survey.*
*C.D.G. Newsletters. (esp. 54 onwards). C.D.G. Derbyshire Sump Index.*
*Cordingley, J.N. & Farr, M. 1981. B.C.R.A. Caves & Caving No.12. pp.10-12.*
*Cordingley, J.N. 1986. The Peak Cavern System - a Caver's Guide. Vitagraph, Didsbury, Manchester.*
*D.C.A. Newsletters. (No. 62 onwards).*
*Gilbert, J.C. 1949. B.S.A. Cave Science Vol.2. No.10. pp.53-62. Survey.*
*Gill, D.W. 1972. E.P.C. Jour. Vol.8. No.1. pp.36-38.*
*Kitchen, G. 1971. Bull. B.S.A. No.4. pp.21-22.*
*Kitchen, G. 1972. Bull. B.S.A. No.6. pp.8-9.*
*Kitchen, G. 1971. Bull. B.S.A. No.3. pp.6-9.*
*Nash, D.A. & Beck, J.S. 1989. The Peak Cavern Bibliography. Published by B.C.R.A.*
*Nixon, D.A. 1992. B.C.R.A. Caves & Caving No.55. pp.2-3*
*Nixon D.A. 1991. Descent No.101. pp.20-22*
*Salmon, L.B. 1962. B.S.A. Cave Science Vol.4. No.31. pp. 288-317. Survey.*
*Salmon, L.B. 1952. B.S.A. Cave Science Vol.3. No.20. pp.177-181. Survey.*
*Simpson, E. 1948. B.S.A. Cave Science Vol.1. No.3. pp.74-81. Survey.*

Overleaf: Titan from the roof dome, 145m above the floor.
Photo by Robbie Shone

### PEAKSHOLE SOUGH
NGR 1482 8268   Grade: 2
Alt. 625ft (188m)
Length: 1200ft (366m) approx
Depth: 100ft (30m)

Gated. Contact Peak District Mining Museum, Matlock Bath.
Entrance in cutting just beyond the last house, below the Peak Cavern Gorge footpath.
A mined system which briefly intersects natural passage. Short drop from entrance into walking sized sough level with shallow water. Level passes under a 40ft (12m) shaft to a junction. Level continued for 84ft (26m) to forefield, now backfilled. Left at junction passes short climb to pipe workings extending for 55ft (16.5m), shortly to reach a three way junction. South west cross cut passage ends after 73ft (22m) at a forefield. Sough continues, passing under higher workings with voice contact to Wall Shaft Mine. Passage continues, enlarging briefly, to a forefield. A section of miners' wooden plankway has been preserved a short distance from the forefield. Third passage at junction is connection to Wall Shaft Mine. 15ft (5m) fixed ladder up narrow stope, then short climb up a pack. Narrow rising passage with loose floor leads to further fixed ladder 25ft (8m) up narrow stope. Short fixed ladder leads into Wall Shaft Mine. Obvious main level passing under Wall Shaft is small and leads to Field Shaft and a short series of workings including a silted phreatic tube. Obscure passage close to Wall Shaft leads to Cottage Shaft, and short workings. All three surface shafts are capped.
References: Penney, D. 1985. Bull. P.D.M.H.S. Vol.9. No.3. pp.171-185. Survey.

### PERRYFOOT CAVE
(Manifold Cave)
NGR 0989 8127   Grade: 3
Alt. 1033ft (315m)
Length: 600ft (183m)
Depth: 97ft (30m)
Status: S.S.S.I.

Permission from Torr Top Farm, Perryfoot.
In hollow immediately north of the road, close to stream sink P1 and Dr. Jackson's Cave. Obvious dry entrance to left of sink.
After short crawl and walk, small chamber has a choice of two ways on, which link up. At floor level a tight crawl in a passage with small pools leads to Iron Maiden Squeeze, which is very tight and must not be attempted by large persons. Beyond, the passage leads on to the final chamber. Alternative route is by delicate climb of 15ft (4.5m) out of the main passage, followed by very tight crawl for 10ft (3m), then series of crawls or walking. Turn sharp left at bottom of very muddy slope. Stream can be heard at bottom of very narrow shaft but cannot be reached. Continue along muddy passage to Backwater Chamber with concrete dams. Baling by B.S.A. led to 200ft (61m) of passage with 25ft (8m) climb down to flooded rift chamber at 940ft (287m) O.D. The sump in Backwater Chamber is at 970ft (296m) O.D. some 180 yards (165m) short of Coalpithole Rake, and about 100ft (30m) above the "Lost Swallet". Water reappears at Russet Well, Castleton.
References: Elliot, D. 1975. Caves of Northern Derbyshire. Part 3. pp.16-19. Survey.
Salmon, L.B. 1963. B.S.A. Cave Science Vol.5. No.33. pp.36-52.
Salmon, L.B. & Boldock, G. 1950. B.S.A.Cave Science Vol.2. No.11. pp.118-123.
Salmon, L.B. & Boldock, G. 1949. B.S.A. Cave Science Vol.2. No.9. pp.15-20. Survey.

### PINDALE CAVE
NGR 157 822
Grade: 1
Alt. 800ft (240m)
Length: 155ft (48m)

Entrance at the uphill end of Pindale Quarry, in the opposite face to Black Rabbit Cave.
A crawl passage aligned on a small calcite vein ran WNW for 50ft (15m). After 23ft (7m) of digging by SUSS a breakthrough was made in 2007 into 23ft (7m) of open stooping passage on the same line, decorated with straws and small stals, ending at a mud choke with small airspace and good draught (the continuing dig – Destiny Passage). A hole through boulders in the floor of the new section led into 11m of nicely shaped crawling passage (Tits) ending at an intermittent sink in mud. A draught rises from a slot in

the floor by this sink. There are some small but vulnerable formations here and further visits to this dead end should be avoided. Opposite Tits further digging gained a tight boulder floored rift, where a 4m high aven ends in a too tight horizontal passage (No Cheese Tunnel). Digging continues. The passage is heading for Dirtlow Rake.

**ROWTER HOLE**
(Longcliffe Caverns)
**NGR 133 823**
Grade: 3-4 (Mine)
Alt. 1450ft (442m)
Length: 400ft (122m)
Depth: 270ft (82m)
Status: S.S.S.I.

Permission from Rowter Farm.

800ft (244m) north east of Rowter Farm. Approach through farm yard. Entrance capped by platform and steel lid.

Belay to lid. Fine 225ft (69m) deep mine shaft driven through solid rock for the first 170ft (52m), then entering a large chamber 60ft (18m) high, 20ft (6m) wide, and 100ft (30m) long. To the west, a steep rubble floored slope leads to a descending crawl into a mine level. This enters a large chamber leading up into the Abyss, a high natural aven with a short level 20ft (6m) up on one wall. Other openings can be seen 50ft (15m) up and at roof level, but as far as is known they have not been explored by cavers. To the east from the entrance shaft a natural passage can be followed up a scree slope to where a stream enters from a bedding plane 30ft (9m) up in the north wall, Hypothermia Passage. This was dug out in 1975 to 80ft (24m) of very tight wet crawling to a larger passage where the stream enters from a boulder choke on the right. To the left a crawl leads to a small decorated chamber containing a blind aven.

From the entrance of the bedding plane a traverse leads upwards to a choke. Above, a chimney can be climbed for 20ft (6m) (beware of loose deads) into the Upper Chamber with unstable workings and shafts in the roof to east and west. 100ft (30m) rope useful for climb back down. Back in the main chamber near the inlet are two shafts 25ft (8m) deep. The first is unstable but the second can be descended into a chamber with the stream entering. A further 25ft (8m) pitch in a rift follows. At the bottom an upward slope leads to a short climbable pitch with a short flooded working at the bottom. This has in the past been wrongly referred to as a sump. At the foot of the second 25ft (8m) pitch a further short climb down enters a crawl containing the stream which sinks in the floor. The crawl is eventually blocked with gravel. Passage at the foot of the entrance shaft was dug by D.C.C. in 1984. The dig in the floor of the boulder choked west chamber is now 18ft (5.5m) deep.

**Tackle:**

| | |
|---|---|
| *Entrance shaft:* | *75m rope. Optional rebelay and deviation. Belay to scaffold bar.* |
| *Lower pitches:* | *35m rope. 1 rebelay.* |

*References: Bentham, K. 1977. D.C.A. N/L No.32. Rucksack Club Journal 1938.*
*Elliot, D. 1975. Caves of Northern Derbyshire. Part 1. pp.1-2. Survey.*
*Randles, J. 1953. The Speleologist (first series) No.1. pp.26-28. Survey.*

**RUSSET WELL**
**NGR 1482 8270**
Dive
Alt. 615ft (187m)
Depth: 82ft (25m)
Status: S.S.S.I.

In private garden on east side of entrance to Peak Cavern Gorge.

Main resurgence for the Castleton area. Water rises from a hole in a mineral vein some 10ft (3m) below the surface of a pool. Pumping into water mains during drought has failed to lower the level more than an inch or so, but clearing of Slop Moll resulted in a cessation of flow for a time. Diving has reached a depth of 82ft (25m), progress being halted by a tight slot.

*References: Cave Diving Group Newsletter nos. 50, 53, 54, 56, 57, 59, 60, 61, 63, 64, 67, 68, 74, 84.*
*Wright, M. undated. S.U.S.S. Jour. Vol.3. No.2. p.18.*

## SHEEPWASH CAVE
(P2 Swallet)

**NGR** 1007 8133
**Grade:** 2
**Alt.** 1064ft (324m)
**Length:** 100ft (30m)
**Depth:** 30ft (9m)

Status: S.S.S.I.

Permission from Perryfoot Farm.

In hollow 200ft (61m) north west of road junction at Perryfoot.

Inconspicuous entrance which takes a stream partly culverted. Entrance passage is a short crawl to an enlarged joint where the stream sinks. Can be descended for 15ft (5m) before it becomes too narrow for further progress. Across the joint a crawl leads to an aven which can be climbed for about 20ft (6m) blocked at the top. Tight high rift follows sloping downwards steeply to an awkward thrutch, immediately followed by a 15ft (4.5m) pitch into the main chamber. Pool at the north end is fed from surface stream re-appearing from tight inlet passage. To the left of the pool a descending tube leads to the terminal sump dived by CDG for 35ft (11m) blocked with silt. Inlet enters above the sump, and can be followed for a short distance before it becomes too tight. Perryfoot stream was diverted into Sheepwash Cave during the working of Coalpithole Mine.

*References: Elliot, D. 1975. Caves of Northern Derbyshire. Part 4. pp.1-3. Survey.*

*Parker, J. 1971. C.D.G. N/L No.19.*

*Salmon, L.B. 1963. B.S.A. Cave Science Vol.5. No.33. pp.38-39.*

*Salmon, L.B. & Boldock, G. 1950. B.S.A. Cave Science Vol.2. No.11. pp,118-120.*

## SIDETRACK CAVE

**NGR** 1168 8152
**Grade:** 3
**Alt.** 1230ft (375m) approx
**Length:** 1570ft (479m)
**Vertical range** 26ft (7.8m)

Status: S.S.S.I.

Discovered 16/08/02 by D.A.Nixon, D.Clucas, R.Shone.

On the top bench in the north east face of Eldon Hill Quarry. Contact DCA for current access conditions.

Extremely fine and vulnerable formations. Care! Please keep to taped pathway.

An obvious entrance at the base of the face reduces in size to a flat out crawl. 525ft (160m) of crawling follows, passing small avens and gradually enlarging to hands and knees. A junction with a major fossil trunk passage, the Litton Stroll is reached. The Litton Stroll can be followed to the right (north) for approx. 200ft (60m) to a complete mud choke, and to the left for approx. 200ft (60m) until it becomes too low in flowstone. A small branch near the north end leads into the Flat-out Walk, and a further 295ft (90m) of small passages and avens.

*Reference: Shone, R. 2002. Descent No. 169. pp.26-27. Survey.*

## SLITHERSTONES MINE NO.1

**NGR** 125 815
**Grade:** 3 (Mine)
**Alt.** 1470ft (448m)
**Length:** 140ft (43m)
**Depth:** 230ft (70m)

Permission from Oxlow House Farm.

South east of Nettle Pot, in the same field.

200ft (61m) deep engine shaft covered with concrete sleepers (please replace). Communications difficult in shaft. Loose workings at bottom extend for a short distance to east and west. To west, slope leads down to pool which has been wrongly referred to in the past as a sump.

*Reference: Elliot, D. 1975. Caves of Northern Derbyshire Part 1. pp.23-25. Survey.*

The Litton Stroll. Sidetrack Cave. Photo by Robbie Shone.

### SLITHERSTONES MINE NO.2

**NGR** 123 815
**Grade:** 2 (Mine)
**Alt.** 1460ft (445m)
**Length:** 100ft (30m)
**Depth:** 180ft (55m)

Permission from Oxlow House Farm.

300 yards (274m) west of Shaft No.1.

Entrance covered with concrete sleepers. Please replace. 150ft (46m) deep shaft. Last 30ft (9m) contains rotten stemples which should be avoided. At bottom high narrow passage leads down to the east to 100ft (30m) of very unstable workings.

*Reference: Elliot, D. 1975. Caves of Northern Derbyshire Part 1. p.26. Survey.*

## SNELSLOW SWALLET
(P10)

**NGR 1125 8231**
Grade: 3 (Dig)
Alt. 1154ft (351.7m)
Length: 140ft (43m)
Depth: Shaft: 187ft (57m).
Swallet: 151ft (46m)

Owned by Peakshill Farm. Access not normally granted.

Southwest of Giants Hole, west of the farm track, 650ft (200m) NE of Christmas Swallet.

A series of parallel fissures. The stream is now diverted to Christmas Swallet. The largest fissure is the original rift entrance, dug via several short climbs to a hole leading westwards into an aven. An excavated rift chamber extends downwards for 65ft (20m), becoming wider at the bottom. On the west side at the bottom is a small passage leading to a further 33ft (10m) narrow pitch, which is choked. An artificial shaft from surface enters the aven, making it a 145ft (44m) pitch to the rift chamber floor.

References: Clarke, J. Bull. B.S.A. No.85. p.4.

Kitchen, G. Bull. B.S.A. Nos. 69-73. Survey in no.73.

Mee, B. Bull. B.S.A. No.82. pp.9-10.

Salmon, L.B. & Boldock, G. 1950. B.S.A. Cave Science Vol.2. No.11. p.121.

## SPEEDWELL MINE AND CAVERN
(Navigation Mine)

**NGR 1392 8274**
Grade: 4 (Part Show)
Alt. 814ft (245m)
Length: 3.5 miles (5.7km) (Incl. Peak Cavern: 10.3 miles/16.5 km)
Depth: 522ft (159m)
Status: S.S.S.I.

Access beyond the show cave not generally allowed.

Show Cave entrance at foot of Winnats Pass. Sealed shaft entrance by the toilets in the car park opposite.

**Warning: The cave carries a large stream directly from the swallets of Rushup Edge to the resurgences of Russet Well and Slop Moll. It is seriously flood prone.**

Flight of steps down to the Canal. The 75ft (23m) shaft drops into the end of the level nearby. The Canal is a straight mine level with static water maintained at about 3ft (1m) depth. The normal means of progression is now by electrically powered boat. Several veins are intersected, but the first passages of interest occur at Halfway House, where the level intersects Longcliffe Vein. Passages to right and left are walled up, but another passage can be followed up a series of mined pitches to the large Justification Chamber, and on into Royce Hall. Stemple Sump was dived to a depth of 52ft (16m) but is choked with silt. 1500ft (460m) south from the entrance is the Bottomless Pit, a large phreatic cavity on Foreside Rake, which marks the end of the show cave. The aven here contains a short choked passage at about 130ft (40m) height, and a 40ft (12m) pitch down from the platform leads to a huge sump pool, choked underwater at 26ft (8m) depth with what is thought to be the spoil from the continuation of the main level. Water reappears at Russet Well in Castleton some 40ft (12m) lower and about 1/2 mile (800m) away. The Bottomless Pit cavern was referred to by Farey (1815) as "The Devil's Hall". The mined passage continues beyond the Pit as wading in Far Canal. 500ft (150m) from the Pit is a low crawl on the right leading to Pilkington's Cavern. This, and the following five pitches have been scaled, and lead via a tortuous passage to Watricle Cavern, with a completely choked mineshaft leading on up. This point is about 400ft (120m) above the Far Canal. A continuing crawl beyond the first pitch of Pilkington's Cavern leads to the Assault Course, a small streamway leading downstream to a small sump, and upstream via a very long and strenuous crawl to an aven. A series of pitches was climbed for 300ft (91m) to a tight draughting continuation. Other routes off the Far Canal are short downstream crawls, and must not be entered to avoid damage to dams maintaining the water level. At the end of Far Canal a large stream is met.

Downstream is an 18ft (6m) pitch down an iron ladder against the dam wall (The Bung Hole) into easy streamway. A large aven immediately on the right is Block Hall, climbed for 250ft (75m) approx. to a connection with the White River Series (see Peak Cavern). The Bung Hole streamway continues easily to a low duck, only passable in dry weather. The duck can be avoided by a dry oxbow 165ft (50m) further back on stream left to rejoin the main route just before Rift Cavern, where the 80ft (24m) high Egnaro Aven (fitted with iron ladders) marks the end of the Wind Tunnel connection with Peak Cavern. Downstream is a deep pool (Puttrell's Pool), followed by an inlet cascade on the left. This is the Long By-pass, and can be followed, mainly crawling, to a dry passage connecting back to the Bung Hole Streamway. The Lower Bung Streamway continues, and is very wet and difficult going except in drought conditions. It ends at the Downstream Sump, dived for 495ft (150m) to a depth of 16ft (5m). Three other passages lead off this streamway; the first is Window Inlet, 650ft (200m) of easy crawls including 53ft (16m) and 10ft (3m) sumps to a boulder blockage. The second passage is on the right, and is a deep canal soon ending at Treasury Sump, an unpleasant 80ft (24m) dive connecting with Treasury Chamber of Peak Cavern. The third passage is Overspill Passage, also on the right, 200ft (60m) from the Downstream Sump. It consists of 330ft (100m) of flood-liable crawl down to a sand choke and very low sump.

Speedwell Streamway.  Photo by Paul Deakin

Main Rising.
Photo by Paul Deakin

Upstream from the end of Far Canal is further wading to The Whirlpool, past a short mined passage on the left with natural chamber reached by climbing through boulders. The Whirlpool is a short but turbulent swim (fixed rope usually in place) if the pulsing stream is entering from Whirlpool Passage on the right. This inlet can be followed by walking and crawling to the ebbing and flowing Whirlpool Rising, dived for 480ft (146m) to where the way on is too small. The first part of the sump can be by-passed via an awkward crawl to reach the first of two airbells. An excavated passage on the right about halfway up Whirlpool Passage connects with the Assault Course. The main route upstream across the Whirlpool is drier walking, past a roof level passage on the right connecting back to Whirlpool Passage, and past the Boulder Piles, with hanging chokes in the roof. A crawl on the right leads to the gated connection with the bottom of Leviathan in James Hall's Over Engine Mine, and a connection with Far Sump Extension of Peak Cavern via Stemple Highway Inlet Sump (now drained). Beyond Boulder Piles the route enlarges considerably. An iron ladder on the right (15ft/5m) leads to Bathing Pool Passage, ending at a large sump pool dived to 60ft (18m) with no way on, and a branch to the smaller Secret Sump (135ft / 41m deep). Further upstream is Cliff Passage, shortly before Main Rising. This large sump has been dived past a deep area at -120ft (-36m) to a point where it rises to only 10ft (3m) depth. Beyond this point the sump descends a large shaft (with airbell above) to 115ft (35m) depth. Tunnel continues to head of another large shaft (the New Leviathan) landing at 210ft (64m) depth. Floor slopes down to choked floor of mobile sand at a final depth of 233ft (71m).

Cliff Passage inlet passes ancient but vulnerable inscriptions on the wall (care!) to an easy crawl ending at a scramble up boulders to Cliff Cavern. At the head of the slope is a 160ft (50m) bolt climb into passages at both ends of the aven. To the west is Cliffhanger Passage, 660ft (200m) of large but very dangerous boulder strewn passage (including an oxbow) to a sump dived to an impossibly tight slot after 130ft (40m). To the east at the top of Cliff Cavern is Joint Effort, another large passage reached by a decidedly airy traverse. 500ft (150m) of varied going ends at avens (which close down at 30ft (9m) height), and two small sumps. The farthest of these sumps is a low 50ft (15m) dive to a climb emerging partway up the 40ft (12m) high Spidros Aven, too tight at the top, and with no way on at base of 26ft (8m) pitch.

**Tackle:**
**The Bung, Bathing Pool Passage, and Egnaro Aven are fitted with iron ladders. Other upward pitches may be rigged, but check the status before the trip.**

*References:* Anon. 1981. *The Lyre* No.5. pp.14-15.
*Cave Diving Group reports. Various from 1970 onwards.*
Cordingley, J.N. 1986. *The Peak Cavern System, a Caver's Guide.* Vitagraph, Didsbury, Manchester.
Ford, T.D. 1956. *Trans C.R.G.* Vol.4. No.2. pp.101-119. Survey.
Nixon, D.A. 1995. *Descent* No. 126. p.12. James Halls Over Engine Mine Survey.
Pilkington, J. 1789. *A View of the Present State of Derbyshire.* pp.72-75.
Puttrell, J.W. 1937. *Caves and Caving* (pre-war series) No.2. pp.44-47. Survey sketch. Puttrell, J.W. 1938. *Caves and Caving* (pre-war series) No.3. pp.85-88. Survey (section) sketch.
Puttrell, J.W. 1938. *Caves and Caving* (pre-war series) No.4. pp.125-126.
Shaw, R.P. 1983. *B.C.R.A. Cave Science* Vol.10. No.1. pp.1-8. Survey.
Simpson, E. 1954. *B.S.A. Cave Science* Vol.3. No.22. pp.267-273.
T.S.G. *Survey of the Peak/Speedwell Cave System.*
Warwick, G. 1947. *British Caver* No.17. pp.49-50.

### SUICIDE CAVE
(Horseshoe Cave)
**NGR 137 827**
Grade: 2
Alt. 898ft (274m)
Length: 450ft (137m)
Status: National Trust. S.S.S.I.

No known access restrictions.

Obvious entrance on the right near the foot of the Winnats Pass, with a second smaller entrance to the left.

First chamber has a boulder slope with a deceptive 15ft (4.5m) drop at the end. The route on is under the start of the slope. Left fork in second chamber leads to muddy crawls. Right to high third chamber. Back and foot traverse upwards at the end leads to rising passage with boulder choke at end, which has been dug upwards into a fissure to the surface.

*Reference: Cordingley, J. 1976. S.U.S.S.Jour. Vol.2. No.5. p.9. Survey.*
*Elliot, D. 1975. Caves of Northern Derbyshire. Part 5. pp.25-27. Survey.*

### THISTLE POT
**NGR 126 812**
Grade: 1
Alt. 1430ft (436m)
Depth: 55ft (17m)

On the moor between Eldon Hole and the top of Conies Dale.

A 45ft (14m) water worn shaft dug by Pegasus Caving Club leads to two squeezes and an 8ft (2.5m) pitch into 80ft (24m) of well decorated rift passage. A 12ft (3.5m) pitch terminates in a flooded bedding plane. Extremely loose in parts.

*Reference: Elliot, D. 1975. Caves of Northern Derbyshire. Part 1. p.27.*
*Jarratt, A.R. 1973. D.C.A. N/L No. 17. p.2-3.*

### TREAK CLIFF CAVERN
(Tray Cliff Cave, The Wonder Caves)
**NGR 136 832**
Show
Alt. 950ft (290m)
Length: 1000ft (305m)
Status: S.S.S.I.

One mile west of Castleton on the Mam Tor Road. Entrance by footpath up Treak Cliff.

An outer series of caves much altered by mining for Blue John stone, with good examples easily seen. An inner series of grottoes with some of the best stalactites in Derbyshire, discovered in 1926.

*References: Ford, T.D. 1954. Trans. Cave Research Group, Vol.3. No.2. pp.123-135. Survey.*
*Guide Book. Story of Treak Cliff Cavern. Survey.*
*Royce, S.J. 1945. Ancient Castleton Caves. pp.42-46. Survey.*

### TREAK CLIFF SEPULCHRAL CAVE
Lost

Immediately above Treak Cliff Cavern, but now quarried away. It contained a Bronze Age burial.

*Reference: Armstrong, A.L. 1923. Jour. R.A.S. Vol.53.*

### TREE HOLE
**NGR 135 832**
Lost
Alt. 1000ft (305m)
Length: 300ft (91m)

On Treak Cliff, to the north west of the show cave and immediately north of the old quarries. Shaft in hollow close to lone tree, now filled in.

A narrow passage led through muddy crawls under stacked deads to two chambers with miners debris. A large collapsed choke formed a west (uphill) wall of the larger chamber, and on the surface above a hollow suggests a former continuation to both the larger rock shelter visible from the valley, and to the small Dielasma Cave.

*Reference: Elliot, D. 1975. Caves of Northern Derbyshire. Part 5. p.31*

## WINDY KNOLL CAVE

NGR 1263 8303
Grade: 1
Length: 213ft (65m)
Depth: 51ft (15.7m)
Status: National Trust. S.S.S.I.

In field between Chapel and Sparrowpit roads west of Mam Tor. A broad entrance adjacent to the old quarry leads to a large passage. A part of the entrance roof collapsed in early 2006. The size is quickly reduced by cones of debris from collapses to surface. A short crawl leads round the first cone to a further short walking sized stretch with a trial dig in the floor at the end. A further low crawl leads to small chambers which can be followed until the fill reaches the roof and progress becomes impossible. Windy Knoll Fissure, which yielded many thousands of animal bones, is now obliterated and is believed to have been backfilled immediately outside the present entrance. Remains in British Museum, and Buxton, Manchester, Derby and Cambridge Museums.

*References: Dawkins, W.B. 1877. Quar. Jour. Geol. Soc. Vol.33. p.724.*
*Elliot, D. 1975. Caves of Northern Derbyshire. Part 4. pp.24-26. Survey.*
*Heath, T. 1882. Derbys. Arch. Jour. Vol.4. pp.167-169. Survey of fissure.*
*Pennington, R. & Dawkins, W.B. 1875. Quar. Jour. Geol. Soc. Vol.31.*

## WINNATS HEAD CAVE

NGR 1314 8282
Grade: 5
Alt. 1325ft (404m)
Length: 2000ft (610m)
Depth: 487ft (148.4m)
Status: S.S.S.I.

Permission from Winnats Head Farm.

Extended 1976 by T.S.G. & O.C.C., 1978 by E.P.C., and 1988 by D.U.G. and T.S.G.

In collapsed cave entrance in old quarry on south side of top of Winnats Pass.

**Warning: Both boulder chokes, below the Main Chamber and below Fox Chamber, are very dangerous, and rescue from beyond would be almost impossible.**

Originally a 20ft (6m) long steeply sloping passage to a dig. Excavated in 1976 to reveal a low crawl leading to a small chamber. Further digging again in a low steeply sloping crawl through water entered the large Main Chamber, floored with boulders, 130ft (40m) from entrance. Large passage in roof to east exhibiting fine roof pendants can be followed for 130ft (40m) to clay choke. Holes in boulder floor can be descended for 50ft (15m) to blockages.

1978 E.P.C. dig in boulders in floor of Main Chamber can be descended through very loose and dangerous boulders to the top of Cornwall Avenue. Great care must be taken as the original pitches have collapsed. From the bottom of the boulder choke a large passage, Cornwall Avenue, can be followed down a steep boulder slope for 60ft (18m) to emerge in Fox Chamber, 150ft (46m) long, 50ft (15m) wide, and 65ft (20m) high. Clay choke at end has been dug.

Holes in the floor can be descended through boulders to the top of a tight slot which drops down 15ft (5m) into a boulder chamber. From this chamber a passage round to the right (following a solid wall) leads through the 1988 dig (now a boulder squeeze) to a chamber with a steeply sloping boulder floor and solid roof and walls. 40ft (12m) down the slope is a 20ft (6m) diam. sump pool which has been dived. The water entering the sump from the boulder choke does not pass through the sump: it flows out to the left hand side into a passage which degenerates after 40ft (12m) into a hands and knees crawl half full of water for 30ft (9m) with the roof lowering for the last five. Once out of the wet crawl, 20ft (6m) of rift passage puts one underneath a 40ft (12m) aven, the top of which is a rock bridge.

A step across a parallel shaft and 15ft (5m) climb up leads to a standing height passage with two climbs of 10ft (3m) leading to crawling passage for 30ft (9m). Sharp left turn, then passage opens out beneath an aven. A stream enters from above, and cascades down the first shaft of 65ft (20m),

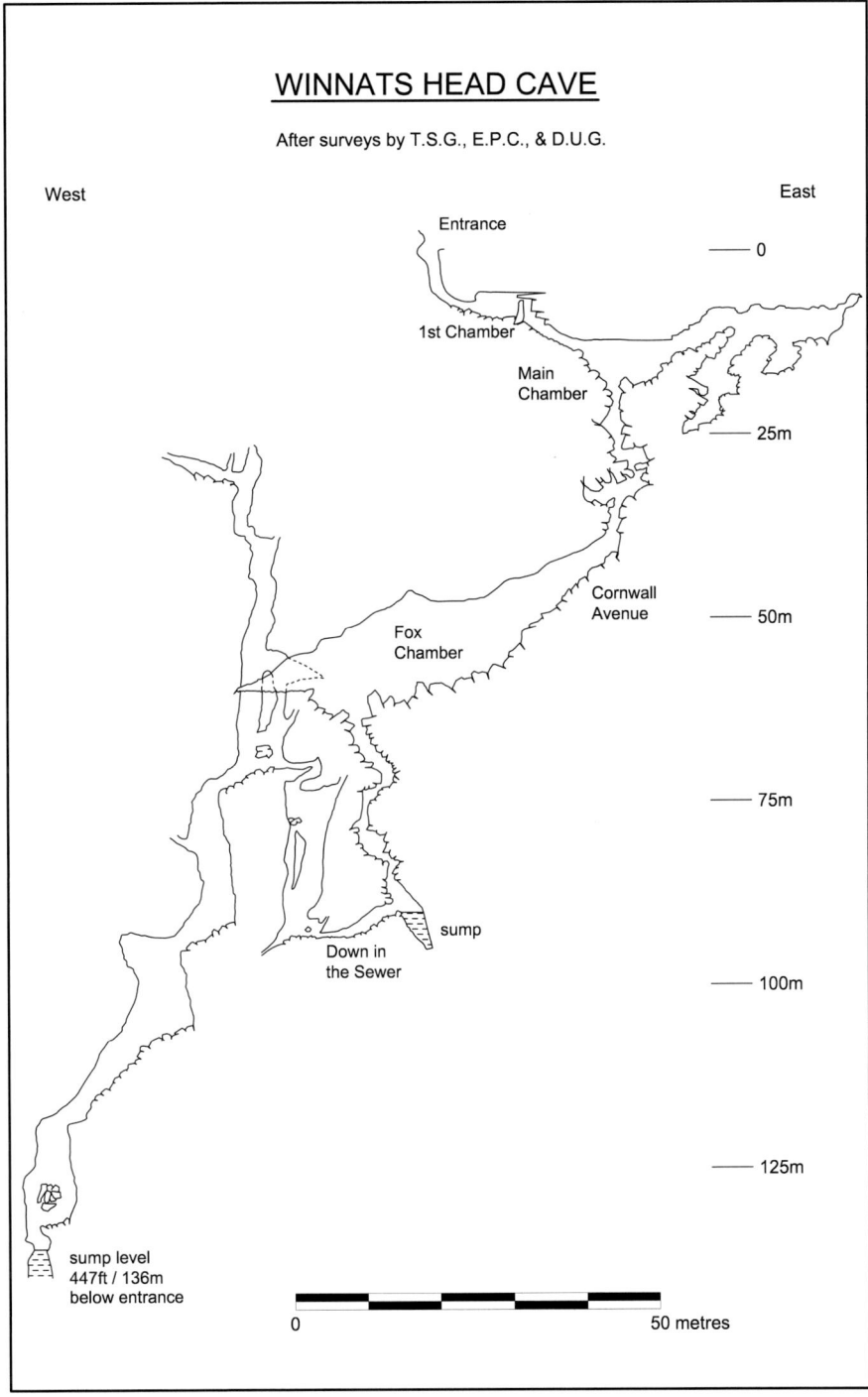

with a ledge on the opposite side of the shaft away from the water. The landing is in a chamber with a boulder floor, 30ft (9m) wide by 50ft (15m) long. At the far end it closes down to 6ft (2m) x 4ft (1.2m) on the lip of the next shaft, 45ft (14m) in a rift 10ft (3m) wide, 25ft (8m) long. The passage continues steeply sloping, walking size, at first with a boulder floor, then down two small climbs to the top of the final shaft. This shaft descends for 30ft (9m) to land on boulders wedged in the shaft, with the water dropping one side and the way on down the other side for a further 15ft (5m) drop. Small passage to sump after 15ft (5m). Water has been seen backed up as far as the wedged boulders. The sump has been dived to a depth of 40ft (12m), where it is silted up.

Upstream the aven divides into two. The dry one can be climbed between blocks to enter a chamber, with a small passage going off to a virtually static sump. By traversing around the left wall, the wet shaft is met again, and continues up for a further 20ft (6m) to a ledge, and a further 10ft (3m) to the base of another aven. The aven is 25ft (8m) high. From the top of the aven, step across the head of a parallel shaft (which takes the water), and climb up a small cascade and into 20ft (6m) of narrow passage with the stream, to the base of a wigwam shaped aven. This aven is 15ft (5m) high, and at the top there are four small continuing avens, which all narrow with no obvious way on. From the head of the 15ft (5m) aven a passage heads off, 15ft (5m) wide, 5ft (1.5m) high, with some fine stalactites. This gradually increases in height and continues for 60ft (18m) until the roof lowers to a choke with water entering. A small amount of water comes in from an immature side passage on the left, not passable.

Harpur Hill Series can be entered by a traverse along a ledge on the right hand wall at the bottom of Cornwall Avenue. A flat out crawl leads to a chamber after 60ft (18m) of passage blocked at the end, but with voice connection to blocked passages at the top of Cornwall Avenue. Straight on is a narrow rift passage over a hole in the floor to a 7ft (2m) climb down, leading to a low passage 17ft (5m) long blocked with clay. Above the 7ft climb two passages can be climbed for about 40ft (12m). The first is blocked with boulders, the second rejoins the Harpur Hill entrance chamber at roof level. A third way on from the chamber is a walking passage on the left leading after 50ft (15m) to a 10ft (3m) climb down. Climb is followed by a further 55ft (17m) of passage containing a small stream to a mud sump, which has been dug.

**Tackle:**
*40ft (12m) climb up to head of 1st Pitch may be rigged, but beware of old ropes of doubtful vintage.*
*1st Pitch downstream:*     *30m rope. Belay to eyehole + bolt. 35ft (11m) to ledge with 2 rebelays.*
*2nd Pitch downstream:*     *22m rope. Bolt behind head at pitch top. Rebelay on opposite wall.*
*3rd Pitch downstream:*     *20m rope. Bolt at pitch head. Rebelay on opposite wall.*
*Final climb: Handline, or thread third pitch tackle down below jammed boulders.*
*If upstream pitches are rigged, old tackle must be viewed with extreme caution.*
*References: Gill, D.W. 1978. D.C.A. N/L No.36. p.9.*
*Gill, D.W. 1978. B.C.R.A. Caves & Caving No.1. p.14.*
*Skorupka, R. 1988. C.D.G. N/L No. 86. p.8.*

# Caving Courses in the Peak District

## www.cavertraining.co.uk

- Introduction to Caving
- Basic Caving
- Ladder & Line
- Introduction to **SRT** (Single Rope Techniques)
- Intermediate SRT
- Advanced SRT
- SRT Pitch Rigging
- SRT Rescue
- Cave/Mine Leader Training & Assessments
- Cave Instructor Training & Assessments
- First Aid Training & Assessments

### Nigel Atkins CIC
**t: 01283 210666    m 07831 449919**

www.cavertraining.co.uk
info@cavertraining.co.uk

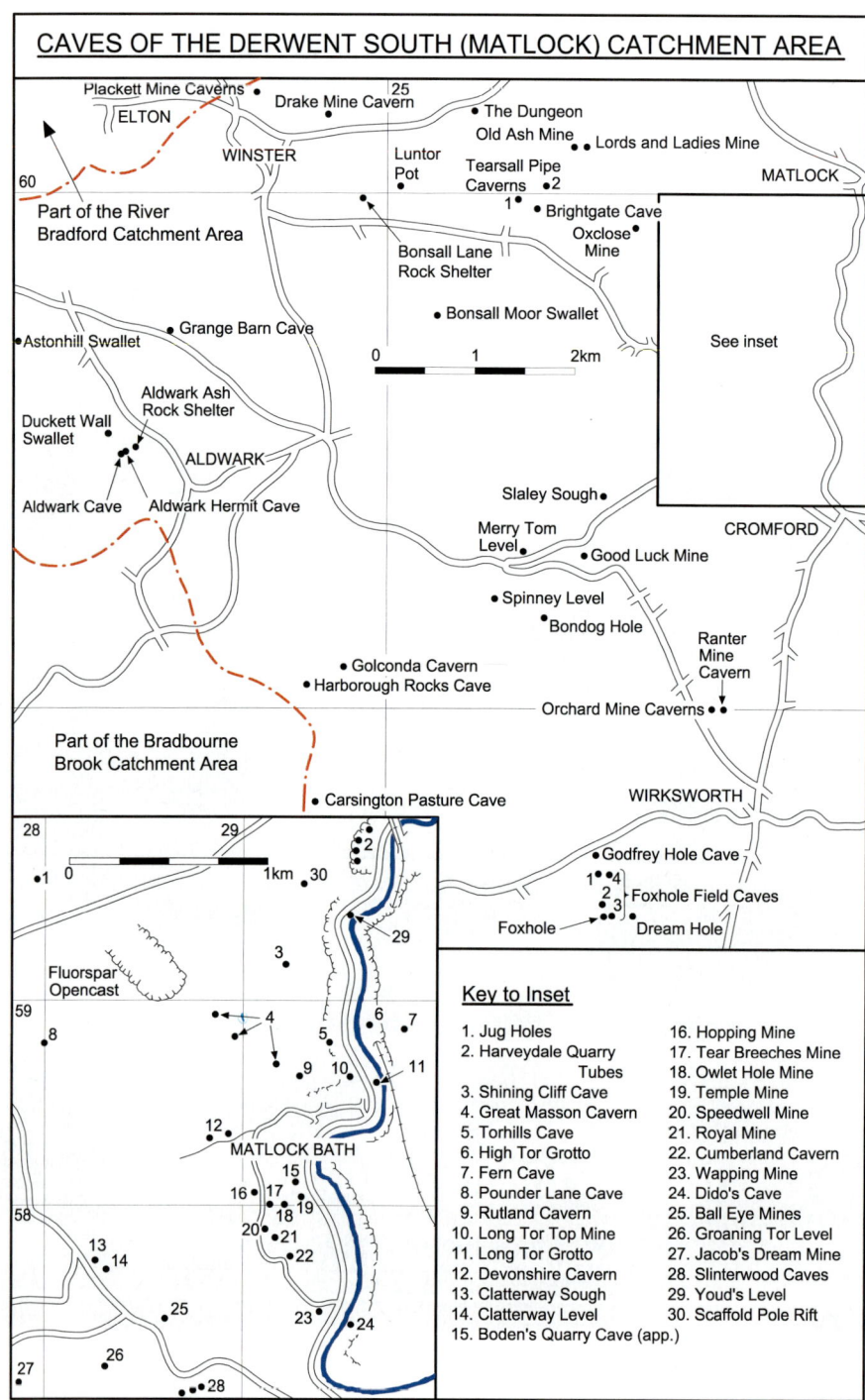

# THE DERWENT SOUTH (MATLOCK) CATCHMENT AREA

High Tor towers over the Matlock Gorge

The deeply incised River Derwent drops below the 100m contour in its course through the spectacular gorges at Matlock, while the limestones rise steeply up dip to over 300m to the west and south west.

Unfortunately large vadose caves and risings are unknown. Drainage and cave development are largely governed by lavas and mineral veins within the limestone, and possibly by the occurrence of dolomitic limestones.

The thermal springs constitute a proportion of the total drainage, along with surface streams and the few steeply dipping but immature stream caves. The greatest proportion of the drainage emerges from lead mine soughs, indicating the extent to which the natural drainage has been modified by mining.

The majority of the known caves have been intersected by the miners, and there are some classic examples of ancient mineralised solution caves.

Dolomitisation of the limestone probably took place during the Permian. This was followed by mineralisation when hydrothermal mineral fluids dissolved limestone along major joints, and deposited the well known range of Derbyshire minerals.

The Tertiary and Pleistocene saw the re-invasion of these cavities by streams flowing under phreatic or epiphreatic conditions, and many were filled with sediment during several glaciations. The source of these sediments is still in some doubt, but a lot of material was undoubtedly derived from the overlying gritstone.

The interesting story of the geological history of the area is not within the scope of this book. A great deal has been written about it elsewhere, and the reader is referred to the cited references for further information.

Many of the mines are still being systematically explored and surveyed, and much work remains to be done.

### ALDWARK ASH ROCK SHELTER
**NGR 2245 5750  Grade: 1**
**Alt. 1050ft (320m)**
**Length: 5ft (1.5m)**

Situated on a ledge some 300ft (100m) before Aldwark Hermit's Cave, behind large ash tree.

A fissure cave which becomes too tight.

*Reference: 2003. OCC N/L Vol. 39, No. 7-10, p.38.*

### ALDWARK CAVE
**NGR 2235 5745**
**Grade: 1**
**Alt. 1066ft (325m)**
**Length: 5ft (1.5m)**

Immediately to the right of Aldwark Hermit Cave.

Small entrance can be followed for 5ft (1.5m) where it divides into fissures.

*Reference: 2003. OCC N/L, Vol.39, No. 7-10, p.38.*

### ALDWARK HERMIT CAVE
**NGR 2235 5745**
**Grade: 1**

Obvious cleft entrance (5ft / 1.5m by 6ft / 2m) in a line of crags 600m west of Aldwark on the edge of a valley.

Walking passage closes down into fissures. No prospects of extension.

*Reference: 2003. OCC N/L Vol.39, No. 7-10, p.38.*

### BALL EYE MINES
**NGR 285 574**
**Grade: 4 (Mine)**
**Alt. 600ft (180m)**
**Length: More than 1 mile (1.6km)**

Van Traverse Level is gated and padlocked. No access at present. Contact D.C.A. for up to date information.

On the hillside on the north of the Via Gellia, a few hundred yards down from the junction with the Bonsall Road.

A complex of mine workings and natural caverns mainly developed on two levels. At the top is the large open 'Hermitage' (also known as Rugs Hall), believed to be the chamber where a fossil elephant was found. Part of chamber is now dangerously unstable owing to adjacent quarrying. Crawl at rear leads to series of low pipe workings which have been intersected by the quarry face and are now very unstable. Danger from quarry blasting! Main lower workings can be entered at several points from ledge about 100ft (30m) above the road. Westernmost entrance is Houghton Pipe, trending north westwards for some 400ft (120m) with two levels. Main entrance from terrace leads into complex of pipe workings and caverns with two blind shafts in the floor. Crawl on right leads to Van Traverse Cavern (see below). Climbing down incline and doubling back to the shaft leads to Foutrabbey Sough, over 1000ft (300m) long, with climbing shaft connection to upper series. Immediately to the right and above Main Entrance is entrance to Ball Eye Rake, with high but partly collapsed stopes. The Rake is intersected by the quarry face just beyond the Hermitage, and can usually be seen to continue on the far side of the quarry. Eastern end of terrace has several short openings, and entrance to Van Traverse series, a single large cavern parallel to the hillside with much fluorspar and a shaft into toadstone in the floor. Several short branches lead off. Inner end of lower series, including Fountrabbey Sough, are under the quarry floor. Exploration at any time when the quarry is working is dangerous!

*References: Buckland, W. 1823. Reliquiae Deluvianae.*
*Dawkins, W. Boyd. 1874. Cave Hunting. pp.284-5.*
*Ford, T.D. 2001. Mining History. Bull. P.D.M.H.S. Vol.14. No.6. pp.1-34. Survey.*
*Heath, T. Derbys. Arch. Jour. Vol.4. p.162.*
*Hurt, L. 1970. Bull. P.D.M.H.S. Vol.4. No.4. pp.289-305. Survey.*
*Oakman, C.D. 1978. Sough Hydrology of the Wirksworth-Matlock-Youlgrave area, Derbyshire. Unpublished M.Phil thesis, Leicester. pp.89-91. Survey.*

The coffin level, Ball Eye Mine
Photo by Paul Chandler

**BODENS QUARRY CAVE**
NGR 293 581
Lost

Exact site no longer known.
A bone cave intersected by quarrying "in a declivity about 20ft above the River Derwent on the east side of the Heights of Abraham". Finds include bones of rhinoceras, hyena, bear, and bison.
*Reference: Law, R. 1878. Trans. Manch. Geol. Soc. Vol.15. pp.52-55.*

**BONDOG HOLE**
NGR 266 559
Lost (Mine)
Alt. 1075ft (325m)
Depth: 240ft (73m)

Listed by Farey (1811) "in 4th Lime-stalactites". Large single cavern at foot of 240ft (73m) deep mine shaft of Bondog Mine. Decorated level off at 150ft (46m). The chamber has now been intersected by Middleton Limestone Mine and largely destroyed.
*References: Farey, J. 1811. A General View of the Agriculture and Minerals of Derbyshire. Vol.1. p.293. (London).*
*Orpheus C.C. N/L Vol.10. No.1. 1974.*

### BONSALL LANE ROCK SHELTER
NGR 2475 5995
Grade: 1. Arch.
Alt. 1112ft (339m)

Twin entrances to a shallow single chambered cave with small fissures leading off it.

### BONSALL MOOR SWALLET
(Greg's Hole)
NGR 255 588
Dig
Alt. 1000ft (300m) approx.
Length: 150ft (45m)
Depth: 65ft (20m)

Excavated 2001-2002.
A small swallet cave approximately 20m deep. The route consists of a series of climbs down narrow rifts with large jammed blocks.
*Reference: Westwood, R. 2002. Descent No. 164. p.13. Survey.*

### BRIGHTGATE CAVE
NGR 265 599   Grade: 2
Alt. 950ft (290m)
Length: 1080ft (329m)
Depth: 85ft (26m)
Status: S.S.S.I.

Call at Brightgate Farm. Access fee payable.
Entrance on south side of head of dry valley below Brightgate Farm, amongst boulders below small outcrop.
An interesting system combining joint maze and bedding passages, unusual in this area in being unmodified by mining. Drop down into entrance chamber with tight inlet on right. 10ft (3m) deep hole in floor drops to narrow descending rift into the Labyrinth, an intricate joint maze in dipping limestone. Various routes through this into 8ft (2.5m) high chamber or into Skid Row, and abandoned inlet with a smooth sloping calcite floor. Both routes rejoin in a sloping bedding chamber with some formations and 18th century miners' inscription. Descending bedding chambers continue on to a final smaller passage, squeeze, and choke. Just before the squeeze a draughting tube on the left leads through a tight squeeze to an aven. Back in the first 8ft (2.5m) high chamber, opposite the main passage is the entrance to the Western Bedding Cave, 50ft (15m) of low bouldery crawl to an earthy draughting choke. One of the main rifts in the Labyrinth can be followed as a traverse at a higher level, and opens into a small chamber with some stumpy stalagmites.
*References: Hurt, L. 1967. British Caver. Vol.47. p.74.*
*Hurt, L. 1968. British Caver. Vol.48. pp.19-21.*
*Ryder, P. 1979. Trans. B.C.R.A. Vol.6. No.1. Survey.*
*Webb, D. 2001. A Cave and Mine Conservation Audit for the Masson Hill area. DCA. Survey.*

### CARSINGTON PASTURE CAVE
NGR 2415 5368
Grade: 2. Arch.
Alt. 1000ft (300m)
Length: 25m approx.
Depth: 25m approx.

Dug by Pegasus Caving Club in 1998. Archaeologically excavated 1998-2002. Subject of a Time Team investigation in 2002.
In the middle of the pasture approx. 1km south east of Brassington.
The low entrance to the cave lies in a hollow, and a second artificial entrance 20ft (6m) to the south (possibly an access shaft created by lead miners) provides the vertical entry to the cave. Immediately inside the walk-in entrance the cave widens into the 16ft (5m) diameter Entrance Chamber, with flowstoned walls and a clay floor. In 1998 Pegasus Caving Club broke through the floor to reveal a series of chambers with copious archaeological remains. In 2002 archaeologists revisited the cave with Channel 4's Time Team, when further archaeological discoveries were made in Yorick and Flasid chambers.
The cave is notable for the large numbers of prehistoric human bones found, showing that the cave

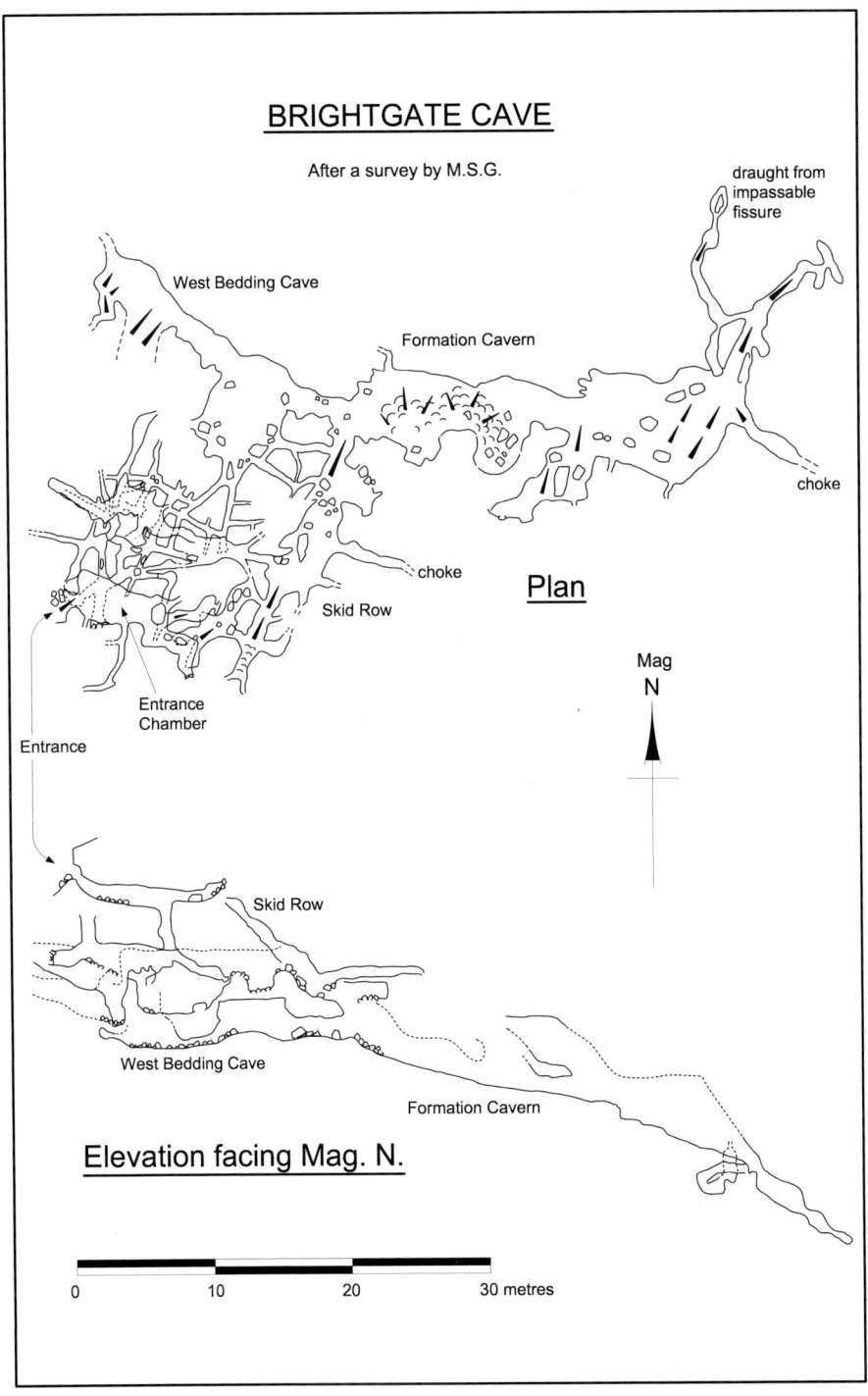

was used for the burial of more than 20 individuals of both sexes and all ages from newborn infants to adults.

The archaeological finds include: Roman period metal artefacts, pottery and animal bones. Iron Age: human bones, pottery and animal bones. Late Neolothic – early Bronze Age: human bones (including some with cutmarks indicating defleshing), bone artefacts and animal bones.

References: Chamberlain, A.T. 1999. CAPRA Issue 1.
Chamberlain, A.T. 2001. CAPRA Issue 3.
Steans, A. and Scothon, M. 1998. Descent 145. p.34.
Tune, R.N. 1967. Bull. P.D.M.H.S. 3. pp 249-252.

### CLATTERWAY LEVELS
(Ball Pie Mine, Brogdale Pipe)
NGR 283 577 (Lr)  282 578 (U)
Grade: 2 (Mine)
Alt. 500ft (150m)
Length: 2000ft (600m) approx.

Upper Entrance: Follow public footpath between stone cottages. Immediately beyond Burton Place Cottage climb up steep bankside and bear left through trees and undergrowth. Lower Entrance: A low opening in the wood south of the first cottages going up the hill from the Pig O' Lead pub to Bonsall. Narrow upper entrance, rediscovered by Masson Caving Group in 1988, leads after 75ft (23m) to 38ft (12m) deep shaft blocked at the bottom. Level off at 20ft (6m) leads after 50ft (15m) to 11ft (4m) deep free-climbable shaft. Level continues over shaft but is soon blind. The free-climb leads into fairly complex pipe workings which continue for a long way to the south east, and lead through to the lower entrance.

References: Chandler, P. 1988. Clatterway Level & Sough, Bonsall. D.C.A. N/L No.68.pp.6-8.
Ford, T.D. 2001. Mining History. Bull. P.D.M.H.S. Vol 14. No.6. pp.1-34.
Knox C.S. 2003. CCPC N/L No.73. pp.1-2. Survey.
Oakman, C.D. 1978. Sough Hydrology of the Wirksworth-Matlock-Youlgrave area, Derbyshire. Unpublished M.Phil thesis, Leicester. pp.89-91. Survey.

### CLATTERWAY SOUGH
(Brogdale Sough)
NGR 282 577
Grade: 2. (Mine)
Alt. 500ft (150m)
Length: 1000ft (300m) approx.

Permission required from Mr D.White, Hollowbrook Cottage.
In garden immediately north of the first cottages going up the hill from the Pig O' Lead to Bonsall.
First 300ft (91m) is 4ft (1.2m) high with 3ft (.9m) of water. Then dry, totalling some 1000ft (300m) of levels with small solution cavities. There are a number of shafts going both up and down (difficult free-climbs, best laddered) in the dry section.

### CUMBERLAND CAVERN
(Former Show Mine)
NGR 2923 5773   Grade: 2.
Alt. 525ft (158m)
Length: 1/4 mile (400m)
Status: S.S.S.I.

Proceed up Wapping Lane or Clifton Road near the Church.
Mined level leads to pipe vein workings and natural caverns, which link with Wapping Mine. The Show Cave is abandoned. The entrance has partly collapsed and is sealed by double steel doors.

References: Adam,W. 1838. The Gem of the Peak. Derby. pp.60-61. (Moorland reprint 1973).
Flindall, R. and Hayes, A. 1972. Bull. P.D.M.H.S. Vol.5. No.2. pp.114-127. Survey.
Barnatt, J. & Webb, D. 2002. Cumberland Cavern & Wapping Mine, Matlock Bath. DCA publication. Survey.
Webb, D. 2001. A Cave and Mine Conservation Audit for the Masson Hill area. DCA. Survey.

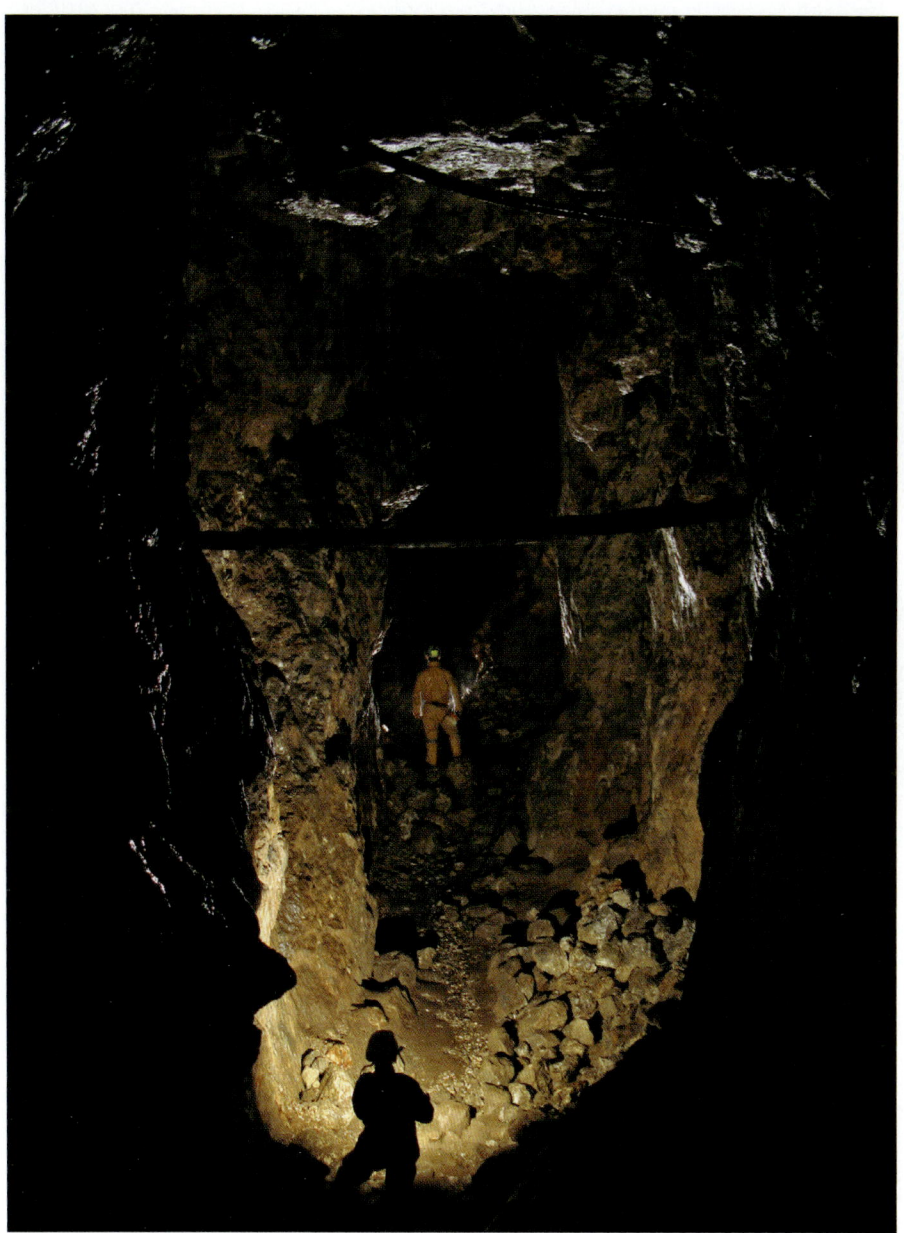
Cumberland Cavern. Photo by Rob Eavis

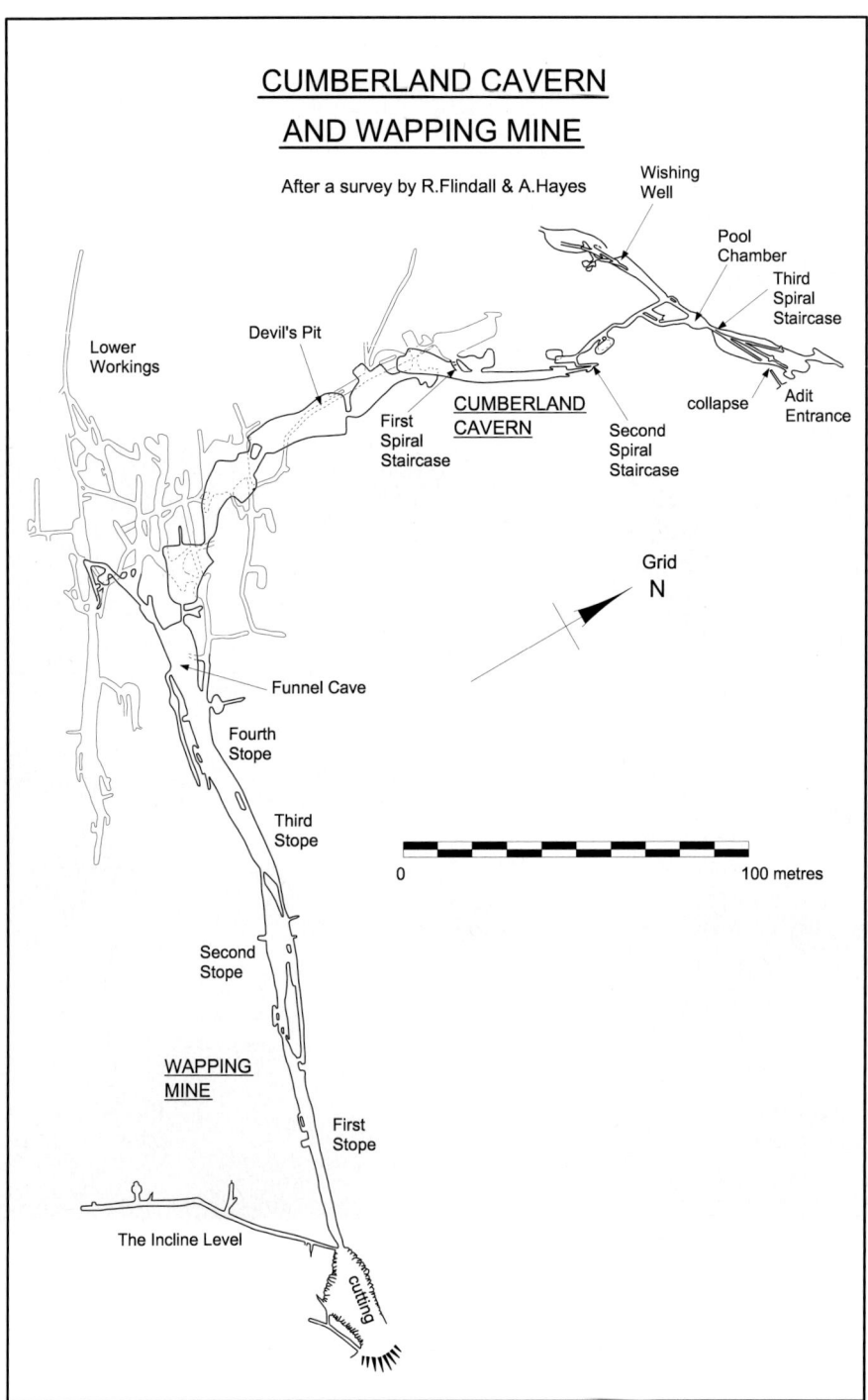

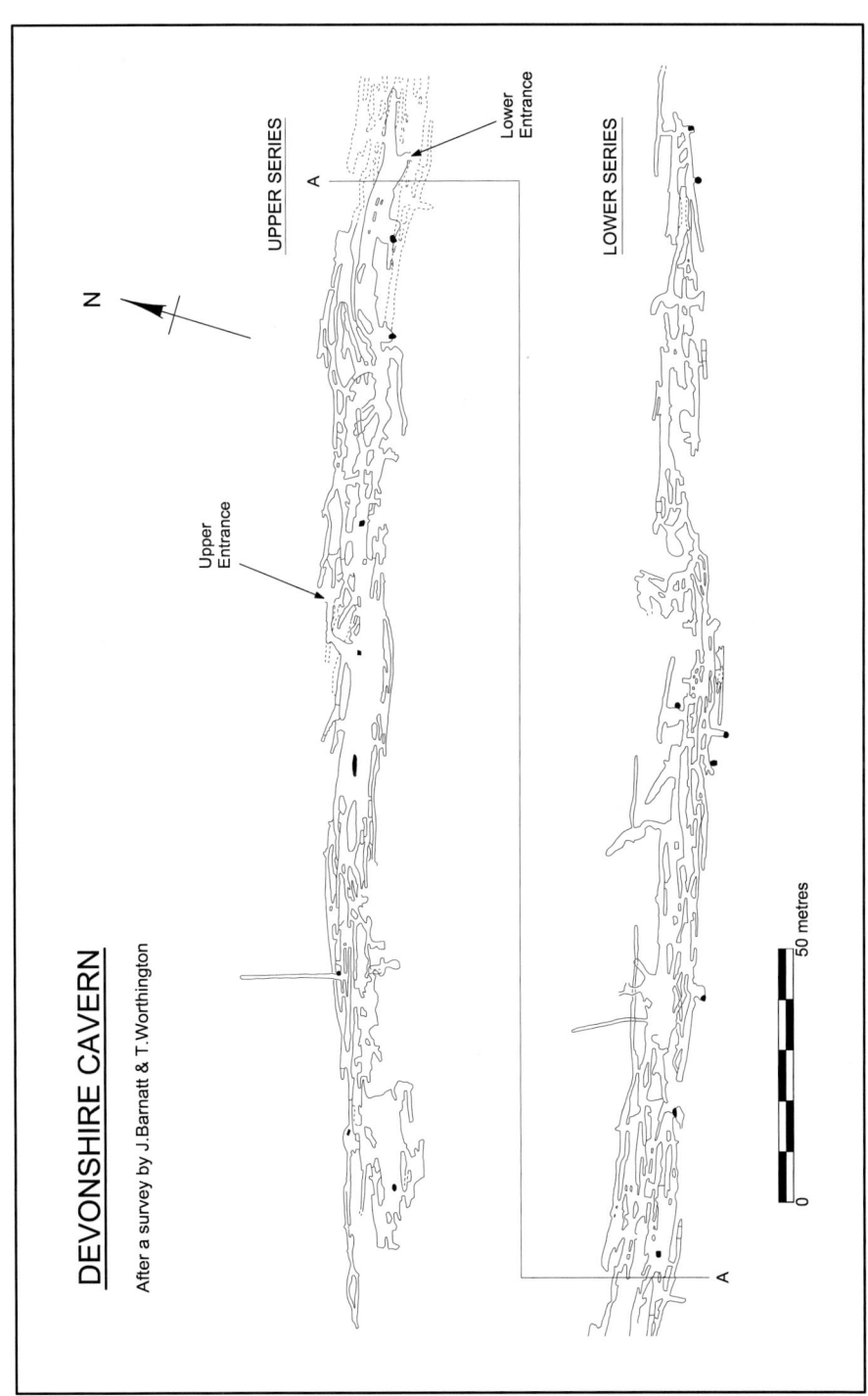

## DEVONSHIRE CAVERN
**NGR 290 584**
Grade: 3. (Mine)
Alt. 700ft (213m)
Length: 1000ft (305m)
Depth: 260ft (80m)
Status: S.S.S.I.

All entrances now blocked except entrance just off the footpath to Bonsall off north end of Upperwood Road. This entrance is gated, and requires an adjustable spanner. Please keep the gate closed. Please park down in the valley rather than fill the turning space in the narrow road.

A complex series of interconnected mine workings (part natural), which go both up and down dip from the entrance. These include chambers, mine galleries and crawls. Close to the bottom end there are two relatively tight wet crawls. The upper series was formerly a show cave. In parts there have been roof falls in the past, choking some passages.

References: Adam, W. 1838. The Gem of the Peak. Derby. p.62. (reprint Moorland Publishing 1973).
Barnatt, J. 2001. Mining History. Bull. P.D.M.H.S. Vol.14. No.5. pp.37-38.
Larson, J. 1954. The Speleologist Vol.1. No.3. pp.121-127. Survey.
Webb, D. 2001. A Cave and Mine Conservation Audit for the Masson Hill area. DCA. Survey.

## DIDO'S CAVE
**NGR 296 574**
Grade: 1 & Dive (Mine)
Alt. 300ft (91m)
Length: 1400ft (426m)

Entrance is set back on the east bank of the Derwent near the weir at Masson Mill.

Totally mined except for short natural sections, its exploration has been the preserve of divers. 200ft (61m) of easy passage leads to a short climb down into The Lake. At the eastern end of The Lake Sump One (25ft/8m) leads to a short section of canal and then into Sump 2 (80ft/25m). There are two air bells in Sump 2, which terminates in a choke and access can be gained to further passage by crawling over boulders.

From The Lake, going north, is the Coffin Level, 56ft (17m) long. This level joins two parallel rifts, surfacing in another "lake". To the west are Sumps 4 & 5 both 20ft (6m) in length, ending with a small airspace called The Teapot. To the east are Sumps 6 & 7, 20ft (6m) and 23ft (7m) long, and finally Sump 8, 218ft (66m) goes to the end of the rift. 110ft (33m) into Sump 8 a passage goes off to the right and surfaces after a short distance in Lord Nelson's Passage, choking after 100ft (30m). There are numerous shafts in the floor in this cave which should be avoided.

References: Bentham, K. 1977. CDG N/L No.45. pp.21-22. Survey.
Bentham, K. 1978. DCA N/L No.37,p.4., and CDG N/L's 37,38,46,57.
Fox, C. 1996. CDG N/L No.119.; Murland, J. 1978. CDG N/L No.49. p.25. Survey.
Phipps, M. 1981. The Lyre No.5. pp.21-22. Survey.

## DRAKE MINE CAVERN
**NGR approx. 244 608**
Lost (Mine)

Listed by Farey (1811). Believed to be near the intersection of Shack Vein and Drake Vein.

Reference: Farey, J. 1811. A general view of the Agriculture and Minerals of Derbyshire. p.293.

## DREAM HOLE
**NGR 275 530**
Grade: 1 (Mine/Arch)
Alt. 800ft (240m)
Depth: 50ft (15m)

North of Sprink Wood, south-west of Wirksworth, on the summit of the hill.

Large open fissure. Partly mined. Scramble down the west end. Crawl, and then climb. Among the remains found was an almost complete skeleton of a rhinoceras, now in Oxford University Museum. No modern excavation of deposits attempted.

*References: Buckland, Rev. W. 1824. Reliquae Deluvianae (with section drawing).*
*Dawkins, W.B. 1874. Cave Hunting. pp.284-285.*
*Heath, T. 1882. Derbys. Arch. Jour. No.4. pp.163-165.*

**DUCKET WALL SWALLET**
(Greenlow Swallet)
NGR 222 577
Dig
Alt. 980ft (299m)

Shaft dug here in 1967 was refilled as too tight.
A small stream sinks under stone troughs.
A second shaft a short distance to the north was on the site of the former sink, among loose material, mostly clay. Only one solid wall. Dug to a depth of 30ft (9m) and refilled and abandoned in 1975.
*References: Farey, J. 1811. A general view of the Agriculture and Minerals of Derbyshire. p.295.*
*Mellors, P.T. 1976. D.C.A. N/L No.27. p.5.*
*Mellors, P.T. 1969. The Speleologist Vol.3. No.19. p.17.*

**THE DUNGEONS**
NGR 259 609   Grade: 1
Alt. 750ft (225m)
Length: 20ft (6m)

Landslips in the limestone south west of Wensley.
Short lengths of bedding and fissure cave exposed by landslip. One is a possible dig.

**FERN CAVE**
(Roman Mine)
NGR 298 588 (Fern Cave) 298 589 (Roman Mine)
Grade: 2 (Show Mine)
Alt. 600ft (180m)
Length: 600ft (180m)

Gated at present. On summit of High Tor, Matlock.
Very old open worked out lead vein. Connects with Roman Mine, which is open.
*Reference: Arnold, F.H. 1881. Science Gossip Vol.XVII, p.283.*
*Ford, T.D. 2001. Mining History. Bull. P.D.M.H.S. Vol.14. No.6. pp.1-34.*
*Pickin, J. 1985. Bull. P.D.M.H.S. Vol.9. No.3. pp.197-199. Survey.*

**FIG'S DIG**
(Astonhill Swallet)
NGR 213 586
Grade: 2. Dig
Alt. 950ft (285m)
Length: 500ft (150m) approx.

An old swallet in a shallow dry valley two fields east of Astonhill Farm. A short free climb leads to a junction in a crawling sized passage. East leads through 485ft (148m) of passage to a dig face. North is unstable and leads almost immediately to a collapse under a large surface excavation and should not be entered.
Dug to present length by the Eric Caving Club.
*References: Mellors, P.T. 1969. The Speleologist Vol.3. No.19. p.17.*

**FLUORSPAR CAVERN**
(Jacob's Cavern)
NGR 291 581
Grade: 2 (Mine)
Alt. 600ft (180m)

Entrance sealed after a fatal accident. Adit close to Upperwood Road above Old Pavilion site.
A series of old "pipe-vein" workings for lead and fluorspar, once a show cave, but more recently mined. Parts are in a dangerous state. Links with the Hopping, Royal, and Tear Breeches Mines.
*References: Frost, R.V. 1953. The Speleologist, Vol.1. No.2. pp.63-67. Survey.*
*Flindall, R. & Hayes, A. 1973. Bull.P.D.M.H.S. Vol.5. No.4. pp.182-189. Survey.*
*Webb, D. 2001. A Cave and Mine Conservation Audit for the Masson Hill Area. D.C.A.*

## FOX HOLES
(Odin Cavern)
**NGR 2723 5300**
**Grade: 2**
**Alt. 800ft (240m)**

Described by Buckland (1833). Reopened by the Odin Club.
Permission needed from Peter Ward on 01629 825842.
Towards the east end of the low limestone outcrop above Sprink Wood, 1/4 mile (0.4km) east of Pittywood Farm.
60ft (18m) crawl to circular domed chamber 30ft (9m) in diameter. Ochreous clayey fill had been mined for ochre. Several small mined levels lead off from the chamber.
*References: Buckland, W. 1833. Reliquiae Diluvianae. p.65.*
*Kirkham, N. 1967. Bull. P.D.M.H.S. Vol.3. No.3. p.166.; Potts, J. 1990. O.C.C. Jour. No.6. Survey.*

## FOX HOLES FIELD CAVES
**Grade: 1**
**Alt. 895ft (235m) approx.**
Permission needed from Peter Ward on 01629 825842

### No.1 Cave
**NGR 2717 5304**      **Length: 15ft (4.5m)**

210ft (64m) north west of Fox Holes. A short bedding plane cave on the west facing slope.

### No.2 Cave
**NGR 2721 5301**

60ft (18m) north west of Fox Holes.
A rock shelter in the west end of the same limestone outcrop.

### No.3 Cave
**NGR 2725 5300**

60ft (18m) east of Fox Holes. A rock shelter in the east facing slope.

### No.4 Cave
**NGR 2727 5304**

170ft (55m) north east of Fox Holes. A short rift cave in the south facing slope.

## GODFREY HOLE CAVE
**NGR 271 536**
**Grade: 1**
**Alt. 750ft (225m)**
**Length: 251ft (76.5m)**
**Depth: 28ft (8.5m)**

Permission from "The Beeches", Godfreyhole.
Bob Liggins and others dug Godfreyhole from 1968 to 1990: 22 years!
Immediately behind cottages of Godfreyhole hamlet.
A large cave entrance surrounded by trees and undergrowth. Appears to have been used as a cowshed, and has had two "rooms" walled off. A trial archaeological dig was fruitless. Roomy entrance passage, containing excavated material, leads past digging equipment and lined shaft 28ft (8.5m) deep on the right (connects to lower level), soon ending in an excavated shaft under wooden floor (partly rotten, care required). 7ft (2.1m) deep shaft (ladder not fixed), followed by short stepped passage, to next shaft 12ft (4m) deep (fixed ladders in place) down to lower level. Facing ladder, short passage to left to bottom of lined shaft to surface. Longer narrow passage to right, walking or stooping size, leads to abandoned dig. Passage on right at entrance is roomy but short, used for storage, and ends in a blind shaft 18ft (5.5m) deep and shaft, now capped, to surface in stone building above.
*References: Pers. Comm. Bob Liggins with P.Chandler, 2006.*

**GOLCONDA CAVERN**
NGR 246 554
Grade: 3 (Mine
Alt. 1160ft (348m)
Depth: 500ft (150m)

Not normally accessible.

To the north east of Harborough Rocks. 400ft (122m) deep shaft.

Lower Golconda shaft, 1/4 mile (400m) to north west, is 290ft (88m) deep and contains a partly collapsed ladder way. The mine consists of a large series of solution cavities close to the junction of the limestone and dolomite. Farey (1811) referred to "A very large cavern in 4th lime".

References: Farey, J. 1811. A general view of the Agriculture and Minerals of Derbyshire. p.294.

Ford, T.D. & King, R.J. 1966. Trans. C.R.G. Vol.7. No.2. pp.91-114. Survey.

Ford, T.D. & King, R.J. 1965. Economic Geology Vol.60. Survey.

Puttrell, J.W. 1960 (Reprint of article in Sheffield Telegraph). Bull.P.D.M.H.S. Vol.1. No.2. pp.8-12.

Cave Pearls, Golconda Cavern. Photo by Paul Deakin

### GOOD LUCK MINE
**NGR 2700 5649**
Grade: 2 (Mine)
Alt. 675ft (206m)
Length: 3540ft (1079m)

The mine is looked after by the Goodluck Preservation Club. Those wanting a trip should e-mail access@goodluckmine.org.uk. Visitors are invited to make a donation towards the upkeep & preservation of the mine.

At top of an obvious spoil heap on the south side of the Via Gellia. An extensive series of narrow adits, crosscuts, and small stopes of the early 19th century, which have intersected a number of small solution caverns. Several other shorter levels lie in the immediate vicinity, and notes can be found in the references given.

*References: Amner, R. & Naylor, P. 1973. Bull.P.D.M.H.S. Vol.5. No.4. Survey.*
*Flindall, R. & Hayes, A. 1972. Bull.P.D.M.H.S. Vol.5. No.1. pp.61-80.*

### GRANGE BARN CAVE
**NGR 2280 5860**
Grade: 1
Length: 13ft (4m)

Halfway between Grange Barn and Aldwark Grange in field to NNE of Via Gellia Road.

A depression some 8-10m in diameter. A low descending crawl in the bottom for approx 4m to an earth fill.

*Reference: Brooks. S, 2005. OCC N/L. Vol.41. No. 7-9. p.33.*

### GREAT MASSON CAVERN
**NGR 292 586**
Grade: 3-5 (Part Show)
Alt. 840ft (256m)
Length: c.3 miles (5km)
Status: S.S.S.I.

Owner is Mr. Pugh, Heights of Abraham, Matlock Bath. Access also via the old fluorspar opencast. Do not enter the show cave. Show Cave entrance close to Victoria Tower on Heights of Abraham.

Entrance is via worked out Great Rake stopes, leading into a northward continuation of the Rutland (Old Nestus) Pipe, with numerous worked out pipe-vein cavities lined with calcite and fluorspar. Masson Cavern at end of Show Cave is large phreatic chamber, with a staircase leading to the Show Cave "back door" at 291588. The so-called "lake" is a flooded level. Extensive workings beyond (gated) lead into workings and pipe veins of Black Ox, Carding's Nestus, and High Loft Mines with continuation into Crichman and Beck Mines. Former links with King Mine and Knowles Mine workings (largely destroyed by opencast fluorspar workings on the summit of Masson Hill). Branch system near Beck Shaft once led ENE into Gentlewoman's Pipe workings, trending downhill towards Matlock, and linking with Youd's Level which discharges into the Derwent at 295594, making this one of the deepest cave-cum mine systems in the country.

*References: Dunham, K.C. 1952. Memoir of the Geological Survey on "Fluorspar" p.99. Survey.*
*Flindall, R. & Hayes, A. 1976. The Caverns and Mines of Matlock Bath. Part 1. Moorland, Hartington. Survey.*
*Ford, T.D. 2001. Mining History. Bull. P.D.M.H.S. Vol.14. No.6. pp.1-34. Surveys.*
*Webb, D. 2001. A Cave and Mine Conservation Audit for the Masson Hill Area. D.C.A. Survey.*

### GROANING TOR LEVEL
(Hallicar Wood Level)
**NGR 2830 5722**
Grade: 1 (Mine)
Alt. 600ft (180m)
Length: 850ft (255m)

At top of field on south side of Via Gellia directly above car park near Pig O' Lead.

An easy walk in adit leads to two small chambers in decomposed toadstone. A small stream rises near the terminal choke and sinks in a small hole in the floor.

*References: Smith, & Ford, T.D. 1971. Bull.P.D.M.H.S. Vol.4. No.5. pp.378-9. Survey.*
*Flindall, R., Hayes, A. & Rieuwerts, J. 1977. Bull. P.D.M.H.S. Vol.6. No.6. pp.275-277. Survey.*

### HARBOROUGH ROCKS CAVE
(Harborough Cave)

NGR 2422 5523
Grade: 1 (Arch)
Alt. 1165ft (355m)
Length: 50ft (15m)

Obvious entrance high in Harborough Rocks above Brassington.

Single chamber 6m x 10m (20ft x 30ft) with chimney to surface and narrowing fissures at back. Excavated Romano-British finds in Derby Museum. Second small cave nearby.

*References: Armstrong, A.L. 1923. Jour. Roy. Anthrop. Trust. Vol.53. pp.402-16. Survey.*
*Brailsford, J.W. 1957. Derbys. Arch. Jour. No.77. pp.54-55.*
*Fox, W.Storrs. 1909. Derbys. Arch. Jour. No.31. pp.89-96.*
*Jackson, J.W. 1929. Naturalist. pp.105-107.*
*Potts, J. 1988. D.C.A. N/L No.67. pp.11-13. Survey.*
*Smith, R.A. 1909. Derbys. Arch. Jour. No.31. pp.97-114.*

Sediments in Masson Cavern.
Photo by Dave Webb

### HARVEYDALE QUARRY TUBES
**NGR 296 598 Grade: 2-3**
**Alt. 350ft (105m)**
**Length: 2100ft (640m)**

Access not normally allowed.
In disused quarry, variously known as Harveydale, Holt, or Hope Quarry. Four tubes, 30-50ft (9-15m) above the quarry floor.
A: Length 1500ft (457m). Long crawl in bedding tube with low meander channel often the only way through. At 375ft (114m) from the entrance is a cross passage. Right is a long wet crawl. Left is walking to another junction. Left (down dip) is dangerously tight and deceptive. Right leads into the side of a deep mine shaft on Seven Rakes Vein, with water some 65ft (20m) below. B: Too tight for entry. C: Hands and knees crawl for 300ft (92m) in a westerly direction to a small shaft 30ft (9m) deep. Cross this and a further 300ft (92m) crawl leads to the same shaft as tube A, but 30ft (9m) higher up. D: A tight tube at the south end of the quarry which closes after a few feet.
*References: Operation Mole reports for 1958-1959. Reprinted in British Caver Vol.31.*

### HIGH TOR GROTTO
**NGR 296 588 Grade: 1**
**Alt. 350ft (106m)**
**Length: 300ft (90m)**

Owner Mr Pugh, Heights of Abraham. Now gated and locked by British Rail.
North of the Colour Works on the east bank of the Derwent.
A large slab has detached from the roof: the railway is 3m above and care is needed.

A former show cave with good calcite crystals, which were largely covered by whitewash when it was used as a pump lodge. The sump at the end was dived for 50ft (15m) to a blank wall. Nearby is Side Mine, also in the factory grounds.
*References: Adam, W. 1838. The Gem of the Peak. (Reprint by Moorland, Hartington, 1973) p.63*
*Ford, T.D. 2001. Mining History. Bull. P.D.M.H.S. Vol.14. No.6. pp.1-34*

### JACOB'S DREAM MINE
**NGR 278 571**
**Grade: 1 (Mine)**
**Alt. 700ft (210m)**
**Length: 500ft (150m) approx.**

In topmost crags on the south side of the Via Gellia directly above the works.
Easy walk-in adit leads to small chamber with faulted wall of toadstone, some small solution features and a small stalactite grotto.

### JUG HOLES
**NGR 2797 5959 Grade: 2**
**Alt. 850ft (255m)**
**Length: Over 1/2 mile (0.8km)**
**Status: S.S.S.I.**

No known access restrictions.
In wood south of Leawood Farm and north of Salters Lane, on summit of Masson Hill.
Large cave entrance in wood leads to workings ahead and to the left. On right near foot of slope is descent into series of muddy caverns, with branches to old workings, and finally out to the adit entrance lower down the hill. At back and to right 12ft (4m) shaft leads to Boulder Maze on left and roomy but dirty stalagmite caverns with limestone roof and floor of green clay (decomposed basalt lava). Once noted for its bats and for the "sound of a barking dog" caused by a small syphon pool no longer operative.
*References:*
*Fiander, G. & Webb, D. 2002. Jugholes Interpretation Pack. DCA publication. Survey.*
*Nash, D.A. 1957. Trans. C.R.G. Vol.5. No.1. pp.13-22.*
*Worley, N.E. and Nash, D.A. 1977. Trans. B.C.R.A. Vol.4. No.3. p.388-401. Survey.*

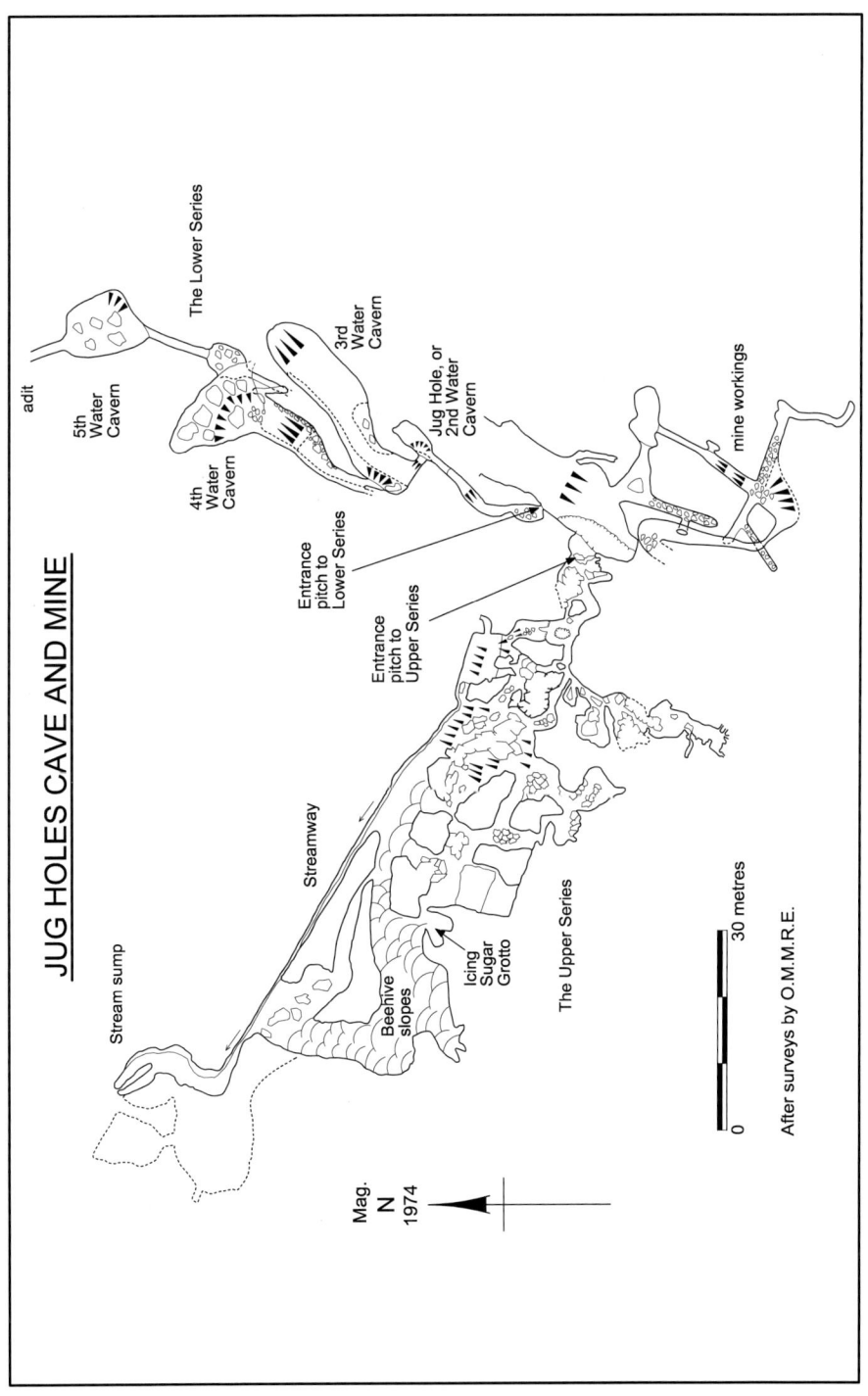

## LONG TOR GROTTO

NGR 297 586
Grade: 2 (Mine)
Alt. 300ft (90m)
Length: 300ft (90m)

Entrance below wicket gate on river bank just north of the footbridge to the paint works.

**Warning: Beware of flooded hole in the floor 16m in from entrance. Danger from Weil's Disease from rats associated with sewage seepage.**

A flood defence "penstock" has been installed over the original entrance but access is retained either via a crawl through a gate in the penstock, or in high water conditions via a grill in the top of a linked tower. A "false" padlock is fitted and the grill can be opened from above, or below for emergency exit if the gate is lowered while you are in. Entrance passage may contain sewage. Sough tunnel runs westwards under the main road. Series of old workings in Great Rake with solutional effects in bedding etc. Difficult to understand why it was called a Grotto, though it appears to have been open to visitors at some time. A mined level to the right, at the foot of the Great Rake stope, leads to extensive mined passages.

*References: Ford, T.D. 2001. Mining History. Bull. P.D.M.H.S. Vol.14. No.6. pp.1-34. Surveys.*
*Webb, D. 2001. A Cave and Mine Conservation Audit for the Masson Hill Area. D.C.A.*

## LONG TOR TOP MINE
(Little Dish Mine)

NGR 2955 5865.
2945 5860 (shaft)   Grade: 2 (Mine)
Alt. 152m
Length: 200m approx.

At the top of Long Tor Quarry, but approached from the footpath above. Follow a hollow downwards with a low cliff to the south side. Entrance just north of the cable car wires, just before the top of the quarry.

A concealed low entrance leads to narrow mine workings, with several junctions and one tight crawl to small mined caverns with a grilled shaft to surface in the wood above.

*References: Barnatt, J. & Worthington, T. 2006. Mining History Bull. P.D.M.H.S. Vol.16. No.3. Survey.*
*Webb, D. 2001. A Cave and Mine Conservation Audit for the Masson Hill Area. D.C.A.*

## LORDS AND LADIES MINE

NGR 270 605
Grade: 2 (Mine)
Alt. 600ft (180m)

Permission from Mr Greatorex, Lobby Farm, Oker.

On the east side of Northern Dale, between Wensley and Snitterton.

A complex series of low cave passages, all extensively modified by mining, with several entrances. A through trip involves a low wet crawl.

*References: Barnatt, J. & Worthington, T. 2006. Mining History Bull. P.D.M.H.S. Vol.16. No.3.   Survey.*
*Nash, D.A. 1957. Trans. C.R.A. Vol.5. No.1. p.22.*
*Riley, P. 1977. Bull. P.D.M.H.S. Vol.6. No.5. p.244.*

## LUNTOR POT

NGR 2513 6007  Grade II
Alt. 1080ft (329m)
Length: 120ft (37m)
Depth: 65ft (20m)

Discovered 2004 by David Whitehouse, pushed by Buster Wright and Iain Barker.

From the lay-by on Bonsall Moor Lane where the Limestone Way crosses it, follow the path towards Winster. The well hidden entrance lies below a dolomite boulder in an elongated depression alongside a broken wall; there are several capped shafts in the immediate area.

The small entrance leads immediately down an earthy slope into a small rift chamber containing some stacked deads. A flat-out crawl at waist height leads to holes in the floor. Below the north wall of the entrance chamber is the head of a 40ft (12m) pitch with passages off to the east and west at a depth of 25ft (8m). West Passage leads under a loose boulder supported by an oak stemple to the head of a pitch of 33ft (10m) which is blocked at the base.

East Passage leads immediately through a tight drop into a sporting pitch of 40ft (12m) liberally strewn with loose rock; this has not been pushed to a conclusion.

The whole cave is in dolomitic limestone.

**Tackle**
    First Pitch: 18m rope
    West Pitch: 14m rope
    East Pitch: free-climbable with care: no belays in-situ.

References: 2004. DCA N/L No.120

**MERRY TOM LEVEL**
(Lower Nimblejack Level. Twenty Friend Vein)
NGR 264 565   Grade: 1
Alt. 650ft (198m)
Length: 350ft (107m)

Bottom and Middle entrances have been gated. Access through Wirksworth Mines Research Group.

Immediately below the Middleton road, near Nimblejack Corner.

Small slabbed entrance soon enlarges to 5ft x 2.5ft (1.5 x 0.75m). After 270ft (82m) a square shaft in the roof discharges a trickle. The level ends at a handpicked stope in the vein.

Reference: Smith, A. & Ford, T.D. 1971. Bull. P.D.M.H.S. Vol.4. No.5. p.381. Survey.

**MILLCLOSE MINE**
NGR Shaft 259 625.
Sough 264 626.
Watts Shaft 257 618
Alt. Shaft 400ft (122m)
Length: Over 1/2 mile (0.8km
Grade: 2 (Mine)

Access strictly by permission of the Works Manager, H.J. Enthoven and Sons Ltd. prior to visit.

Half a mile north west of Darley Bridge, in the outbuildings.

Shaft boarded over and locked. Entrance shaft has fixed iron ladders to the only accessible level at a depth a 60ft (18m). The shaft continues down for over 800ft (244m) but is full of water and boarded over. From shaft a passage leads to a T-junction. Right leads to a water filled passage and old pumping shaft (which is not boarded over). Left at the T-junction leads to Yatestoop Sough, along which water rushes to the exit and into the River Derwent. Interesting ochreous deposits in the roof and on the sides of the sough. Sough can be followed into the mine until roof fall prevents progress. Very strong current of water pours over the top of the fall. Digging here enabled some progress to be made, but divers reported the level reducing in size beyond, with little hope of further exploration. Flooded caverns below the water table contained a lining of lead ore etc.

Watts Shaft is a large open shaft 190ft (58m) deep to water. Level at 157ft (48m) heads south for 540ft (165m), and is the pumpway into Old Millclose Sough. It is driven in shale, ventilation is poor, and it is silted at the far end. A side passage leads east, then turns south, passing the Fire Engine Shaft (covered at the surface) with old ladders still in place. The silted end of the level is just beyond.

### NEW SPEEDWELL MINE

Royal Mine and Pavilion Mine (qv) are names for workings dating from the 1950's on the site of New Speedwell. New Speedwell was obliterated.

### OLD ASH MINE
NGR 269 605  Grade: 2
Alt. 600ft (183m)
Length: 800m approx.

Now gated - permission and key to be sought by phone from Mr Greatorex. Lobby Farm, Oker (Tel: 01629 733575). Note that the footpath down Northern Dale is not a public footpath.

Gated adit on the west side of Northern Dale, opposite Lords' and Ladies' Mine, roughly midway between Wensley and Snitterton.

An adit leads into a complex system of mined and natural passages. A very tight squeeze was pushed in 1982 to discover a further 300ft (91m) of mostly natural passage with some fine formations, further evidence of entry by miners via a now run-in shaft, and a blind 12ft (3.6m) deep sump. Mud Shaft leads to short lower levels. A 150ft (46m) capped shaft on the hill top at 268 605 enters the system at Bridge Cavern, where a pendulum is required to get onto the rock bridge 30ft (9m) above the bottom of the shaft.

References: Barnatt, J. 2001. Mining History. Bull. P.D.M.H.S. Vol.14. No.5. p.38.

Barnatt, J. & Worthington, T. 2006. Mining History Bull. P.D.M.H.S. Vol.16. No.3. Survey.

Gibson, R. & Ryder, P. 1983. B.C.R.A. Caves & Caving No.20.p.16.

Nash, D.A. 1957. Trans C.R.G. Nol.5. No.1. p.22.

### ORCHARD MINE CAVERNS
NGR 283 550 approx.
Lost

No longer known. In one of many veins lying parallel to and on the east side of the Middleton - Wirksworth road. Farey's description appears to be confused with Orchard Pipe Caverns at Winster on page 264.

Reference: Farey, J. 1811. A general view of the agriculture and minerals of Derbyshire. p.294.

### OWLET HOLE MINE
(Victoria Cavern)
NGR 292 580  Grade: 1 (Mine)
Alt. 500ft (152m)
Length: 400ft (122m)

Gated. Owned by P.D.M.H.S. Keys obtainable from the Mining Museum. Entrance is close to a footpath: please close the lid after entering.

High on the hillside just south of Matlock Bath. Shaft entrance is 200 yards down the footpath from the Upperwood Layby.

The shaft entrance is rigged with iron ladders (of doubtful provenance: lifeline essential), and enters the mine 50ft (15m) from the main passage. The system consists of a mined pipe vein.

Reference: Ford, T.D. 2001. Mining History. Bull. P.D.M.H.S. Vol.14. No.6. pp.1-34.

Maddocks, C. 1957. The Lyre No.2. pp.42-43. Survey.

Webb, D. 2001. A Cave and Mine Conservation Audit for the Masson Hill Area. D.C.A.

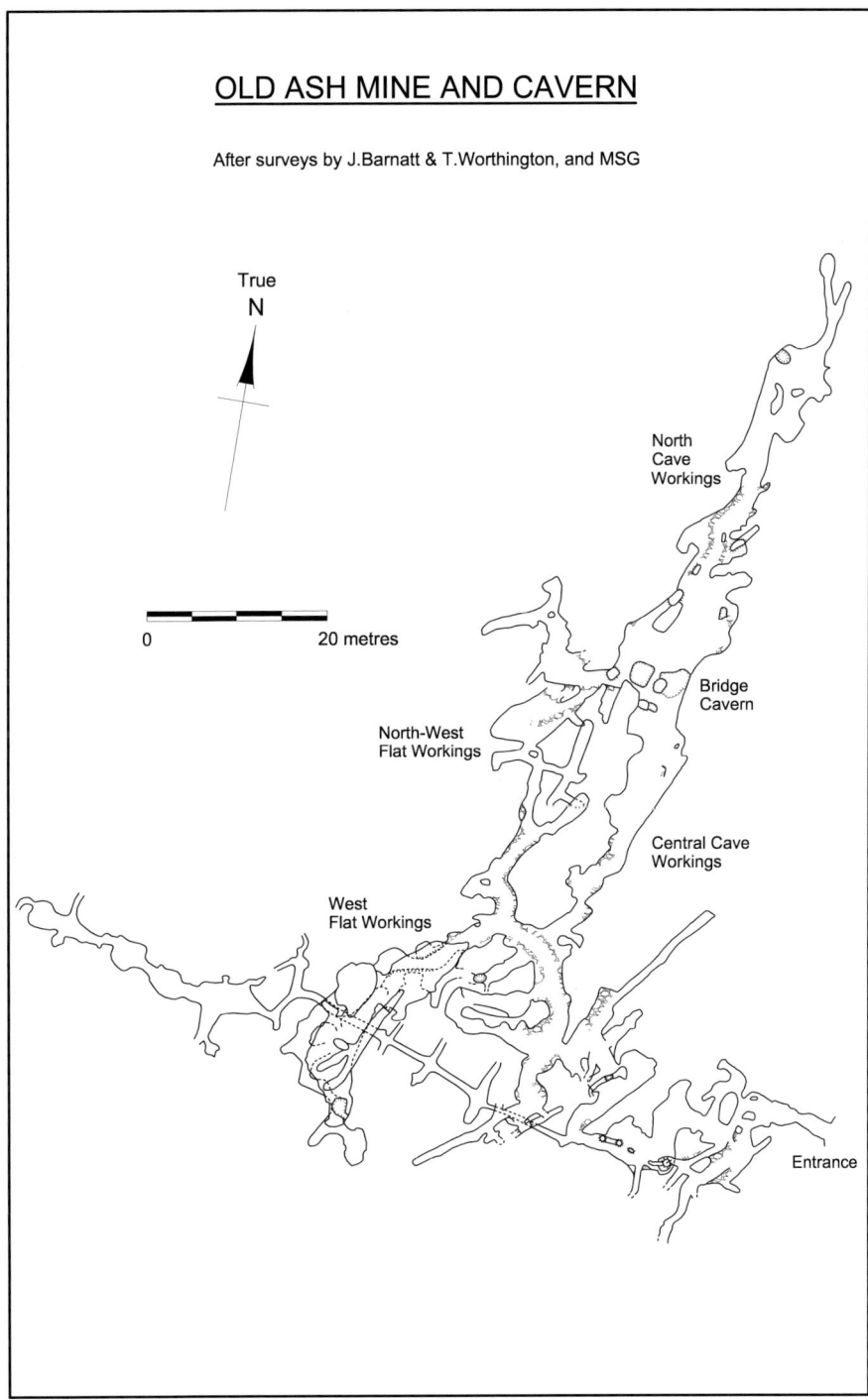

## OXCLOSE MINE

**NGR 275 597  Grade: 4 (Mine)**
**Alt. 730ft (223m)**
**Length: 5000ft (1500m) approx.**
**Depth: 350ft (107m)**
**Status: S.S.S.I.**

Access not normally granted.

Escape Route shaft in field behind Leawood Cottage, Snitterton. Main Shaft in next field downhill.

The first pitch of the Escape Route is a 60ft (18m) shaft, with ladder belayed to rail to avoid ginging. Short crawl to the second pitch of 25ft (8m). From the foot of the pitch proceed down dip for 700ft (213m) along a complex route. Take care to avoid an 80ft (24m) shaft in the floor. A mined area around the Engine Shaft is reached at the 200ft (61m) level. Shaft continues to 300ft (92m) level. Workings continue down dip, passing a 10ft (3m) pitch, and the Phosphorescent Pool shaft (reflecting daylight from surface). A large chamber can be reached, flooded at its lower end. This is a sump, passed after a short dive to emerge in G.O.N. Mine. Another route leads to the Engine Shaft at the 300ft (92m) level.

*Reference: Nash, D.A. 1957. Trans. C.R.G. Vol.5. No.1. pp.19-20.*

## PLACKETT MINE CAVERNS

**NGR 237 610   Grade: Mines**
**Alt. 700ft (213m)**
**Depth: Over 300ft (91m)**

Permission rarely given. North west of Winster. Main Shaft at 237 610, another at 239 608.

A vast cavern 120 yards (110m) high was recorded by Farey (1811). Recent exploration revealed an extensive series of pipe-vein workings.

*Reference: Farey, J. 1811. A general view of the agriculture and minerals of Derbyshire. p.294.*

## POUNDER LANE CAVE
(Pounder Cave)

**NGR 280 588  Grade: 1**
**Alt. 870ft (265m)**
**Length: about 100ft (30m)**
**Depth: 30ft (9m)**

Triang Pot dug by Jackpot Caving Group 1975/6. Further work by Masson Caving Group 1988.

In crags east of Pounder Lane.

Small arch entrance enlarged by mining. Walking size passage for 20ft (6m) to Triang Pot, dug out to 28ft (9m) depth, with low bedding passage at the bottom. Artificially enlarged without success. East passage continues across top of pot for 30ft (9m) to 7ft (2.5m) blind pot.

*Reference: Allen, L. 1977. Descent No.37.pp.14-15. Survey.*

## RANTER MINE CAVERN

**NGR 284 550**
**Lost**

Grid reference given is for Ranter Mine shaft.

A "lost" cavern listed by Farey, 1811. Probably in the vein running parallel to and east of the Middleton and Wirksworth road. Orchard Mine Cavern is probably close by.

*Reference: Farey, J. 1811. A General view of the Agriculture and Minerals of Derbyshire. Vol.1.p.265.*

## ROYAL MINE
(New Speedwell Mine, Pavilion Mine)

**NGR 2915 5784  Show**
**Alt. 600ft (183m)**
**Status: S.S.S.I.**

A complex incorporating Tear Breeches Mine, Hopping Mine, and Speedwell Mine, Matlock. Old lead mine workings and 20th century fluorspar workings, intersecting sand filled caverns. Outer parts have been developed as a guided mine tour, with taped commentary and automatic lighting effects.

*References: Adam, W. 1838. Gem of the Peak. 1973 reprint by Moorland Publishing, Hartington. pp.63-63.*

*Flindall, R. & Hayes, A. 1973. Bull. P.D.M.H.S. Vol.5. No.4. pp.182-199. Survey.*

### RUTLAND CAVERN
(Old Nestus Grotto. Nestus Mine)
NGR 2925 5858
Show (Mine)
Alt. 675ft (206m)
Length: 560ft (171m)

On Heights of Abraham, approached through grounds off Upperwood Road.
Artificial passage for 240ft (73m) leads to chamber 300ft (91m) long. Branches into two near the end. On the left is Old Nestus Cavern, one of the oldest lead mines in Derbyshire, with good evidence of pick work. Good mineralisation features in upper galleries up Roman Stairs. Also various rare minerals found in the Lower Nestus workings down shaft (now blocked) below Tower House.

References: Barnatt, J. & Rieuwerts, J. 1998. Mining History. Bull. P.D.M.H.S. Vol.13. No.5. pp.51-64. Survey. Flindall, R. & Hayes, A. 1976. The Caverns and Mines of Matlock Bath. Moorland Publishing, Hartington. Hurt, L. 1968. Bull. P.D.M.H.S. Vol.3. No.6. pp.369-379.

### SCAFFOLD POLE RIFT SHAFT
NGR 293 596  Grade: 3
Alt. 655ft (200m)
Depth: 33ft (10m)

On north-eastern slope of Masson Hill adjacent to a hedgerow. Shaft top covered by loose boulders.
An enlarged rift with levels off at 15ft (4.5m) and base.
Reference: 1996. OCC N/L, Vol. 32, No.1. p.1 & 5. (Survey).

### SHINING CLIFF CAVE
NGR 292 592  Grade: 2
Alt. 700ft (213m)
Length: 200ft (61m)

Difficult to find among crags and undergrowth, at the foot of a small bluff forming part of Shining Cliff.
An 8ft (2m) drop between boulders into a low passage trending north via small chambers to a terminal crawl. There is some evidence of mining at the far end. From the main passage one can enter high narrow rifts. The left hand one has a flowstone wall and leads via a climb to a short choked inlet passage, the right hand one is a blind traverse.

### SLALEY SOUGH
NGR 2719 5710
Grade: 2 (Mine)
Alt. 675ft (206m)
Length: 2269ft (691.6m)
Depth: 151ft (46m)

Adit entrance near the top of the North side of the Via Gellia, about 200ft (61m) above the A5012 road about 50 yards east of the conspicuous entrance to Bonsall Leys Level.
From the 3ft (1m) square entrance a crosscut 6ft (2m) high and 3ft (1m) wide leads northwestwards. Initially the floor has a few inches of water, but soon becomes dry. After 150ft (46m) the level is 5ft (1.5m) high and 2ft (0.6m) wide, and continues to close until it is only 3ft (1m) square. Great Rake is intersected 460ft (140m) from the entrance. Easy walking to the right for 40ft to the top of a winze 52ft (16m) deep and partly backfilled. A small level continues for 20ft (6m) to a forefield. To the left of the T-junction is the foot of the First Raise, and the main level, 6ft (2m) high and 3.5ft (1m) wide, runs for 330ft (100m) to the Second Raise. Here the main level turns north west, and a crawl continues ahead into a larger passage which turns south east 145ft (44m) beyond the raise.
The main level soon turns west-north-west again, passing a zone of calcite strings and vugs after 180ft (55m). 40ft (12) further, a branch on the right leads to a 151ft (46m) blind pitch. The main level continues past the base of the Third Raise as a crawl over fallen toadstone, and continues larger again for 445ft (136m) to Parson Rake. The Fourth Raise lies 150ft (46m) further, and the main level continues for a further 500ft (152m) to the Western Forefield.
Reference: Flindall, R.B. & Hayes, A.J. 1971. Bull. P.D.M.H.S. Vol.4. No.6. pp.431-437. Survey.

### SLINTER WOOD CAVES
**NGR 288 571  Grade: 1**
Alt. 550ft (165m)
Depth: 100ft (30m)

In the cliff almost opposite Ball Eye Mine.

Three small caves. The floor of one collapsed to reveal a 100ft (30m) deep hole. Various mine levels in the same area have been described by Flindall et al, 1977.

*Reference: Flindall, R.B., Hayes, A.J., & Rieuwerts, J.H. 1977. Bull. P.D.M.H.S. Vol.6. No.6.  pp.263-279. Surveys.*

### SPEEDWELL MINE
**NGR 2907 5788  Mine**
Alt. 550ft (168m)

Incline sealed after a fatal accident.

Adit entrance now partly concealed by rubbish in road fork at Upperwood. All entrances blocked.

Old lead mine, formerly a show cave. Parts more recently worked for fluorspar and calcite via adits, as Royal Mine from top of Old Pavilion grounds, and accessible via adits from there. Also known as New Speedwell Mine, or Angelina's Cavern, though that name more strictly applied to a chamber now mined away. Whole system is somewhat unstable, and parts are in a dangerous state. Link route to Fluorspar Cavern.

*Reference: Flindall, R. & Hayes, A. 1973. Bull. P.D.M.H.S. Vol.5. No.4. pp.182-199. Survey.*

### SPINNEY LEVEL
(Anglo-Saxon Mine)

**NGR 261 561  Grade: 2 (Mine)**
Alt. 700ft (210m)
Length: c.1000ft (305m)

Behind the only large hillock close to the road from Nimblejack corner in the Via Gellia south to Hopton.

Flooded entrance. The level trends westwards. The first hundred feet (30m) is low with 2ft (60cm) of water and a partial roof collapse, then a well decorated section leading to dry levels with a blind shaft in the floor and two short upper series. Also known as Anglo-Saxon Mine from the four letter inscriptions near the end!

*Reference: Smith, A. & Ford, T.D. 1971. Bull. P.D.M.H.S. Vol.4. No.5. p.382.*

### TEAR BREECHES MINE
**NGR 2912 5800**
Grade: 3 (Mine)
Alt. 600ft (183m)
Status: S.S.S.I.

No access at present.

Most entrances except Royal Mine, which is a show cave, are blocked. Three main entrances.

1) Hopping Mine adit above Upperwood Road.

2) Jacob's (or Angelina's) Adit and steps immediately across and below the road (also known as Fluorspar Cavern).

3) Speedwell Mine (also known as New Speedwell, Royal, or Pavilion Mine) in old opencast fluorspar pit at the top of the Pavilion grounds.

A complex system of mined out fluorspar deposits and old solution caves. Once a group of separate mines, there have been other adits and at least 8 shafts, though the mines were all finally linked in the course of mining operations in the 1950's. The names have all been variously applied to whole mines or individual chambers, but the original, according to mine records, was Tear Breeches Mine. Various parts have been show caves at times. Hopping Adit branches into an incline down into Jacob's Cavern, and a level straight ahead into a large muddy cavern. Levels from both meet in stopes at the foot of Jacob's entrance steps; a series of stopes leads on through the former Speedwell Cavern into the workings developed from the adit in the top of the Pavilion grounds. These contain a striking fault-bounded chamber with toadstone clays. The whole complex is rather unstable and sewage has leaked in at one point.

*References: Frost, R.V. 1953. The Speleologist (Derbyshire) Vol.1. No.2. pp.63-67.*
*Flindall, R. & Hayes, A. 1973. Bull. P.D.M.H.S. Vol.5. No 4. pp.182-199.*

## TEARSALL PIPE CAVERNS NO.1
**NGR 263 600  Lost**
**Length: Over 1000ft (305m)**

The mine consisted of a series of sub-parallel levels connected by steep shutes down from the bedding, with buddle pools and sledge runs. Most of the complex has now been quarried away.
*Reference: Flindall, R. 1974. Bull. P.D.M.H.S. Vol.5. No.6. pp.373-382. Survey.*

## TEARSALL PIPE CAVERNS NO.2
(Dalefield Mine (part)?)
**NGR 266 602  Grade: 3 (Mine)**
**Alt. 800ft (244m)**
**Length: Sump Series: 1700ft (518m).**
**Pool Series: 1000ft (300m)**

A key and box spanner for both shafts are kept by Mr Walker at Brightgate Farm. A £2 deposit is payable for the key.

Pool and Sump shafts are both lidded and locked. Other shafts are covered with concrete sleepers. 15 shafts in a field downhill and north of Tearsall Farm.

### Sump Series:
Entered by Sump Shaft (60ft/18m) at the bottom extremity of the field, or by Wall Shaft (55ft/17m) adjacent to the dry stone wall at the top of the field. Sump Shaft leads to a large natural and mined passage 12ft (4m) high running north-south. Northerly leads to a meander passage with a stream sinking in the floor. The stream rises from an upstream sump which was baled to allow excavation of a submerged choke to provide a connection to Pool Series.

Near to where the stream sinks a tight rift gives access to Ridgeways Series and Rift Chamber, some 40ft (12m) high and rather dangerous. From the shaft bottom the passage south goes through the Gnasher Crawl to the Main Chamber, and thence up a wet crawl, Thrutchers Paradise, to the base of a small climbing shaft. This leads to the base of Wall Shaft and a series of mined passages continues westwards with at least three shafts to the surface, but all sealed.

### Pool Series:
Situated adjacent to Sump Series and entered by four shafts, Pool Shaft (47ft/14.4m), Line Shaft (44ft/13.5m), Fern Shaft (36ft/11m) and Short Drop Shaft (15ft/4.6m). Pool shaft is now lidded and locked. From Pool Shaft, upstream is short series of mined / natural passages, which basically form a short round trip starting and ending at Stal Chamber. Downstream over miner's clay dam into Main Chamber. There are three ways off - large obvious passage to the left, a rope climb to the left, and a short climb straight ahead. The short climb is followed by a climb down into mined passage with stacked deads. There are two ways off - ahead is a crawl to a small chamber with small but pretty formations, or scramble over small boulders to a junction. Straight on down under deads (care) is T'Owd Man's Passage, which reaches a dead end after 80ft (24m). Near the end are two short branches to the left (Webb's Way) and right. Right at the junction leads to the bottom of Line Shaft and another choice. Left is soon blind. Right leads under small hole into passage containing cave pearls, and after a short step up the passage gets tight and muddy. In 1994 the Masson Caving Group baled the upstream sump in the Sump Series and forced a tight connection to the Line Shaft area of the Pool Series to link the two systems and make a through trip possible. The sump can be baled from the Sump Series side. Up the small hole, left leads back to Line Shaft, right closes down after a very tight crawl, and a low crawl through a muddy pool leads past small stalactites to a junction. Left rises quite steeply to a dead end. The other route is a climb down a fixed rope back into Main Chamber. Following the large obvious passage from Main Chamber, clamber over fallen deads to a collapse. Climb to a small narrow passage leading to the New Extension (1987). Shaft just beyond narrow section is Fern Shaft. Large walking sized passage closes down after short drop. Crawl on right near Fern Shaft leads to a boulder choke which draughts (possibly from a shaft nearby). A climb on the left leads to bottom of Short Drop Shaft. Just before Short Drop Shaft, a narrow passage on the right is Mick's Amazement, which soon enlarges to walking size, and after a

short stooping section reaches a fairly large cross passage with a few formations. Obvious passage straight on leads to an unstable area with rotten timbers, a blocked shaft to surface, and a shaft to a lower level. (Lower shaft can be free-climbed with care, or use 15ft (5m) ladder and belay). The other way on from the cross passage leads up to a boulder choke on the right, and a small rising passage to the left with drops back to Mick's Amazement.

References: Beeston Mines Research Group Report No.1.
Derbyshire Caving Club N/L 1960, 1961, 1964,1965.
Peakland Archaeological Society Journal No.21. 1966.
Survey by Derbyshire Caving Club, W.2. Pool and Sump Series.
Survey Pool Series & New Extensions 1987 by Phil Ingham & Masson Caving Group.
Webb, D. 1995. Caves & Caving No.68. p.6. Survey.
Webb D. 1995. Descent No. 122. p.8. Survey.

### TEMPLE MINE
(Temple Pipe Cavern)
NGR 292 581  Show (Mine)
Alt. 400ft (122m)
Length: 500ft (152m) approx.

Owned by P.D.M.H.S. Access controlled by the Mining Museum. Small charge made.

Entrance is an adit off Temple Road, opposite the Peak District Mining Museum.

A series of fluorspar workings with numerous small sand-filled caverns. One level was driven into a thick clay wayboard and into the top of a lava flow.

### TORHILLS CAVE
(Dark Hole Mine. Primrose Mine)
NGR 2943 5879
Grade: 2 (Mine)
Alt. 500ft (152m)
Length: 250ft (76m)

Two entrance at different levels in the crag opposite High Tor.

Part cave, part mine, on the line of Great Rake. Bottom entrance leads to Clay Cavern, with climb into upper series of mined and natural passages and grottos reached from upper entrance. A small stream flows in wet weather and backs up in terminal chambers, which contain interesting sediments and rock formations. Draught connects to blocked surface workings on rake just below footpath from Matlock Bath.

References: Barnatt, J. & Worthington, T. 2006. Mining History Bull. P.D.M.H.S. Vol.16. No.3. Survey.
Findall, R. & Hayes, A. 1976. The Caverns and Mines of Matlock Bath. pp.27,44,48.

### WAPPING MINE
NGR 2939 5749  Grade: 2 (Mine)
Alt. 400ft (122m)
Status: S.S.S.I.

No access at present.

In the wood close to the Wapping footpath.

The first section is a high mined out vein, with an unstable roof in places. Where the vein gives way to pillar and stall workings climb up to left into higher natural passages which link with Cumberland Cavern. Lower Mine workings continue under part of this and there used to be several link routes.

References: Flindall, R. & Hayes, A. 1972. Bull. P.D.M.H.S. Vol.5. No.2. pp.114-127. Survey.
Ford, T.D. 2001. Mining History. Bull. P.D.M.H.S. Vol.14. No.6. pp.1-34. Survey.
Barnatt, J. & Webb, D. 2002. Cumberland Cavern & Wapping Mine, Matlock Bath. DCA     publication. Survey.

> **YOUD'S LEVEL**
> NGR (Main entr.) 2955 5945
> Grade: 3 (Mine)
> Alt. 295ft (90m)
> Length: 1.2 miles (1.9km)
> Status: S.S.S.I.

Key available from Peak District Mining Museum, Matlock Bath (01629 583834). Access to all shafts on the system is via Greenhills Farm (294 598), off Salters Lane on the way up to Masson Quarry. The farmer is Mr Frank Kirkum, from whom permission must be sought.

Main entrance lies at back of public toilets on Artists Corner.

**Warning: Danger from Weil's Disease from rats associated with sewage seepage in adit entrance.**

### Railway Shaft, Greenhills Farm
**NGR 29425956**
**Alt: 532.79ft (162.40m)**

Large shaft mound surrounded by trees. Shaft is 6ft (2m) diameter & 150ft (46m) deep, where it is blocked. 80ft (24m) of fill between here and coffin level of main system. Level at 95ft (29m) going 400ft (122m). No connection with the sough.

### Day Shaft, Greenhills Farm
**NGR 29215959**
**Alt: 576.31ft (175.66m)**

Large shaft mound surrounded by trees. 4ft 6ins x 2ft 6ins approx. (1.4 x 0.75m). 266ft (81m) deep to main system coffin level. Level at 90ft (27m), small opening, hard to get into. Driven in toadstone wayboard, low and wet for 400ft (122m), but not yet followed to a definite end.

### Overseer Shaft, Greenhills Farm
**NGR 28975928**
**Alt: 774.64ft (236.11m)**

2ft 6ins (0.75m) dia. air ducting for the first 16ft (4.9m), then into solid rock 4ft x 2ft (1.2 x 0.6m). 20ft of rubble was removed from the top of the shaft, and the ginging replaced by air ducting to leave a shaft 200ft (61m) deep. There are no side levels. All the above shafts are covered with concrete railway sleepers.

### Main Level

Entrance is a short shaft into the level, which goes north under the road. Size increases to walking height after 230ft (70m). Stream is met just beyond, flowing into a flooded stope, 33ft (10m) deep to an unexplored level. Of two further stopes the second was dived to 30ft (9m) with no way on. A short trial leads to a dog leg shaft blocked 82ft (25m) up. The passage then turns left into the longest coffin level in Derbyshire, 1200ft (365m). Shortly after the turn a shaft in the roof leads up to the Waterfall Series. The level is silted here, and is a low crawl in water for 65ft (20m). A short trial on the right leads to the bottom of the blocked Railway (Haslam) Shaft. The coffin level now averages 4ft 6ins (1.4m) high by 1ft 8ins (0.5m) wide. A short trial is passed, and approx. 655ft (200m) beyond the Waterfall Series shaft, a further trial goes for 312ft (95m) to the south west. A "Y" junction is reached. Right leads to the bottom of Day (Deep) Shaft. The sough continues in a south westerly direction, through a number of low crawls over miners' backfill, passing through an 80ft (25m) long chamber. Eventually the level splits at an area of workings known as Old Jant Mine. Right follows the stream into a small area of ramifying workings. Left steps up and climbs steeply, passing a short shaft to higher workings on the right. At the top of the steep rise, a very low tight crawl is followed by a hands and knees section and another tight section. Just beyond is the Overseer Shaft Chamber (shaft also known as Upper Close Shaft). The passage continues to rise steeply through old stopes to a forefield. A climb up into the stops above leads on upwards and forwards to the bottom of Gentlewoman's Shaft, a stepped shaft blocked from surface to the step. Beyond, large passages trend south westwards. It was possible to follow a crosscut and continue into the Masson Mine complex, but the connection has been severed by quarrying. A shaft a short distance back from this point, on the edge of the quarry, is open to surface but covered with a large rock. Waterfall Series. A difficult 82ft (25m) climb up the Waterfall Shaft against the flow of water gives access to a level in a toadstone wayboard. A short distance into the level, a climb leads up into ramifying workings. Main level continues low and wet for 400ft (122m) to a fall with the stream flowing from one side of the level.

*Reference: Warriner, D., Willies, L., & Flindall, R. 1981. Bull. P.D.M.H.S. Vol.8. No.2. pp.65-108.*

## Features listed as potential archaeological sites

1: NGR 2423 5521   Alt: 361m   A 1m wide fissure narrowing to 0.40m before being blocked with sediment and rocks.
2: NGR 2424 5521   Alt: 358m   A 1.10m wide cleft narrows to 0.60m.
3: NGR 2433 5515   Alt: 353m   A long fissure 9.50m deep.
4: NGR 2458 5509   Alt: 342m   A cave only visible by two very small holes, possibly rabbit holes appears to be full of sediment.
5: NGR 2462 5516   Alt: 345m   An 11m long narrow fissure in the limestone pavement on top of a crag.
6: NGR 2424 5537   Alt: 356m   A small phreatic tube in a rock shelter.
7: NGR 2417 5553   Alt: 355m   A level floored fissure choked at the back with rocks.
8: NGR 2416 5554   Alt: 350m   A letterbox slot in a cliff face. Choked to within 0.40m of the roof.
9: NGR 2442 5511   Alt: 351m   A deliberately blocked up fissure.

# THE RIVER DOVE CATCHMENT AREA

The River Dove below Thorpe Cloud

The River Dove can conveniently be divided into two areas, North and South. The upper 10kms of the river generally follows the strike along the shale / limestone boundary, the limestones dipping approximately 18 degrees to the south west.

At the northern end is Dowel Resurgence, fed by a group of sinks high in the reef limestone. Some have been inconclusively dug, but digging at Owl Hole revealed a mature cave.

The two major risings further south, the Crowdwell and the Ludwell, both have high discharge figures of roughly 50 l/sec., but are not fed from any known sinks. No extensive digging has been carried out at these sites or in the numerous dolines in the Dove catchment as a whole.

North - south faulting and folding gives rise to some striking limestone scenery along the course of the Dove, and leakage seems to have been prevented by the building of wiers with clay-puddled floors to improve the fishing. This has effectively prevented the river from disappearing underground.

Incision of both the Dove and the Manifold took place during the Pleistocene, the pre-glacial river downcutting in a series of stages to preserve a number of river terraces.

From Wolfscote Grange the river cuts through the upper reef limestones for the next 8 kms, doubling in size at the Milldale Risings. Although no dye tests have been carried out, it is suspected that these risings are partly fed from the sinks to the north west, Gateham and Plantation Swallets. It is possible that an extensive system awaits the determined digger here.

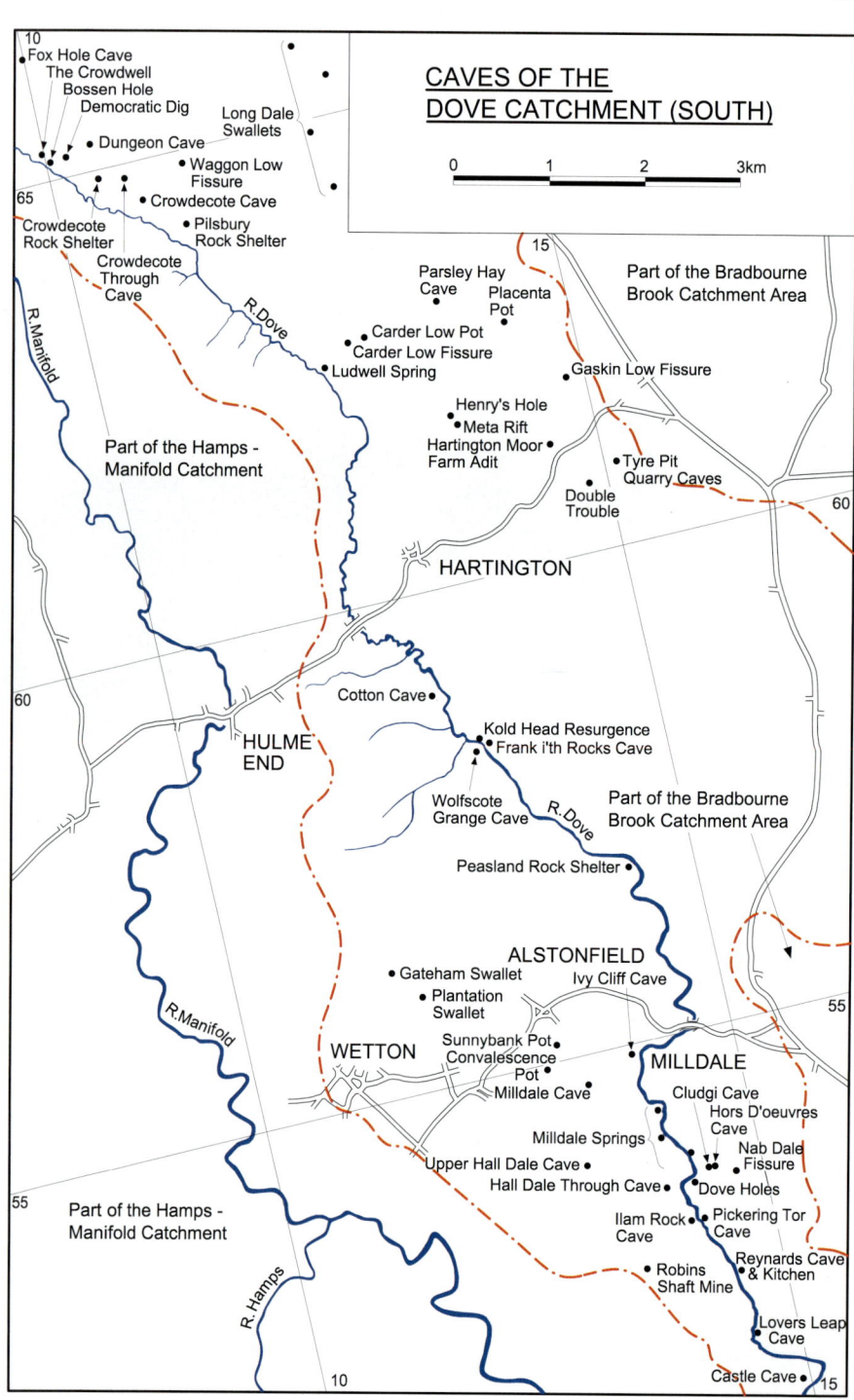

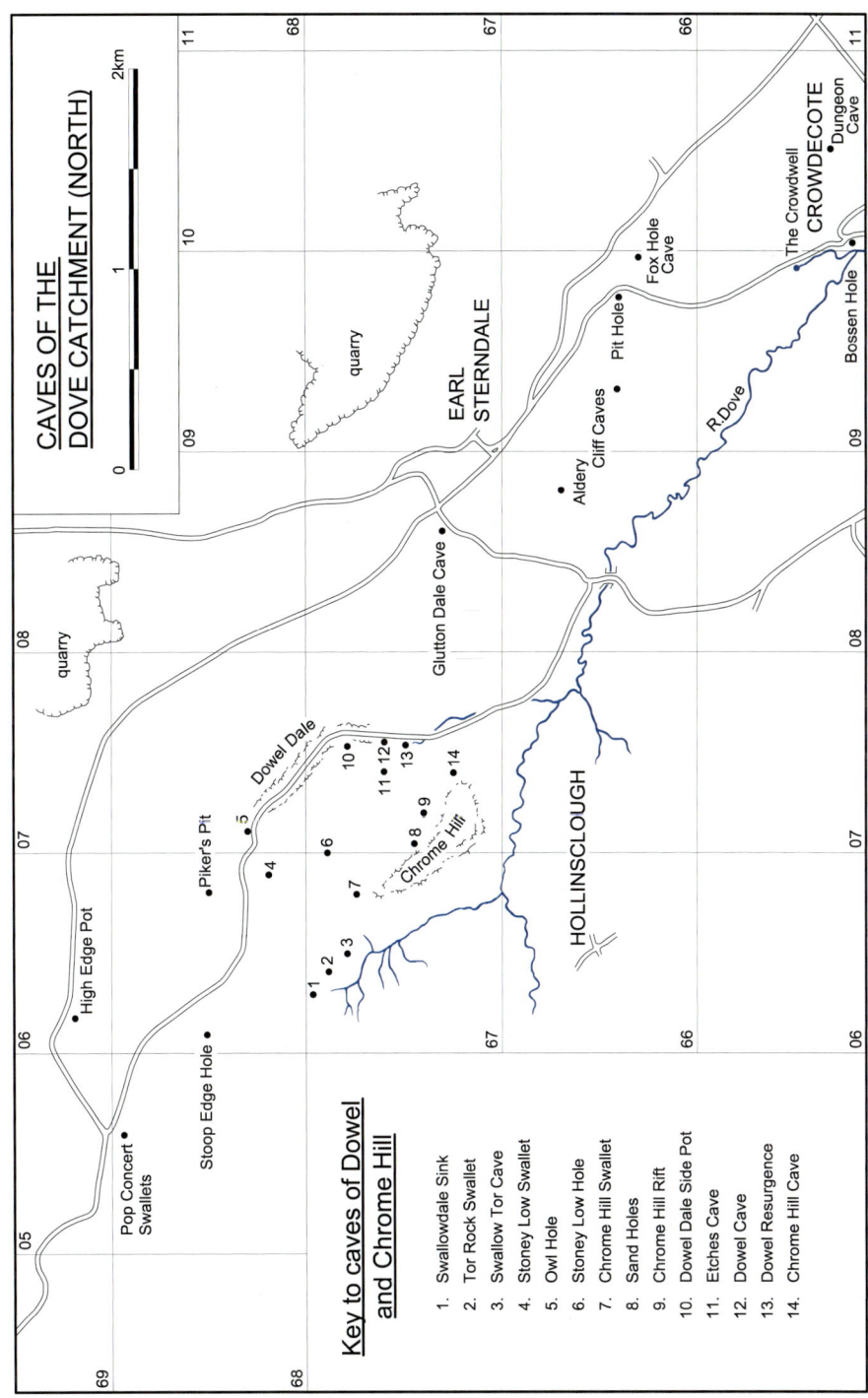

### ALDERY CLIFF CAVE
**NGR 088667 Grade: 1. Digs**
Alt. 1000ft (300m)

On west slopes of Aldery cliff, half a mile south west of the village.
One small cave above Underhill Farm.
Reference: Tottle, P. 1959. The Lyre, Vol.1. No.3. p.60

### ALDERY CLIFF FISSURE
**NGR 0975 6630 Grade: 2**
Alt. 985ft (300m)
Length: 100ft (31m)
Depth: 56ft (17m)

At the extreme southern end of Aldery Cliff Quarry above an overgrown spoil heap.
A sporting fissure cave extended by the Orpheus Caving Club. Rift entrance leads to squeeze up to a higher level in rift whereupon rift becomes too tight after 16ft (5m). Hole down in floor just inside entrance drops (25ft/8m ladder required) into spacious rift that is choked. Seepage water backs up in wet weather. Entrance gated at request of BMC. Please replace gate after visit.
*Reference: 2003. O.C.C. N/L, Vol.39, No. 7-10, p. 46.*

### BOSSEN HOLE (Crowdecote)
**NGR 100 652 Grade: 1**
Alt. 800ft (240m)
Length: 114ft (34m)

200ft (61m) south east of Crowdwell Spring.
A hands and knees crawl. Contains a small shattered chamber and ends at a small hole in the floor. Liable to flooding.
Reference: Crabtree, P.W. 1970. Jour.S.U.S.S. Vol.1. No.6. pp.238-9. Survey.

### BOTTLE POT
**NGR 0665 6807 Grade: 3**
Alt. 1310ft (400m)
Length: 196ft (59.8m)
Depth: 95ft (29m)

Dug by OCC in 2009. Named 'Bottle Pot' on account of the fact that several intact Offiler's Beer Bottles were found.
Located in a shakehole near to Stoop Farm. Named 'Bottle Pot' on account of the fact that several intact 'Offiler's Beer Bottles were found whilst it was being dug in 2009.
An entrance rift descends for 10ft (3m) to reach a sloping bedding crawl that opens onto a 25ft (7.6m) deep Rift/Pot that can be free climbed (ladder useful). At the base of this Pot a tight (enlarged) descending Rift Passage quickly leads to the top of a fine 46ft (14m) deep Aven Pitch (14m ladder and 30m lifeline or 20m SRT Rope essential). At the base of this 80ft (24m) of good size (12ft/3.5m high x 10ft/3m wide) silt floored phreatic relic passage can be followed that terminates in a silt choked fissure that takes a small misfit stream that flows along the passage. Further digging would be difficult and lack of stacking/storage space for spoil would disfigure this fine lower passage. In a silt floored alcove just beyond the base of the second pitch a well preserved skeleton of what is believed to be a 'Hare' can be found.

### CARDER LOW FISSURE
**NGR 127 627 Dig**
Alt. 1050ft (320m)

Above the Ludwell.
A choked fissure apparently on a vein or fault, with a noticeable draught in cold weather. A possible dig. Further down the hill are choked shafts, and on a continuation is Carder Low Mine. Below is the Ludwell, a major resurgence.

## CARDER LOW POT
NGR 129 627  Dig
Alt. 1050ft (320m)

Adjacent to a boundary wall.
A choked pot. Digging would involve removal of small boulders.

## CASTLE CAVE
NGR 1491 5128  Grade: 1
Alt. 550ft (167m)
Length: 15ft (5m)

At top of scree in crags 200 yards (182m) south west of Dovedale stepping stones.
An inviting large cave entrance which closes completely 15ft (3m) in.

## CHROME HILL CAVE
NGR 074 673  Grade: 1
Alt. 1150ft (349m)
Length: 20ft (6m)

On north side of Chrome Hill, visible from Dowell Farm.
A stooping height entrance soon closes down. Corroded flowstone visible on the walls.
*Reference: Smith, P. 1960. The Lyre No.3. p.61.*

## CHROME HILL RIFT
NGR 072 674  Grade: 1
Alt. 1175ft (358m)
Length: 25ft (8m)

Above and to the right (west) of Chrome Hill Cave.
A tight sporting rift descends to a crawl blocked by dripstone.
*Reference: Smith, P. 1960. The Lyre No.3. p.61.*

## CHROME HILL SWALLET
NGR 068 678  Grade: 2
Alt. 1200ft (366m)
Length: 93ft (28m)
Depth: 30ft (9m)

Difficult to find.
An active swallet with a tight letter-box entrance. A low crawl leads to a narrow descending slot which is difficult to reverse. Progress is halted after another drop by a large wall of mud 40ft (12m) along Magic Hammer Passage, a promising streamway. Rabbit Inlet on the left can be climbed and followed back close to the entrance.
*Reference: Phipps, M. 1981. The Lyre No.5. pp.4-5.*

## CLUDGI CAVE
NGR 1443 5360  Dig
Alt. 673ft (205m)
Length: 13ft (4m)

30m to the west of Hors D'oeuvres Cave. An obvious cave entrance leads to a hands and knees crawl. Possible dig at floor level at the end of the passage.
*Reference: 2001. OCC N/L Vol.37, No.7-8-9, p.37.*

## CONVALESCENCE POT
NGR 130 550  Grade: 1
Alt. 800ft (240m)

200ft (61m) south of Sunnybank Pot.
Short pitch into earth-choked section of Sunnybank Pot.

## COTTON CAVE
NGR 127 589  Grade: 1
Alt. 710ft (213m)

In the grounds of Beresford Estate, Hartington. Entrance well hidden.
Contains one small chamber. Charles Cotton is said to have hidden there. Three small rock shelters nearby.

## CROWDECOTE CAVE
NGR 109 646  Dig
Alt. 850ft (255m)

A small rising on the limestone/shale junction at the base of a small outcrop adjacent to the Crowdecote-Pilsbury bridle path.
To gain access boulders must be removed from a fissure. A very tight descending crawl which might be forced further.

## CROWDECOTE ROCK SHELTER
NGR 105 649  Dig
Alt. 790ft (237m)

At the foot of a limestone outcrop.
A probable old resurgence cave, now blocked by silt.

## CROWDECOTE THROUGH CAVE
NGR 1075 6485  Grade: 1
Alt. 1000ft (300m) approx.
Length: 16ft (5m)
Depth: 5ft (1.5m)

Situated at foot of a prominent rib of limestone that looks southwards down into Upper Dove Valley. Obvious landmarks are three large sycamore trees that are growing near to entrance.
The cave has two entrances. The first (left facing the hillside) is a rift 5ft (1.5m) deep and 4ft (1.4m) long by 2ft (0.6m) wide. Ahead is a fissure that closes but could be dug. To right is a triangular section passage 4ft (1.2m) wide and 3ft (0.8m) high that goes for 6ft (1.8m) to emerge at second entrance, which is a 4ft (1.2m) diameter pot 5ft (1.5m) deep. Minimal prospects for further extension. May be used as an occasional fox lair.
*Reference: O.C.C. Log Book. Sept. 2006.*

## THE CROWDWELL
NGR 100 653  Dig
Alt. 800ft (240m)

Large resurgence in Upper Dove Valley. Water emerges from buried culverts below growing rubbish heap.
*Reference: Smith, P. 1960. The Lyre No.3. p.60.*

## DEMOCRATIC DIG
NGR 1021 6520  Grade: 2
Alt. 920ft (280m)
Length: 108ft (33m)
Depth: 40ft (12.3m)

Situated in a small stone quarry on the west side of the Upper Dove at the side of the Hurdlow to Longnor Road some 100ft (30m) above the village of Crowdecote.
From the back of the quarry a 4.5ft (1.4m) diameter phreatic tube descends steeply for 20ft (6m) to reach a small chamber. A low crawl to the SW passes through a small chamber before reaching a 6.5ft (2m) x 13ft (4m) chamber with shoring in the roof. At the far end of the chamber a scaffold shored shaft through mud and boulders drops for 13ft (4m) to reach a steeply descending 1m diameter scalloped phreatic tube that enlarges slightly before levelling out to end in small rift chamber that marks the current end of the dig. The mud and boulder filled passage continues beyond and is currently being dug.
*References: Brooks, S. 2006. OCC N/L Vol.42 No.9-12 pp.59-60. Survey*

Democratic Dig.
Photo by Simon Brooks

### DOUBLE TROUBLE
NGR 1480 6070   Dig
Alt. 1065ft (325m)
Length: 30ft (9m)

In the disused Tyre Pit Quarry. The first cave is situated at the base of the quarry wall just inside quarry on the north side of the gap where the Quarry opens on to the Tissington Trail.

A boulder filled rift was dug by O.C.C. to reveal a pleasant calcite coated rift-pot. This descends to a depth of 26ft (8m) where it pinches out. With no obvious draught and the only prospect of further extension being by serious rock removal this site has now been capped.

### DOVE HOLES CAVES
NGR 1425 5353   Grade: 1
Alt. 700ft (210m)
Status: National Trust. S.S.S.I.

On the left bank of the River Dove, south east of Hanson Grange, opposite Hall Dale.

Two large entrances 55ft (17m) and 30ft (9m) wide and high. Both close almost immediately.

### DOWEL CAVE
NGR 075 676   Grade: 1 (Arch)
Alt. 1025ft (308m)
Length: 50ft (15m)

50 yards (45m) up the dale from the present rising.

An old resurgence cave, consisting of a fissure descending inwards, choked at the bottom. Archaeological excavation uncovered the remains of ten Neolithic inhumations.

References: Bramwell, D. 1957-60. P.A.S. N/L Nos.14-17.

Bramwell, D. 1959. Derbys. Arch. Jour. No.79. pp.97-109. Survey.

Bramwell, D. 1960. The Lyre No.3. pp.13-15 & 67.

Bramwell, D. 1977. P.A.S.Bull. No. 30. p.8.

Hart, C.R. 1984. North Derbyshire Archaeological Survey.

### DOWEL DALE SIDE POT
NGR 075 678   Grade: 3
Alt. 1100ft (335m)
Depth: 210ft (64m)

Discovered and dug in 1985. Further excavation by TSG 1996-1999. 20ft (6m) above the road.

Fissure passage and climbs lead to major dig down through boulders for 100ft (30m) - care needed with shoring. Large descending chamber leads to choice of steep bouldery fissure or tube. Avoid fissure by entering tube and rigging short pitch on left after 10ft (3m) to choke, currently being dug.

Across top of pitch is Upstream Sump, water from which descends the pitch. Sump has been explored for 315ft (96m) to depth of 33ft (11m). 121ft (37m) into sump is small unexplored passage on right which presumably connects with nearby Static Sump (dived for 30ft / 9m), reached by 80ft (24m) crawl along continuation of tube from pitch head. Two further junctions in Upstream Sump at 196ft (60m) and 295ft (90m) from base have small passages leading off on left, both continuing very small (as does main continuation). The 60m junction is the only turn round spot. Whole of lower series is probably flooded when Dowel Resurgence is flowing. The destination of the stream in low-water conditions is unknown. The Crowdwell has been suggested.

References: Cordingley, J.N. 2000. Diving in Dowell Dale Side Pot. T.S.G. Jour. 17. p. 27. Survey.

Gibson, R. 1986. E.P.C. Jour. Vol.9 No.5. pp.4-5. Survey.

Kinge, N. 2000. Dowel Dale Side Pot. Survey. T.S.G. Jour. 17. p.19

Smith, P.B. 1997. Dowel Dale Side Pot. T.S.G. Jour. 16, pp.8-11. Survey.

### DOWEL RESURGENCE
NGR 075 675   Grade: 2
Alt. 950ft (290m)
Length: 50ft (12m)

At the foot of Dowel Dale opposite the farm.

Main rising for the Dowel Area. Fissure entrance which has been enlarged soon degenerates to 30ft (9m) of very tight rift passage leading to a sump blocked with boulders. Only for thin people who like spiders!

Reference: Gibson, R. 1981. D.C.A. N/L No.47. p.4. Smith, P. 1960. The Lyre No.3. p.67.

### DUNGEON CAVE
NGR 105 653   Dig
Alt. 1200ft (365m)

Formerly dug by Orpheus Caving Club.

High on the hill east of Crowdecote.

### ETCHES CAVE
NGR 074 676   Grade: 1
Alt. 1025ft (308m)
Length: 300ft (90m)
Status:   R.I.G.S. (Dowel Dale)

100 yards (91m) west-north-west of Dowel Resurgence, and 75ft (23m) above it.

A short rift cave was dug by Orpheus Caving Club into a series of well decorated rifts connected by muddy crawls.

References: Smith, P. 1960. Lyre No.3. pp.65-66. Survey.

Harrison, H.R. & Haskew, M.T. 1965. The Lyre No.4. pp.25-28. Survey (post-extension).

Pernetta, J.C. 1966. P.A.S. N/L No.21. pp.11-16.

### FOX HOLE CAVE
(High Wheeldon Cave)
NGR 100 663   Grade: 1 (Arch)
Alt. 1360ft (408m)
Length: 180ft (56m)
Status: National Trust. S.S.S.I.

The cave is gated and a key can be obtained from the NT on 01335 350503

In small outcrop on north west end of High Wheeldon.

Drop 8ft (2.5m) into passage leading to chamber 20ft (6m) long where there is a branch to the right leading to a second chamber. Zigzag passages beyond. Excavated remains in Buxton Museum.

*References: Bramwell, D. 1962-1977. P.A.S. N/L No.18. pp.1-6 & 32. No.19. pp.10-12. No.20. pp.8-10 and 11-12. No.21. pp.6-7 & 10. No.22. pp.5-6. No.23. pp.5-6. No.24. pp.7-8.*
*Bramwell, D. 1970-1977. P.A.S. Bull. No.25. p.8-10. No.26. pp.1-4. No.27. pp.1-3. No.29. pp.7-8. No.31. pp.5-6. No.30. pp.4-6.*
*Bramwell, D. 1971. Derbys. Arch. Jour. No.91. pp.1-19. Survey.*
*Gee, S. 1958-1960. P.A.S. N/L No.15. pp. 17-18. Survey. No. 16. p.25. No.17. pp.13-14.*
*Jackson, J.W. 1951. Derbys. Arch. Jour. 71 (New Series Vol.24) pp.72-77.*
*Jones, R.T. 1977. P.A.S. Bull. No.30. pp.2-3.*
*Shimwell, D.W. 1971. P.A.S. Bull. No.26. pp.7-13.*

### FRANK 'ITH ROCKS CAVE.
NGR 1317 5843.
Grade: 1 (Arch).
Alt. 765ft (233m).
Length: 150ft (46m)
Status: National Trust. S.S.S.I.

South of the footbridge on the east side of Wolfscote Dale. A large cave entrance leads to a chamber with a crawl on the right, which leads through the cliff to emerge close to the entrance of a second cave. This consists of a rising muddy rift passage blocked after 100ft (30m). Archaeological remains in Buxton Museum.

*References: Palmer, L.S. 1926. Proc. Univ. Bristol Spel. Soc. Vol.11. No.3.*
*Jackson, J.W. 1926. N.W. Naturalist, p.193.*

### FRIDAY NIGHT DIG
NGR 1480 6076   Dig
Alt. 1065 (325m)
Length: 8ft (2.5m)

In Tyre Pit Quarry. In the face of the buff of limestone that forms the south side of the gap that opens on to the Tissington Trail.

An obvious rectangular entrance 4ft x 4ft (1.2m x 1.2m) leads to a passage that is 8ft (2.5m) long and continuing, albeit in a not too encouraging fashion.

### GATEHAM SWALLET
(Dumble Hole)
NGR 1165 5628   Dig
Alt. 830ft (253m)
Length: 30ft (9m)
Depth: 50ft (15m)

**WARNING: Great care should be taken due to the unstable nature of the walls and the many large, loose boulders throughout the cave.**

Access restricted at landowners request. For current access situation contact The Eldon Pothole Club.

Explored: 1949 - 1958, Birmingham Cave & Crag Club. Reopened 2010, Eldon Pothole Club.

Gated entrance situated in the base of a large swallow hole next to the Hulme End - Wetton Road, 300m south-west of Gateham Farm.

Entrance pitch 20ft (6m) is followed by a short, inclined crawl down to the head of 6ft (2m) climb into a small rift chamber. South-west end of chamber ends after 10ft (3m) at an unstable

boulder choke with a strong draught issuing from gaps between boulders in the floor. At base of climb a short crawl heads north-west to a boulder choke after 16ft (5m).
Reference: Warwick, G.T. (1965) Geographical Journal, 131 (1), p.49.
Afford A.B. (1982) History of the Birmingham Cave and Crag Club, Chapter 1: 1947-1950.

### GASKIN LOW FISSURE
**NGR 148 618  Dig**
**Alt. 1243ft (379m)**

In the plantation on the summit of Gaskin low.
At the northern end of the plantation is a 16ft x 3ft (5m x 1m) fissure choked with small rocks.

### GLUTTON DALE CAVE
**NGR 086 673  Dig**
**Alt. 1050ft (320m)**

A road drain is channelled into a small cave mouth which was excavated for 30ft (9m) but has since been filled in.
Reference: Smith, P. 1960. The Lyre Vol.1. No.3. p.61.

### HALL DALE THROUGH CAVE
(Au Pair Cave)
**NGR 1395 5350  Grade: 1**
**Alt. 721ft (220m)**
**Length: 25ft (7.7m)**
**Depth: 6.5ft (2m)**
Status: National Trust. S.S.S.I.

Situated in low rib of limestone on the north side of Hall Dale some 500ft (150m) before the River Dove is reached.
A rift entrance concealed by an Ash Tree leads to a comfortable 4.25ft (1.3m) x 6ft (1.85m) rift passage that runs through the rib of limestone to exit at a second entrance 2.3ft (0.7m) x 3.3ft (1m).

### HARTINGTON MOOR FARM ADIT
**NGR 145 612**
**Grade: 2 (Mine)**
**Alt. 985ft (300m)**
**Length: 975ft (297m)**

Permission from Hartington Moor Farm.
Entrance at end of obvious "cutting" in field.
Large mined passage is followed for 600ft (180m) approx. passing some small but pretty formations after 400ft (120m) approx, to reach an almost total blockage. Unpleasant flat out crawl over farm refuse on right for 8ft (2.4m) leads to more large mined passage. Two short branches: one on the right is walking size and contains formations, and leads through a shallow wet section to a forefield. Main level continues to a forefield. Mined for iron ore.

### HENRY'S HOLE
**NGR 1355 6170  Grade: 2 Dig.**
**Alt. 1010ft (308m)**
**Length: 43ft (13m)**
**Depth: 23ft (7m)**

Dug by Eldon Pothole Club. On the western rim of Long Dale.
A fluted shaft was dug to a depth of 23ft (7m), then a horizontal passage for 20ft (6m). Digging continues.
Reference: Dearman, R. 1998. BCRA Caves and Caving No. 79. p.11.

### HIGH EDGE POT
**NGR 062 692  Dig**
**Alt. 1350ft (405m)**
**Depth: 10ft (3m)**

A few yards south of the road.
A swallet taking a little water, dug out to a depth of 10ft (3m).

### HORS D'OEUVRES CAVE
NGR 1445 5360
Grade: 1 (Dig)
Alt. 655ft (200m)
Length: 23ft (7m)

200m up Nab Dale from the junction with Dove Dale at the point where the dale narrows. 50ft (15m) south of the path (over the wall) an alcove can be seen in a rocky rib.
A bedding crawl showing signs of solutional activity.
*Reference: 2001, OCC N/L Vol.37, No.7-8-9, p36.*

### ILAM ROCK CAVE
NGR 1418 5311
Grade: 1
Alt. 525ft (158m)
Length: 30ft (9m)
Status: National Trust. S.S.S.I.

Inside the detached Ilam Rock.
Entrance 4ft (1.2m) high rising to 30ft (9m) inside. Overhanging walls have much tufa inside.

### IVY CLIFF CAVE
NGR 139 549   Dig
Alt. 570ft (174m)   Length: 8ft (2.5m)

Follow the tarmac footpath upstream from the Milldale bridge to the road. A further 200ft (60m) reaches an ivy covered crag. The cave entrance is 26ft (8m) above the road (a slippery scramble).
A 3ft (1m) diameter phreatic tube blocked by silt/clay fill.
*Reference: 2001 OCC N/L Vol.37, No.7-8-9, p38.*

### KOLD HEAD RESURGENCE
NGR 131 584   Dig / dive
Alt. 682ft (208m)

A rising which issues a considerable flow in wet weather, and could be worth a dig if permission could be obtained.
*Reference: Carter, R.L. 1986. CDG N/L. No.81. p.16.*

### LONG DALE SWALLETS
NGR 128649, 128658, 129643, & 131654  Digs
Alt. 1050 - 1100ft (320 - 335m)

A series of small inactive swallets in the floor of Long Dale
The first listed occasionally takes water from a dew pond. Little hope of extension as mineshafts nearby give no encouragement.

### LOVERS LEAP CAVE
NGR 1448 5182   Grade: 1
Alt. 500ft (150m)
Length: 10ft (3m)
Status: National Trust. S.S.S.I.

Just above river level below Lovers Leap.
A small resurgence cave, blocked at the end with calcite.
*Reference: Potts, J. 1976. D.C.A. N/L No.27. p.6.*

### LUDWELL SPRING
NGR 124 625   Dig
Alt. 750ft (229m)

Water supply. Permission must be sought before interfering with the spring.
A large resurgence below the road.
Water issues from an impenetrable slot. A short mine level is nearby, with good flowstone.

### META RIFT
NGR 136 616   Grade: 1
Alt. 975ft (297m)
Length: 20ft (6m)

At the foot of one of the larger scars on the west side of Long Dale.
A narrow rift cave about 20ft (6m) long and 14ft (4m) high.
*Reference: Phipps, M. 1974. O.C.C. N/L Vol.10. No.3. pp.20,22,23. Survey.*

### MILLDALE CAVE
NGR 134 547  Grade: 1
Alt. 950ft (290m)
Length: 6ft (2m)

Situated below a small rock face 330ft (100m) above the road on the south side of the dale.
The key-hole entrance leads into a small chamber. A squeeze on the left leads to a second smaller entrance.
*Reference: Brooks. S, 2001, OCC N/L, Vol.37, No. 7/8/9.*

### MILLDALE SPRINGS
NGR 141 541  Springs
Alt. 525ft (160m)
Status: National Trust. S.S.S.I.

Both banks of the River Dove from 141 543 down to Doveholes. A group of resurgences from both banks, responsible for a large part of the river's flow below Milldale.

### NAB DALE FISSURE
NGR 1470 5350  Grade: 1
Alt. 820ft (250m)
Length: 26ft (8m)
Status: National Trust. S.S.S.I.

2300ft (700m) up Nab Dale, where the dale becomes narrower and swings to the North-North-East between two ribs of rock. To the west of the footpath two rock shelters can be seen, from these a faint path to the South-West along a grassy terrace reaches the cave after 100ft (30m).
A 20ft (6m) high slip-feature on a calcite vein can be followed for 7.4m.
*Reference: 2001, OCC N/L Vol.37, No.7-8-9, p.38.*

### NASH RISING
NGR 144 527  Dig / dive
Alt. 495ft (151m)
Length: 10ft (3m)

A small cave on a joint issues a small stream. Has been dug inconclusively to 3ft (1m) depth.
*Reference: Peak District Sump Index update 1997. p.17.*

### OWL HOLE
(Dove Pit)
NGR 0710 6830  Grade: 1
Alt. 1225ft (373m)
Length: 850ft (259m)
Depth: 136ft (41.4m)
Status:  R.I.G.S. (Dowel Dale)

No prior access permission needed, but park on the unfenced grass area downhill from the pot (don't block the gate). Walk to the uphill end and go through a narrow gap in the fence adjacent to the wall. Cross the rough area, and climb over a stile in the far corner.
Prior to 1993 the shakehole had become filled with rubbish, but was emptied by the National Park Authority. The cave was discovered after digging by O.C.C. in the late 1990s.
By the road at the top of Dowel Dale.

One of Derbyshire's largest natural open potholes. Ringed by large sycamore trees along its northern fringe the 82ft (25m) by 45ft (13m) pot is 40ft (12m) deep, and can be easily descended by a short scramble and walking down a rubble slope from the southern side. Five passages lead off the north end of the pot and are described from left (west) to right (east).

1) Small draughting rift at floor level can be penetrated for 16ft (5m) before becoming tight. Voice connection to Crystal Pallas Extension.

2) Crystal Pallas Extension - Reached by a slippery 23ft (7m) climb (bolt ladder in place - 65ft (20m) rope or 25ft (8m) electron ladder required). 3ft (1m) x 5ft (1.5m) entrance on a ledge leads to a rift passage 50ft (15m) long that reduces in size until a well decorated chamber is reached. Ahead the chamber becomes a bedding passage and continues for 60ft (18m) to reach an aven chamber (Hoggmorton Aven). A low crawl beyond become too tight after 23ft (7m). Take care of formations in this section of the cave. Left from chamber a hole down leads to a short passage that opens onto a balcony overlooking 50ft (15m) x 33ft (10m) Crystal Pallas Chamber. A 16ft (5m) pitch descends

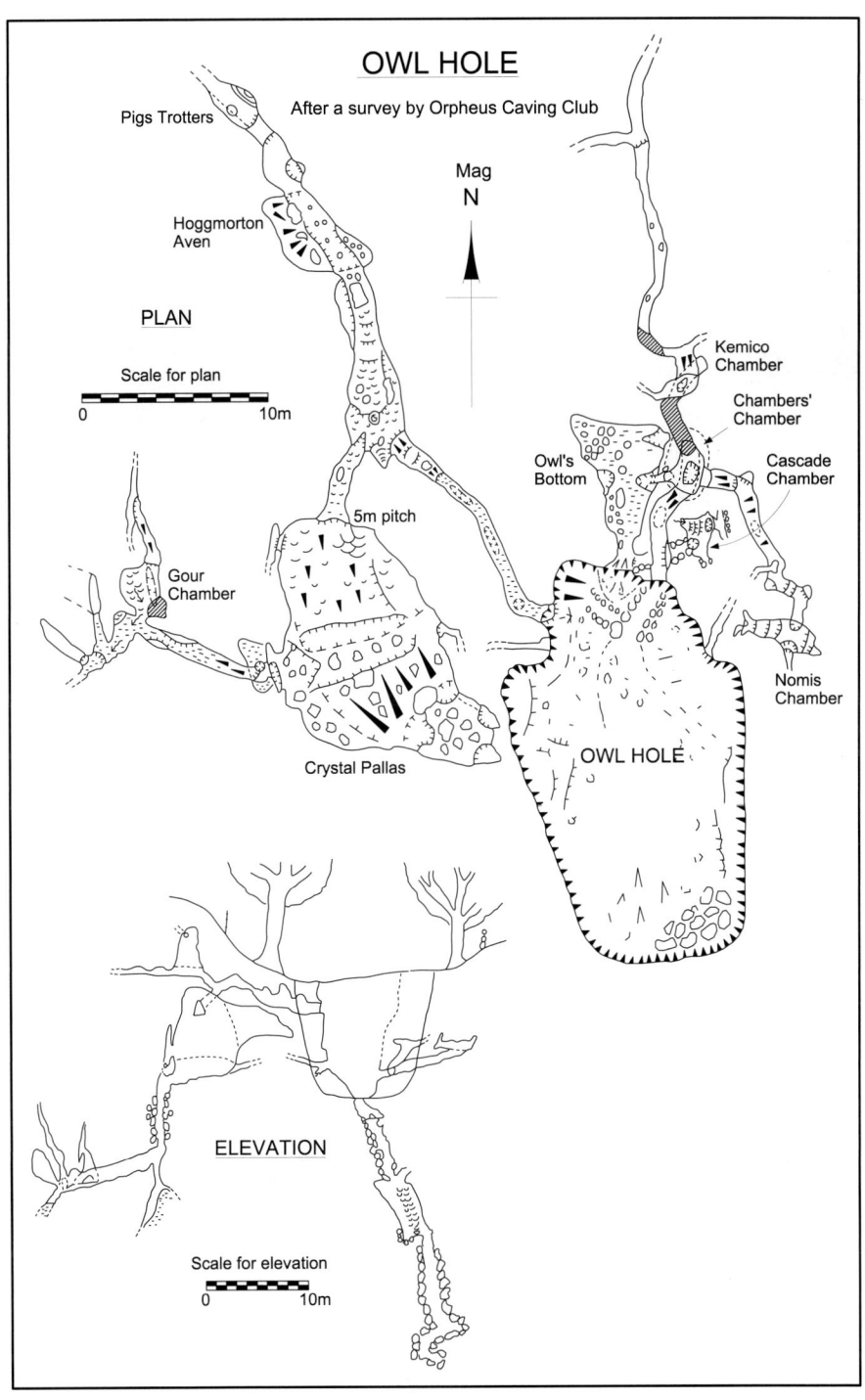

Crystal Pallas. Photo by Simon Brooks.

into the well-decorated chamber. To the south the chamber ascends to a higher section before closing at which point it is less than 7ft (2m) from the side of the Owl Hole Pot. From the lowest point of Crystal Pallas Chamber a rift descends for 26ft (8m) to reach a horizontal passage. A further tight hole down leads to a chamber largely filled by a large silt bank. The horizontal passage leads to the pretty Gour Chamber and a series of rifts. In wet weather water enters via a small aven in Gour Chamber and sinks in a mud choke further down the passage.

3) Owl's Bottom and Cascade Chamber - An obvious hole in the base of Owl's Hole at its northern end leads to a 30ft (9m) long bedding chamber with what could be miners hand written inscriptions (names) in pockets in the roof. Just inside the chamber is the Cascade Chamber Extension. A descent through scaffolded boulders reaches a rift chamber that has a 23ft (7m) high calcite cascade down the north wall (Cascade Chamber). From here it is possible to descend a further 50ft (15m) though scaffolded boulders to the deepest point in the cave some 100ft (30m) below the base of Owl Hole. Care should be taken in this section of the cave as it is still being dug and is still settling.

**Tackle:**
**Climb down to Cascade Chamber: 10m handline. Belay to scaffold bar.**
**Climb up to Crystal Pallas: Bolt ladder in place. 8m ladder + 20m lifeline.**
**Pitch down to Crystal Pallas: 5m tether to belay to bolt and calcite boss. 8m ladder + 15m lifeline.**

4) Orpheus (Three Chambers Extension) - A small 2.5ft (0.8m) x 4ft (1.2m) arched passage leads after 20ft (6m) to a small chamber (Chamber's Chamber) with a false floor. To the right a small ascending tube turns left and reaches another small decorated chamber (Nomis Chamber) after a further 40ft (12m). Ahead from Chamber's Chamber the passage continues for a further 33ft (10m) before a climb up through a hole in a false floor leads to the small and decorated Kemico Chamber. From here a short 7ft (2m) climb up flowstone reaches a further 65ft (20m) of very low and well-decorated passage that eventually becomes to tight. Progress beyond Kemico Chamber should be avoided to preserve the fragile formations in this part of the cave.

5) Burnt Tube - on a ledge 7ft (2m) up the east wall of Owl Hole is a small blackened tube that is 8ft (2.5m) long and has an audible connection to the passage that leads to Nomis Chamber.

*References: Brooks, S. and others. OCC N/L Vol.40 No.7-9. pp.37-43. Survey.*
*Smith, P. 1959. The Lyre No.3. pp.60-67.*

Hoggmorton Aven.
Photo by Simon Brooks

**PARSLEY HAY CAVE**
**NGR 137 629  Grade: 1**
**Alt. 1000ft (305m)**
**Length: 20ft (6m)**

In Long Dale in disused quarry south of Vincent House. Entrance high up in quarry.

12ft (4m) crawl then very tight into small chamber. No way on. Only to be attempted by thin men.

**PEASLAND ROCK SHELTER**
(Iron Tors Cave)
**NGR 1434 5689  Grade: 1**
**Alt. 650ft (198m)**
Status: National Trust. S.S.S.I.

On the east bank of the River Dove, 15ft (4.5m) above the path, opposite Peasland Rocks, a few hundred yards downstream from Biggin Dale.

A large cave entrance which is little more than a rock shelter with a small blocked tube at the end.

### PICKERING TOR CAVE
NGR 1424 5312
Grade: 1
Alt. 550ft (168m)
National Trust. S.S.S.I.

Opposite Ilam Rock, 100ft (30m) up Pickering Dale.
A small cave.

### PIKERS PIT
NGR 068 685   Grade: Dig
Alt. 1225ft (373m)

525ft (160m) west of Greensides Farm.
A large collapsed swallet. Boulder ruckle penetrable for only a few feet. Water resurges at Dowel Resurgence.
*Reference: Smith, P. 1959. The Lyre No.3. p.62.*

### PILSBURY ROCK SHELTER
NGR 113 643   Grade: 1
Alt. c.1000ft (c.300m)

Well above the Crowdecote to Pilsbury bridle path.
Difficult to find, close to a small tree. A rocky shelter. It might be extended by excavating among loose blocks.

### PIT HOLE
NGR 098 664   Grade: 1
Alt. 1000ft (305m)

In south corner of quarry.
A choked tube. A grating in the road nearby covers a natural fissure.
*Reference: Smith, P. 1959. The Lyre No.3. pp.60-61.*

### PLACENTA POT
NGR 1435 6250   Grade: 2
Alt. 985ft (300m) approx
Depth: 85ft (26m)

Dug by O.C.C. to its present depth.
Approx. 1000ft (300m) south of the Orpheus C.C.cottage.
A hading shaft on a mineral vein, modified by mining.
*References: Brooks, S. 1997. O.C.C. N/L Vol 33 No.8/9 pp.35 & 38-9. Survey.*

### PLANTATION SWALLET
(Rakes Wood Swallet)
NGR 1195 5600
Grade: 5. Dig
Alt. 900ft (274m)
Length: 272ft (83m)
Depth: 180ft (55m)

Dug over a period of years to a depth of 40ft (12m) by Birmingham Cave and Crag Club and O.C.C. Dug by Eldon Pothole Club to reach a depth of 180ft (55m) through a lethal boulder choke. Reopened 2007 by Darfar P.C.
Situated in the centre of Rakes Wood Plantation.
A large swallet taking several streams in wet weather. Resurgence is not known. 16ft (5m) entrance shaft, (metal lid over, please replace), leads to a 10ft (3m) climb down, (found blocked in 2007 and subsequently re-opened), into a sloping passage. Downslope on the left after 12ft (4m) is a short drop into the Main Chamber, some 35ft (11m) long, up to 10ft (3m) wide and 10ft (3m) high. The stream enters in the right-hand (highest) corner. Just before the lowest part of the chamber, off to the right is a short drop and crawl to the head of a 20ft (6m) pitch (tight at the top). At the bottom of this is an enlargement under dangerous boulders with two solid walls. Against one of these walls a tightish descent can be made into the boulder choke proper, where some proper shoring is needed. The final stream sink is a steeply descending muddy passage which is very difficult to reverse, and where the air quickly becomes stale.

*Tackle:*
*5m ladder advisable on entrance shaft.*
*References: Bentham, K. 1987. BCRA Caves and Caving No.38. p.2.*
*Milner M. 2007. The Derbyshire Caver (D.C.A.) No. 126.*

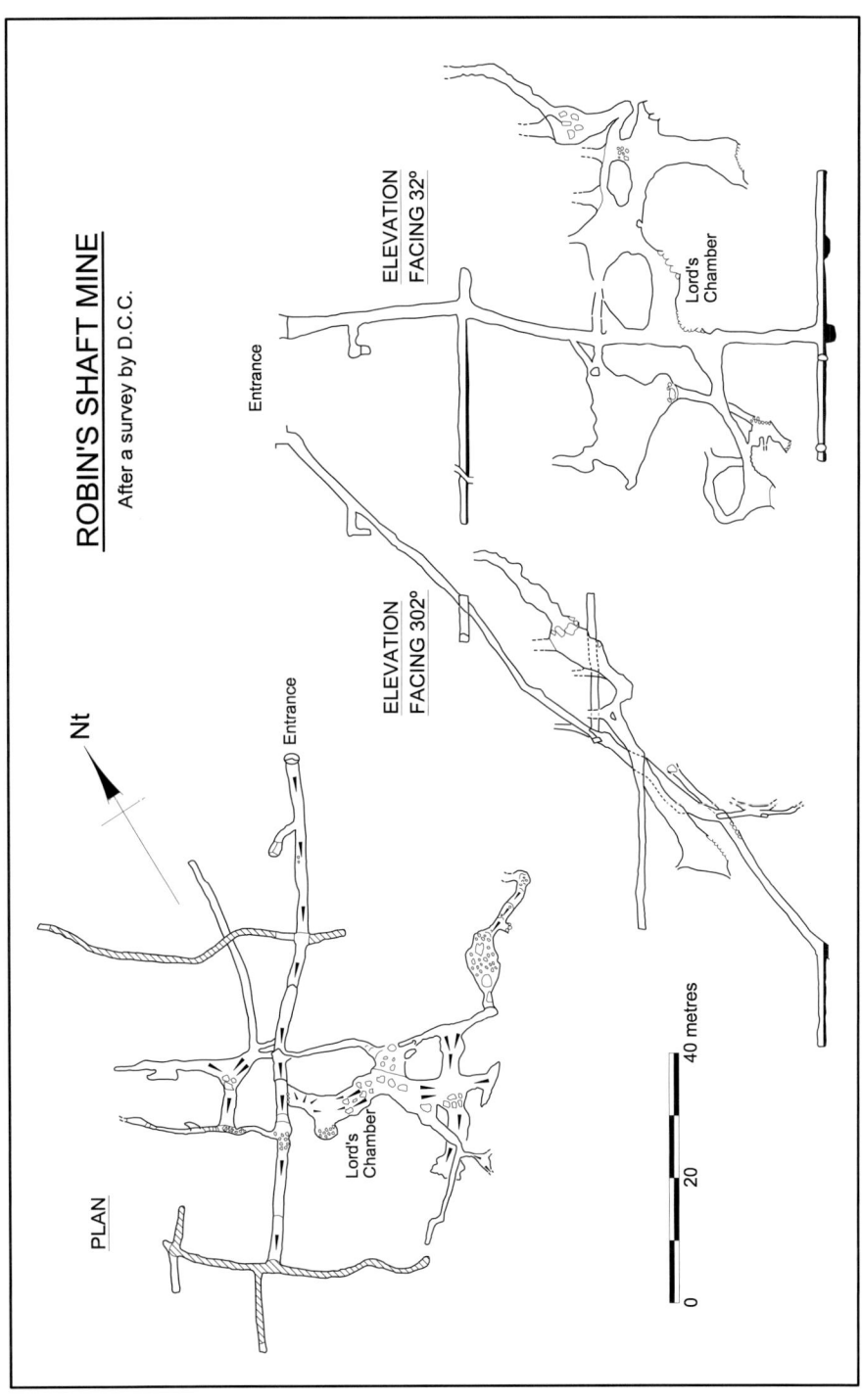

### POP CONCERT SWALLETS
NGR 056 689
Alt. 1330ft (405m)

South west of High Edge Raceway, 500ft (150m) south of the road.

A line of six swallets/shake holes (the furthest filled with farm refuse). Could be promising digs.

*Reference: 1996. O.C.C. N/L Vol.32, No.3, pp21 & 25*

### REYNARD'S CAVE
NGR 1452 5252
Grade: 1. (Arch)
Alt. 360ft (110m)
Length: 40ft (12m)
Status: National Trust. S.S.S.I.

High on the east side of Dovedale. Between Bostern Grange and Sharplow Dale.

A natural arch and cave. Two smaller caves behind. The larger is Reynard's Cave, the other Reynard's Kitchen (qv). Archaeologically excavated.

*Reference: Adam, W. 1838. Gem of the Peak. 1973 reprint by Moorland Publishing, Hartington. pp.215-216.*

### REYNARD'S KITCHEN
NGR 1452 5252    Grade: 1
Alt. 370ft (113m)
Status: National Trust. S.S.S.I.

High on the east side of Dovedale, above and behind the large natural arch.

A small cave with a short climb in the roof.

### ROBIN'S SHAFT MINE
NGR 1355 5276    Grade: 3
Alt. 1075 (328m)
Depth: 320ft (97m)

Permission from Hill Top Farm. Small fee.

Close to Hill Top Farm, Ilamtops Low.

**Warning: There have been instances of a $CO_2$ build-up in the lower parts of the mine.**

Large mine shaft inclined at between 45 and 60 degrees. A short level is passed after 60ft (20m), with two further blind levels at 145ft (44m). Between 260ft (79m) and 295ft (90m) are various entrances to a system of impressive part-natural phreatic chambers and passages up to 60ft high, roughly inclined down from east to west. Several high avens have been climbed to a height of approximately 150ft (46m). There are possible digs in the floor at the lowest points. The main shaft continues down to 400ft (122m) (300ft/91m depth) to end in partly flooded mine workings.

**Tackle:** 100m rope. Belay to multiple fence post supports with deviation to wooden beam. Rebelays to eco hangers.

*References: Boardman, P. 1982. B.C.R.A. Caves and Caving No.16. pp.2-4. Survey.*
*Darroch, C. 1981. Descent No.48. pp.16-17.*
*Darroch, C. 1981. D.C.A. N/L No.47. pp.2-3.*

### SANDHOLES SWALLET
NGR 071 675    Dig
Alt. 1200ft (366m)
Depth: 30ft (9m)

1000 yards (914m) west of Dowell Farm under the north face of Chrome Hill.

A dig in a choked swallet has been pushed to a depth of 30ft (9m) in very unstable ground. Water reappears at Dowell Resurgence.

*References: Phipps, M. 1981. The Lyre No.5. p.4.*
*Smith, P. 1960. Lyre No.3. pp.63 & 65.*

### SPARKLOW SWALLET
(Waggon Low Swallet)
NGR 131 654    Dig
Alt. c.1150ft (350m)

Permission from Cronkston Grange Farm.

Ambitiously excavated in 1992/3 to narrow fissures.

In small blind valley adjacent to a wall.

A swallet blocked by easily removable boulders. Emits a draught in cold weather.

### STONEY LOW HOLE
(Tor Rock Cave)
NGR 070 679   Grade: 1
Alt. 1325ft (404m)
Length: 50ft (15m)
Depth: 25ft (8m)

A fissure in a scarp.
Fissure leads to tight 25ft (8m) pitch. A constricted dig is possible at the bottom.
*References: Smith, P. 1960. The Lyre No.3. p.63.*
*Phipps, M. 1981. The Lyre No.5. p.4.*

### STONEY LOW SWALLET
NGR 069 682   Dig
Alt. 1275ft (389m)

A swallet which has been unsuccessfully dug. Dye took 44 hours to reach Dowel Resurgence only 1000 yards (914m) away and 325ft (99m) lower.
*Reference: Smith, P. 1960. The Lyre No.3. pp.63-64.*

### STOOP EDGE HOLE
NGR 061 685   Grade: 2
Alt. 1425ft (434m)
Depth: 50ft (15m)

A tight fissure dug in 1957.
50ft (15m) deep. No ladder required.
*Reference: Smith, P. 1960. The Lyre No.3. p.62. Sketch survey.*

### SUNNYBANK POT
NGR 132 552   Grade: 2
Alt. 800ft (244m)
Length: 150ft (46m)
Depth: 20ft (6m)

Vertical entrance under a small tree.
A 20ft (6m) pitch leads to a very narrow rift where progress can only be made by traversing halfway up.

### SWALLOWDALE SINK
NGR 063 680   Grade: 2
Alt. 1150ft (350m)
Length: 115ft (35m)
Depth: 40ft (12m)

A letter box entrance below Stoop Farm.
Slit entrance leads to a narrow passage where a small hole can be descended in the floor to a tiny chamber. A squeeze enters a short length of stream passage ending at a silted sump. A 10ft (3m) climb leads via an awkward vertical tube to a chamber close to the surface.
*References: Smith, P. 1959. The Lyre Vol.1. No.3. p.61.*
*Phipps, M. 1981. The Lyre No.5. p.5. Survey.*

### SWALLOW TOR CAVE
NGR 065 678   Arch
Alt. 1000ft (305m)

A small cave excavated archaeologically.
*Reference: Smith, P. 1960. The Lyre No.3. p.61.*

### THORSWOOD SWALLET
NGR 117 473   Dig
Alt. 960ft (293m)

In a hollow on the north side of the road near Thorswood House.
A choked sink taking a small stream.

### TOR ROCK SWALLET
NGR 064 679   Grade: 1
Alt. 1250ft (381m)

South of Stoop Farm, a few hundred feet above and to the east of Swallow Brook.
A small stream sinks down a very low bedding plane. Has been pushed by Eldon P.C., but too narrow for further progress. Resurges a few hundred feet lower down in valley floor.

### TREE STUMP POT
NGR 093 664  Grade: 1 (Dig)
Alt. 285ft (300m)
Length: 40ft (12m)
Depth: 13ft (4m)

Originally explored by the Orpheus Caving Club.
On the crest of the ridge.
A fissure pot with two small phreatic tubes connecting from lower down the hillside.

### TYRE PIT QUARRY CAVE 1
NGR 1499 6059   Dig
Alt. 1100ft (335m)
Length: 80ft (24m)

See also Friday Night Dig and Double Trouble.
A small vadose passage becomes a crawl over clay for 50ft (15m) to a small chamber. Becomes too tight 20ft (6m) further.
*Reference: Allwright, P. 1972. O.C.C. N/L Vol.8. No.5. pp.1-2. Survey.*

### TYRE PIT QUARRY CAVE 2
NGR 1502 6061          Dig
Alt. 1115ft (340m)
Length: 8ft (2.5m)

40ft (12m) along and 15ft (4.5m) up the face from cave no.1.
A small cave only 8ft (2.5m) long developed on a small calcite vein.

### UPPER HALL DALE CAVE
NGR 132 539  Grade: 1
Length: 16ft (5m)
Status: National Trust. S.S.S.I.

In the upper part of Hall Dale, on the north side, at the base of a small cliff just before second stone stile on footpath.
Cave entrance 2ft (0.6m) x 3 ft (1m) high. After 8ft (2.5m) a small aven connects with surface. Extends for another 8ft (2.5m).
*Reference: Brooks. S, 2005, OCC N/L. Vol.41. No. 10. p. 43.*

### WAGGON LOW FISSURE
NGR 114 649   Dig
Alt. 1150ft (350m)

At the back of a small quarry.
A fissure choked with rocks.

### WATSON'S SWALLET
NGR 065 678   Grade: 2
Alt. 1065ft (325m) approx.
Depth: 75ft (23m)

Dug in the 1990s by M.Bennett, B.Major, R.Westwood, A.Wilson.
On Tor Rock, south of Stoop Farm.
Entrance pitch 4 oil drums deep (14ft/4.4m) continues through a squeeze into a chamber for another 13ft (4m). Crawl at floor level into a rift with small inlets in roof. Down slope to short free-climbable pitch (6ft/2m). A squeeze leads to a further short drop into a small chamber. The entrance drums are believed to have collapsed.

### WOLFSCOTE GRANGE CAVE
NGR 131 584          Digs
Alt. 725ft (221m)

South of the footbridge, opposite Frank I'th Rocks Cave.
Small blocked cave entrances.

## Features listed as potential archaeological sites

1: NGR 1450 5253 Alt: 183m. A wide cave mouth near Reynard's Cave, closing down to a single tube going back for 10m.
2: NGR 1452 5254 Alt: 176m. A long open fissure near Reynard's Cave..
3: NGR 1450 5252 Alt: 157m. A low entrance into a chamber. A phreatic tube continues for over 30m.
4: NGR 1426 5299 Alt: 140m. An obvious entrance at the top of an eroding bank.
5: NGR 1427 5301 Alt: 140m. An obvious fissure 5m from the path.
6: NGR 1417 5310 Alt: 221m. A shallow rock shelter on a detached rock up past Ilam Rock.
7: NGR 1420 5309 Alt: 148m. A tall open cave in a crag next to Ilam Rock.
8: NGR 1422 5308 Alt: 148m. A wide fissure coming to a stop after 1.90m.
9: NGR 1412 5346 Alt: 143m. An open rock shelter near the path.
10: NGR 1460 5216 Alt: 150m A single chamber cave at Tissington Spires.
11: NGR 1424 5362 Alt: 157m. A small rock shelter near the Dove Holes.
12: NGR 1436 5330 Alt: 199m. A single chamber opposite and visible from the Dove Holes.
13: NGR 1419 5360 Alt: 210m. A small rock shelter.
14: NGR 1423 5360 Alt: 215m A large shallow cavity.
15: NGR 1415 5358 Alt: 212m. A shallow cave.
16: NGR 0747 6757 Alt: 327m. A small cave near to Etches Cave. A single chamber with a low passage running off at the back.
17: NGR 1319 5836 Alt: 250m. A shallow cavity up a steep scramble.
18: NGR 1327 5815 Alt: 250m. A low rock shelter high on the dale side above the footpath.
19: NGR 0640 6790 Small cave next to track.
20: NGR 0663 6790 Alt: 391m. Square cut fissure with narrow passage at the back.

# THE GRITSTONE CAVES

Stanage Edge

The White Peak limestone outcrop is almost completely surrounded by escarpments of the overlying Namurian gritstones. There are no known solution caves in the gritstone: most of the drainage, apart from local percolation down joints, remains on the surface.

All the caves listed here are formed either by wind erosion along major joints, by the partial detachment of huge blocks from the scarp faces, or have been artificially excavated. Most provide a useful shelter for climbers and walkers from the harsh conditions that can prevail on the high gritstone moorlands.

# Gritstone Caves

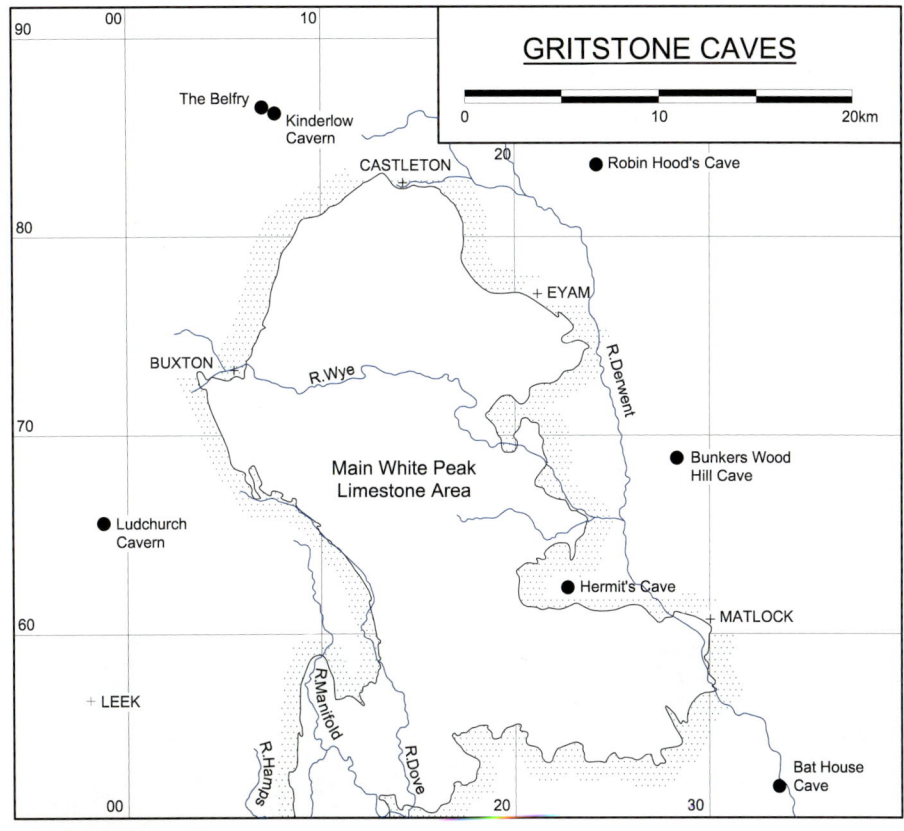

**BAT HOUSE CAVE**
NGR 335 523    Arch
Alt. 550ft (167m)

In Shining Cliff Woods, near Alderwasley.
A gritstone fissure which yielded a Roman brooch and pottery.
*References: Haverfield, F. 1905. Victoria County History of Derbyshire. p.236.*
*Ward, J. 1899. The Reliquary. Vol.V. S.*

**THE BELFRY**
NGR 072 866    Lost
Alt. 1800ft (549m)

On the south edge of Kinderlow, just below the edge.
A maze caused by the splitting off of gritstone blocks.

**BUNKERS HILL WOOD CAVE**
NGR 284 690    Arch
Alt. 1050ft (320m)

In the gritstone scarp south east of Chatsworth.
An archaeological cave in gritstone. Middle Bronze Age remains have been found.
*Reference: Radley, J. & Cooper, L. 1966. Derbys. Arch. Jour. Vol.86. pp.93-98. Survey.*

**HERMIT'S CAVE**
NGR 227 623   Grade: 1
Alt. 800ft (240m)

In Cratcliffe Tor, near Birchover.
A semi-artificial enlarged joint in gritstone. Formerly used by a hermit who carved a Crucifixion in the wall. Now used by climbers as a shelter.

### KINDERLOW CAVERN
NGR 072 867  Grade: 1
Alt. 1800ft (549m)

1/4 mile (0.4km) east of shooting hut near top of Oaken Clough on Kinderscout.

In gritstone. Entrance among tumbled blocks, difficult to find. A series of fissures in the gritstone.

### LUDCHURCH CAVERN
NGR SJ 987 657  Grade: 1
Alt. 1025ft (312m)

No known access restrictions.

In woods high above the River Dane, west of Gradbach. Accessible by footpath from Gradbach Mill (now a Youth Hostel).

A series of fissures in the gritstone up to 50ft (15m) deep, in places 10-13ft (3-4m) wide. Stone steps lead down from the footpath at each end of the main fissure. The sheer walls adorned with ferns and overhung with trees make this an impressive place.

### ROBIN HOOD'S CAVE
NGR 243 837  Grade: 1
Alt. 1350ft (411m)
Length: 50ft (15m)

In the gritstone scarp of Stanage Edge.

A series of wind eroded holes in the gritstone scarp. Used by climbers for camping. A number of other small caves lie on the same stretch of the Edge.

Robin Hood's Cave. Photo by John Beck

# THE HAMPS / MANIFOLD CATCHMENT AREA

The Manifold Valley at Thor's Cave

As in the case of the River Dove, the Rivers Manifold and Hamps accumulate on the Namurian Grits and Shales to the west. To the north of Wetton, adverse folding together with the shaly nature of the limestones keeps the Manifold on the surface. On reaching reef limestones at Wetton Mill, however, the river sinks underground, and during the summer months, the river bed is dry as far as the risings at Ilam. As water levels increase, the river migrates downstream, successively overpowering the various swallets. Thus for the majority of the year, the swallet caves in the river bed are inaccessible. The Wetton Mill sinks have been dye tested to the Main Rising at Ilam.

The river Hamps sinks in a similar manner at Waterhouses, and this water has been tested to the Hamps Spring and the Upper Rising, both near Ilam. The sinks along the limestone/shale boundary to the south west have been dye tested to the Hinkley Wood Risings, although there appeared to be a connection between these risings and the Upper Rising at Ilam.

The Wetton Mill - Ilam system is unlikely to be penetrable for great distances. The gradient is shallow, and the known caves are all terminated by sumps, although determined pushing in drought will undoubtedly reveal more open passage.

The Waterhouses - Ilam system is a rather better prospect. The straight line distance is roughly 4km (2.5 miles), and the fall is in the order of 70m (230ft). This gives a gradient of just under 100ft per mile, which suggests a significant length of vadose cave passage carrying the entire River Hamps. The intermediate Waterways Swallet was always regarded as a promising site, and significant discoveries have been made here.

The hydrology of the area is fascinating, and the reader is referred to the cited references for further information on the structural geology and geomorphology.

Included in this chapter is a small area of limestone which drains into the River Churnet. The stream found in the Ribden Mine probably drains to the Weaver Hills Rising, but this is not known to have been tested. Also included is the small area of limestone which drains south eastwards to the lower River Dove, where there are small sinks and risings about which little is known.

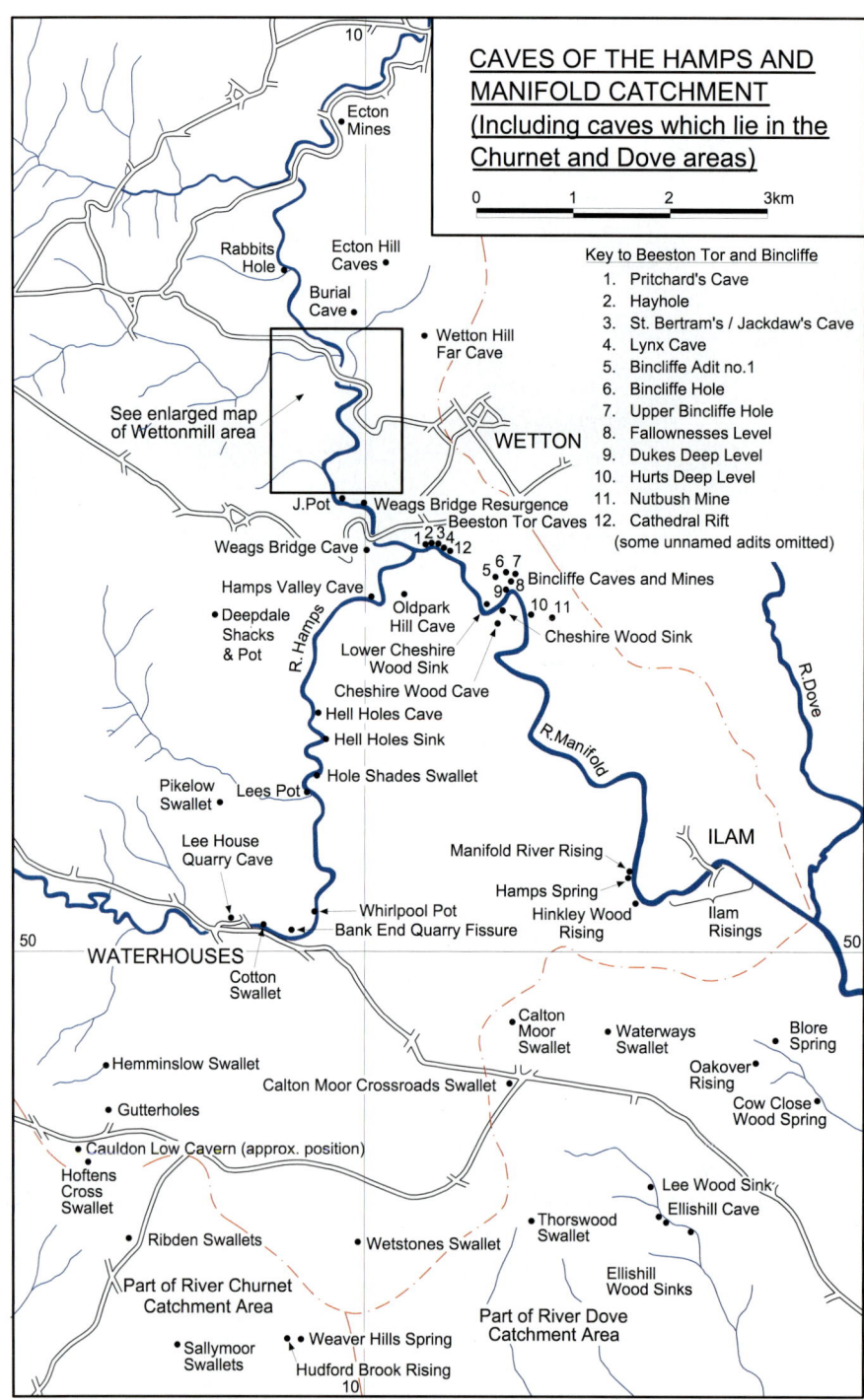

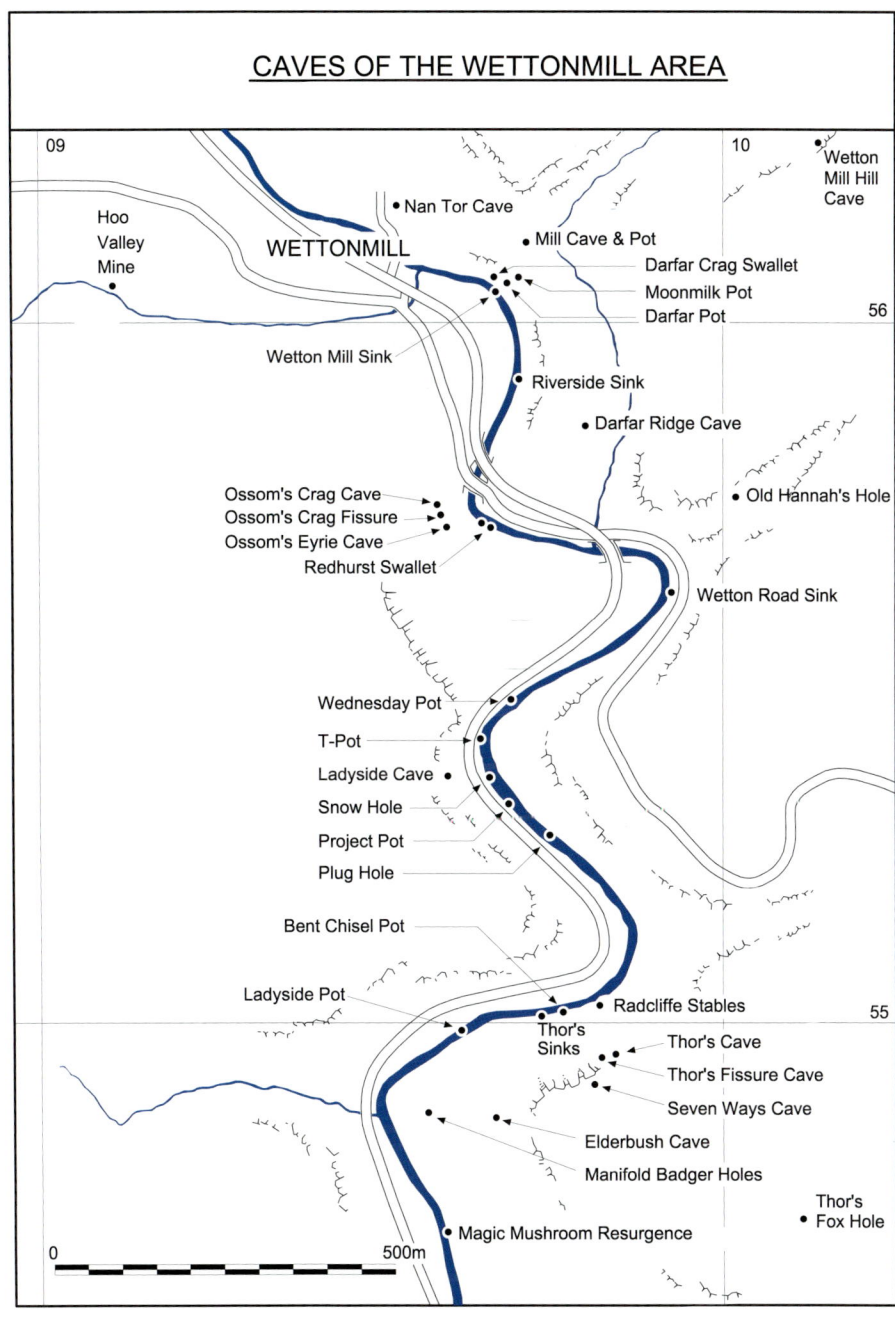

### BANK END QUARRY FISSURE
**NGR approx. 092 502  Lost**

Now largely quarried away.
*Reference: Brown, E. 1865. Trans. Midland Scientific Association. pp.34-38.*

### BEESTON CAVE
**NGR 1069 5405    Grade: 1**
**Alt. 750ft (233m)**
**Length: 50ft (16m)**
**Status: National Trust. S.S.S.I.**

Difficult to find in the undergrowth, especially during the summer months.
Series of tight interconnecting rift passages gradually getting too tight.
*References: Milner, M. 2005. A Cave and Mine Conservation Audit for the Manifold and Hamps Valleys. p24.*

### BENT CHISEL POT
**NGR 0977 5498    Dig**
**Alt. 560ft (171m)**
**Depth: 10ft (3m)**

100ft (30m) downstream of Radcliffe Stables on the same side of the river at the foot of a small crag.
Filter gate on entrance. Please replace. Originally a thick concrete plug, a 1.5ft (0.3m) hole was made in this and a rift excavated for about 10ft (3m). Acts as a sink or resurgence when river is flowing.
*References: Milner, M. 1985. D.C.A. N/L No.60. p.9.*
*Milner, M. 1984. The Manifold Caver. p.32.*

### BINCLIFFE HOLE
**NGR 114 538 Grade: 1**
**Alt. 900ft (274m)**
**Length: 25ft (8m)**

In topmost outcrop above Bincliffe Mine Levels..
A badger lair. Flat out crawling as far as possible (about 25ft/8m).

### BINCLIFFE LEVELS
**Grade: 2 (Mines)**
**Alt. 550 - 1000ft (167 - 305m)**

A group of eleven adits (two blocked) mostly well hidden in thick scrub vegetation on a steep hillside.

Adit 1:
NGR 11303 53786  Length: 357ft (109m)
Adit 2: Fallownesses Level, Fallows Level
NGR 11480 53756  Length: 1425ft (434m)

Adit 3: Dukes Deep Level.
NGR 11464 53628  Length: 1300ft (396m)
Adit 4:
NGR 11571 53754  Length: 300ft (91m)
Adit 5:
NGR 11574 53811  Length: 105ft (32m)

Adit 6:
NGR 11594 53573  Length: 18ft (5.5m)
Adit 7: Hurts Deep Level.
NGR 11630 53382   Length: 1099ft (335m)
Adit 8:
NGR 11548 53807  Length: 108ft (33m)
Adit 9: Nutbush Mine.
NGR 11833 53385  Length: 216ft (66m)
Adit 10:
NGR 11535 53804  Length: 10ft (3m)
Adit 11:
NGR 11525 53814  Length: 52ft (16m)

Two entrances are close to river level and lead to long adits. The third long adit is high in the hillside between two miners' coes. Most of the adits are easy walking and some lead into natural solution cavities. Some penetrate old stempled workings with dangerously unstable stacked deads, and some go under choked shafts on the hilltop. Several of the levels contain good cave pearls, which should not be trodden on!
*References: Pedrick, P.D. and Chapman, C.J. 1974. Bull. P.D.M.H.S. Vol.5. No.5. Survey.*

### BINCLIFFE MINE, UPPER
NGR 115 538
Grade: 3 (Mine)
Alt. 975ft (292m)

The most northerly of three shafts near a sycamore tree.
A 40ft (12m) pitch with a chamber 25ft (7.5m) down containing large dog tooth spar. A further descent of 15ft (5m) to a scree heap with passages running north and south leading to several parallel passages with cave pearls and stalactites. Several short drops need care, and unstable deads require considerable caution.

### BREDON BROOK SINKS
NGR 085 515    Digs
Alt. 700ft (213m)

Stream was positively dye tested to Ilam in June 1990.
Brook loses water in its bed at a number of points between Back o' th' Brook and its confluence with the River Hamps near Lee House. In prolonged dry weather the bed progressively dries up as far as a point roughly one third of a mile (0.5km) below the ford at Back o' th' Brook.
*References: Harvey, F.A. 1977. Waterfall of Yesterday. p.40.*
*Milner, M. 1984. The Manifold Caver. p.6.*
*Mellors, P.T. 1989. D.C.A. N/L No.71. p.3.*

### BURIAL CAVE
NGR 0988 5643    Grade 1
Length: 13ft (4m)
Status: National Trust. S.S.S.I.

At the top of the gully containing Darfar Pot top entrance and Moonmilk Pot.
A small cave in which human remains were found by cavers in the 1980's.

### CALTON MOOR CROSSROADS SWALLET
NGR 116 487    Dig
Alt. 1000ft (305m)

Small swallet near crossroads. Poor possibilities.
*Reference: Beasley, F. 1975. D.C.A. Newsletter No.24.pp.2-4*

### CALTON MOOR SWALLET
NGR 115 493    Dig
Alt. 1035ft (315m)
Length: 12ft (4m)

Dug out by D.S.G.
A dig in an inclined bedding passage. Possibilities are poor. Rising unknown.
*References: Beasley, F. 1975. D.C.A. N/L No.24.*

### CATHEDRAL RIFT
NGR 1069 5404
Grade: 1(Arch)
Alt. 750ft (233m)
Length: 105ft (32m)
Status: National Trust. S.S.S.I.

Difficult to find in the undergrowth, especially during the summer months.
Large rift passage similar to Old Hannah's Hole. Progress needs to be made at varying levels in the rift, which eventually becomes too small. Bones and a decaying trowel are among the evidence of past archaeological attention by persons unkown.
*References: Milner. M. 2005. A Cave and Mine Conservation Audit for the Manifold and Hamps Valleys. p.24.*

### CAULDON LOW CAVE
**NGR 07 48**
Lost

Exact position not known.
Bone cave now completely quarried away.
*Reference: Trans. North. Staffs. Field Club Vol.XL p.85. & Vol.XLI p.92.*

### CHESHIRE WOOD CAVE
See also Lower Cheshire Wood Cave
**NGR 1132 5330    Grade: 1**
**Alt. 800ft (240m)**
**Length: 40ft (12m)**
**Depth: 18ft (5.5m)**

Situated some 800m below Beeston Tor and above wooded area in a small crag just below upper edge of valley.

An impressive entrance 21ft (6.5m) wide by 13ft (4m) high narrows to reach a point where the passage divides. To left the cave closes in a tight tube after 7ft (2m). To right a 5ft (1.5m) climb up through a body sized hole leads to a bedding chamber 8ft (2.5m) dia that contains some white flowstone and stalagtites and closes in a narrow tube after another 13ft (4m). There are limited prospects for further extension.
*Reference: North Staffs. Field Club Journal, Vol.4. 1964.*

### COTTON SWALLET
**NGR 089 502    Lost**
**Alt. 690ft (210m)**
**Length: 25ft (8m)**

In bed of River Hamps, 450ft (140m) below the bridge.
Had a solid rock roof and ran south under river and road. Ended in a choke. Sink has been dye-tested to Hamps Spring and Ilam Upper Rising.
*Reference: Clark, 1917. Trans. North Staffs. Field Club Vol. 52. pp.25-33.*

### DARFAR CRAG CAVE
(Darfar Badger Caves)
**NGR 0971 5590  Grade: 1 (Digs)**
**Alt. 750ft (229m)**
**Length: 100ft (31m)**
**Depth: 10ft (3m)**
Status: National Trust. S.S.S.I.

Entered in 1987.
Several badger holes (in use) in the trees halfway along the ridge.
Left hand (northerly) entrance leads to short descending phreatic passage. Immediately inside on the right a small muddy passage can be followed via several small muddy chambers to second entrance. Shaft in floor here descends for 10ft (3m) to natural fill blockage.

### DARFAR CRAG SWALLET
**NGR 0967 5607 Grade: 2 (Dig)**
**Alt. 625ft (191m)**
**Length: 130ft (40m)**
**Depth: 30ft (9m)**
Status: National Trust. S.S.S.I.

Lower sections flood prone with water rising from below.
Large sloping entrance shaft 25ft (8m) deep leads to choke (dig). On right a way may be open to a continuation passage via a crawl. Right leads to narrow rifts approaching the river, left leads for 40ft (12m) to a mud choke, passing a dig on the right which draughts, and is less than 30ft (9m) from the end of the Wind Tunnel in Darfar Pot. Entrance now gated and needs an adjustable spanner to open.

**Tackle:**
**Entrance shaft: 8m ladder. Short belay. 20m lifeline.**
*References: Milner, M. 1984. D.C.A. N/L No.56, p.13.*
*Milner, M. 1984. The Manifold Caver pp. 13-14. Survey.*

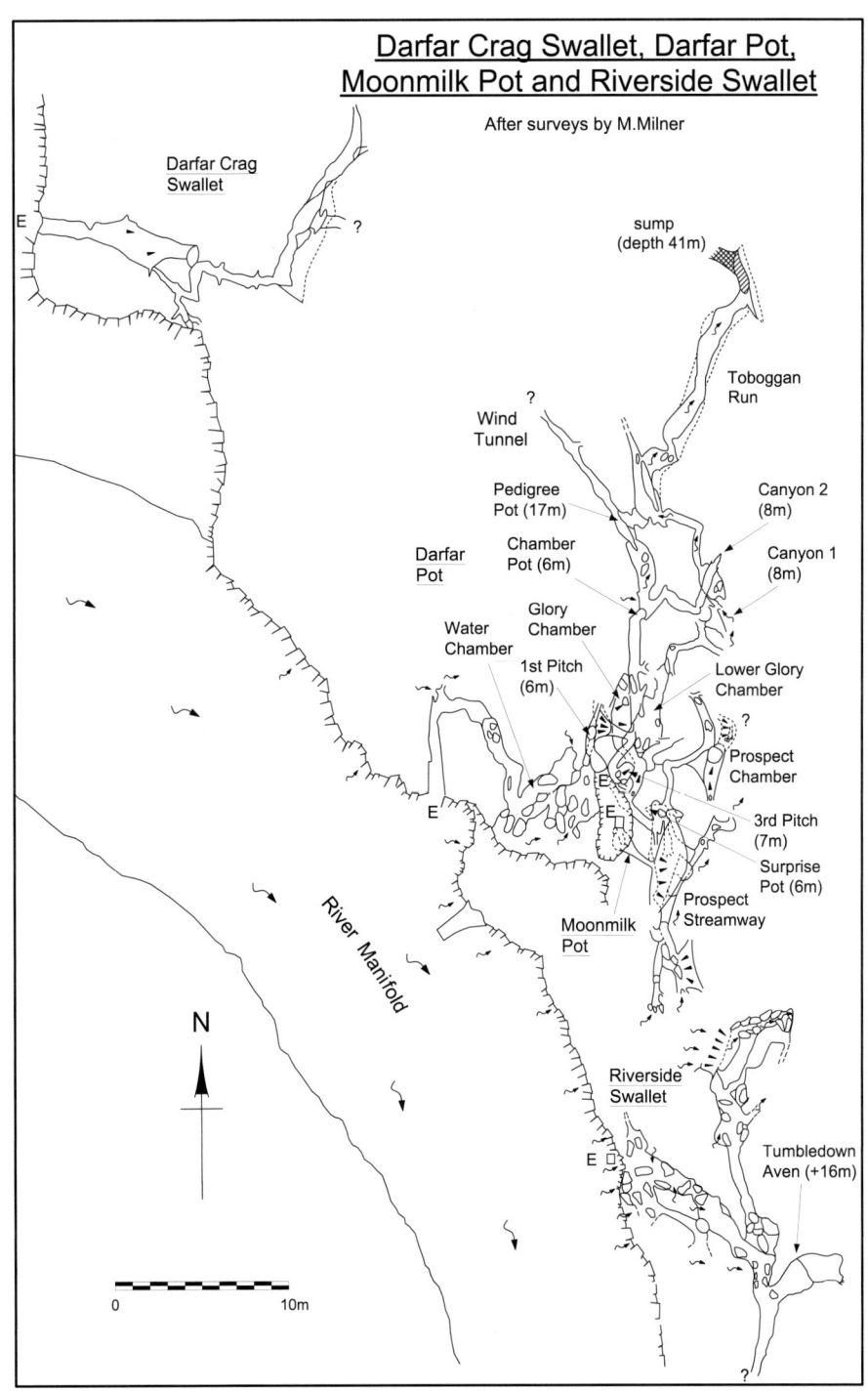

## DARFAR POT

**Grade: 4  Stream sink**
NGR 0968 5604
Alt: 610ft (186m)
**Top entrance (Spider Cave)**
NGR 0972 5603
Alt: 635ft (194m)
Length: 1200ft (366m)
Depth: 175ft (53m)

Status: National Trust. S.S.S.I.

Discovered in 1979 by Trent Valley Caving Group. Extended by same in 1980 and 1983. The top entrance was linked to main cave in 1996 by members of Darfar P.C.

**Warning: The cave is very flood prone, and is the first cave to be affected if the river floods. Only descend below Glory Chamber in settled conditions. The sump backs up to river level (ie. fills the cave to the foot of the 1st top entrance pitch) and does so very quickly.**

Original entrance is in cliff face at river level in the upstream corner of Wetton Mill Main Sink, filter gate on entrance. Top entrance is 23ft (7m) above river in gully a few metres downstream, behind the entrance shaft of Moonmilk Pot. This should be used in preference to the river entrance as it is much safer in the event of the river flooding. (And doesn't need unblocking every summer.)

The top entrance route consists of three pitches. The first, just inside the entrance is 25ft (8m) deep, the second one is about 15ft (5m) deep and broken by ledges, with the third following immediately and around 20ft (7m) deep (eyebolt belay) directly into Glory Chamber.

Just before the top of the third pitch, a new passage on the right was opened up in 2007 by members of Darfar P.C. revealing many new passages heading back towards the river. A 6ft (2m) climb down leads immediately on the left to a bypass to the third pitch, (entering Glory Chamber near the eyehole into Prospect Chamber), while straight on is a sloping passage leading to Glazebrooke Junction where there are 3 ways on.

Straight on leads to Prospect Chamber by-passing the original way in via the eyehole in Glory Chamber. To the right at floor level is a squeeze into the upward trending Dan's Passage. Immediately to the left is the top of Surprise Pot, 20ft (6m) deep (eyebolt belay), which drops into the 30ft (10m) long and up to 20ft (6m) high Prospect Streamway.

Right (upstream) at the base of the pitch leads under a wedged block to where the river enters through boulders from the direction of Riverside Swallet. (A passage also ascends towards Moonmilk Pot above the wedged block.) Left (downstream) leads quickly to a descending twisty passage carrying the water towards the descending rift in the floor of Prospect Chamber.

Back at the foot of the third pitch in Glory Chamber, right (south) leads down to where the river sinks into the boulder floor. Right here leads up a mud slope and through a vertical upward squeeze into Water Chamber with the lower end of the river entrance passage entering from the right-hand side just before the river enters and immediately sinks into boulders.

Left back in Glory Chamber leads via a 10ft (3m) climb (fixed handline) to the bottom end of the 3rd pitch bypass on the right and on the left the eyehole leading via an awkward squeeze and climb down (fixed handline) into Prospect Chamber, parallel to and slightly lower than Glory Chamber. In the floor at the lowest point is a slope down into another smaller 'chamber' above a (yet to be entered) descending rift which can be seen to enlarge a short distance down. The roar of water can be heard in the distance.

From Glory Chamber hole in floor at far end leads down to Lower Glory Chamber and squeeze on left near bottom leads to top of Canyon 1, a narrow 25ft (8m) pitch. Tight squeeze on left (downstream) at bottom leads to bottom of Canyon 2, while to the right is the bottom of an as yet unreached waterfall. At top of Canyon 1, a very tight squeeze down to the right of the pitch (as yet unpassed) leads to the top of the waterfall.

Above the hole down to Lower Glory Chamber is a 10ft (3m) climb with fixed rope to squeeze into Darfar 2, discovered in 1983. Immediately right is tight descending passage which is very hard to get out of. Straight on is a hole in the floor to the top of Chamber Pot, 20ft (6m) deep. This is the main way to the bottom. Over the top of this the passage goes left and right. Left is awkward slide down to the Wind Tunnel, which can be reached easier from the top of Chamber Pot. The Wind Tunnel is a silty joint-controlled passage which draughts and ends in a dig within 50ft (15m) horizontally and 20ft (6m) vertically of Darfar Crag Swallet. The right hand way goes via a right then left hand bend and 7ft (2m) climb down to Canyon 2, a larger hading rift. After a sloping descent of 25ft (8m) (use belay round chockstone), climb down through boulders to reach the river again (via a tight squeeze). To the right (upstream) is the link to Canyon 1. Left a short passage 3/4 full of water can be followed round a left hand bend to the top of the Toboggan Run. Note this has only about 1ft of air space. Do not attempt it if there is less than this.   Chamber Pot is free-climbable, (though a ringbolt has been installed at the top for the less confident), to a waterfall. Beyond this is the top of another pitch, Pedigree Pot, which is 55ft (17m) deep. Top 10ft (3m) is tight and sloping, but widens downwards. Fixed rope in place, but advise lifeline from below the narrow section. At the bottom is 20ft (6m) long, 10ft (3m) high passage with the river (from Canyon 2) entering on the right. A climb down at the downstream end of this passage enters the Toboggan Run, a steeply descending clean washed tube about 5ft (1.5m) wide and 3ft (1m) high carrying the river into the terminal sump after 70ft (23m) (in low water). Was dived in 1989 and found to be too tight to continue after 130ft (40m) at a depth of 50ft (15m). Toboggan Run has a fixed rope due to the large volume of water which flows down it in anything but very dry conditions.

*Tackle:*
*Upper Entrance:*
          1st Pitch   25ft (8m) ladder + lifeline. Ringbolt belay.
          2nd Pitch  25ft (8m) handline in place. Ringbolt belay.
          3rd Pitch  25ft (8m) ladder + lifeline but by-pass exists. Stemple belay.
*Prospect Chamber:*  20ft (6m) handline.
*Surprise Pot:*  20ft (6m) ladder + lifeline.
*Canyon 1:*  25ft (8m) ladder + lifeline.
*Canyon 2:*  20ft (6m) ladder + lifeline. Chockstone belay.
*Pedigree Pot:*  **55ft (17m) rope in place but advise lifeline below narrow section. Jammer useful for return.**
*Toboggan Run:*  100ft (30m) handline.

*References: Brooks, S. 1989. O.C.C. N/L Vol.26. No.9/10. p.36.*
*Johnson, S. 1983. Caves & Caving No.22. pp.10-11. Sketch survey.*
*Milner, M. 1981. D.C.A. N/L No.48. pp.1-2.*
*Milner, M. 1983. The Manifold Caver. pp.11-16. Survey.*
*Milner, M. 1984. D.C.A. N/L No.56. p.13.*
*Milner, M. 1984. The Manifold Caver. pp.9-11. Survey.*
*Milner, M. 1987. D.C.A. N/L No.64, pp.14-15.*
*Milner, M. 1996. D.C.A. N/L No.93. p.12.*
*Milner, M. 1997. Descent No. 135 p.19.*
*Milner, M. 2007. Descent No. 197 p.15. Survey.*
*Milner, M. 2007. A Cave & Mine Conservation Audit for the Manifold & Hamps Valleys - 2nd edition p.37. Survey.*
*Pointon, S. 1993. Descent No. 114. p.10. Survey.*

## DARFAR RIDGE CAVE
(Bone Cave)

**NGR** 0980 5588 **Grade:** 1 (Arch)
**Alt.** 750ft (228m)
**Length:** 350ft (107m)
**Status:** National Trust. S.S.S.I.

Owned by the National Trust. To get the key, please contact the South Peak Estate Office on 01335 350503 during office hours, or email <mailto:ilampark@nationaltrust.org.uk>. No more than four people in the cave at any one time for conservation reasons. Much conservation work has been carried out within the cave, so please respect the taping and avoid spreading mud on recently cleaned formations.

In crest of spur above Darfar Crag.

10ft (3m) entrance climb drops into large passage. Left into Old Series, a large muddy bedding plane. Right leads for 16ft (5m) to left hand bend and into New Series via muddy crawl to enter Aussie Chamber. Slide down on right into Link Passage to the Graveyard, because of skulls of small birds found here. At end on right is crawl to Root Chamber, near the surface. 7ft (2m) drop leads via short squeeze and crawl to Final Chamber. New Series was well decorated when found in 1981 by T.V.C.G. Pleistocene and Neolithic remains.

References: Milner, M. 1981. D.C.A. N/L No. 48. pp.3-4.
Milner, M. 1981. T.V.C.G. Review. pp.9-14.
Milner, M. 1983. The Manifold Caver. pp.25-28. Survey.
Nicholson, S. 1966. Peakland Archaeological Society N/L No.21. pp.20-25.
Thomas, F.H. & Moore, R. 1962. Peakland Archaeological Society N/L No.18. pp.7-9.

## DEEPDALE POT
(Deepdale No. 5)

**NGR** 0839 5342  **Dig**
**Alt.** 1000ft (305m)
**Depth:** 40ft (12m)

Situated to the east of the road outside Deepdale Farmhouse a couple of metres away from the drinking trough at the head of Deepdale. Metal lid over, please replace.

Originally dug to a depth of 20ft (6m) via a 15ft (5m) free-climbable entrance shaft in calcited boulders by members of Orpheus C.C. during the 1970's and 1980's. In 1991/2 members of Darfar P.C. increased this to a depth of 40ft(12m) via another 20ft (6m) shaft shored by scaffolding to a loose boulder floor. Resurgence as for Deepdale Shacks. Cave draughts strongly outwards and has a potential depth of around 400ft (122m) to Ladyside Wood (1/2 mile away) alone.

References: Milner, M. 1992. D.C.A. Newsletter No.77. p.5.
Milner, M. 1994. The Manifold Caver 1994. p.17.

## DEEPDALE SHACKS

**NGR** 084 534  **Digs**
**Alt.** 1000ft (305m)

Beside Deepdale Farm.

Two active sinks, both silted up. The more northerly takes a fair amount of water off the shales. One has been opened up as a dig by Orpheus Caving Club and Birmingham Carabiner Club. The current Eldon P.C. dig is roughly 40ft (12m) deep, with a strong draught. Water was dye tested in 1992 to the Upper (Hamps) Rising at Ilam in normal flow and the foot of Ladyside Wood in the Manifold Valley in high water conditions.

## DONKEY HOLE
One of "Radcliffe Stables"

**NGR** 0978 5498  **Grade:** 3
**Alt.** 570ft (171m)
**Length:** 130ft (40m)

Extended 1991 & 1992 by Darfar P.C.

The smaller and more northerly of two caves known as Radcliffe Stables directly below Thor's Cave, about 30ft (9m) above the river bed.

The entrance is of the rock-shelter type. There is a crawl ahead to a chamber with water and a choked passage to the right. Now extended round a couple of tight sharp corners for 30ft (10m)

before breaking into the sizeable Main Chamber up to 20ft (6m) high, 10ft. (3m) wide and 30ft (10m) long. A dig in the lowest part of the chamber looked promising, but ran in after winter floods.
*References: Milner, M. 1994. D.C.A. N/L No. 85. p.6.*
*Milner, M. 1994. The Manifold Caver. p12.*

| ECTON COPPER MINES |
|---|
| Grade: 2 to 4 |
| Alt. 600-1000ft (183-305m) |
| Length: c.3/4 mile (1.2km) |
| Status: S.S.S.I. |

Most of former entrances sealed. Bag Mine shaft is now filled. Access is currently not normally granted.

These old copper mines are well known to cavers for their cave pearls and other formations in adits extending as much as 3/4 mile (1.2km) into the hill. Beware of flooded shafts in the floor, which once led into workings 900ft (274m) below river level.

**Apes Tor Level**        **NGR 0999 5862**
Now blocked but formerly connecting Deep Ecton with the north end of the hill at river level.

**Bag Mine**        **NGR 1021 5774**
Shaft entrance high on the east side of the hill requires 30ft (9m) ladder. Ginging partly collapsed and unstable. Steeply sloping stopes lead to long adit going north west. Further 25ft (8m) ladder pitch into Goodhope/Dutchman Level, with climb up into Goodhope stopes on the left, at foot of Goodhope Shaft (110ft/34m) to surface.

**Clayton Adit**        **NGR 0959 5808**
Adit on road side, up to knee deep in water. Now gated. Leads to underground winding and pumping chamber and long adit to Waterbank Mine. Beware flooded shafts. Turn right at Clayton Engine Chamber, then left into Chadwick Mine workings. Cross flooded shaft by plank to reach Chadwick Cascades, which can be climbed to old workings at the foot of Chadwick Shaft 100ft (30m) from the surface.

**Dale Mine Adit**        **NGR 0945 5845**
Most of the Dale Mine is now inaccessible, but the adit is open for 1150ft (351m), at which point falls prevent further progress. Sumped passage off main adit 590ft (180m) from entrance explored for 82ft (25m) and is dangerously loose. 165ft (50m) beyond sumped passage in main adit is flooded shaft on right in large chamber, dived to false floor at 141ft (43m) depth. The pipe workings appear to have been very extensive.

**Deep Ecton**        **NGR 0962 5813**
Adit entrance gated. Up to 3ft (0.9m) of water, leads into Engine Chamber and extensive series of level and stopes. Beware flooded shafts, one of which has been dived to a depth of over 100ft (30m). Also accessible via 150ft (46m) of fixed ladders from Salts Level.

**Dutchman Level**        **NGR 0981 5818**
Close to largest hillock high on hillside. Half flooded and with good cave formations, links through to Goodhope and Bag Mines. Four flooded shafts have been explored by divers. Gated. No access - private water supply.

**Fly Mine**        **NGR 0988 5809**
Above and to the south of Dutchman Level. A sloping series of pipe workings.

**Salts Level**        **NGR 0971 5829**
Behind Ecton House. Leads into deep Ecton workings via a fixed ladderway. Gated.

**Waterbank Mine**        **NGR 1031 5755**
A climbing shaft leads into the sough. Long hands and knees crawl leads to stopes on two levels.

**Whey Level** (Birch's Level)   **NGR 0956 5805**   **Grade 1**
Altitude: 700ft (213m)                              Length: 700ft (213m)

Obvious entrance at side of road. The level is easy walking with an occasional wet floor, ending at a forefield. The remains of valve gear can still be seen, from the storing of whey. It was used as a store for the Ecton Creamery in the 1920's - 1930's.
References: Kirkham, N. 1967. P.D.M.H.S. Special Publication. Survey.
Robey, J.A. & Porter, L. 1972. Bull. P.D.M.H.S. Vol.5. No.2. pp. 93-106. Surveys.
Robey, J.A. & Porter, L. 1972. The Copper and Lead Mines of Ecton Hill. 92pp. Moorland Publ. Co., Hartington.
Robey, J.A. & Porter, L. 2000. The Copper and Lead Mines around the Manifold Valley, North Staffordshire. Landmark Publishing.

**ECTON HILL CAVES**
(Sycamore Cave)
NGR 102 570    Grade: 1
Alt. 1025ft (312m)
Length: 17ft (5m) & 20ft (6m)

On a crag at summit of south east end of Ecton Hill.
Two entrances. One 3ft (0.9m) high becoming very tight before short descent to small chamber. The other is to the south in the same crag, longer, with one chamber.

**ELDERBUSH CAVE**
NGR 0978 5488  Grade: 1
(Arch)
Alt. 900ft (274m)
Length: 150ft (46m)
Status: S.S.S.I.

In south west end of Thor's Crag.
Entrance chamber completely excavated. Fissure leads to lower series with good formations. Animals and human remains from Pleistocene to Romano-British.
References: Bramwell, D. 1947-1950. P.A.S. N/L Nos. 1-6 & 8.
Bramwell, D. 1950. Trans. C.R.G. Vol.1. No.4. pp.47-52.

Elderbush Cave. Photo by John Beck

### ELLISHILL CAVE
NGR 1303 4739  Grade: 1
Alt. 770ft (240m)
Length: 10ft (3m)

Overlooking Ellishill Brook on the west side of the gorge.
A short walk-in cave. In low flow conditions the brook is dry for nearly a mile from a sink point nearby.

### ELLISHILL WOOD SINKS
NGR 131 473 to 134 472
Digs
Alt. 700ft (213m)

Private grazing land adjoining steeply wooded flank of Ellishill area. Crossed by two North - South footpaths linking Swinscoe & Stanton villages.

Sinks occur between points where paths (mentioned above) cross Ellishill Brook. Tributary from direction of Bullgap Lane (west) sinks on reaching dry bed of Ellishill Brook. Downstream course of brook becomes divided and less clearly defined for a distance of some hundred metres. Under conditions where Lee Wood Sink (1295 4763) overflows, brook may peter out along this section. In flood flow continues down brook's full length.

### GUTTERHOLES
NGR 0729 4839  Grade: 4
Alt. 970ft (295m)
Length: 200ft (61m)
Depth: 40ft (12m)

On west side of road past Cauldonlow Quarries. Entrance lies under concrete slabs which should be replaced.

A series of tight squeezes down between boulders leads to a steep slide to lip of The Funnel, a blind 25ft (8m) descent in the floor overhung by collapsed boulders. Way on is to the right via an awkward squeeze, then a brief climb into the roof, and through another squeeze before sliding down into a tall narrow rift. 10ft (3m) hole in floor drops into stooping sized phreatic passage, soon ending at Amatt's Rift, a 15ft (4.5m) easy descent. Extension from west end of rift leads back under valley floor into extensive collapse area. Digging has made a through route possible from here to the top of The Funnel, but care is needed in route finding, and with unstable rock. Parts of the cave are active, depending on where the stream is sinking. Dye testing has shown that the water resurges at Ilam.

*References: Mellors, P.T. 1975. D.C.A N/L Nos.26. p.1-2 and 29. pp.1-3. Survey.*
*Mellors, P.T. 1989. D.C.A. N/L No. 71. pp.2-9.*

### HAMPS VALLEY CAVE
NGR 1003 5350  Dig
Alt. 550ft (168m)

On north bank (left bank) of the River Hamps half a mile upstream of the confluence with the River Manifold. Just above the 3rd bridge.

A small cave entrance to a tight crawl that could be dug out.

### HAYHOLE
(The Hayloft)
NGR 1064 5407  Grade: 1
Alt. 700ft (213m)
Status: National Trust. S.S.S.I.

High in the face of Beeston Tor.

An obvious crescent shaped opening on a prominent joint in the reef limestone. Not to be confused with Jackdaw's Cave.

### HELL HOLES CAVE
NGR 0943 5243
Grade: 1
Alt. 630ft (192m)

On right bank of River Hamps, downstream from Hell Holes Corner (marked on old two and a half inch maps) and 100ft (30m) above river level. Between bridges 5 & 6 from the confluence with the River Manifold.

A small cave in the cliff on the opposite side of the river from the Waterhouses to Beeston footpath.

### HELL HOLES SINKS
NGR 0952 5211    Digs
Alt. 600ft (183)
Status: National Trust. S.S.S.I.

In river bed, with limited access.

In river bed and right hand bank of the River Hamps between the 6th and 7th bridges upstream from the confluence of the Hamps and Manifold.

A few small sinks in the river bed with obvious signs that once the sinks were much larger as there are large limestone blocks with eye bolts and holes for bolts in the bed of the river. Also upstream the river bed is lower than that downstream.

### HELL HOLES SWALLET
NGR 0952 5212    Dig
Alt. 600ft (183m)
Length: 13ft (4m)
Depth: 6ft (2m)

Dug by members of Darfar P.C. in the late 1990's

Just downstream of Hell Holes Sinks in the right-hand side of the river bed. (Looking downstream.) Manhole cover over, please replace.

Dug for around 13ft (4m) getting too small and requiring enlarging. Takes a large quantity of water when river flowing which resurges at Ilam Risings.

*References: Milner, M. 1998. Descent 140. p11.*

### HEMMINGSLOW SWALLET
(Hemminslow Swallet)
NGR 0730 4882    Grade: 3
Alt. 940ft (286m)
Length: 150ft (46m)
Depth: 45ft (14m)

In prominent blind valley on west side of road past Caldon Quarry, barely half a mile (0.8km) north of Gutterholes.

**Warning: The stream rises rapidly with the onset of rain and can make the entrance pitch impassable.**

Area is fenced and entrance fitted with hinged grill. Stream is culverted to base of 10ft (3m) lidded concrete shaft through road widening rubble. Shaft is presumed to stand on site of original main sink, but digging here has been unproductive, with no sign of bedrock. In flood streamwater backs up in shaft and overflows to sink in northern corner of valley at foot of solitary limestone outcrop. Digging here in 1988 by members of Darfar P.C. revealed a squeeze to the top of a tight pitch which can be free-climbed into a narrow phreatic rift, with several ways on including a 20ft (6m) high aven. The southerly routes soon become too tight or choked with clay or boulders, but the northerly way on entered a tight, vadose passage with cross-rifts, two levels and holes in the floor in the lower one which after about 33ft (10m) splits into several ways on. In 1989, digging by the same team here broke into the clean-washed Rift Chamber which was about 15ft (6m) long, 6ft (2m) wide and up to 20ft (6m) high. Unfortunately, all ways on in the floor in this area proved to be too tight.

The stream was positively dye tested to Ilam in June 1990. The next hollow north also takes a small stream.

*References: Mellors, P.T. 1973. D.C.A. N/L No.18. p.2.*
*Mellors, P.T. 1989. D.C.A. N/L No.71. pp.2-9.*
*Milner, M. 1988. D.C.A. N/L No.68. p.15.*
*Milner, M. 1994. The Manifold Caver. p18-19. (Survey.)*

### HOFTEN'S CROSS SWALLET
(Red Scar Swallet)
**NGR 071 479**   **Grade: 1**
**Alt. 1040ft (317m)**
**Length: 30ft (9m)**

Opened up in 1975 by Derbyshire Speleological Group. Lidded by C.C.P.C. & Staffs. Moorlands D.C. Two small lidded swallets in stream bed.

A short length of low passage in solid rock from the foot of a brief pitch. Floor of shingle and inwashed domestic refuse from disused tip. Considerable flow in wet weather. Water is believed to resurge at Ilam, 4 miles (6km) away and over 500ft (152m) lower.

*References: Beasley, F. 1975. D.S.G. Bulletin Vol.1. Part 1. p.6.*
*Beasley, F. 1975. D.C.A. N/L No.24 pp.2-4.*
*Beasley, F. 1976. D.C.A. N/L No.27. p.4.*
*Farey, J. 1811. A General View of the Agriculture and Minerals of Derbyshire. Vol.1. p.295.*

### HOLE SHADES SWALLET
**NGR 0950 5178**
**Grade: Dig**
**Alt. 610ft (186m) approx.**

A sink just downstream of the first bridge below Lee House in the right-hand side of the river bed (looking downstream). Takes a significant quantity of water when river flowing. Resurgence currently unknown, but probably Ilam Risings.

*References: Milner, M. 1997. Descent 135. p.18*

### HOO VALLEY MINE (NORTH)
**NGR 0912 5605 Grade: 1 (Mine)**
**Alt. 653ft (199m)**
**Length: 417ft (127m)**
**Status: National Trust. S.S.S.I.**

Just to the right of the footpath following the brook up the valley.

Stooping entrance leads to a 6ft (2m) climb down on the left. At bottom left is choked within a few feet, but right is stooping sized level with water. Soon enlarges to walking size. Cross 8ft (2.5m) deep flooded shaft on right with care, and continue for 80ft (25m) to foot of run in shaft from which a stream issues. Pass on right hand side at roof level to regain walking passage to junction. Right for 80ft (25m) through water to dead end. Ahead for 100ft (30m) to another dead end. Another mine directly opposite on the south side of the valley (NGR: 0912 5601) consists of a walking size trial roughly 200ft (61m) long.

*References: Milner, M. 1984. The Manifold Caver. pp.30-31. Survey.*

### HUDFORD BROOK RISING
**NGR 092 461**   **Spring**
**Alt. 750ft (229m)**

A small spring below the Weaver Hills, source of the Hudford Brook.

### ILAM RISINGS
**Dives   Alt. 450ft (135m)**
Status: National Trust. S.S.S.I.

#### Hamps Spring    NGR 1270 5078

Upstream from the Main Resurgence on the opposite (west) bank. The water rises through the muddy floor of a hollow with no obvious place to dig. Dye tests have proved a source at Waterhouses Sink (0916 5012). Dye takes 3 to 6 days and comes out at both the Hamps Spring and Ilam Upper Rising on opposite sides of the Manifold. Air bubbles appear in high water conditions and may indicate the proximity of air-filled passages.

#### Manifold River Rising    NGR 1273 5078

The river seeps up out of its bed a few metres up from the Hamps Spring. Probably an overflow from the Main Rising but dye tests have not confirmed this.

### Hinkley Wood Resurgence    NGR 1283 5046

Two small risings 50ft (15m) apart on the west bank between Ilam Main Risings and the Hamps Spring. Dye tests have proved a connection with Waterways Swallet 1 mile (1.6km) away and 470ft (143m) higher, and Gutterholes. Also connected to Ilam Main Rising. A possible dig?

### Ilam Wier Rising    NGR 1315 5056

A small culverted rising on the east bank just below the weir. Source unknown but alleged connections to the cellars of Ilam Hall and to Main Rising were not confirmed by dye testing. Too small for divers.

### Ripple Rising

Previously hidden, digging allowed access to a small silty chamber. After 52ft (16m) Fat Frog Squeeze leads to a bedding plassage. Squeeze at 39ft (-12m) into easy passage to 125ft (38m) from base passing two small pots. At 125ft (38m) a silt bank (Choc 'n' Choc squeeze) at -28ft (-8.5m) to a junction with a possible connection with nearby Wier Rising. Squeeze under flake at 213ft (65m), then low cherty passage to 360ft (110m) at 3ft (1m) depth, where it becomes smaller.

### Main Rising    NGR 1314 5057

The main rising of the River Manifold from its sink at Wetton Mill, 4 miles (6.4km) away. Water comes from beneath the path on the east bank close to Ilam Hall. Diving by C.D.G. members has passed a low area around 150ft (46m) in. Pushing in 1993 reached a limit 623ft (190m) from base, at a depth of 99ft (30.1m), and the limit is now 889ft (271m) at 177ft (54m) depth.

### Raspberry Rising    NGR 1313 5057

Immediately upstream of Main Rising. Small pot gives access to 100ft (30m) of constricted bedding passage to a tight rift.

### Ilam Upper Rising (Well Rising) NGR 1309 5055

A few feet upstream of Raspberry Rising, and dye tests have proved a source in the River Hamps. Underwater digging enabled divers to reach a small chamber and 53ft (16m) of constricted passage.

### Quazie's Well

Some 300ft (100m) downstream from Main Rising. Excess water flows via two small passages to St Bertrams Well, 33ft (10m) away.

### St.Bertam's Well    NGR 1325 5060

Close to Quazie's Well. A well leads to two short passages which have been dived in vain.

### Flow Gauge Rising    NGR 1396 5074

By the road some 300ft (100m) from Ilam Cross. Small rising with no diving prospects.

### Ilam Village Rising    NGR 135 512

### Okeover Risings    NGR 1440 4890

Small petrifying springs.

### Cowclose Wood Springs    NGR 1465 4850

*References: Ammatt, S., Drakeley, K., & Potts, J. 1981. Lyre No.5. pp.26-41.*
*Brooks, S. 1987. C.D.G. N/L No. p. Survey.*
*Brooks, S. 1986. D.C.A. N/L No.62. pp.2-6. Survey.*
*Cave Diving Group. Various newsletters.*
*Gill, D.W. 1973. British Caver No.60.p.62-64.*
*Mellors, P.T. 1989. D.C.A. N/L No.71. pp.2-9.*

## J-POT
**NGR 097 545  Sink/rising**
**Alt. 500ft (152m)**

In the bed of the River Manifold
A small sink which becomes a rising under certain flow conditions.

## JACKDAWS CAVE
(Jackadaws Cave, Beeston Tor Cave, St Bertrams Chimney)
**NGR 1065 5408    Grade: 1**
**Alt. 700ft (213m)**
Status: National Trust. S.S.S.I.

High above St Bertram's Cave in the face of Beeston Tor.
An enlarged joint, similar to Hayhole, but less conspicuous. Connected to St. Betram's Cave by a very tight squeeze.

## LADYSIDE CAVE
**NGR 0960 5534    Grade: 1**
**Alt. 650ft (198m)**
**Length: 40ft (12m)**
Status: National Trust. S.S.S.I.

100ft (30m) above the valley floor. In thick undergrowth and difficult to find.
A rift entrance. A high passage some 30ft (9m) long diminishes in size and becomes mud choked.

## LADYSIDE POT
**NGR 0960 5498    Grade: 5**
**Alt. 550ft (168m)**
**Length: 1500ft (457m)**
**Depth: 70ft (21m)**
Status: S.S.S.I.

Entered June 1975 by O.C.C. Extended 1976/7 by O.C.C. & C.D.G.
In the bed of the River Manifold, 750ft (228m) upstream of Ladyside Brook.
The entrance is in the bed of the river, and therefore the whole cave fills to the roof. No descent should be contemplated except in very dry settled weather.
The entrance is covered by a metal grid. The descent is tight, and the return is difficult for large cavers. The rift widens out, and reaches the silt-covered floor of the stream passage after a total descent of 50ft (15m). Upstream (north) leads to a fine phreatic passage with large silt banks to Upstream Sump 1, passed after 30ft (9m) (not free-diveable) to a further 250ft (76m) of phreatic passage heading in the direction of Redhurst Swallet, and ending at Sump 2. A rift descends to -20ft (-6m) to a low passage followed for 13ft (4m) to the north. Sump 2a lies in a parallel rift, 24ft (7m) deep to a further low bedding.

Downstream (south) from the entrance, a hands and knees crawl passes an aven to two sumps. The first can be passed in drought (not free-diveable) to a sharp narrow climb, The Rasp, then a crawl to the Great Rift at the foot of which are two sumps with poor prospects. Traversing over the Great Rift leads to Deterred Series. A pitch of 35ft (11m) rejoins the streamway which sumps in both directions. Downstream has been dived for 26ft (8m). A high level by-pass here leads to a number of rifts in the floor.

The widest can be laddered for 60ft (18m) to a further 100ft (30m) of narrow stream passage to another undived sump. The muddy and arduous nature of the cave, despite its short length, make this an unpleasant spot.

**Tackle:**    Entrance:  50ft (15m) rope. Tight. Jammer & sling useful
              Deterred Series:    1st Pitch:  50ft (15m). 60ft (18m).
                                  2nd Pitch: 75ft (23m). 90ft (27m).  Long belay.

References: Allwright, P. 1977. O.C.C. N/L Vol.13. No.9. pp.46-47. Survey.
Amatt, S. & Drakeley, K. 1975. O.C.C. N/L Vol.11. No.6. pp.33-35. Surveys.
Drakeley, K. 1975. O.C.C. N/L Vol.11. No.5. pp.27-29. Survey.
Drakeley, K. 1981. The Lyre No.5. pp.41-47. Survey.

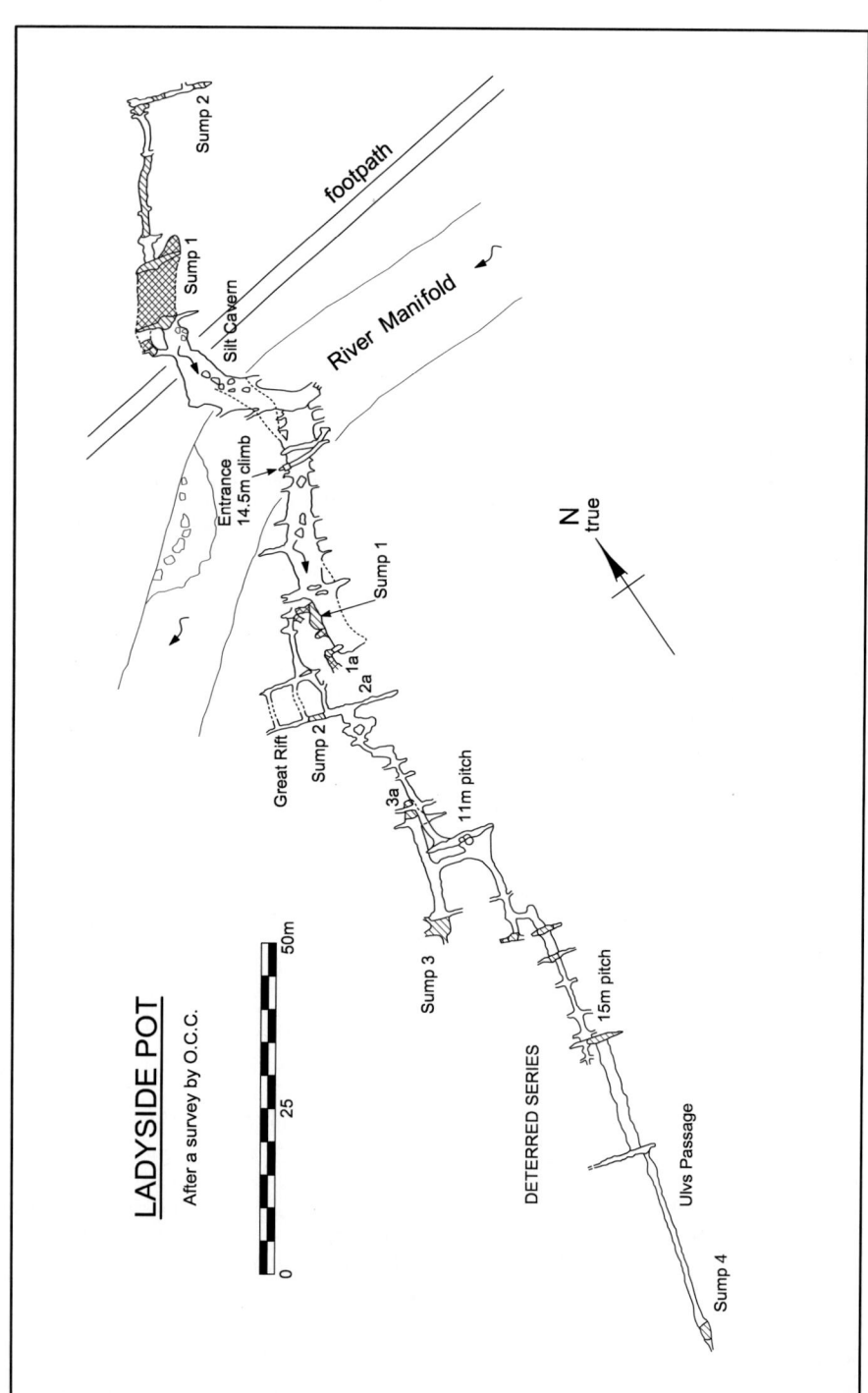

## LEE HOUSE QUARRY CAVE
(Waterhouses Fissure?)
**NGR 086 503**     Arch
**Alt. 730ft (219m)**

High in disused Lee House Quarry on the north east of the village.

Cave entrance difficult of access and has unstable roof. Easily visible. Has cave-earth fill just inside awaiting excavation. May be the same as Waterhouses Fissure recorded by Heath, 1882. It is also possible that Waterhouses Fissure may have been Bank End Quarry Fissure.

*References: Aitken, J. 1873. Trans. Manch. Geol. Soc. Vol.12.*
*Brown. 1864-5. Trans. Midland Scientific Assoc. p.34.*
*Heath. 1882. Derbys. Arch. Jour. pp.164-5.*

## LEES POT
**NGR 0940 5158**     Dig
**Alt. 620ft (189m) approx.**

A sink immediately below the footbridge across the river in the left-hand side of the river bed. (Looking downstream.) Took a lot of water when originally dug in the early 1980's. The cave was extended down the bedding for several metres, before a sudden flood refilled the cave before a lid could be installed. The cave draughted strongly outwards and was very reminiscent of parts of Waterways Swallet.

*References: Milner, M. 1983. D.C.A. Newsletter No.51. pp.2-6.*

## LEE WOOD SINK
**NGR 1295 4763**     Dig
**Alt. 800ft (244m)**

In bed of Ellishill Brook, where water passes from Bullgap Shales to Ellishill reef limestones.

Site difficult to approach due to undergrowth. Under low flow conditions brook sinks completely into mud, stones, and crevices, not always at exactly the same spot. In wet weather brook flows on to Ellishill Wood Sinks or beyond. Bed can be dry from Lee Wood Sink to downstream end of Catholes Wood where there is a gradual reappearance of water, with volume not fully restored till limestone beds are crossed again below Limestone Hill (east of Stanton village).

## LOWER CHESHIRE WOOD CAVE AND SINK
**NGR 1120 5335**     Grade: 1
**Alt. 575ft (175m)**
**Length: 80ft (24.5m)**
**Depth: 5ft (1.5m)**

Extended by OCC to present length in April/May 2009.

Situated some 800m below Beeston Tor on south bank of Manifold some 60m below remains of an old concrete foobridge

The entrance is 23ft (7m) above the riverbed above some obvious anticlinal folded limestone in the valley side. A arched entrance (8ft / 2.4m x 3ft / 0.9m) leads to a low crawl that enters a small chamber after 18ft (5.5m) where the passage divided. To the left the passage continues as a hands and knees crawl for another 26ft (8m) to reach a choke. To the right a short 10ft (3m) long passage ends in a silt choke. Limited prospects for further extension. The roof for much of the cave is a single bed of limestone anticinally folded.

### LYNX CAVES
(Toad Hole)
NGR 1067 5407  Grade: 1 (Arch)
Alt. 700ft (213m)
Length: 150ft (46m)

Status: National Trust. S.S.S.I.

20 yards (18m) downstream of St. Bertram's Cave, a climb up a steep gully leads to the Lynx Caves at the same altitude as Hayhole.

Upper Lynx Cave is a short old phreatic passage with remains of formations, eventually becoming too narrow. Lower Lynx Cave a short distance to the east is a collapsed continuation of the upper cave, and contains only a short crawl. Archaeological excavations revealed lynx, polecat, and reindeer remains. Finds in Natural History Museum, London.

*References: Wilson, G.H. 1926. Some Caves and Crags of Peakland. pp.54-55.*

### MAGIC MUSHROOM RESURGENCE
NGR 0960 5470
Grade: 1 (Dig)
Alt. 545ft (169m)
Depth: 12ft (4m)

Situated half way between the Ladyside Brook Sinks and Weag's Bridge Resurgence near the east bank of the river.

A 5ft (1.5m) diameter sloping tube descends for for 12ft (4m) to narrow fissure a few inches wide which would need enlarging to make further progress. Issues impressive volumes of water in flood. Filter gate/grille over. Please replace.

*References: Brooks, S. 1991. D.C.A. N/L No. 75. p.5.*
*Milner, M. 1994. The Manifold Caver. p.17.*

### MANIFOLD BADGER HOLES
NGR 0958 5486    Digs
Alt. 650ft (198m)

Opposite Ladyside Wood and Brook, 100 yards (91m) down valley from Ladyside Pot. 50-100ft (15-30m) above river level.

Several ancient sinks, now used (or have been used) as badger holes. Possible digs.

### MILL CAVE AND POT
NGR 0965 5609  Grade: 1 (Arch)
Alt. 680ft (207m)
Length: 40ft (12m)
Depth: 25ft (8m)

National Trust. S.S.S.I.

Cave now gated. An adjustable spanner is required to open.

On east bank of river 150 yards (137m) south of Wetton Mill, about 100ft (30m) above river level.

Two small entrances close together. First is to cave with large fallen roof block. Beyond is pot with 21ft (6m) pitch into passage apparently leading behind cave but choked. Some stalactite formations. Various domestic animal remains as well as human remains and Middle-Late Bronze Age pottery.

**Tackle: 6m ladder + lifeline.**

*References: Ryder, Longworth, & Gunstone. 1971. N. Staffs. Jour. Field Studies, Vol.11.*

### MOONMILK POT
NGR 0970 5603    Grade: 1
Alt. 630ft (192m)
Length: 58ft (18m)
Depth: 30ft (10m)

Status: National Trust. S.S.S.I.

In gully near Darfar Pot top entrance.

A 12ft (4m) concreted shaft, (manhole cover over - please replace), leads via awkward descending passage to chamber at river level 12ft (4m) long, up to 6ft (2m) wide and 10ft (3m) high with moonmilk on the walls. To the north (left) is a 6ft (2m) climb up to an eyehole overlooking the chamber. To the south (right) is a descending mud slope which should link with Darfar Pot and/or Riverside Swallet and could be dug.

*References: Johnson, S. 1980. T.V.C.G. Review. p.18-20. Survey.*
*Milner, M. 1981. D.C.A. N/L No. 48. p.1. Survey.*
*Milner, M. 2007. The Derbyshire Caver (D.C.A.) No. 126. p15.*

### NAN TOR CAVE
(Wetton Mill Rock Shelter)
NGR 0953 5615
Grade: 1 (Arch)
Alt. 640ft (192m)
Length: 115ft (35m)
Status: National Trust. S.S.S.I.

Just north of Wetton Mill Farm.
A limestone hummock riddled with holes from which one can emerge in the most unexpected places. A fossil swallow hole, probably once connected to a small cave above Wetton Mill Sink. Rock shelter on north side was excavated to reveal a late glacial to Iron Age sequence.
*References: Kelly, J.H. 1976. Stoke Museum Publication.*
*Warwick, G.T. 1953. Proc. 1st Int. Spel. Congr., Paris. Tome 2. pp.1-10.*

### OLD HANNAH'S HOLE
NGR 1002 5575
Grade: 1 (Arch)
Alt. 800ft (244m)
Length: 45ft (14m)
Status: National Trust. S.S.S.I.

Human remains excavated in 1896 are in the Hanley Museum, Staffs.
On the west side of Redhurst Gorge, south of Wetton Mill.
A fissure entrance 10ft (3m) high and narrowing. Supposed natural explosions took place here and at Darfar Ridge Cave.
*References: Bramwell, D. 1950. Trans. C.R.G. Vol.1. No.4. pp.47-52.*
*Wardle, T. 1899. Trans. N. Staffs. Field Club. No.33. pp.97 & 105.*

### OLDPARK HILL CAVE
(Falcon Low Cave)
NGR 1040 5360    Arch
Alt. 984ft (300m) approx.
Status: National Trust. S.S.S.I. Scheduled Monument.

An archaeological cave that produced skeletons of two adults and four children that may be of prehistoric date but no dateable artefacts accompanied them.
*Reference: Emery, G. T. 1962. North Staffs Journal of Field Studies 2, 33-36.*

### OSSOMS CHIMNEY
NGR 0960 5572    2 (Arch)
Alt. 720ft (220m)
Length: 53ft (16.2m)
National Trust. S.S.S.I. Scheduled Monument.

Situated on the far right hand (NW) end of the Crag is a remnant cave that gives the crag its name. This feature is also described in Climbing Guides as a 'Moderate' Chimney Climb.
An obvious (10ft / 3m x 13ft / 4.0m) arched entrance rises steeply as a fine phreatic passage that swings right and soon reaches a second 4m diameter entrance overlooking the valley.

### OSSOMS CRAG CAVE
(Yellersley Tor Cave)
NGR 0958 5576  Grade: 1 (Arch)
Alt. 700ft (213m)
Length: 60ft (18m)
Status: National Trust. S.S.S.I. Scheduled Monument.

The name is variously spelled Ossoms, Ossom's or Ossums: the spelling on the 1:25000 OS map is used here.
100ft (30m) up on the west side of the Manifold above Darfar Road bridge at the foot of a crag.
An obvious (9ft / 2.7m x 10ft / 3.0m) triangular entrance leads to a fine phreatic passage that soon narrows and leads to a pool. Through this leads via a muddy rising passage to a hading rift. A small passage on the right is the continuation of the entrance passage, and has been dug for 7ft (2m). Fill blocks the way on. Late Palaeolithic remains found.
*References: Bramwell, D. 1954. P.A.S. N/L No.11. pp.5-7.*
*Bramwell, D. 1955. P.A.S. N/L No.12. pp.13-16.*
*Bramwell, D. 1956. P.A.S. N/L No.13. pp.7-9.*
*Bramwell, D. 1957. Lyre No.2. pp.20-22. Survey.*
*Warwick, G.T. 1953. Proc. 1st. Int. Congr. Spel. Paris. Tome II. pp.1-10.*

## OSSOMS CRAG FISSURE

NGR 0960 5575     Dig
Alt. 700ft (214m)
Length: 10ft (3m)
Depth: 10ft (3m)
Status: National Trust. S.S.S.I.

In Ossom's Crag.
Narrow waterworn passage with a large boulder partly obscuring the entrance has been dug to a corner which needs enlarging.
*References: Trent Valley Cave Exploration Group N/L.*

## OSSOMS EYRIE CAVE

NGR 0960 5573     Arch
Alt. 780ft (234m)
Length: 35ft (10.6m)
Depth: 20ft (6.2m)
Status: National Trust. S.S.S.I.

Discovered by P.A.S. in 1956.
Situated on a sloping ledge on the face of Ossoms Crag. Best reached by abseiling from the top of the Crag.
A small archaeological bone cave. Noted for bird remains. The 7ft (2m) x 7.5ft (2.3m) entrance soon reduces in size and after 10ft (3m) rises steeply to terminate in a calcite blockage. Contains flowstone and a large birds nest at the end.
*References: Bramwell, D. 1956. P.A.S. N/L No.13. pp.10-11.*
*Bramwell, D. 1957. P.A.S. N/L No.14. pp.8-15.*
*Bramwell, D. 1958. P.A.S. N/L No.15. p.8.*
*Gee, S. 1956. P.A.S. N/L No.13. p.11.*

## PIKELOW SWALLET

NGR 085 515     Dig
Alt. 790ft (240m)

Dye tested inconclusively in 1988.
Between Waterfall village and the summit of Pike Low.
Overflow from a mere sinks in a cluttered hollow at the head of a steep dry valley.
*References: Mellors, P.T. 1989. D.C.A. N/L No.71. pp.1-9*

## PIKE LOW SWALLETS

NGR 0850 5150     Digs
Alt. 775ft (236m)

In field just west of Pike Low overlooking Bredon Brook.
Two small choked swallets taking drainage from shales. An attempt to trace the more southerly of these to Ilam Risings in 1988 proved inconclusive.
*References: Mellors, P.T. 1989. D.C.A. N/L No.71. pp.3-9.*

## PLUGHOLE

NGR 0973 5525     Dig
Alt. 500ft (152m)

A mud filled joint in the bed of the River Manifold.
Digging caused the river to be engulfed in a large whirlpool during high flow.

## PRITCHARD'S CAVE

NGR 1058 5407     Grade: 1
Alt. 630ft (192m)
Length: 60ft (18m)
Status: National Trust. S.S.S.I.

A low entrance amongst brambles.
Entrance leads to two parallel joint passages which soon end after 60ft (18m) although digging may be possible.
*References: O.C.C. N/L Vol.13. No.6.*
*Phipps, M. 1981. The Lyre No.5. p.48. Survey.*
*Wilson, H. 1926. Some Caves and Crags of Peakland. pp.35 & 55-58.*

### PROJECT POT
**NGR 0969 5531 Grade: 1 (Dig)**
**Alt. 500ft (152m)**
**Length: 70ft (21m)**
**Depth: 12ft (4m)**

In middle of bed of River Manifold.

Draughts strongly. Entrance (with grille over - please replace) is a 10ft (3m) climb down. At bottom 2 ways on. Left leads to a very narrow rift. Right leads to an enlarged section ending in a bedding lane which is currently too tight for further progress. This is approx. 45ft (14m) from West Passage in T-Pot. Lowest sections sump in flood. Water originates from Redhurst Swallet via Wednesday Pot and T-Pot.

*References: Milner, M. 1984. The Manifold Caver. p.16.*
*Milner, M. 1985. D.C.A. N/L No.60. pp.8-9.*

### RABBITS HOLE
**NGR 0906 5686 Grade: 2 (Dig)**
**Alt. 670ft (204m)**
**Length: 150ft (46m)**

Discovered 1979 by T.V.C.E.G.

Low entrance 10ft (3m) above the left side of the road.

The entrance chamber leads up dip for 30ft (9m) to a tight squeeze through boulders into a small chamber. A low passage straight on leads after 10ft (3m) to a tight sloping squeeze down on the left. At the bottom a short passage leads to another, tighter squeeze, the Supermangle, which needs helmet and battery off to pass. Beyond a larger muddy chamber 10ft (3m) round is gained with low passages off which draught. Currently occupied by badgers.

*References: Milner, M. 1980. D.C.A. N/L No.43. p.1.*
*Milner, M. 1983. The Manifold Caver. pp.33-34.*

### RADCLIFFE STABLES
**NGR 0977 5498      Grade: 1**
**Alt. 570ft (174m)**
**Length: 50ft (15m) & 130ft (40m)**

Directly below Thor's Cave, some 30ft (9m) above the river.

Two small caves. Name is applied either to the more southerly or both of the caves. The northern cave is known as Donkey Hole (qv). Once used by a refugee from the Jacobite rebellion. During 1991 and 1992, digging by members of Darfar P.C. extended the northerly passage round a couple of tight, sharp corners for 30ft (10m) before breaking into the sizeable Main Chamber up to 20ft (6m) high, 10ft (3m) wide and 30ft (10m) long. A dig in the lowest part of the chamber looked promising, but ran in after winter floods.

*References: Milner, M. 1994. D.C.A. N/L No.85. p.6.*
*Milner, M. 1994. The Manifold Caver. p.12.*

### REDHURST SWALLET
**NGR 0967 5570      Grade: 4**
**Alt. 610ft (186m)**
**Length: 950ft (294m)**
Status: National Trust. S.S.S.I.

A number of small entrances on the south side of the river 1/4 mile (400m) upstream of Redhurst Bridge.

The first major swallet downstream of Wetton Mill, and therefore extremely liable to flooding. One hour's respite only. The cave between the Knifedge and Sump 4 floods very easily, with Sumps 2 & 3 rising BEFORE the others. Do not get cut off! Only go beyond Sump 1 in dry settled weather.

Only one entrance is open, and is covered by a metal grid (adjustable spanner needed). Just inside the entrance, right leads back towards the crag, with a narrow climb down to Puke Sump (which dries up in summer) on the left. Back at the entrance, left soon enlarges to walking size, and after a sharp right hand bend a climb down (The Knifedge) leads to Sump 1. A passage to the right of this can be followed back to the other side of Puke Sump. Sump 1 drains in summer and leads to a high narrow rift with the passage continuing on the left at the far end and soon reaching Sump 2. Half way along the rift on the left is Shredder Passage, which is tight and nasty for 80ft (24m) to a 13ft (4m) pitch with a sump at the bottom. At the far end of the rift a narrow continuation was enlarged

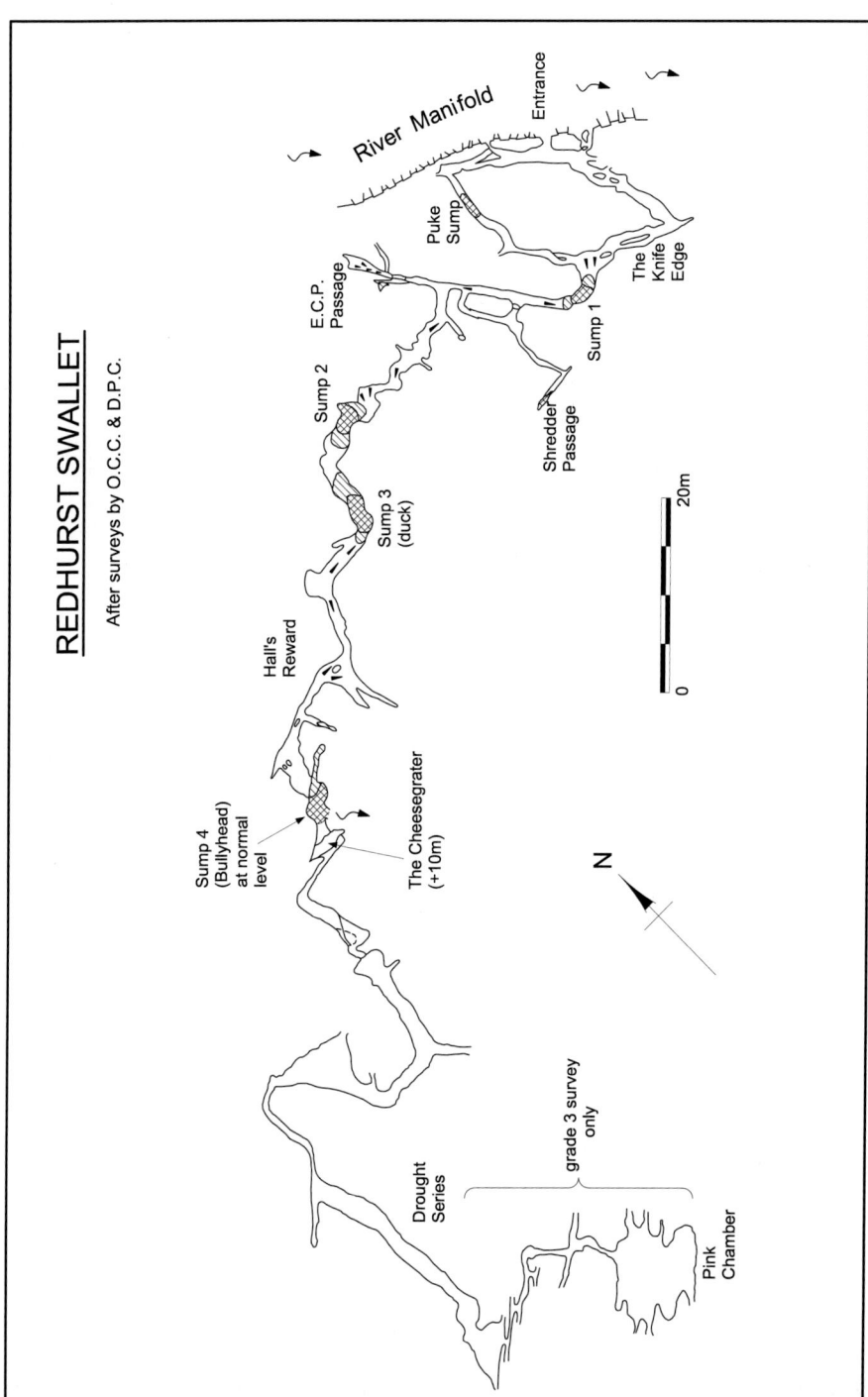

by members of Darfar P.C. and in 1992 ECP Passage was entered. A 25ft (8m) pitch leads to a larger sloping passage with a narrow draughting rift on the right heading back towards the river. At the foot of the pitch is a deep looking sump. Sump 2, passed by siphoning in 1959, drains in summer, and Sump 3 followed within a few feet. Sump 3 never drains, but an airspace may be present in a dry summer, when it is a short duck.

Beyond, the passage rises to a large section with stal deposits in the roof. A tight rift on the left leads to Sump 4a, which is 7ft (2m) deep but too tight. Straight on is a slope down to Sump 4 (Bullyhead Sump), which has been dived for 7ft (2m) to a tight bedding. A 20ft (6m) climb up to the right leads to Drought Series. A wide bedding passage leads via a Z-bend to a slope down for 40ft (12m). A sandy floored passage is then followed to a steeply rising sandy slope. At the top left soon gets too low, but a crawl under flakes reveals a short larger section. From here turn right and through a low archway to a rift. Left and then right leads to a larger section with many rifts leading off. Pink Chamber can be reached by going up the slope to the right of the deep muddy rift in the floor, and after crossing over it a crawl leads to a muddy slope on the right into Pink Chamber, 20ft (6m) wide and up to 50ft (15m) high, approaching the surface.

***Tackle:***
***ECP Passage pitch: 25ft (8m) ladder + lineline.***

*References: Jarvis, E. 1965. The Lyre No.4. pp.28-35 & 38. Survey.*
*Knox, C.S. 2005. C.C.P.C. N/L No.86. pp.8-9.*
*Milner, M. 1984. The Manifold Caver. pp.21-23.*
*Milner, M. 1985. D.C.A. N/L No.60. pp.9-10 & 1987 No.64. p.14.*
*Milner, M. 1992. D.C.A. N/L No. 77. p.5.*
*Potts, J. 1981. The Lyre No.5. pp.36-36.*

### REDHURST UPPER CAVE
**NGR 0967 5569  Grade: 1 (Dig)**
**Alt. 670ft (193m)**
**Length: 20ft (6m)**
Status: National Trust. S.S.S.I.

Discovered by T.V.C.E.G. in 1986.
On the crag top directly above the entrance to Redhurst Swallet.
A large mud-filled phreatic tube 20ft (6m) long. Could be dug further.

### RIBDEN SWALLET No.1
**NGR 075 471  Grade: Dig**
**Alt. 1000ft (305m)**

In a depression near the road in a private garden.
The main swallet. There is no obvious entrance but water sinks among boulders.

### RIBDEN SWALLET No.2
**NGR 075 471  Grade: 4**
**Alt. 1000ft (305m)**

Permission required from Ribden Farm.
Across the road from (1) to the east. A large open mine shaft with a wall round it.
**Warning: The air in the shaft can be dangerous - a caver passed out on the rope here.**

Fine free hanging descent for 169ft (51.5m) to land on rubbish. A mined level leads off 5ft (1.5m) from the bottom, immediately breaking into natural passage, and forks. Right via a short crawl to the high Fourways Aven. Ahead from here leads to a choke through which the stream enters. Climb on left via tight squeeze to a junction. Right leads to the same choke: left is too tight. Right from Fourways Aven leads to Manimal Passage, which splits into several silted tubes. Back at the fork, left opens into walking sized passage scattered with refuse. A steep muddy ramp descends past deep holes in the floor to a rock bridge, the head of the second pitch, 21ft (6.5m) deep, landing in the large Chernobyl Chamber. A steeply descending tube leads shortly to a sump. This may dry up, but water backs up into the entrance shaft in wet weather. The shaft is still being filled with rubbish.

**Tackle:**
| | |
|---|---|
| Entrance Pitch: | 55m rope. |
| Slope above Chernobyl Chamber: | 10m handline. |
| Chernobyl Chamber: | 8m ladder + lifeline. |

*References:* Gill, D.I. 1966. E.P.C. Jour. Vol.7. No.1. pp.68-72. Survey.
Robey. J.A. & Porter, L. 1971. Bull. P.D.M.H.S. Vol.4. No.6. pp.417-428. Survey. Robey, J.A. & Porter, L. 1972. Bull. P.D.M.H.S. Vol.5. No.1. pp.14-30. Survey.
Tucker, S.J. 1987. D.C.A. N/L No.65. pp.6-9. Survey.

### RIBDEN SWALLET No.3
NGR 075 471  Dig
Alt. 1000ft (305m)

In the fields adjacent to the farm about 100 yards (91m) to the south of (1).

A group of shakeholes. No obvious entrances, although five of them have been seen to take water in wet weather. The water from the swallets reappears at the foot of the Weaver Hills at 092 461, some 250ft (76m) lower in altitude.

### RIVERSIDE SINK
(Riverside Swallet)
NGR 0969 5602    Grade: 2
Alt. 610ft (186m)
Length: 210ft (65m)
Depth: 50ft (15m)
Status: National Trust. S.S.S.I.

50ft (15m) downstream of Wetton Mill Sink.

The lower areas near the end are very unstable.

Scaffolded entrance shaft, (manhole cover over - please replace), 10ft (3m) deep leads to a steep clamber down a phreatic passage with water normally entering from the roof in many places. At bottom, right leads up slope for several metres before turning sharp left to enter the foot of Tumbledown Aven, 50ft (16m) high, dug into in 1988 by members of Darfar P.C. On the left a squeeze down leads to an enlargement with a mud sump in one corner. Left of the squeeze over a mud bank enters a

The very wet entrance to Riverside Swallet. Photo by M Milner

continuation. Straight on part of the river enters down a slope on the left and runs away through the boulders towards Darfar Pot. Right is a tight squeeze into another small muddy continuation where the water is last seen. The water reappears in Prospect Chamber in Darfar Pot.
References: Milner, M. 1984. D.C.A. N/L No.56, p.13.
Milner, M. 1984. The Manifold Caver. pp.25-26. Survey.
Milner, M. 1994. The Manifold Caver. p.11.
Potts, J. 1975. O.C.C. N/L Vol.11. No.9. p.43.

### RIVERSIDE TWO
NGR 0970 5600  Grade: 1 (Dig)
Alt. 610ft (186m)
Depth: 30ft (9m)
National Trust. S.S.S.I.

30ft (9m) entrance shaft (manhole cover over - please replace) leads to rift becoming too tight both upstream and downstream. River sinks all around.
References: Brooks, S. 1991. D.C.A. N/L No. 75. p.5.
Milner, M. 1994. The Manifold Caver. p.11.

### ST. BERTRAM'S CAVE
NGR 1066 5407
Grade: 2 (Arch)
Alt. 600ft (183m)
Length: 700ft (213m)
Status: National Trust. S.S.S.I.

Archaeological excavations revealed evidence of occupation, including a hoard of Saxon coins. Remains in Buxton Museum, and British Museum London.
On the north bank of the River Manifold, opposite Beeston Tor Farm.
Two obvious entrances. The left hand one involves a short climb into a short blind joint passage. The right hand and larger entrance, formerly furnished with a door, leads to a small network of old phreatic passages, including a climb into the lofty Skull Rift (rope useful) and crawls into the "Cellars". An exit from the cave can be made by climbing a 30ft (9m) high rift, to emerge via a squeeze through the window higher in the cliff face, known as Jackdaw's Cave, or St.Bertram's Chimney.
References: Amatt, S. 1975. D.C.A. N/L No.24. pp.7-8. Survey (grade 1).
Amatt, S.N. 1981. The Lyre No.5. p.49. Survey.
Holmes, F.A. 1909. Climbers Club Journal No.44. (Reprinted in P.A.S. N/L No.8. pp.10-12).
Wilson, G.H. 1926. Some Caves and Crags of Peakland. pp.38-47.
Wilson, G.H. 1934. Cave Hunting Holidays in Peakland. pp.47-56.

### SALLYMOOR SWALLETS
NGR 08 46  Digs
Alt. 850-950ft (259-290m)

To the west and northwest of Kevin Quarry, below the main limestone escarpment of Wredon.
Several small intermittent swallets, all choked. Resurgences not known.
References: Beasley, F. 1975. D.C.A. N/L No.24. pp.2-4.
Mellors, P.T. 1973. D.C.A. N/L No.18. p.2.

### SEVEN WAYS CAVE
NGR 0982 5490  Grade: 1 (Arch)
Alt. 900ft (274m)

On back of hill containing Thor's Cave, close to Elderbush Cave.
A short series of passages with seven branches or entrances. Dug archaeologically.
References: Anon. 1952. P.A.S. N/L No.8. pp.4-5.
Bramwell, D. 1952. P.A.S. N/L No.8. pp.6-8, & No.10. pp.6-7.

**SNOW HOLE**
(Station Sinks)
**NGR 0965 5536   Dig**
**Alt. 550ft (168m)**
**Length: 15ft (4.5m)**
**Depth: 15ft (4.5m)**

On right hand bend in River Manifold below Ossom's Crag.
A series of sinks in fissures. One was dug to a depth of 15ft (4.5m) in a narrow joint where water could be heard ahead. Also dug horizontally for 10ft (3m) to narrower part under concrete in river bed (Approaching the new entrance of T-Pot.) Manhole cover over - please replace.

References: Amatt, S. 1981. The Lyre No.5. p.48.
Milner, M. 1983. The Manifold Caver. p.29.
Milner, M. 1994. The Manifold Caver. p.6.
Warwick, G.T. 1953. lst Congr. Int. Speleo. Paris, Vol.2. Sect.1. pp.59-68.

**T POT**
**NGR 0966 5538        Grade: 5**
**Alt. 585ft (178m)**
**Length: 695ft (212m)**
**Depth: 25ft (8m)**

Old entrance lies in bed of River Manifold on the right of the main stream channel, approximately 30ft (9m) downstream of Kyles Folly.
The old entrance passage is awkward and tiring. The whole cave can flood to the roof. Do not descend in unsettled weather, or when the river is sinking downstream of the stone bridge near Redhust Swallet.

Manhole cover over entrance. Please replace. Tight, inclined bedding entrance. At bottom, right (downstream) is an awkward squeeze (head first) into continuing passage. Follow via upward sloping bedding to a squeeze down to a pool. Over this leads quickly to main passage. Left, East Passage, is walking size for 22ft (7m) to boulders. Straight on through the boulders is small phreatic tube which has been pushed for 60ft (18m). Left at the boulders leads after 12ft (4m) to narrowing rift with way on through flakes to the right (North Passage). Beyond this slide over the mud slope to the left to regain larger passage. Beyond the mud slope is a confusing series of draughting joint-controlled passage which have so far been pushed for 150ft (46m) and are heading towards Wednesday Pot with which a voice connection has been established. Back at the junction with the entrance passage, turning right is West Passage. Stooping for 20ft (6m) leads to larger section 10ft (3m) high and up to 15ft (5m) wide. On the left here is Pool Passage which can be followed for 30ft (10m) past a muddy pool befoe getting too low, but straight on is a step down to 30ft (10m) of clean walking-sized passage. After a squeeze onto a ledge a wide bedding passage (West Passage) continues for another 100ft (30m) towards Project Pot, gradually getting too low. Route finding is made difficult by silt banks and large flakes of chert. Back at the largest part of West Passage (just before the step down) is the 'Hole in the Floor' dig which takes the whole flow of the river in moderate flood and is about 15ft (5m) deep. In the far (north-east) corner the new entrance passage enters the main cave. The new entrance, connected to the main cave in May 1992 by members of Darfar P.C. is situated about 20ft (7m) downstream of the old entrance at the downstream end of the concreted area. Manhole cover over - please replace. A 6ft (2m) climb down leads after 15ft (5m) to narrower section. Squeezing past this leads to another 15ft (5m) of passage and a small enlargement. In the left-hand corner a squeeze over a block enters the main cave near the 'Hole in the Floor' dig.

References: Milner, M. 1983. T Pot. The Manifold Caver. pp.19-22. Survey.
Milner, M. 1984. The Manifold Caver pp.16-17. Survey.
Milner, M. 1981. D.C.A. N/L No.48. pp.2-3.
Milner, M. 1994. D.C.A. N/L No.85. p.6.
Milner, M. 1994. The Manifold Caver. p.5.

### THOR'S CAVE
(Thyrsis's Cavern)
**NGR 0986 5496  Grade: 1** (Arch)
**Alt.** 870ft (265m)
**Length:** 150ft (46m)

Very obvious entrance in prominent crag south west of Wetton.
A large chamber, archaeologically excavated. Daylight penetrates most of it from the "West Window".
*References:* Bramwell, D. 1950. Trans. C.R.G. Vol.1. No.4. pp.47-52.
Brown, E. 1865. Trans Midland Scientific Assoc. pp.1,19, & 70. Survey.
Carrington. 1866. The Reliquary Vol.6. pp.201-212.
Dawkins, W.B. 1874. Cave Hunting. pp.127-129.
Heath, T. 1882. Derbys. Arch. Jour. Vol.4. p.165.
Warwick, G.T. 1947. P.A.S. N/L No.1. pp.4-5.

### THOR'S FISSURE CAVERN
(Fissure Cave)
**NGR 0985 5496  Grade: 1** (Arch)
**Alt.** 850ft (259m)
**Length:** 60ft (18m)

Below and to the south of Thor's Cave West Window.
A fissure cave which has been archaeologically excavated. Late Palaeolithic to Roman sequence found.
*References:* Bramwell, D. 1974. Archaeology in the Peak District.
Bramwell, D. 1950. Trans C.R.G. Vol.1. No.4. pp.47-52.
Wilson, G.H. 1934. Cave Hunting Holidays in Peakland. pp.13-46.
Wilson, G.H. 1937. B.S.A. Caves & Caving No.2. pp.61-69. Survey.

### THOR'S FOX HOLE
**NGR 1012 5472  Grade: 1**
**Alt.** 870ft (265m)
**Length:** 60ft (18m)

Entered by O.C.C. in 1976.
Small cave entrance in base of 6ft (2m) cliff on south side of Wetton Valley in hill that contains Thor's Cave. Entrance faces road from Wetton Mill as it turns to face Thor's Cave.
A small phreatic cave. Became impossible to push due to the smell (occupied by foxes).

### THOR'S SINKS
**NGR 0974 5500      Digs**
**Alt.** 710ft (216m)

Several sinks in joints in the side and centre of the bed of the River Manifold below Thor's Cave between Donkey Hole and Radcliffe Stables.
Mostly filled with concrete and iron pipes. Some of the concrete has been removed, and water continues to sink.

### WATERWAYS SWALLET
(Waterings Swallet)
**NGR 1260 4917  Grade: 3**
**Alt.** 935ft (285m)
**Length:** 1725ft (526m)
**Depth:** 410ft (125m)
**Status:** S.S.S.I.

Park in gated area just up the road on the opposite side to Waterings Farm. Use stile opposite the farm drive to reach the cave.
Entrance under iron lid inside fenced area at end of blind valley 200ft (60m) beyond present stream sink.

**Warning: After prolonged heavy rain or rapid snowmelt, the stream overflows into the cave. Entrance Series and parts of Top Passage become impassable. Take care.**

Entrance is short drop among boulders. Steeply sloping gap through boulder pile soon leads to sharp dogleg bend, and route then follows one solid wall down-dip to brink of climb down into first small chamber. A succession of short climbs and scrambles followed by a crawl across a steeply inclined bedding plane leads to a hole in the roof. This soon gives access to a descent into the large Main Chamber, 20ft (6m) square and boulder-strewn. From Main Chamber a number of passages lead off. Ahead, hidden behind a fallen block, is 30ft (9m) pitch to large impressive sloping passage (The Gallery). To the right is Rift Passage, which can be followed by climbing down ledges. This is usual route to reach far end of The Gallery. Small slot on right next to Rift Passage rejoins main route via a choice of two dry waterfalls (Swirl Passage). Obvious opening above Rift Passage leads to tight and arduous uphill inlet route between boulders (Top Passage) which crosses over entrance series and ends at Omega Aven close to surface. The Gallery is scene of a number of digs attempting to

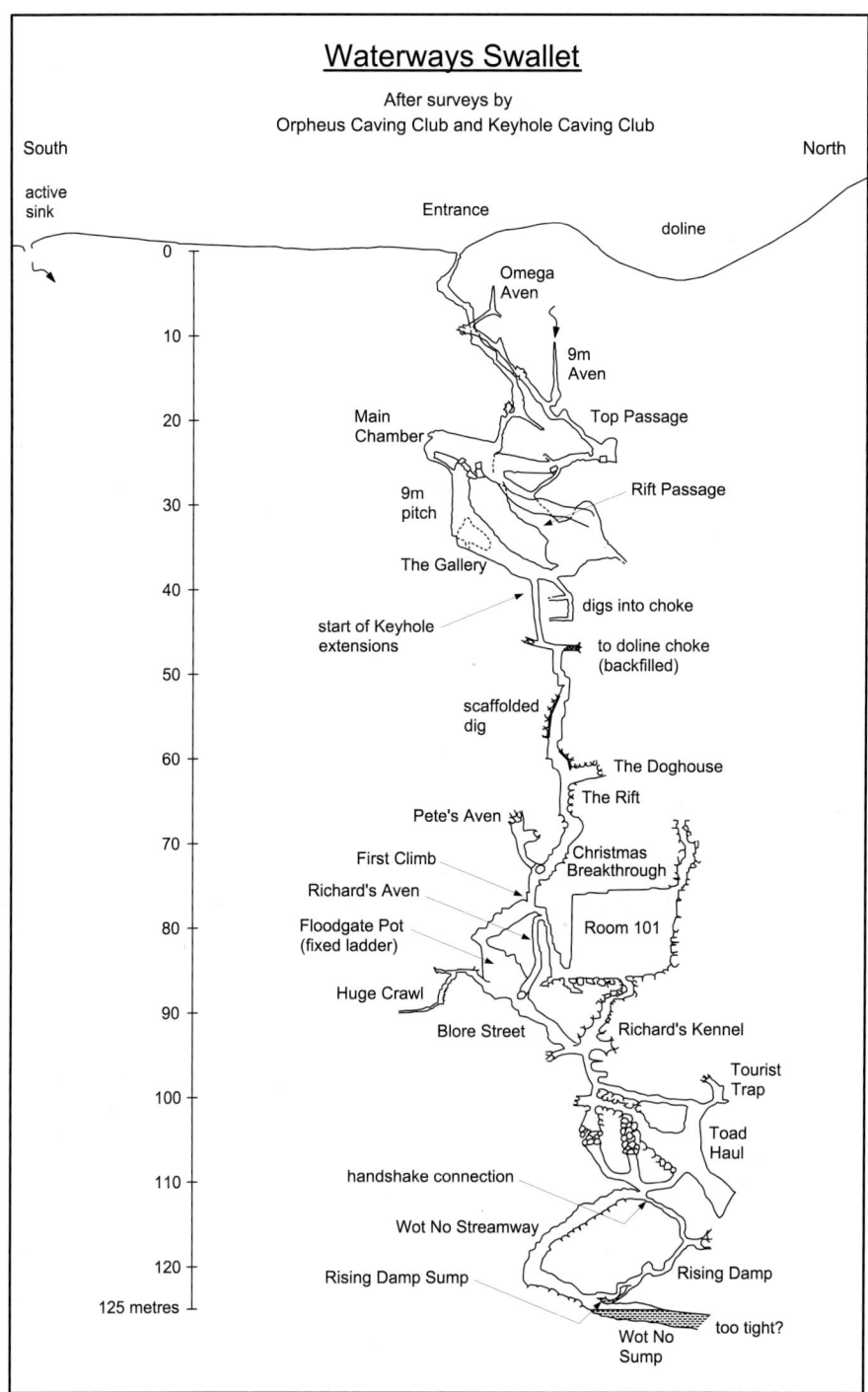

bypass massive terminal boulder collapse which underlies large shakehole seen on the surface near the cave entrance. Longest dig is via obvious inclined stooping passage which soon becomes flat out crawl past and under boulders jammed against solid left wall and into tight bedding plane. The stream has been traced to Hinkley Wood Risings at Ilam.

From the Gallery, an enlarged rift descends to a short crawl and a short climbable pot. Around the corner at the bottom, a series of scaffolded climbs lead through a squeeze to the top of a narrow vertical scaffolded rift, (The Doghouse). Descend this and crawl though the choke, with a solid wall on the right, to a small cavity. From here, the route doubles back below itself to emerge in standing passage and the start of the lower streamway. This is followed down a couple of climbs to reach the top of Floodgate Pot, 16ft (5m) deep and laddered on the right. From the bottom a large passage (Blore Street) leads down a couple of climbs to a choke. A route down through the choke or a squeeze on the left both reach the same chamber from which a further crawl leads out. This is followed to emerge half way up a large, impressive chamber, Toad Haul.

A dig into a rift 23ft (7m) down under the first climb in Blore Street emerges into Room 101, a collapse chamber about 40ft (12m) x 26ft (8m) x 33ft (10m) high, A tube at the top has voice connection with Richard's Aven. A dig in the floor led through a dangerous choke to the bottom end of Blore Street. An upward dig into the choke draughts strongly.

A lifelined climb leads to the floor of the chamber. Immediately at the foot of the climb, a squeeze between boulders leads to sizeable phreatic tube (Wotno Streamway) descending for 230ft (70m) to Wotno Sump. Just before the sump, a low duck on the right leads to further passage, heading back up under the floor of Toad Haul. This has a number of crawls off of it, and a further sump (Rising Damp). Back in Toad Haul, a gulley on the far wall leads to a fixed rope and climb into a short passage. This leads through a very tight squeeze (The Tourist Trap) and into a small dry streamway. This emerges back in the roof of Toad Haul and gives a 50ft (15m) pitch back to the floor. The lowest point in Toad Haul is still being dug, as are a crawl near the foot of Floodgate Pot and a number of other choked inlets.

**Tackle:**
*Most of the cave is free-climbable. Fixed ropes should be assessed by those using them.*
*Climb down to Room 101 should be lifelined.*
*Descent from Room 101 to Blore Street has a fixed ladder, but check condition.*
*Climb down to Toad Haul is exposed and should be lifelined.*
*Climb up to Tourist Trap may have a fixed rope. Jammer useful.*

*References: Anon. 1974. O.C.C. N/L Vol.10. No.4. p.32.*
*Drakeley, K. 1981. The Lyre No.5. pp.54-56.*
*Mayer, D. 1962. British Caver No.36. p.48.*
*Milner, M. 1987. D.C.A. N/L No.65. p.17.*
*Potts, J. 1981. The Lyre No.5. pp.36-37.*
*Potts, J. 1981. The Lyre No.5. pp.50-53. Survey. Potts, J. 1981. O.C.C. N/L Vol.10. No.6. p.49.*

### WEAG'S BRIDGE CAVE
**NGR 100 540**     Grade: 1
**Alt. 540ft (165m)**

100 yards (91m) downstream from the bridge, by the track. A small rift cave.

### WEAG'S BRIDGE RESURGENCE
**NGR 0995 5446**     **Grade: 1**
**Alt. 540ft (165m)**
**Length: 72ft (21m)**

In the north bank of the River Manifold.
A tight crawl for 60ft (18m), then a descent down a tight vertical chimney. Acts as either a sink or a resurgence depending on river flow conditions. The start of the crawl was widened by members of Darfar P.C. during the 1990's who then extended the cave by several metres down a tight, descending rift at the end to an enlargement and parallel rift with water.
References: Allwright, P. 1976. O.C.C. N/L Vol. 12. No.5. pp.18-19. Survey.
Milner, M. 1998. D.C.A. N/L No. 97. p.1.

### WEAVER HILLS SPRING
**NGR 093 461**     **Dig**

A very small rising. The source of the Hudford Brook, which drains southwards to the River Churnet.
References: Beasley, F. 1975. D.C.A. N/L No.24.

### WEDNESDAY POT
**NGR 0967 5544**     **Grade: 3**
**Alt. 585ft (178m)**
**Length: 180ft (56m)**
**Depth: 15ft (5m)**

In right hand side of river bed under trees.
The cave can quickly flood to the roof. Do not descend if the river is sinking below the stone bridge near Redhurst Swallet.
Manhole cover over - please replace. 10ft (3m) climb down entrance rift leads to 2 ways on. Down and left is the upstream passage, 20ft (6m) of crawling becoming tight. In the floor just before the end, a descent can be made to a lower passage, which was enlarged by Darfar P.C. during the 1990's for about 30ft (10m) in the direction of Redhurst Swallet. The cave continues in the same direction, draughting strongly, but just too tight to negotiate and needs enlarging. Removal of spoil a problem.
Right at the bottom of the entrance shaft is a squeeze along a bedding into larger downstream passage averaging 4ft (1.3m) wide and 3ft (1m) high. Follow to a pool and crawl through to larger section with perched sump on right. Passage can be followed for some distance until it gets too low approaching T-Pot (qv). Part way along here at a cross-rift, a voice connection with North Passage in T-Pot has been established. Sometimes a stream is active along the whole downstream passage, its source being the perched sump. The river can be heard roaring below the known cave under certain conditions, and when flooded has been traced to Redhurst Swallet. It flows to Project Pot via T-Pot.
References: The Manifold Caver 1984. p.19. Survey.
The Manifold Caver 1983. p.23. Survey.
Milner, M. 1995. D.C.A. N/L No. 89. p.12.
Milner, M. 1996. D.C.A. N/L No. 93. p.12.

### WETSTONES SWALLET
**NGR 0985 4710**     **Grade: 2**
**Alt. 1060ft (323m)**
**Length: 20ft (6m)**

In the plantation between Walk and Weaver Farms.
A small stream, fed from meres, sinks at the foot of a low crag. Digging has uncovered a short length of cave from the back of which it is possible to climb up into a loose roof area or down into a choked pot. Water has been traced to Ilam. The crag bears traces of old flowstone and embedded pebbles, and cavity behind overhang at one end contains remains of old stalactites.
References: Mellors, P.T. 1973. D.C.A. N/L No.18. p.2.
Mellors, P.T. 1989. D.C.A. N/L No.71. pp.2-9.
Mellors, P.T. 1993. Descent No. 110. p.14.

### WETTON MILL COOPE CAVES
**NGR 0985 5645**    Digs
Alt. 1,033ft (315m) approx.
Status: National Trust. S.S.S.I.

A number of small draughting badger holes around the summit of the ridge north and above Wetton Mill.

### WETTON HILL FAR CAVE
**NGR 106 562**    Grade: 1
Alt. 1070ft (325m)
Depth: 30ft (10m)
Status: National Trust. S.S.S.I.

6ft (2m) climb down into entrance chamber up to 10ft (3m) long, 10ft (3m) high and 6ft (2m) wide. 10ft (3m) climb down in northern corner leads to descending rifts in solid rock, gradually getting too tight for further progress. Carries a lot of percolation water after heavy rain. Entrance has grille over to deter livestock. Please replace. (Adjustable spanner required.)

*Milner, M. 2006. The Derbyshire Caver (D.C.A.) No. 125. p13.*

### WETTON MILL HILL CAVE
**NGR 102 562**    Grade: 1
Alt. 900ft (274m)
Status: National Trust. S.S.S.I.

In crag at top of west side of Wetton Hill near two isolated thorn trees.

A short muddy fissure passage.

### WETTON MILL SINK
**NGR 0970 5603**    Dig
Alt. 610ft (186m)
Status: National Trust. S.S.S.I.

500ft (152m) downstream from Wetton Mill Bridge.

A large volume of water, the entire river in dry weather, is engulfed by the river bed. Digging over many years has confirmed that the site is a huge boulder choke. Water can be heard roaring below. The nearby Darfar Pot (qv) has by-passed this choke, and meets the river underground. In wet weather the river overflows to sink at Redhurst Swallet, and progressively further downstream.

### WETTON ROAD SINKS
**NGR 0991 5562**    Digs
Alt. 595ft (181m)

Just below road from Wetton Mill to Wetton Village, in river bed, 100 yards (91m) downstream from Redhurst Bridge where the road starts to rise (on bend) to leave river level.

A large hollow in river bed that has been completely concreted up and contains iron pipes to relieve pressure arising during flooding of the cave beneath. Some fissures have been dug, and the roar of water can be heard under certain conditions. All are too narrow for further progress.

### WETTON ROAD SINK
**NGR 0992 5560**    Grade: 1 (Dig)
Alt. 610ft (186m)
Length: 10ft (3m)

Situated at the downstream end of the large concreted area. Manhole cover over - please replace.

A clean-washed passage descends down the beds for about 10ft (3m) until it gets too tight. Needs enlarging.

*References: Milner, M. 1996. D.C.A. N/L No. 93. p.12.*

### WHIRLPOOL POT
**NGR 0945 5040**    Grade: Dig
Alt. 670ft (204m) approx.
Depth: 16ft (5m)

A large sink at the foot of a crag behind the sewage treatment works in the right-hand side of the river bed (looking downstream). Originally dug to a depth of around 13ft (4m) in thinly bedded rock in the early 1980's. Cave subsequently collapsed after floods and is need of re-opening.

*References: Milner, M. 1983. D.C.A.Newsletter No.51. pp.2-6.*

## Features listed as potential archaeological sites

1: NGR 1068 5407  Alt: 171m  At the base of Beeston Tor, 5m above river bed. Narrows to the base. Small tube 2m above the floor.
2: NGR 1070 5404  Alt: 205m  A small cave on the western side of Beeston Tor.
3: NGR 1070 5406  Alt: 230m  A large shelter towards the top of a cliff. A low crawl leads off to the West. Fissure at back is blind.
4: NGR 1076 5403  Alt: 195m  A very small entrance leading to a larger chamber.
5: NGR 1076 5405  Alt: 215m  A large fissure open to the sky.
6: NGR 1081 5400  Alt: 195m  A single chamber, with passage off to the west.
7: NGR 0950 5611  Alt: 193m  A small low cave next to the footpath.
8: NGR 0958 5576  Alt: 202m  A narrow mouthed fissure.
9: NGR 0979 5488  Alt: 286m  A shaft entrance 1.50m deep to the rear of Elderbush and Seven Ways Caves.

# THE RIVER LATHKILL CATCHMENT AREA

Upper Lathkill Dale

The Lathkill area has always been rather frustrating to cavers, for the most extensive caves are only accessible in drought. However, abandoned high level caves such as Water Icicle have started to yield their secrets, and suggest the existence of an extensive high level network.

Lathkill Dale drains the structural basin centred on Monyash, and the risings from Lathkill Head Cave down to Cales Dale owe their position to a saddle-like structure on the eastern rim of the basin. Lavas outcrop in the valley floor further to the east, and this would keep the drainage on the surface were it not for the soughs which capture it in dry conditions.

There are no large allogenic sinks in the Monyash area, but a few small trickles which accumulate above the lavas do sink round the edge of the outcrop.

Lathkill Head Cave and Lower Cales Dale Cave are the most extensive systems. Both discharge a large volume of water in flood, and both are flooded after a short distance in all but very dry weather. Prospects for extension are good in both cases. At the limit of Lathkill Head Cave, long considered to be unpushable, a way was found through the choke in 1990 to enter a continuation which soon needed more digging. In the same year, the length of Lower Cales Dale Cave nearly doubled, and there is still a very powerful draught at the farthest limit.

Opposite Lathkill Head Cave lies Critchlow Cave, more frequently accessible, and pushed to a draughting choke after a gruelling crawl for some 2000ft (610m), where determined pushing revealed more low passage, and another "final" choke. Critchlow Cave can also discharge a large stream in very severe floods, suggesting a connection with the main drainage system somewhere far to the west.

The only other connection with the main drainage is in the Knotlow Mine, north west of Monyash. Here the miners have intersected natural passages carrying a large stream which disappears into a very deep sump, and is thought to reappear at Lathkill Head Cave.

Careful investigation of other mines in the area, and some determined digging, may well reveal extensive (and large) vadose passages to the west of the known system. Further prospects have opened up in Water Icicle, and there is the chance of superbly decorated high level cave here.

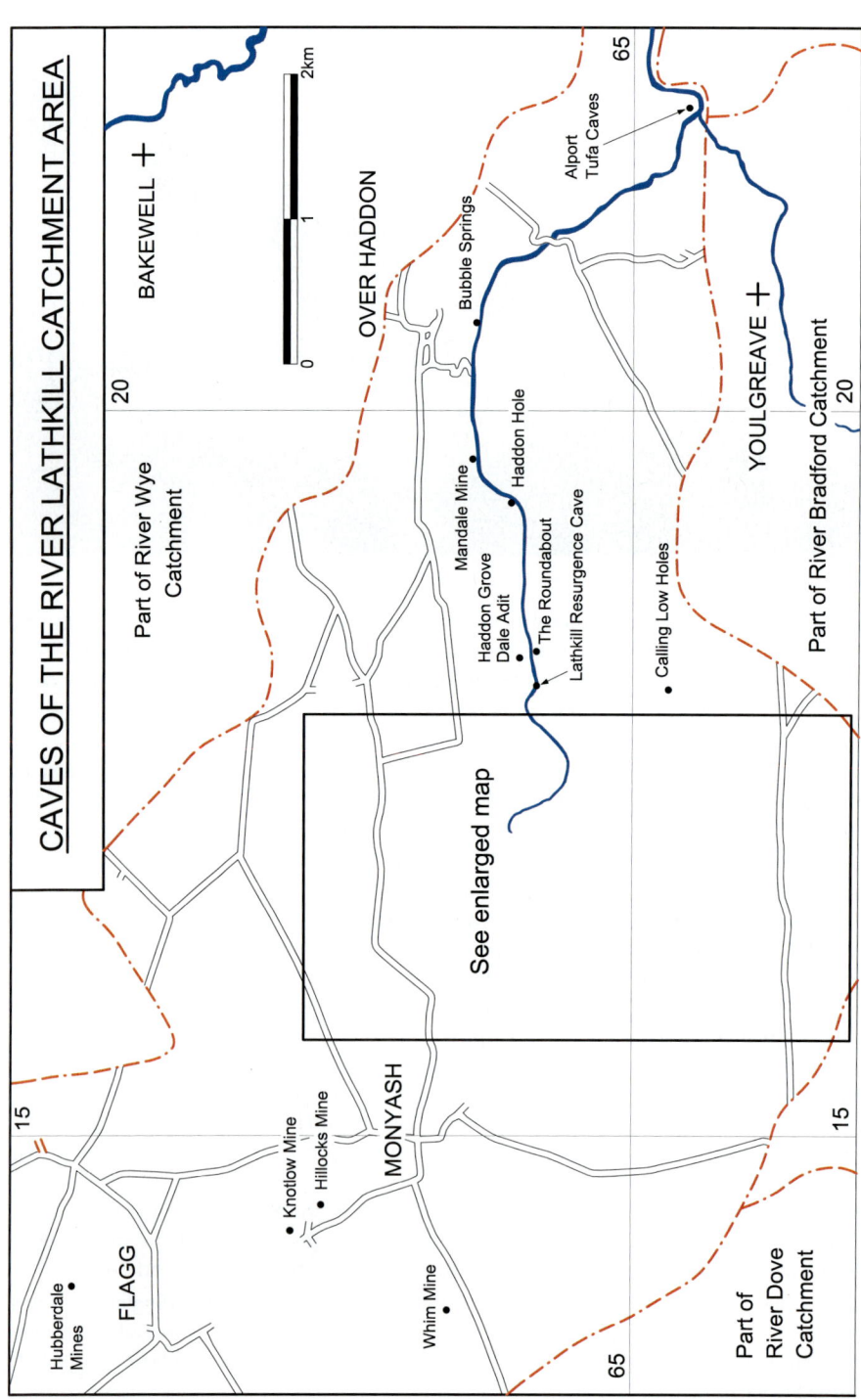

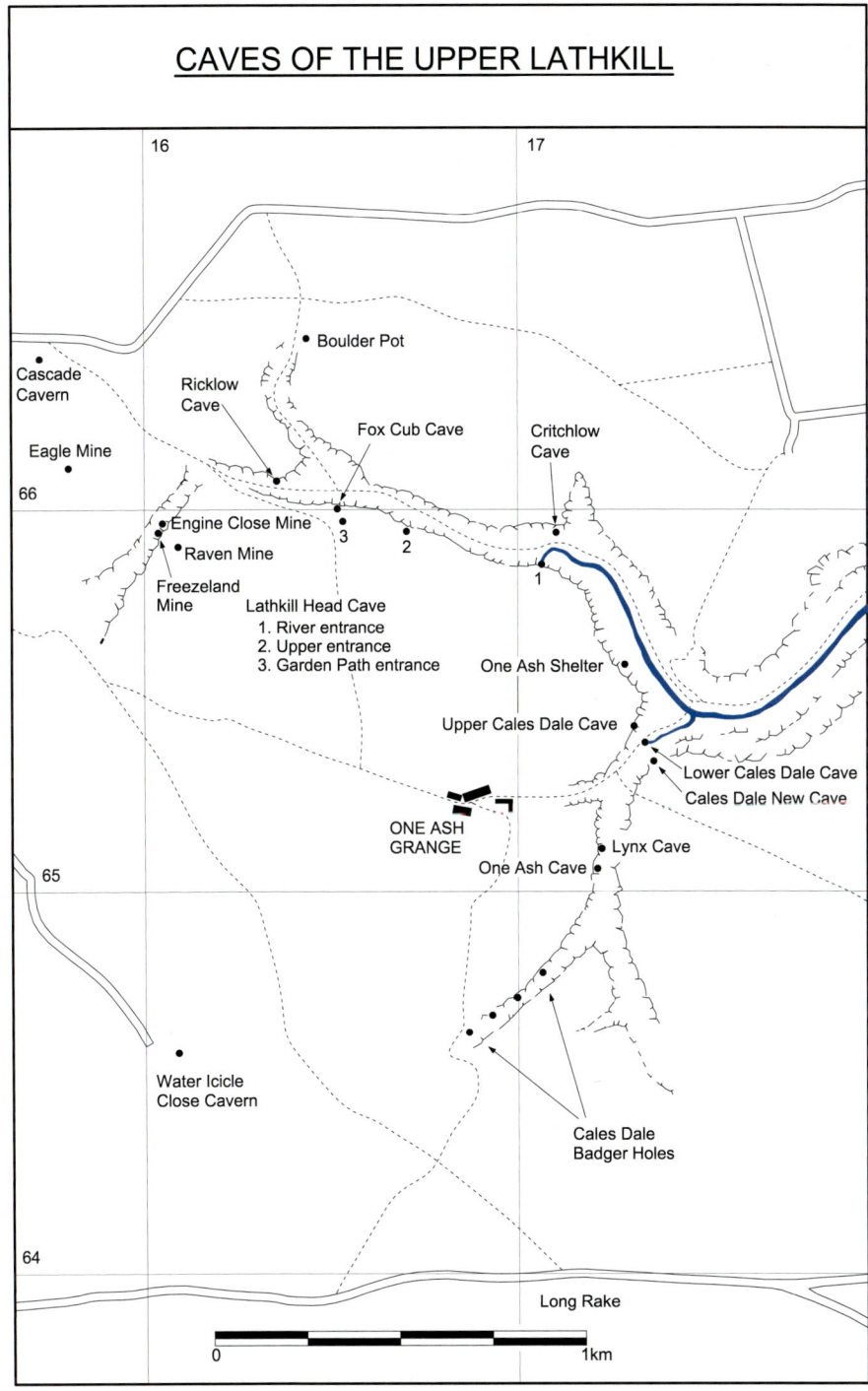

### ALPORT TUFA CAVES
NGR 221 646     Grade: 1
Alt. 450ft (137m)
Length: 20ft (6m)

Alport by Youlgrave. Situated immediately north of the road.

A unique series of small rock shelter type caves in late Pleistocene tufa. Variously used as hen houses and cart park, but potentially of archaeological interest. One cave partly collapsed after 1963 frosts exposing moonmilk in cavities in tufa.

### BOULDER POT
NGR 164 665     Grade: 2
Alt. 875ft (267m)
Length: 320ft (37m)
Depth: 110ft (34m)

On left of track to Ricklow Quarry from Bakewell-Monyash road, among large boulders.

Please keep the entrance closed. Narrow entrance leads to small bone chamber and a further descent to crawls. A series of tight climbs allow access to the original terminal choke, which was passed by Dave Arveschoug, Pete Brocklehurst, Mike Sutton, Ben Bentham in 1993 to 200ft (60m) of passage with two free-climbable pitches. Whole place is rather unstable. The strong draught may come from Critchlow Cave.

### BUBBLE SPRINGS
NGR 206 661     Springs
Alt. 605ft (185m)

In the bed of the River Lathkill, close to the tail of Lathkill Dale Sough.

Water rises from beneath tufa in the bed of the Lathkill, above toadstone. In dry weather it can be seen that there is nothing enterable.

### CALES DALE BADGER HOLES
NGR 167 646 - 172 648     Digs
Alt. 900-1000ft (270-300m)

On both sides of the south west branch of Cales Dale.

Five or six small badger holes, some large enough to enter. Require digging.

### CALES DALE CAVE (LOWER)
NGR 174 654     Grade: 2-5
Alt. 675ft (206m)
Length: 3460ft (1055m)
Status: S.S.S.I.

Extended 1971 by P.T.Mellors and Eldon Pothole Club, and in 1976 and 1990 by the Technical Speleological Group.

Two low entrances below the footpath up Cales Dale, a short distance from the confluence with Lathkill Dale.

**Warning: Almost the whole cave floods to the roof in wet weather, and beyond Figures of Eight chamber in all but drought. Trips to the end are extremely arduous.**

Two entrances unite inside. Low phreatic passage for 125ft (38m) to the First Chamber. On the right the floor rises to Stalactite Chamber with closed avens above and 50ft (15m) of passage, blocked at the end. To the left of the First Chamber the passage can be followed for 40ft (12m) to the Second Chamber. A 40ft (12m) crawl on the right leads to the Rathole, dug through loose boulders in 1971 to a large chamber, the Dog House. A 32ft (10m) climb up the far wall leads to a junction after 25ft (8m). Passages to left and right are both blocked after 20ft (6m). A crawl at floor level in the Dog House draughts strongly, and was partly dug in 1990 in the hope of by-passing the sump. From the Second Chamber 70ft (21m) of muddy passage can be followed to Figures of Eight Chamber, which is as far as can be explored in normal weather.

**Beyond the Sump**                                                              **Grade 3-5**

A tight descending squeeze to the left at the start of Figures of Eight Chamber leads to where the sump is normally met. Sump was passed in 1959 drought, but little progress was made. The sump was again passed in the 1976 drought. 100ft (30m) of glutinous muddy passage leads to a crawl on

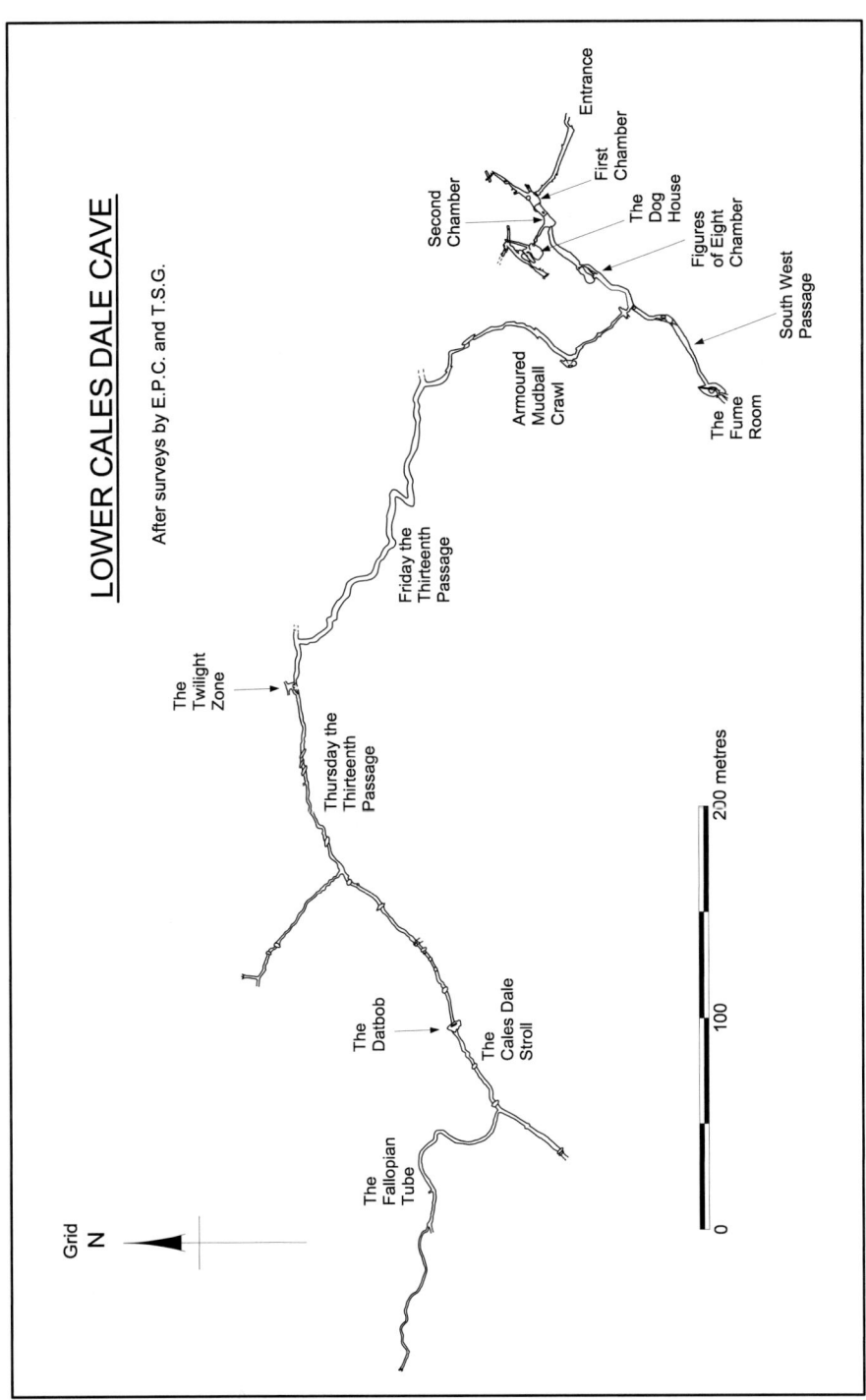

the right, but the main route can be followed through a boulder choke for 180ft (55m) to a second choke. This was passed in 1997 to the Fume Room, and a short continuation to the final choke. The arduous crawl on the right, Armoured Mudball Crawl leads to a small blind aven on the left after 130ft (40m). The crawl continues for a further 180ft (55m) to an aven 26ft (8m) long and about 40ft (12m) high. A crawl at the top may be the other end of the dig in the Dog House. Beyond the aven a further 100ft (30m) of muddy crawling arrives at a low wide bedding plane on the right, too low to enter, the outlet for the stream. Friday the Thirteenth Passage continues as a hands and knees crawl over a gravel floor to a T-junction after 525ft (160m). Right is blocked with clay immediately while left can be followed for 65ft (20m) to a boulder choke, which was passed in the 1990 drought. A squeeze leads up into an aven. Two possible leads high in the aven are unpushed. A further squeeze down through boulders rejoins the main passage, Thursday the Thirteenth Passage, which continues for 330ft (100m) to a junction. The crawl on the right is thought to be the other end of Dawkes' Crawl in Lathkill Head Cave. It can be followed for 220ft (67m) to a junction. Left is silted while right ends after 20ft (6m) at a draughting choke. Main passage continues for 155ft (47m) to a squeeze through boulders below a chamber. Another 155ft (47m) leads past more unpushed avens and inlets to a further choke. A very awkward upward squeeze leads into a chamber, and a climb down rejoins the main passage. The passage soon becomes walking sized for the first time. The Cales Dale Stroll continues to a further choke 265ft (81m) beyond the chamber. Two parallel rifts immediately before the choke lead up through loose boulders into a low bedding plane which becomes too low for progress in all directions. A crawl on the right 120ft (37m) before the choke has been pushed to a junction. The left hand branch is unsurveyed, but the right branch, the Fallopian Tube, leads to a choke in a rift 560ft (171m) from the main passage.

References: Butcher, N.J.D. 1985. Jour. T.S.G. No.11. 1985. p.23
Coates, P. & Wicken, F. 1956. The Speleologist Vol.1. No.4. Survey.
Gill, D.W. 1972. D.C.A. N/L No.12. p.3.
Gill, D.W. 1977. Descent No. 35. p.8.
Gill, D.W. 1976. D.C.A. N/L No.30. pp.10-12.
Westlake, C.D. 1972. Eldon P.C. Journal Vol.8. No.1. pp.31-33. Survey.

### CALES DALE CAVE (UPPER)
(Churn Hole)
NGR 1730 6544   Grade: 1 (Arch)
Alt. 775ft (232m)
Length: 200ft (60m)

Above and to the left of Lower Calesdale Cave on a shelf at the base of a small crag high on the west side of the dale.

There has been considerable confusion between this cave and One Ash Cave, One Ash Shelter, and Lynx Cave, all at about the same altitude and given different names by cavers and archaeologists. A stooping passage divides after 75ft (23m). Left is a blocked crawl, while right is a crawl terminating in a low clay-filled passage. The right hand passage may connect to a low clay-filled entrance on a shelf to the right of the main entrance. Excavated material includes Iron Age and Roman pottery and animal remains, now in the Manchester Museum.

References: Coates, P. & Wicken, F. 1956. The Speleologist No.4. pp.174-175.
Jackson, J.W. & Storrs Fox, W. 1913. Geol. Mag. Vol.60. pp.259-262.
Pennington, R. 1875. Quart. Jour. Geol. Soc. Vol.31. pp.238-240.

### CALES DALE NEW CAVE
NGR 1736 6538  Grade: 2
Alt. 670ft (204m)
Length: 65ft (20m)

Excavated in 1982 by O.C.C.
Almost opposite Lower Cales Dale Cave entrance.
A bedding crawl which became too low for progress.
*References: Morton, K. 1984. D.C.A. N/L No.56. p.2.*

### CALLING LOW HOLES
NGR 181 648  Digs
(Callenge Low Holes)
Alt. 1025ft (312m)

Situated east of the head of Cales Dale south of the farm.
A group of large shakeholes. One leads to a partially collapsed chamber, with small inlets and a rubble floor, said to have been dug out some years ago. Now partly filled in. A small un-named cave lies nearby in the field overlooking the head of Cales Dale. A stooping entrance soon reduces to a tight crawl.
*References: Farey, J. 1811. A general view of the Agriculture and Minerals of Derbyshire. Vol.1.    (London). p.293.*
*Mellors, P.T. 1971. D.C.A. N/L No.10. pp.2-3.*

### CASCADE CAVERN
(Rumbling Hole)
NGR 157 664  Grade: 2
Alt. 820ft (250m)
Length: 125ft (41m)
Depth: 60ft (18m)

Permission from Mr Mycock, Rowson House Farm, Monyash.
At the top of the slope behind the toilet block on the south side of Lathkill Dale close to the Monyash - Bakewell road.
It has been wrongly referred to as Eagle Mine, which lies at 158 661. It is likely to be Eagle Mine whose alternative name was Rumbling Hole. A 40ft (12m) pitch lands on a steep slope of rubble and farm debris leading down into a natural chamber, with an inlet high on the left. In the opposite direction, a mined passage leads under dangerous stacked deads into an area of unstable workings with a dangerous false floor on rotten timbers. Down the steep slope (handline useful) the roof lowers to walking height, and on the right is a steep, descending passage to a clay choke (dug intermittently). Ahead, the main passage crosses a mined shaft in the floor, excavated to a blind face at 16ft (5m) depth, but now completely refilled, and ends just beyond in a series of small worked out mineral pockets.

**Tackle:**
**Entrance pitch: 50ft (15m) rope.**
*References: Gee, S. 1957. The Lyre, Vol.1. No.2.*
*Knox C.S. 1998. CCPC N/L.*

### CRITCHLOW CAVE
NGR 1710 6593  Grade: 4
Alt. 680ft (204m)
Length: 2200ft (670m) approx.
Status: S.S.S.I.

Inside the Lathkill Dale Nature Reserve, which is managed by the Natural England. Evidence of membership of a club with BCA affiliation may be asked for by the wardens.
Entrance crawl excavated by B.S.A. in 1947.
Directly opposite Lathkill Head Cave, but higher up the bank, by a lone bush.

**Warning: The whole cave can fill to the roof in flood, and a stream can flow from the entrance. The cave often sumps in wet winter months at Eccles' Limit, cutting off the draught. A trip to the far end is an arduous undertaking even in dry conditions, and rescue would be extremely difficult.**

Downward sloping entrance crawl for 20ft (6m) then sharp left turn through unpleasant muddy duck, and right turn with squeeze into Warren Chamber. Right hand crawl ahead leads through narrow channel with pools to a further chamber containing muddy flowstone. Continuing crawl develops into wide low bedding cave which veers to right (avoid obvious earlier right turn which is blind), through two small grottoes and over a gravelly floor to a fallen block. Squeeze down under the block (occasionally gravel-choked) into a wide low descending phreatic passage with gravel and stal floor and good formations. Branch to left at end after crawl through pool levels out but is muddy, and marks the limit of exploration by Eccles Caving Club in 1963. From Eccles' limit the way on is a squeeze into a tight and awkward section with extensive breakdown. Wide low easier passage is regained beyond. A further 850ft (260m) (Critchlow 2) was discovered in 1984. It is mostly crawling, but has some fine formations, and leads to two chambers. A low arch at the foot of a mud slope from the roof emerges into a boulder collapse area, where a breakthrough was made in 1991 to further arduous passages totalling over 850ft (260m) and not completely surveyed. A strong draught blows throughout the cave.

References: Beck, J., Gill, D., & Butcher, N. 1980 & 1984. Critchlow Cave. Survey.
Eccles Caving Club. 1963. D.C.A. N/L No.8.
Mellors, P.T. 1985. D.C.A. N/L No.57. pp.2-3.

### EAGLE MINE
NGR 158 661    Dig. (Mine)

A blocked mineshaft which has been confused with Cascade Cavern.

### ENGINE CLOSE MINE
NGR 1605 6596    Grade: 2
Alt. 825ft (251m)
Length: 150ft (46m)
Depth: 30ft (9m)

In Ferndale, a south branch of Lathkill Dale.
A 10ft entrance shaft leads to a short level, with a blocked way out to the valley side. A 20ft pitch leads to a lower level 100ft long. Small natural solution cavities.
References: George, T. 1989. Descent No.86. p.14.

### FOX CUB CAVE
NGR 1655 6600    Dig
Alt. 835ft (255m)

In the back wall of the eastern quarry just below the northern edge of the field containing the Lathkill Head Garden Path entrance.
Foxes have partly excavated a clay-filled phreatic passage. The opening is about 2ft (0.6m) wide and 1ft (0.27m) high. There is a slight, cool outward draft. A second, much smaller hole, lies approx. 5 metres to the right.
References: Knox,C. 2006. CCPC N/L No.90.

### FREEZELAND MINE
NGR 1608 6594    Grade: 2
Alt. 840ft (256m)
Depth: 20ft (6m)

In the field immediately south east of Fern Dale.
A 20ft shaft intersects a phreatic tube, backfilled with rubble. Shaft is presumed to have been deeper.
References: Milner, M. 1988. D.C.A. N/L No.68. p.15.

### GREEN COWDEN CHERT QUARRY CAVE
NGR 200 678    Lost
Alt. 870ft (260m)
Length: 20ft (6m)

In disused chert quarry, north of the Bakewell-Monyash road.
A small crawl passage with a boulder floor goes round two bends and is then choked with boulders. Cave now buried by quarry infilling.

## HADDON GROVE DALE ADIT

**NGR** 183 658   **Grade:** 2 (Mine)
**Alt.** 590ft (180m)
**Length:** 213ft (65m)

Situated on the western side of Haddon Grove Dale, a small subsidiary dale of the Lathkill. Entrance obscured by a lone thorn bush.

An adit, possibly on Gank Hole Vein, terminating in a squeeze that may be passable.

## HADDON HOLE

**NGR** 194 659   Lost
**Alt.** 550ft (167m)
**Length:** 30ft (9m)

In the bed of the Lathkill, east of the ruined Mandale Aqueduct. A short crawl. Accessible only in drought, and often blocked by debris. Cannot now be located.

## HILLOCKS MINE
(Whalf Mine, Whalf Pipe)

**NGR** Climbing shaft 1449 6729: Engine shaft 1448 6729
**Grade:** 3
**Alt.** 937ft (285m)
**Length:** 1963ft (598m)
**Depth:** 168ft (51m)
**Status:** S.S.S.I.

No prior permission necessary but please use stile.

**Warning: CO$_2$ build-up can occur in the lower parts of the mine.**

North west of Monyash just south of the lane, 400ft (122m) east of junction with Green Lane. Capped climbing shaft in the small walled copse on the north side of Blackwell Lane. Capped engine shaft lies on the west side of the boundary wall of the walled copse, reached by a second stile.

Entrance is through oil drum in bottom of old open working. Easy walking for 310ft (94m) then flat crawl opening abruptly onto 9ft (3m) climb down. Squeeze through into 47ft (14m) straight coffin level to First Pitch of 23ft (7m). Several short scrambles lead to Second Pitch, an involved series of short climbs and steep slopes. At the bottom a low arch leads to big levels. Left becomes water filled after 90ft (27m), dived for 13ft (4m) to base of run-in shaft. Right chokes after 60ft (18m) but half right is large 19th century level with the older coffin level in the roof.

After 30ft (9m) rubble slope to right, beyond which very steep rubble slope descends to the left, ending in a coffin level and a flooded area (dived for 16ft (5m) to impassable squeeze), the lowest point in Hillocks Mine. Large level continues through shallow pool to Main Chamber, 30ft (9m) in diameter and 130ft (40m) from arch at foot of Second Pitch. In roof is 190ft (58m) Engine Shaft capped at surface. To right (SE) is roomy passage and up to left after 30ft (9m) to the bottom of the climbing shaft entrance. Main route continues to end of workings 340ft (103m) from Main Chamber. Halfway along is a coffin level on the right, 55ft (16m) long to a choke. To left (NW) in Main Chamber is comfortable undulating passage for 280ft (85m) passing Pool Chamber, but 130ft (40m) before the end is an obscure passage on the right which leads through several tight, loose, muddy crawls to Meccano Passage in Knotlow Cavern.

Climbing shaft was reopened in 1998. A 125ft (38m) pitch lands in a short cross cut to the head of a 23ft (7m) pitch, then a series of short climbs and passages lead to the Main Chamber.

Engine shaft can be rigged as a 190ft (58m) drop to the Main Chamber, or enter a bedding at 128ft (39m) to the head of a 62ft (19m) pitch to the Main Chamber.

**Tackle:**
**Hillocks Mine:**

|  |  |
|---|---|
| *First Pitch:* | *15m rope. Eco hanger and Y hang at pitch head.* |
| *Second Pitch and slopes:* | *35m rope. Eco hanger, eyebolt, Y hang at pitch head, rebelay to jammed boulder for slope.* |

**Climbing Shaft:**
    First Pitch: 45m rope. Belay to bar in shaft lid. Backup to ring. 3 rebelays.
    Second Pitch: 10m rope.
**Walf Pipe Engine Shaft:**
    Direct descent: 70m rope. Belay to rings in shaft lid.
    Alternative route: 55m rope to head of parallel shaft.
    35m rope with 1 rebelay and 1 deviation.

References: Gilbert, J.C. 1952. Cave Science Vol.3. No.21. pp.223-226. Survey.
Knox, C.S. 1998. Caves & Caving No.80. p.8.
Knox, C.S. 2000. C.C.P.C. N/L No.65. pp.3-6.
Mellor, D. 1983. Eldon P.C. Journal Vol.9. No.3. pp.1-6.
Robey, J.A. 1961. Bull. P.D.M.H.S. Vol.1. No.5. pp.30-36.
Robey, J.A. 1962. Bull. P.D.M.H.S. Vol.1. No.6. pp.29-35.
Robey, J.A. 1963. Bull. P.D.M.H.S. Vol.2. No.1. pp.51-56.

### HUBBERDALE PIPE CAVERNS
**NGR 14 69. Sough tail in Deepdale at 161 695   Lost**

A pipe vein said to be 150 yards (137m) wide, running a little west of north, intersected by the level from Deepdale at 46 fathoms depth. No details known, and all shafts and level blocked (the latter about 1000ft (305m) in). Old accounts suggest that it would be very extensive and interesting if access could be gained. Two Gins Shaft (190ft / 58m deep to water) was dived to 20m depth to a short unstable passage.

References: Worley, N. et al. 1978. P.D.M.H.S. Bull. 7 (1) pp.31-39. Survey.
Kirkham, N. 1958. P.D.M.H.S. Bull. 2 (4) pp.206-209.
Smith, P. 1957. Lyre No.2. pp.54-68.

### KNOTLOW CAVERN
**NGR 1438 6739 (climbing shaft)**
**Grade: 3-5 (Mine)**
**Alt. 960ft (290m)**
**Length: 1.25 miles (2km)**
**Depth: 250ft (76m)**
Status: S.S.S.I.

The climbing shaft is fitted with a lid. Large adjustable spanner required. Permission for Crimbo Hollow Engine Shaft from Knotlow Farm. Access via Cross Lane, turning off B5055 at double bend just west of Monyash. Park at junction of Cross and Blackwell Lanes.

Reopened by Eccles Caving Club in 1959. Extensions by E.P.C., S.U.S.S., and B.S.A. (T.P.U.) 1968-1972.

Various entrances between Dale House and Knotlow Farm, northwest of Monyash. Crimbo Hollow Engine Shaft is amongst trees towards Knotlow Farm.

**Warning: Crimbo Swallow and Crimbo Pipe inlet are dangerous except in dry weather. There can be $CO_2$ build-up in the lower parts of the system.**

#### Entrance to Rift Chamber   Grade 3

Very interesting system with both natural and mined passages, including some of the finest coffin levels in Derbyshire. First Pitch is climbing shaft 50ft (15m) deep, followed by a low arch to Second Pitch of 25ft (8m) into Pearl Chamber. Muddy passage leads to a climb down, and a hole on the right opens partway down the 210ft (64m) Chapel Dale Engine Shaft. Further scrambles lead to a wide low chamber with the route ahead to the Bung Series. To the right, more scrambling leads to a 30ft (9m) pitch into Waterfall Chamber, wet on lower part. Meccano Passage, high in the wall of the chamber, can be reached by a pendulum from Waterfall Engine Shaft, and is 350ft (107m) of difficult caving with squeezes, mud and loose boulders to the north east passage of Hillocks Mine. Waterfall

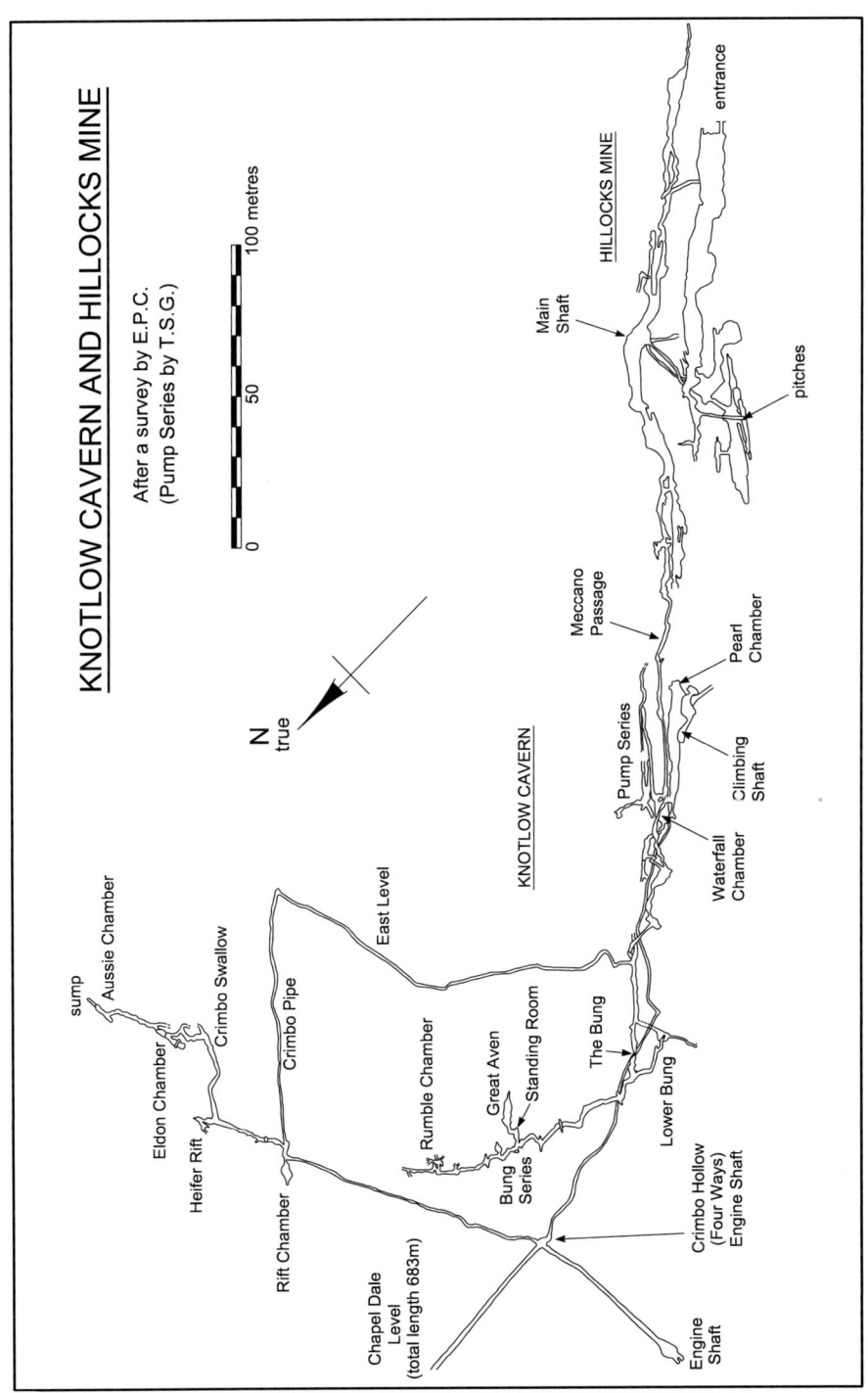

Chamber can also be reached direct by 210ft (64m) Chapel Dale Engine Shaft. The flooded shaft in the floor of Waterfall Chamber has been pumped out by TPU and EPC to find 500ft (152m) of levels normally completely submerged. A tub and rag-and-chain pump were recovered. Water can be followed 502ft (153m) downstream from Waterfall Chamber through coffin level (with deep water towards the end) to the foot of Crimbo Hollow Engine Shaft ("Fourways Shaft"), 175ft (53m) deep, an alternative entrance. On the left is 180ft (55m) of large mine level to the foot of another big engine shaft. Ahead is Chapel Dale Level, very dull paddling for 2291ft (698m). To the right (downstream) is another coffin level 300ft (92m) long with deep water. On the left at the end is Rift Chamber, 25ft (8m) long and 10ft (3m) wide.

### Crimbo Pipe Inlet and Crimbo Swallow — Grade 5

Turning right at Rift Chamber, a big inlet is met with all the water disappearing under the left wall. The water can be followed downstream in dry weather through a long duck, then a part-mined passage. On the left is a low passage leading to Heifer Rift, probably another miners' route in, but now blocked. Surface shaft approx. 100ft (30m) deep is closed at surface and connection blocked by about 10ft (3m) of fill (Knox, 1991). Stream flows into low crawl, Crimbo Swallow. 128ft (39m) of very wet crawling (water backs up on return) leads to Eldon Chamber, with a high aven and very wet pitch to a sump. Traverse across and partway down the pitch to another long crawl to Aussie Chamber. A 15ft (5m) climb rejoins the stream, which immediately sumps. This has been dived to 56ft (17m) depth and continues down. Upstream from the junction with Crimbo Pipe is Crimbo Pipe Inlet, a fierce passage with tight ducks in fast flowing water, leading to the foot of a waterfall. Beyond is a further squeeze and bouldery crawls to East Level, a coffin level 1253ft (381m) long, ending at a T-junction. To the right is the Bung Series, while left up an 8ft (2m) climb leads back to the chamber near the Waterfall Pitch.

### Bung Series — Grade 3

Beyond the junction with East Level the passage contracts to a squeeze, The Bung. A T-junction follows. Left leads to a very tight pitch into a sump, or into a small chamber in drought. Right is 196ft (59m) of flat out crawling to Standing Room 10ft (3m) high from the top of which a traverse back over the rift leads to a crawl to a high narrow aven. Other way is straight on with Great Aven on right. A 70ft (21m) flat crawl leads to Rumble Chamber. In the floor is the Lower Bung Series. A 13ft (4m) pitch and tight squeeze lead to bedding plane, usually with a stream, which probably goes to Crimbo Pipe Inlet. Beyond Rumble Chamber a crawl can be followed for 40ft (12m) until it is too low.

**Tackle:**
*Entrance Shaft:* 25m rope. Belay to rings in lid with backup to stake.
*Second Pitch:* 20m rope. Eco hangers. Y hang on left wall of chamber, deviation from right wall.
*Waterfall Chamber:* 25m rope. Thread belay. Eco hangers. Y hang and 1 deviation.
*Chapel Dale Engine Shaft entrance:*
　　*Direct descent:* 75m rope. Belay to rings in lid with backup to stake.
　　*To avoid pool:* 40m rope to Chain Passage, + 40m rope from Y hang.

References: Batey, J. 1969. S.U.S.S. Jour. Vol.1. No.5. pp.221-223.
Cooper, G.W. & Westlake, C.D. 1970. E.P.C. Jour. Vol.7. No.3. pp.9-28.
Mellor, D. 1983. E.P.C. Jour. Vol.9. No.3. pp.1-6. Survey.
Robey, J.A. 1961. P.D.M.H.S. Bull. Vol.1. No.5. pp.30-36.　　1962. Vol.1. No.6. pp.29-35.
　　　　　　　　　　　　　　　　　　　　　　　　　　　　　　1963. Vol.2. No.1. pp.51-56.
Saville, B. 1960. The Lyre No.3. pp.37-41. Survey.
Westlake, C.D. 1966. E.P.C. Jour. Vol.7. No.1. p.20.
Westlake, C.D. 1970. E.P.C. Jour. Vol.7. No.3. pp.48-52.
Westlake, C.D. 1970. S.U.S.S. Jour. Vol.1. No.6. pp.236-237.

**LATHKILL HEAD CAVE**
(Lathkill House Cave)

**Grade: 2 - 4**
**River Entrance:**
NGR 1707 6588.
Alt. 680ft (207m)
**Upper Entrance:**
NGR 1671 6596.
Alt. 815ft (248.4m)
**Garden Path Entrance:**
NGR 1653 6597.
Alt. 860ft (262m)
**Length: 5000ft (1525m)**
**Depth: 180ft (55m)**
Status: S.S.S.I.

For access to the Garden Path contact DCA for details.
The Upper Entrance needs a large adjustable spanner.
Extended 1965 by E.P.C., 1969 by S.U.S.S. and E.P.C., 1974 by O.C.C., 1976 by E.P.C., 1990-1996 by T.S.G. . A connection was made to Ricklow Cave in 1995.

The only large obvious entrance on the south side of Upper Lathkill Dale. Wet weather resurgence of the River Lathkill.

Almost the whole system floods to the roof in wet weather, and the further limits are full in normal weather. Some of the chokes are loose and dangerous.

**Entrance Series        Grade 2**

The large entrance soon reduces to a 200ft (61m) long bedding plane crawl over large slabs to Rift Chamber. Crawl on right leads to The Spiral, a descent among boulders to a low wide bedding cave. Straight on and then to right is squeeze down into lower bedding plane. In normal weather the stream is soon met at a junction after a short crawl.

**Puttrell's Chamber & Dawkes Crawl    Grade 3**

Left soon sumps, but in dry weather can be followed for 150ft (46m) to a junction. Right leads back to Puttrell's Chamber via a very tight crawl over and between boulders (Mullen's Mistake). Left is Dawkes Crawl, 500ft (152m) of flat out crawling explored in 1976 by E.P.C. to a choke, passed in 1977 to a further 30ft of very tight crawl. Strong outward draught in drought. Right at the first junction leads upstream and again soon sumps, but in dry weather Oval Pot can be reached after 150ft (46m) of crawling. Climb Oval Pot and along low bedding with boulders to Puttrell's Chamber, limit of exploration up to 1965. Left leads through boulders to Mullen's Mistake.

Lathkill Head Cave. Photo by John Beck

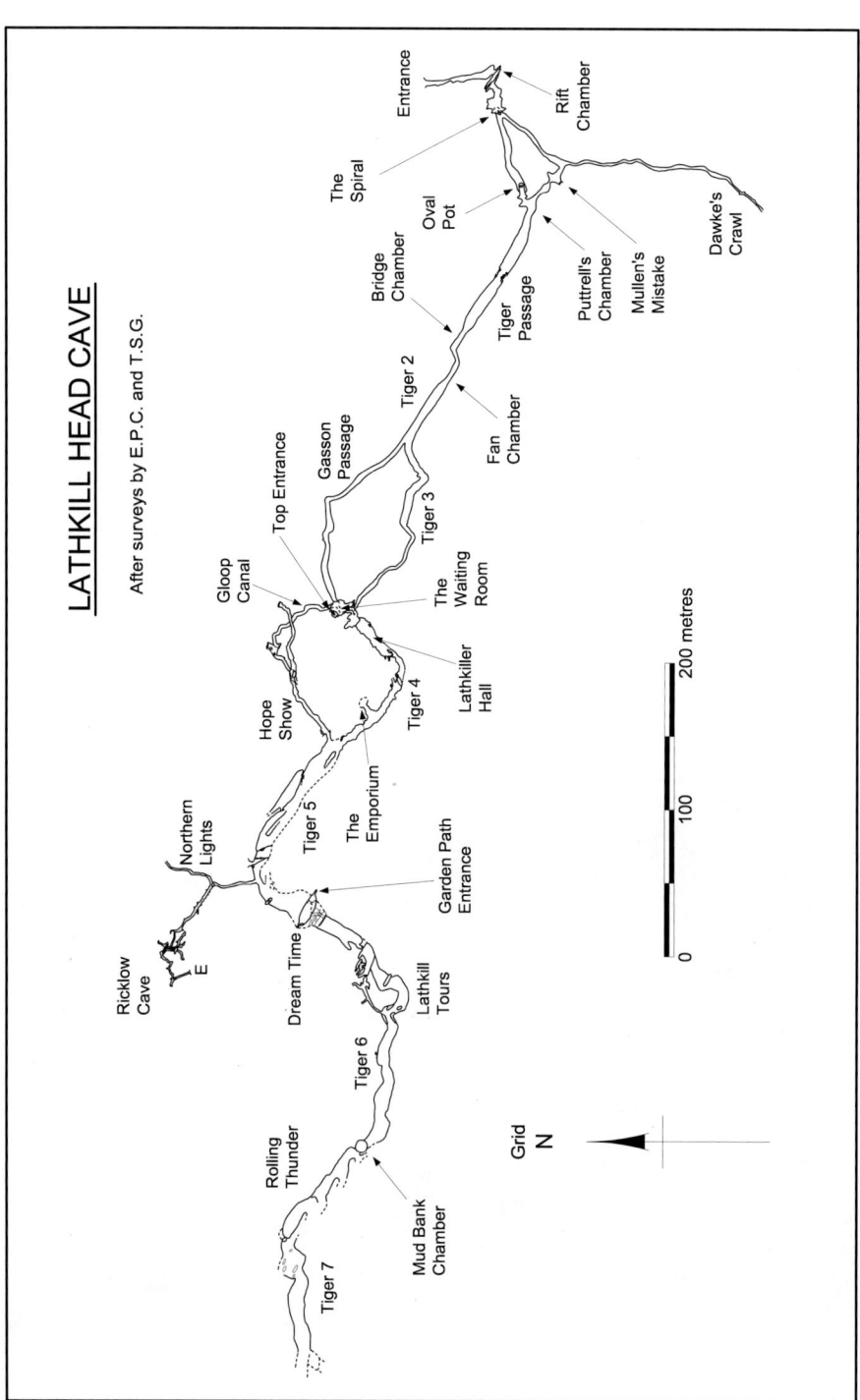

## Beyond Puttrell's Chamber  Grade 4

Straight on from Puttrell's Chamber E.P.C. dig leads to 350ft (107m) of flat out crawling (Tiger Passage) leading to Bridge Chamber, followed by Fan Chamber. This is the only section where it is possible to walk. The rest of the cave is only accessible in drought.

Low bedding plane crawl (Tiger 2) continues for 200ft (61m) to a junction, the limit of exploration up to 1969. Left leads to 480ft (146m) of flat out crawling (Tiger 3) leading to Handshake Chamber. Right at the junction is Gasson Passage, a 500ft (152m) bedding plane crawl which also leads to Handshake Chamber. Just before Handshake Chamber a small hole on the right leads to Gloop Canal, which can be followed on hands and knees through water for 180ft (55m) to Surprise Aven. An exposed climb up of 35ft (11m) enters a small chamber with a silted inlet passage. Another passage to the south west is blocked after 60ft (18m). The side passages draught strongly.

## Beyond The Lathkiller  Grade 4

There are two entrances to the system beyond The Lathkiller, the Top Entrance and the Garden Path. The Upper Entrance was opened in 1991, and leads via a 65ft (20m) pitch into a large chamber, the Waiting Room. A short crawl and climb lead down into Lathkiller Hall, and the top of the Lathkiller choke. Upstream degenerates to flat-out crawling after 130ft (40m), and a blasted squeeze leads to an awkward 6ft (2m) drop into a 30ft (9m) high aven. 100ft (30m) of crawling leads to the Emporium on the right, but the choke is unstable and should be avoided. 130ft (40m) further is the Hope Show on the right, 410ft (125m) of mainly walking passage to a choke of scree. Beyond Hope Show is Tiger 5. A crawl over a mudbank leads to a crawl between boulders, the Electric Crab. After 80ft (25m) a short squeeze down to the right drops into a bouldery crawl with pools, leading after 195ft (60m) to a large fallen block. A climb up and over leads to large passage. On the right is the Northern Lights, dug to create easier access via Ricklow Cave, but it is a flat out crawl in sticky mud, the Beresford Link. Beyond Northern Lights the cave swings south west past a 23ft (7m) high aven, and after 100ft (30m) an ascending crawl through boulders is the base of the impressive Dream Time chamber. The crawl ascends to a climb and some nasty squeezes with awkward turns, then up a 16ft (5m) rift and through a tight squeeze into a calcited chamber. A way into Dream Time is on the right, and to the left another chamber contains a ladder leading back to the streamway and Tiger 6. Dream Time is a magnificent 115ft (35m) high decorated rift at the bottom of the Garden Path entrance.

From Dream Time the way on is through the bedding up on the south west wall, pass through the decorated middle chamber and continue to the third chamber and down the fixed ladder to the streamway. Tiger 6 begins as a flat out crawl in a wide bedding, then through rocks to a blasted squeeze. The passage becomes higher, with a choice of routes. Easiest is to the right, through another squeeze into a narrow sandy passage, followed by the only walking sized passage, Lathkill Tours. Walking continues past a 10ft (3m) aven and a slope down to where there is normally a lake at the start of Tiger 7, rarely accessible. When the lake drains, Tiger 7 begins with crawling along a wide rocky passage, past a 5ft (1.5m) aven. After 195ft (60m) is a round chamber with a central mudbank, Mudbank Chamber. Beyond is another squeeze, with an alternative crawl to the left. More flat-out crawling for 130ft (40m) reaches a blasted trench which is the start of Rolling Thunder. Another 130ft (40m) reaches a squeeze into a small circular chamber, and the final stretch of passage, which now turns to the west. Another 330ft (100m) and several small avens, and the passage ends in a choke with a second ascending choke on the left.

References: Bamber, H.A. 1948. B.S.A. *Cave Science. Vol.1. No.5. pp.148-150.*

Bamber, H.A. 1951. B.S.A. *Cave Science Vol.2. No.15. pp.293-301.*

Bentham, K. 1997. *Descent No. 138. pp.10-11. Survey.*

Drakeley, K. 1974. *D.C.A. N/L No.22. p.6.*

Drakeley, K. 1974. *O.C.C. N/L Vol.10. No.8. pp.65-67.*

Ford, T.D. (ed) 1977. *Limestones and Caves of the Peak District. Chapter 20. Geo Books. Norwich.*

*Gasson, I.D.H. 1970. E.P.C. Jour. Vol.7. No.3. pp.62-3. Survey.*
*Gill, D.W. 1976. D.C.A. N/L No.30. pp.10-12.*
*Gill, D.W. 1974. D.C.A. N/L No.22. p.4.*
*Lord, P.J. 1971. S.U.S.S. Jour. Vol.2. No.1. pp.26-27.*
*Lord, P.J. 1969. S.U.S.S. Jour. Vol.1. No.5. p.224. Survey.*
*Westlake, C.D. 1966. E.P.C. Jour. Vol.7. No.1. p.20.*

The Garden Path, Lathkill Head Cave. Photo by Paul Deakin

### LATHKILL RESURGENCE CAVE
(Pudding Springs)
NGR 1813 6568
Grade: 2
Alt. 600ft (183m)
Length: 200ft (61m)

First entered during the 1959 drought.

About 1 mile downstream of Lathkill Head Cave, below a waterfall.

The entrance and the whole cave are normally under water. The cave consists of a long crawl with small chambers, eventually becoming too low. Developed entirely in tufa below the valley floor. Formations consist of tufa-encased roots.

*References: Commander, B. 1983. T.S.G. N/L No.10. pp.11-14. Survey. Mort, J.B. 1956. The Lyre No.2. pp.11-12 & 14. Survey.*

### LYNX CAVE
NGR 1723 6509
Grade: 1 (Arch)
Alt. 775ft (232m)
Length: 30ft (9m)

Two obvious entrances on a shelf some 15ft (4.5m) above the valley floor on the north side of the buttress containing One Ash Cave on its south side.

Higher entrance drops into roof of lower tube a few feet inside. A stooping passage leads to a partial blockage of rotten flowstone after 30ft (9m). Believed to be the cave excavated by Storrs Fox to reveal remains of Lynx.

*References: Storrs Fox, W. 1906. Proc. Zool. Soc., Vol.1. pp.65-72 & 77.*

### MANDALE MINE
NGR Incline: 197 661 Grade: 3 (Mine)
Alt. 550ft (165m)
Length: 1/4 mile (0.4km) approx.
Status: S.S.S.I.

There is no access to Mandale Founder Shaft at present.

Incline entrance at cliff foot above the sough tail. Mandale Founder Shaft lies on the rake at 190 663.

One of the oldest lead mines in Derbyshire. The incline leads into the main level, usually knee deep in water. Various old stopes can be reached along it, and evidence of sand filled solution cavities seen in places. The sough tail by the footpath can be followed under the old engine house, but is blocked beyond. Workings extend 1 mile to the north west, beneath Mandale Founder Shaft, over 300ft (91m) deep.

*References: Ford, T.D. & Worley, N.E. 1976. Bull. P.D.M.H.S. Vol.6. No.3. pp.141-143. Survey. Rieuwerts, J. 1963. Bull. P.D.M.H.S. Vol.2. No.1. pp.9-30. Survey.*

*Rieuwerts, J. 2000. Lathkill Dale, Derbyshire. Its Mines and Miners. Landmark Publishing Ltd.*

*Thornton, D.R. 1960. Bull. P.D.M.H.S. Vol.1. No.3. pp.3-4. Sketch survey. Tune, R. 1969. Bull. P.D.M.H.S. Vol.4. No.1. pp.67-74. Survey.*

### ONE ASH CAVE
NGR 172 651    Grade: 1
Alt. 780ft (234m)
Length: 100ft (30m)

On the west side of the dale in the narrow gorge section, some 325 yards (297m) east south east of One Ash Grange, on the south side of a buttress.

The cave is on a shelf some 30ft (9m) above the dale floor. A stooping size tube lowers to a crawl which has been dug. Blocked with corroded flowstone. There is an unnamed cave on the same shelf a little way to the south, blocked with clay. Not to be confused with Lynx Cave on the north side of the buttress.

*References: Mellors, P.T. 1969. Bull. B.S.A. No.83. pp.5-6.*

### ONE ASH SHELTER
**NGR 1730 6556**
**Grade: 1. (Arch)**
**Alt. 775ft (232m)**

At base of crag high up and northwest of footbridge.

A rock shelter with a low blocked phreatic tube. Archaeologically excavated to reveal remains of late Upper Palaeolithic Man and animals.

### RAVEN MINE
**NGR 1609 6590  Grade: 2 (Mine)**
**Alt. 880ft (268m)**
**Depth: 190ft (58m)**

First pitch was blocked, but was reopened by Darfar P.C. in 1989. Dug to present depth by Ben Bentham, Mike Sutton and others 1993.

On the south east side of Fern Dale.

**Warning: The eyehole opens directly onto the Third Pitch. Be roped!**

A partly natural shaft 35ft (11m) deep leads very soon to a second pitch of 50ft (15m), further excavated to a total depth of 115ft (35m). Shored shaft continues to an eyehole 125ft (38m) down. 15ft (5m) down the second pitch, natural passages lead off. Up and then down a small hole to a passage with a false floor and bedding crawls off to the left. This opens onto a 55ft (17m) pitch to flooded workings and natural cavities at the elevation of Lathkill Head Cave. At the top of the 55ft (17m) pitch a choke (by-passed by a new shaft) leads to a natural passage up to 15ft (4.5m) high, with a deep pothole in the floor. 10ft (3m) above is a short crawl to the base of a 16ft (5m) climb with a collapse ahead. At the top is a small chamber, and a dig through the Poled Choke led to further natural. Left is a rising boulder choke. Right leads after 100ft (30m) to a choke of deads. A climb up leads into a large passage which closes in one direction and ends at a the base of a choked shaft in the other.

*References: Bentham, K. 1993. Descent No.112. p.18. Survey.*
*Bentham, K. 1993. D.C.A. N/L No.81. pp.6-9.*

### RICKLOW CAVE
(Beresford's Level)
**NGR 1636 6607     Grade: 2**
**Alt. 750ft (225m)**
**Length: 431ft (131m)**
**Depth: 51ft (16m)**

Fitted with a self-locking gate. No spanner or key required.

Small entrance at base of cliff on north side of valley floor immediately below Ricklow Marble Quarry tip.

Short passage leads to 15ft climb down. Water sinks at bottom in wet weather. Was excavated for 14ft (4m) by Fourways Club in 1962 and backfilled from dig in left hand crawl. Dig progressed for 60ft (18m) in mud and water. Right hand crawl leads through pools to 12ft (3.5m) pitch into small pot. Three passages enter in roof but all close shortly. A tight rift at one end of the pot has been enlarged down to a small passage, which was also enlarged to give access to a flooded rift. Small passages continue, extensively dug. A connection with the Northern Lights of Lathkill Head Cave was made by digging the passage in the bottom of the flooded rift in dry weather. The quarry above has a partly collapsed choked cave entrance at the extreme east end which may be worth digging, as well as marble mines which are now in a dangerously unstable condition.

*References: Anon. 1962. D.C.A. N/L No.3. p.1.*
*Milner, M. 1985. D.C.A. N/L No.57. p.20.*
*Milner, M. 1985. D.C.A. N/L No.58. pp.2-3. Survey.*

### THE ROUNDABOUT
**NGR 183 657**
**Grade: 1 (Mine)**

At the junction of Haddon Grove Dale and Lathkill Dale on the western side.

A low wide entrance leads immediately to a crawling passage around a circular pack. Strange.

Water Icicle Close Cavern

## WATER ICICLE CLOSE CAVERN

NGR 1610 6460    Grade: 2
Alt. 1065ft (325m)
Length: 700ft (213m)
Depth: 105ft (32m)
Status: S.S.S.I.

No known access restrictions. Park at end of green lane.

**Warning: High levels of $CO_2$ have been encountered on occasions.**

A capped and lidded shaft in the field north of the end of the green Derby Lane, close to a plantation.

The shaft is 105ft (32m) deep in solid limestone, and descends through the roof of a chamber at the junction of three large passages. The south passage leads into a mined out vein about 120ft (37m) long and 70ft (21m) high. The north passage is about 320ft (98m) long, gradually descending into a clay fill. The north west passage is about 350ft (107m) long with deads stacked at the sides and remnants of stalagmites and some small avens.

The choke at the end was dug over many years, first into a high aven, and in 2009 a scaffolded shaft down the far side led to a continuation. This section is now gated: contact DCA for access details. A further 975ft (297m) of walking sized passage was found. The route splits, and each ends at a choke providing a possible dig. Near the northern limit a pitch, the Elevator, was descended for 69ft (21m) into a very unstable rift, with the way on down choked with broken rock.

**Tackle:**
Entrance Shaft:    40m rope. Scaffold bar in place + backup to stake.

*References: Lord, P.J. 1971. S.U.S.S. Jour. Vol.2. No.1. pp.27-28.*
*Lord, P.J. & Batey, A. 1970. S.U.S.S. Jour. Vol.1. No.6. pp.247-248.*
*Phipps, M. 1981. The Lyre. No.5. pp.12-13.*
*Smith, M.E. 1968. Bull. P.D.M.H.S. Vol.3. No.5. pp.281-284. Survey.*
*Westlake, C.D. 1970. E.P.C. Jour. Vol.7. No.3. pp.57-58. Survey.*
*Brooks, S. 2010. Descent No 212. p.20. Survey*

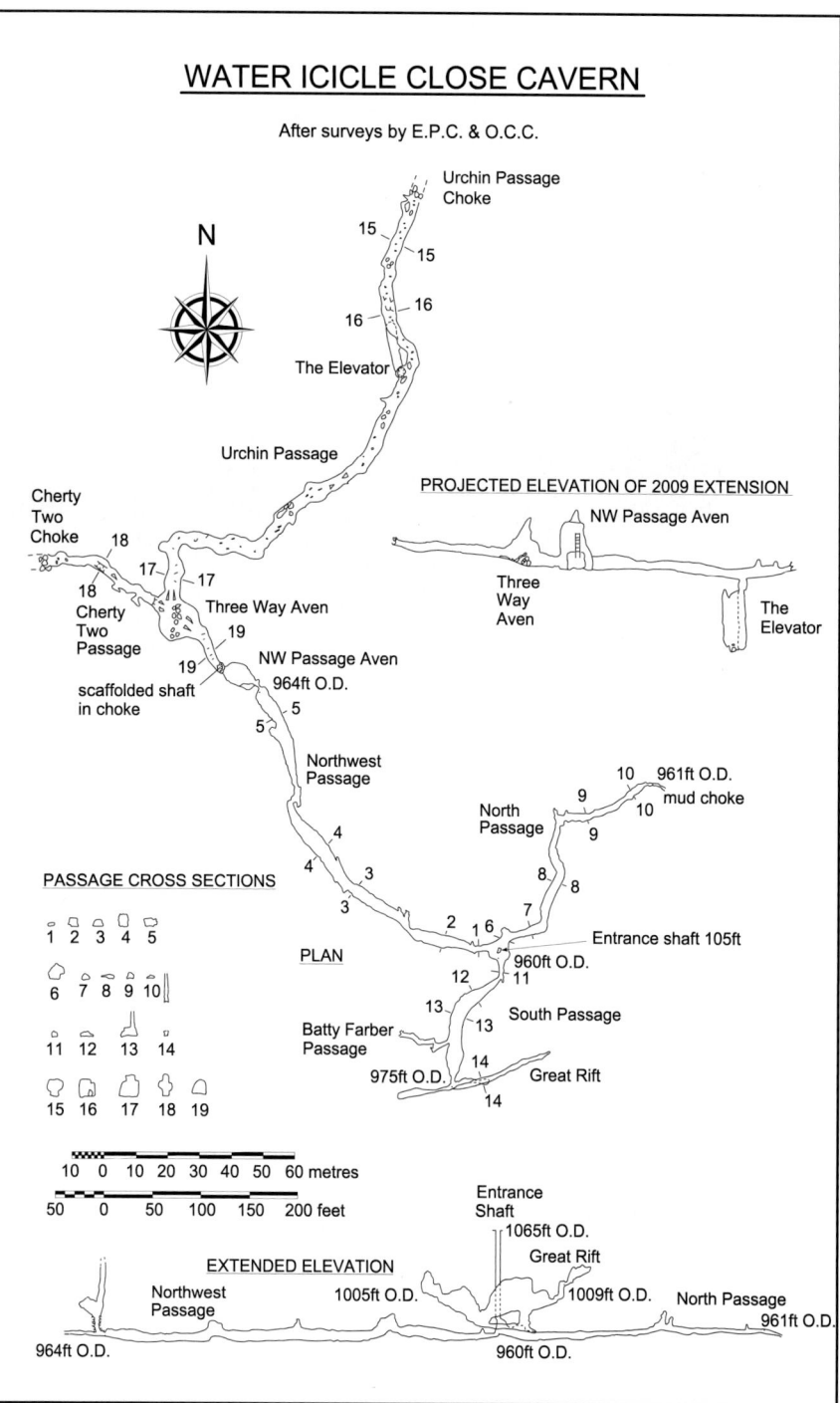

> **WHIM MINE**
> NGR 138 664    Grade: 3
> Alt. 1080ft (330m) approx.
> Depth: 145ft (44m)

Permission should be sought from The Whim, Monyash.

Situated 820ft (250m) east of The Whim, Monyash.

Lies in a narrow, walled line of trees. Six shafts are covered by sleepers. They are numbered from west to east.

Shaft 1: A depression with no apparent shaft.

Shaft 2: 48ft (14.5m) deep, and muddy.

Shaft 3: Connects with Shaft 2, but is dangerous.

Shaft 4: The major shaft on the vein. A 51ft (16m) pitch lands on a narrow ledge. A short traverse to the west passes an eyehole to a second pitch of 66ft (20m), with fine views of a large and partly natural chamber on the vein. At the bottom, a climb over rubbish leads to a low entrance to a second natural chamber, off the line of the vein. Climbed for 69ft (21m) with no passage found. The mine has excellent examples of both stone and wooden stempling.

Shaft 5: Also enters the mine. Superbly ginged on stone stemples.

Shaft 6: Appears to enter the mine, but is too dangerous to descend.

Shaft 7: Completely filled.

References: Bentham, K. 1995. Descent No. 123. p.12.

## Features listed as potential archaeological sites

1: NGR 1620 6610    Alt: 237m    An obvious overhang above a rock shelter.
2: NGR 1681 4594    Alt: 248m    An obvious shelter high in the dale.
3: NGR 1681 6601    Alt: 240m    A small rift cave choked at the back with rocks, with a small off shoot.
4: NGR 1680 6601    Alt: 237m    A small cave.
5: NGR 1687 6598    Alt: 241m    A small entrance choked at the back.
6: NGR 1696 6596    Alt: 225m    A long shallow rock shelter half way up the dale side.
7: NGR 1714 6609    Alt: 233m    A small triangular entrance in a tributary dale.
8: NGR 1715 6609    Alt: 227m    A long high rock shelter in a tributary dale.
10: NGR 1734 6554    Alt: 236m    A good sized cave entrance high above the dale floor.
11: NGR 1730 6556    Alt: 230m    A long low rock shelter.
12: NGR 1732 6543    Alt: 227m    A long low rock shelter high in the dale.
13: NGR 1721 6526    Alt: 251m    An obvious shelter next to the path.
14: NGR 1723 6514    Alt: 247m    An obvious rock shelter on the west side of the dale.
15: NGR 1722 6512    Alt: 246m    A large open entrance which shuts down very quickly.
16: NGR 1692 6595    Alt: 228m    A narrow rift just below the top crag in Lathkill Dale.
17: NGR 1673 6599    Alt: 221m    A low cave behind a bank of soil and nettles.
18: NGR 1836 6541    Shallow cave which has been dug into.
19: NGR 1835 6541    Shallow cave dug from surface.
20: NGR 1838 6544    Long shelter with small cave towards the north end.

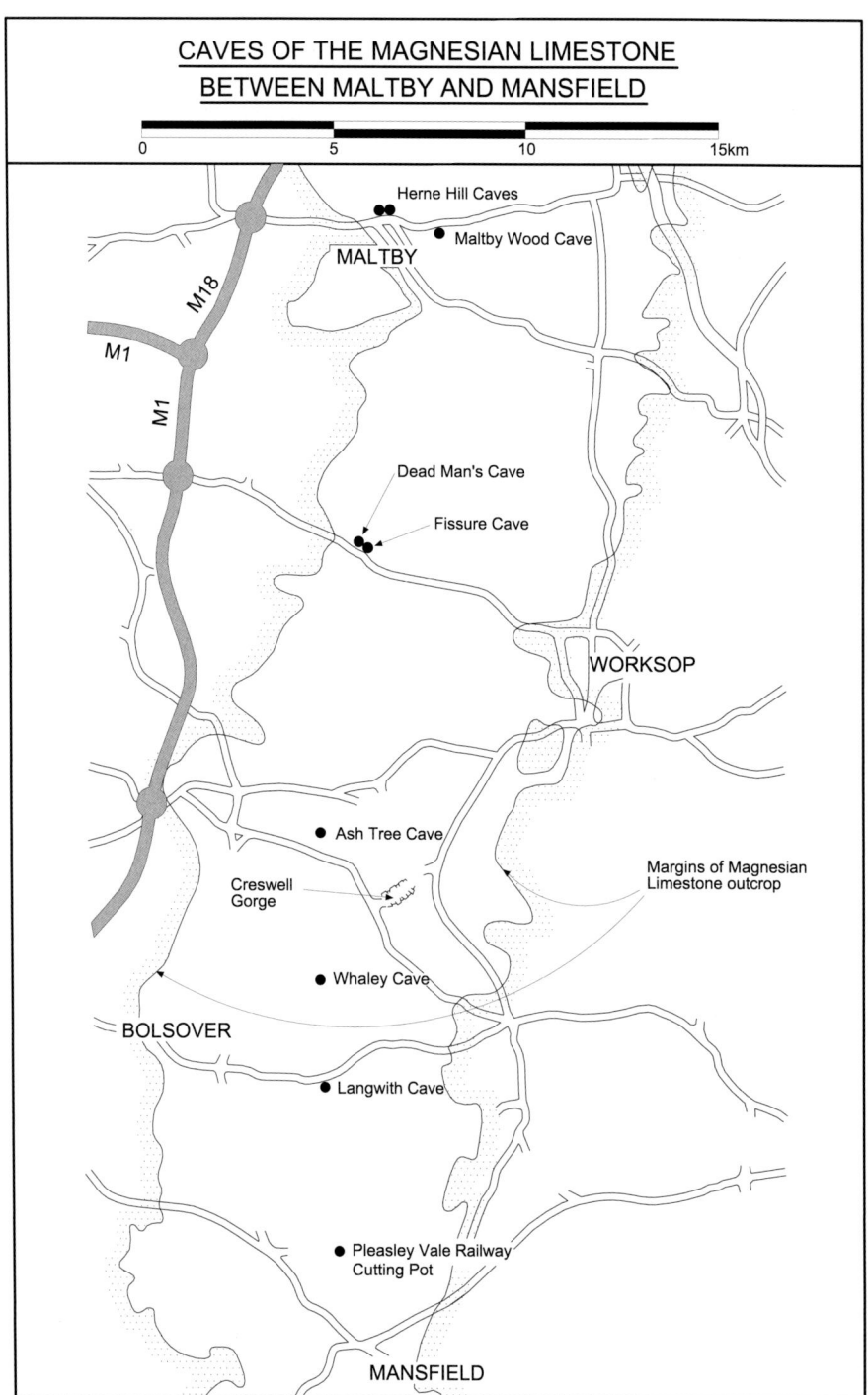

# CAVES OF THE MAGNESIAN LIMESTONE

Cresswell Gorge

A number of caves, mostly of archaeological importance, occur in the Magnesian Limestone of East Derbyshire. Creswell Gorge and its caves are now a National Nature Reserve. The caves are gated and locked, and guided public visits are run at weekends from the Creswell Crags Visitor Centre (at the east end of the gorge) which has displays of archaeological material from the caves. Important prehistoric cave art was found in Church Hole Cave at Creswell in 2003 and 2004. Access to the Herne Hill Caves at Maltby is now controlled by D.C.A., and for this reason they are included here.

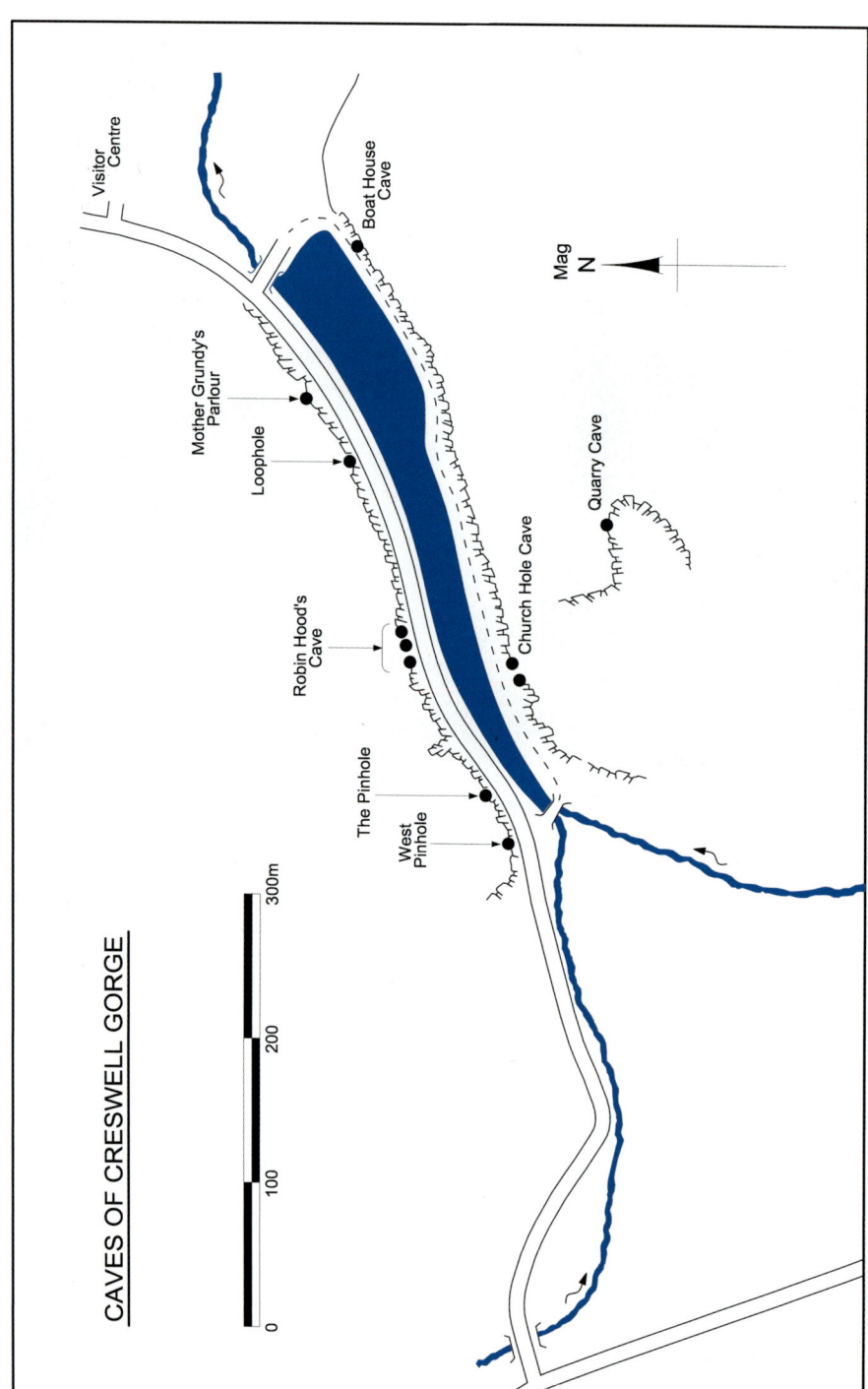

Magnesian Limestone  Caves of the Peak District • Page 249

### ASH TREE CAVE
**NGR 515 762   Grade: 1. (Arch)**
Alt. 395ft (120m)
Length: 23ft (7m)
Depth: 10ft (3m)

Obvious entrance in cliff on south side of shallow valley 650 ft (200m) west of road.
Slope down into chamber. Continuation is choked by fill although further open passage can be glimpsed beyond. Neolithic burial found.
*References: Armstrong, A.L. 1950-1955. Derbys. Arch. Soc. Jour.*
*Armstrong, A.L. 1956. Derbys. Arch. Soc. Jour. 76. pp.57-64.*

### BOAT HOUSE CAVE
**NGR 537 742   Grade: 1. (Arch)**
Alt. 250ft (75m)
Length: 180ft (55m)

Near the east end of the crags on the south side of Creswell Gorge.
Obvious low arched entrance. At rear of entrance chamber gently winding passage 4ft (1.2m) high leads beneath a variety of small avens to a sandy choke. Important archaeological site. Do not disturb fill or deposits.
*References: Armstrong, A.L. Derbys. Arch. Jour. Vol.57. p.129.*

### CHURCH HOLE CAVE
**NGR 534 741   Grade: 1. (Arch)**
Alt. 250ft (75m)
Length: 250ft (75m)

Obvious large entrance on south side of gorge. Gated. Smaller entrance a short distance to the west.
Entrances unite in a roomy tunnel, gradually lowering, to easy climb up sloping tube into final small chamber and calcited choke. Important archaeological site. Do not disturb fill or deposits. Excavated material now in British Museum.
*References: Armstrong. Reports in Derbys. Arch. Jour. from Vol.55. onwards.*
*Heath, Thomas. 1882. Derbys. Arch. Jour. Vol.4. pp.173-176.*
*Mem. Geol. Surv. 1913. The northern part of the Derbyshire Coalfield. pp.107-108.*

### DEAD MAN'S CAVE
**NGR 533 831   Grade: 1 (Arch)**
Alt. 280ft (85m)
Length: 30ft (9m)

Wide entrance in Anston Stones crags next to the A57 road.
Passage constricts to a crawl leading to a low chamber. Archaeological remains found. Take care not to disturb sediments.

### FISSURE CAVE
**NGR 535 830   Grade: 2 (Arch)**
Alt. 170ft (52m)
Length: 33ft (10m)

Entrance in small depression in Anston Stones crags next to the A57 road.
A squeeze leads to a chamber 25ft (8m) long and 10ft (3m) high, with a tight crawl continuing. Archaeological remains found. Take care not to disturb sediments.

### HERNE HILL CAVE 1
**NGR 533 922   Grade: 2**
Alt. 350ft (107m)
Length: 550ft (168m)
Depth: 35ft (11m)

Discovered M.S.G. 1973.
Behind the supermarket on the north side of the main street in Maltby. Gated. Two adjustable spanners needed.
Crawl entrance drops steeply for 15ft (4.5m) to First Chamber, 20ft (6m) by 12ft (4m), and up to 10ft (3m) high. At upper end of chamber a shaft drops 15ft (4.5m) into Second Chamber, also reached down obvious boulder slope. Narrow rift on left of slope enters small blind chamber. On right of Second Chamber

two short passages unite in a low chamber. To the left a squeeze up into a rift leads to 70ft (21m) of passage below the quarry floor. Main route from Second Chamber is a crawl into the Third Chamber. Small passages to the right are blind, while those to the left lead to the Fourth Chamber, about 30ft (9m) by 15ft (4.5m). Beyond Fourth Chamber route lowers, with holes to the left to a parallel passage. Route steps up into Fifth Chamber. On the right of the Fifth Chamber a squeeze leads to a further chamber 25ft (8m) long.

References: Ryder, P. 1974. M.S.G. Journal No.7. pp. 16-17. Survey.

Ryder, P. 1979. M.S.G. Journal No.10. pp.23-24. Survey.

### HERNE HILL CAVE 2
NGR 533 922　　Grade: 2
Alt. 350ft (107m)
Length: 210ft (64m)

Discovered 1980. Entrance lies between the supermarket wall and the cliff face.

Entrance drops into a low chamber. A narrow rift descends into a second chamber with three routes leading on. Crawling and squeezing over concrete (poured down a borehole) leads to a further chamber with small speleothems. A tube on the left leads to a wide low bedding chamber, and via a squeeze into a larger passage leading back to the second chamber. The other way on from here led back under the entrance chamber to a choke.

References: Ryder, P. 1980. B.C.R.A. Caves & Caving No.11. p.6 & p.26. Survey.

### HERNE HILL CAVE 3
(Gateways Cave)
NGR 533 922
Length: 83ft (25m)

Discovered 1993 by Tony & Stuart Gibbs and Steve Gray.

At the back of the Gateway supermarket.

A squeeze leads down a rift into a chamber. Short crawls lead to the second and third chambers. The continuing dig draughts but is constricted.

References: Gibbs, T. 1995. D.C.A. N/L No.88. p.15. Survey.

### LANGWITH CAVE
NGR 518 695　Grade: 1. (Arch)
Alt. 295ft (90m)
Length: 100ft (30m)

Large entrance on north bank of River Poulter, a short distance west of a public footpath and almost due north of Upper Langwith Church.

Entrance drops into a roomy chamber from which much material has been removed by archaeologists. Several sandy crawls lead off. The longest is to the left, ending in a small chamber with tree roots. A Neolithic burial was found.

References: Hinton, M.C.A. 1913. Derbys. Arch. Jour. No.35. pp.157-158.

Keith, A. 1913. Derbys. Arch. Jour. No.35. pp.155-157.

Kennard, A.S. & Woodward, B.B. 1913. Derbys. Arch. Jour. No.35. pp.153-155.

Mullins, E.H. 1913. Derbys. Arch. Jour. No.35. pp.137-153.

### LOOPHOLE
NGR 535 742　Grade: 1. (Arch)
Alt. 250ft (76m)
Length: 50ft (15m)

Small entrance at cliff foot east of Robin Hood's Cave.

Small spidery cave with upper entrance on ledge. Important archaeological site. Do not disturb fill or deposits.

## MALTBY WOOD CAVE
NGR 549 917  Grade: 1
Length: 131ft (40m)

Obvious entrance in the north wall of a mineral railway cutting. Entrance crawl forks almost immediately. Left is a crawl down a slope into a chamber 25ft (8m) x 13ft (4m). The right hand passage is a crawl into a bouldery chamber, then a further crawl 10ft (3m) wide and 3ft (1m) high. After 20ft (6m) a crawl up a rubble slope leads into a chamber 16ft (5m) in diameter. A draught blows from the rubble round the edge of the chamber.
*References: Ryder, P. 1987. M.S.G. Jour. No.11. p.32. Survey.*

## MOTHER GRUNDY'S PARLOUR
NGR 5358 7426  Grade: 1. (Arch)
Alt. 280ft (85m)
Length: 50ft (15m)

Large obvious rock shelter near east end of north side of Creswell Gorge.
Small passage at rear soon ends on a little chamber. Important archaeological site. Do not disturb fill or deposits. Flints and bones excavated can be seen in British Museum, London.
*References: Campbell, J.B. 1969. Derbys. Arch. Jour. Vol.89. pp.48-52. Survey.*
*Campbell, J.B. 1970. Peakland Arch. Soc. Bull. No.25. pp.13-15. Survey.*
*Geological Survey Memoir 1913. The Northern Part of the Derbyshire Coalfield. p.108.   Heath, T. 1882. Derbys. Arch. Jour. Vol.4. p.176.*
*Mello, Rev. J.M. 1880. Trans. Manch. Geol. Soc. Vol.XV. pp.290-314.*

## PINHOLE CAVE
NGR 533 741  Grade: 1. (Arch?)
Alt. 300ft (91m)
Length: 170ft (52m)

Obvious large entrance, gated.
High but narrow passage opens into lofty chamber, with short low branch to right. Ahead, climb through wedged boulders into narrow passage with stalagmite flows, choking after a squeeze and a 6ft (2m) drop. The cave furnished the most complete record of animal and human occupation of any British Caves. Finds can be seen in Derby Museum, Manchester University Museum, The British Museum London, and Middlesborough Museum.
*References: Heath, T. 1882. Derbys. Arch. Jour. No.4. p.169.*

## PLEASLEY VALE RAILWAY CUTTING POT
(Yew Tree Cave?)
NGR 520 649  Grade: 3 (Arch?)
Alt. 450ft (137m)
Length: 295ft (90m)
Depth: 75ft (23m)

Obvious entrance on south side of disused railway cutting.
Continuing rock movements mean that visits to the chamber below Rift Chamber Pitch are not recommended.
An unusual slip-rift system. May be the same as the "Yew Tree Cave" mentioned in early archaeological literature. Drop of 10ft (3m) into rift. Straight ahead is rift with hole in floor leading back into Main Rift. Back under cutting is T-junction with Main Rift. Right is climb down to feet-first squeeze into chamber, with various short rift passages beyond. Left is climb down through boulders onto 15ft (4.5m) Rift Chamber Pitch. Belay to any safe boulder above. Ahead is unsafe high level chamber, rift on left to choked chamber, and scramble up to lip of 20ft (6m) Second Pitch into final chamber.
*References: Dawkins, W.B. 1869. Quar. Jour. Geol. Soc.*
*Ransom, 1866. Report of the British Association.*

### QUARRY CAVE
**NGR 535 740  Grade: 1**
Alt. 295ft (90m)
Length: 50ft (15m)

In north wall of large disused quarry 295ft (90m) south of Creswell Crags.
Obvious entrance drops into large passage with much sandy fill, which meets roof after a short distance in each direction.

### ROBIN HOOD'S CAVE
**NGR 5341 7419**
**Grade: 1. (Arch)**
Alt. 300ft (91m)
Length: 950ft (290m)

Three obvious entrances in Creswell Gorge, all gated.
A series of roomy dry chambers and galleries, owing much of their size to removal of fill by archaeologists. At end of passage running straight in from east entrance is 20ft (6m) aven leading only to short choked passage. Two routes from rear of large chamber just inside central entrance connect in an interesting round trip, including an easy chimney and a squeeze. In floor of large chamber is climbable 11ft (3.5m) shaft to short lower passage. More complex low level series is reached via 8ft (2.5m) shaft at the side of the portal of the west entrance. An important archaeological cave. Do not disturb fill or deposits. Finds in British Museum, London, and Manchester Museum.
*References: Geological Survey Memoirs. 1913. The Northern part of the Derbyshire Coalfield. p.106-107. Survey.*
*Campbell, J.B. 1969. Derbys. Arch. Jour. No.89. pp.52-57. Arch. Survey.*
*Campbell, J.B. 1970. P.A.S. Bull. No.25. pp.11-12. Arch. Survey.*
*Heath, T. 1882. Derbys. Arch. Jour. No.4. pp.170-173.*

### WEST PINHOLE
**NGR 533 741  Grade: 2. (Arch)**
Alt. 245ft (75m)
Length: 200ft (60m)

Several entrances near the west end on the north side of Creswell Gorge.
Entrance to the right into semi-daylight chamber, that to the left into high rift passage pinching out after 50ft (15m). On right of rift passage is a low chamber. On left two routes into a series of low crawls with a squeeze and small avens. Between West Pinhole and Pinhole, and between Pinhole and Robin Hood's Cave are a few short small caves up to 30ft (9m) in length. All the caves are important archaeological sites. Do not disturb fill or deposits.

### WHALEY CAVE
**NGR 511 721  Grade: Arch**

Two archaeological caves excavated by A.L.Armstrong. Nearby are some rock shelters.
*References: Radley, J. 1967. Derbys. Arch. Jour. No.87. pp.1-17. Survey.*

# THE STONEY MIDDLETON CATCHMENT AREA

Chimney Rock, Stoney Middleton Dale

The easily accessible caves of Stoney Middleton Dale have provided many cavers with their first introduction to the sport.

The geology is ideal for the formation of an extensive cave system. A series of swallets on the shale / limestone junction to the west of Eyam take streams which must follow the strike eastwards beneath Eyam. The drainage is uncomplicated by lavas in the area, for the highest of these, the Cressbrook Dale Lava, lies well below the floor of Stoney Middleton Dale.

Four periods of downcutting have occurred in the area, and this is reflected by the four cave levels in Stoney Middleton Dale. The older caves are generally silt filled, but even some of these are penetrable for several hundred feet (ie. Ivy Green Cave).

The original risings undoubtedly lay in the floor of Stoney Middleton Dale, but the water has been captured by soughs. The Resurgence Entrance to Carlswark Cavern can still discharge a large stream in flood. Only two swallets have been penetrated for any distance (Waterfall Swallet and Hungerhill Swallet) and neither gives access to the major cave which must lie beneath.

Carlswark is the largest system. Together with Streaks Pot and parts of Merlin Mine it represents the downstream end of a system whose most distant feeder swallets lie far to the west beyond Foolow.

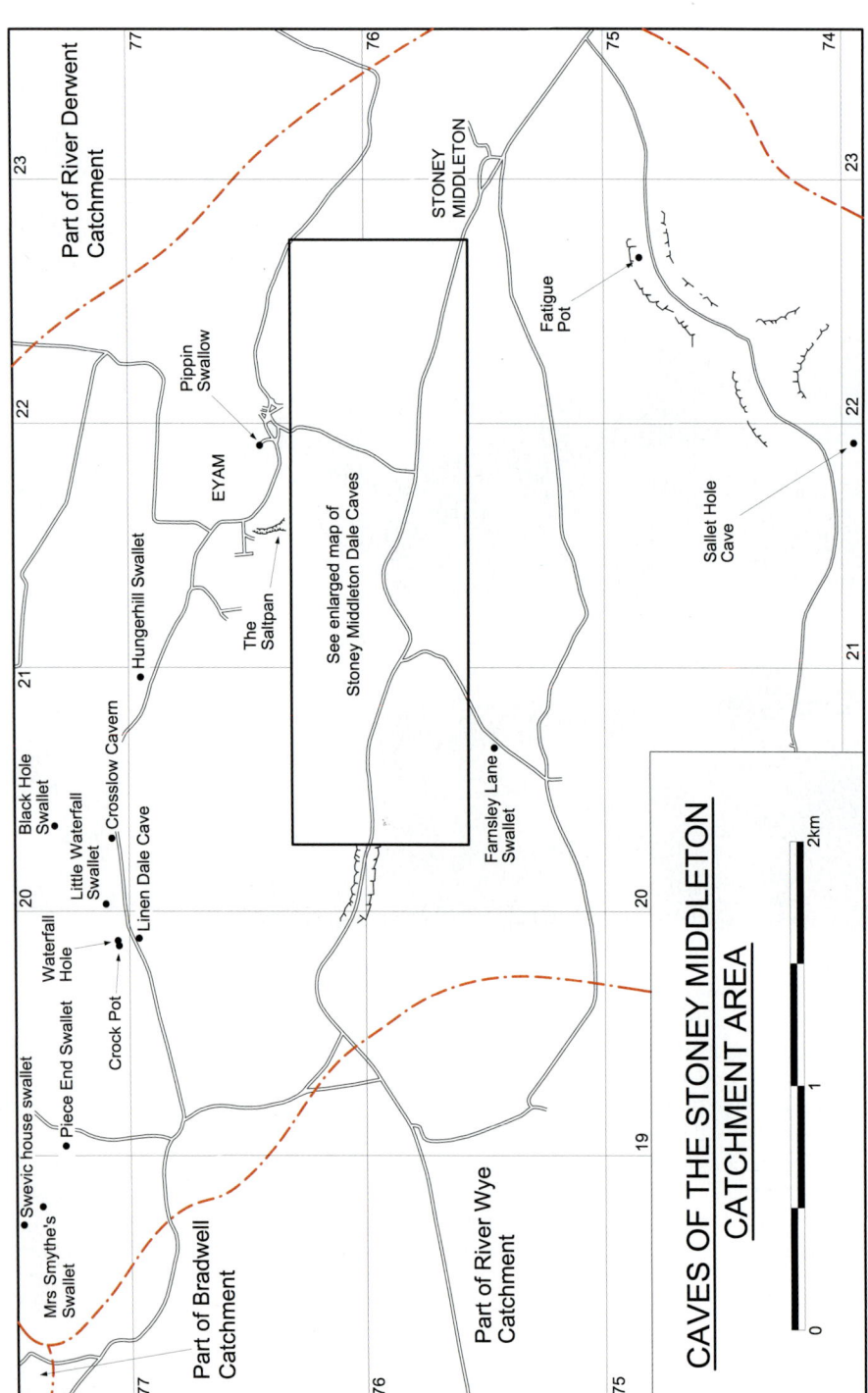

## CAVES OF STONEY MIDDLETON DALE

1. Lay-by Shaft 2
2. Lay-by Pot (Shaft)
3. Lay-by Pot (Oil drum entr.)
4. Lay-by Shelter
5. Hanging Flat Mine
6. Hobbit Hole
7. Well Shaft
8. The Hole in the Wall
9. Rubble Rift
10. Hangover Hole
11. Paracetam 'Ole
12. Hale Bopp Pot
13. Farnsley Lane Cave
14. Beech Fell Cave
15. Watergrove Sough Tail
16. Farnsley Lane Quarry Caves
17. Bagshot Row
18. Yoga Cave (Rubbish Bag Entr.)
19. Yoga Cave (Shaft Entr.)
20. Yoga Cave (Crawl Entr.)
21. Streaks Cave
22. Streaks Pot (Top Entr.)
23. Streaks Pot (Lower Entr.)
24. Mine Level no.8
25. Aaron's Entrance
26. Sunday Mine
27. Mine Level no.9. (Friday Mine)
28. Mine Level no.11. (Monday Mine)
29. Monkey Rock Cave
30. Nicker Grove Mine (adit)
31. Nicker Grove Mine (shafts)
32. Cucklet Delph Upper Cave
33. Upper Cucklet Delph Swallet
34. Cucklet Church Cave
35. Delph Hole
36. Lower Cucklet Delph Swallet
37. Mine Level no.7
38. Hawkenedge Well
39. Beech Tree Hole
40. Merlin Mine
41. Crackpot Cave
42. Carlswark (Eyam Dale Shaft)
43. Carlswark (top shaft)
44. Fireset Mine
45. Mine Level no.12
46. Carlswark (Flower Pot Entr.)
47. Eyam Dale House Cave
48. Mine Level no.6
49. Bamforth Hole
50. Carlswark (Gin Entr.)
51. Carlswark (Resurgence Entr.)
52. Mine Level no.5
53. Mine Level no.4
54. Ivy Green Cave
55. Mine Level no.3
56. Keyhole Cave
57. Cavaliers' Hole
58. Mine Level no.2
59. Mine Level no.10
60. Bossen Hole
61. Mine Level no.1
62. Rock Cottage Tubes

Only a small proportion of this system is known, although many new discoveries have been made in the last thirty years.

Caves are occasionally met in the quarries on the south side of Stoney Middleton Dale. They tend to be penetrable only for short distances, but are often well decorated (ie. Sarah's Cave). The discoveries of Hangover Hole, Paracetam 'Ole, and Rubble Rift in the early 1990s began to indicate a large though possibly fragmented system on the south side of the valley.

Prospects for a large breakthrough are still good, though the digs tend to be remote (ie. the West Choke of Streaks Pot and the Dynamite Series of Carlswark Cavern). There is still a potential drop of just over 200ft (61m) from the lowest point reached in Waterfall Swallet to the Bedpan Sump of Carlswark Cavern.

Although included in the Stoney Middleton area, the drainage of Coombs Dale, to the south, is really separate. The only significant cave is Fatigue Pot, which ends at a very small passage with a tantalising draught. It is still possible that a penetrable system exists beneath Coombs Dale.

Cavers at Stoney Middleton c.1950. The only identified one is Stan Gee (kneeling).
Photo by Bernard Chandler

## BAGSHOT ROW
NGR 2109 7584    Grade: 1
Alt. 673ft (205.1m)
Length: 35ft (11m)

Three entrances in the lowest cliff on the north side of the A623 immediately west of the sharp bend.

The right hand entrance is a crawl for 25ft (8m) to emerge at the middle entrance. The left hand entrance is a larger tube, dug sporadically for many years. Muddy crawl descends past blind tube on right to where roof rises temporarily, passing beneath unstable area. A T-junction is reached: right is blind, left is a flat-out crawl. Before the T-junction a branch on left appears to be the main way on.

## BAMFORTH HOLE
NGR 2205 7580  Grade: 1. Dig
Alt. 600ft (183m)
Length: 30ft (9m)

Somewhat confused. There has been a great deal of argument over this cave, first referred to by Short (1734) as a narrow passage at the end of which was a climb into a cave. The cave corresponds with the east end of Eyam Passage in Carlswark Cavern (Oyster Chamber). The most likely entrance is a small mine level approximately 100ft (30m) west and slightly above Carlswark's Lower (Resurgence) Entrance. A short descending passage ends at roof falls after 30ft (9m). If dug for a considerable distance, it probably connects with the Gin Entrance to Carlswark Cavern.

References: Gill, D.W. 1976. Eldon P.C.Journal Vol.9. No.1. pp.11-12.
Kirkham, N. 1948. British Caver Vol.18. pp.21-26.
Pilkington, J.A. 1789. A View of the Present State of Derbyshire. 2 Vols.
Short, T. 1734. A History of the Mineral Waters of Derbyshire, Lincolnshire, and Yorkshire. p.34 & 95.
Smith, M.E. 1971. Bull.P.D.M.H.S. Vol.5. No.5. pp.370-374. Survey.

## BEECH FELL HOLE
(Birch Fell Hole)
NGR 2090 7563    Grade: 2
Alt. 865ft (264m)
Depth: 50ft (15m)

Discovered by Derek "Teapot" Stables 1993.

Adjacent to the track up to the derelict Farnsley Farm.

A 50ft (15m) deep mineshaft leads down into draughting natural cavities. Digging has so far been unsuccessful.

References: Arveschoug, D. 1994. Caves & Caving No.65. p.3.

## BEECH TREE HOLE
NGR 2171 7585    Grade: 1
Alt. 646ft (196.9m)
Length: 55ft (16.7m)

Excavated by Chesterfield Caving Club for 135ft (41m) 1989 - 1992.

Between Eyam Dale and The Delph, just west of trial workings on Old Oak Scrin.

A silted cave passage at the base of the Lower Shell Bed runs northwards and then north westwards towards natural cavities in a nearby mine on Stub Scrin (Middleton Dale Mine Level No. 7).

References: Chesterfield C.C. 1992. D.C.A. N/L No.77. p.8. Location plan.

## BLACK HOLE SWALLET
NGR 2035 7732   Lost
Alt. 1000ft (300m)

100 yards (90m) south west of Black Hole Mine. Now filled in. The shakehole was a large one, but only occasionally took a stream.

## BOSSEN HOLE
(Badger Hole, Tacko Hole, Windy Ledge Cave)
NGR 2233 7573   Grade: 1
Alt. 625ft (190.5m)
Length: 263ft (80m)
Status: S.S.S.I.

On north side of Stoney Middleton Dale. A footpath leads to an exposed ledge midway up the Castle Buttress. The cave is at the east end of the ledge.

After walking a few feet and climbing up 8ft (3m), rest of cave is a crawl right through the buttress. A left hand branch becomes too tight. The through tube may be too draughty for naked lights at times. Care is needed on the ledge.

*References: Smith, M.E., Jour. S.U.S.S. Vol.1. No.2. Survey.*

## CARLSWARK CAVERN
(Carleswark, Charleswork, The Wonder Cavern)
Grade: 2 - 5
**Resurgence Entrance:**
NGR 2207 7580
Alt. 572ft (174.5m)
**Eyam Dale Shaft:**
NGR 2184 7596
Alt. 644ft (196.3m)
**Gin Entrance:**
NGR 2207 7581
Alt. 623ft (190m)
**Stub Scrin Shaft:**
NGR 2184 7603
Alt. 757ft (230.6m)
**Flower Pot Entrance:**
NGR 2193 7609
Alt. 676ft (206m)
Length (Merlin/Carlswark combined): 10641ft (3243m).
Vertical Range: 200ft (61m).
Status: R.I.G.S. (Eyam Dale) / Status: S.S.S.I.

No known access restrictions.

First desribed by Short (1734) as passing "clean through the mountain to emerge in Eyan (Eyam) Dale" and also "by another of its grottoes it emerges near Fowlow (Foolow) passing quite under Eyam Church".

Explored systematically by cavers early 20th century. Extended by BSA in 1959 to discover the BSA New Series. Extended LCC 1970 to discover the Dynamite Series. Extended by EPC 1973 (Gimli's Dream) and connected to Merlins Mine: connection blocked to preserve formations. Extended by TSG in 1979 to discover the Big Dig Series.

**The Lower (Resurgence) Entrance** lies at the foot of a cliff midway between Stoney Middleton and the Eyam road turning on the A623. **The Gin Entrance** lies about 50ft (15m) vertically above, and slightly west of the Lower Entrance, reached by a rough track. **Eyam Dale Shaft** lies opposite the electricity sub-station in Eyam Dale. **Stub Scrin Shaft**, now partly collapsed and dangerous, lies high above Eyam Dale Shaft, a little further to the north. **The Flower Pot Entrance** lies on the right of Eyam Dale, shortly before the high garden wall of Dale Cottage begins, visible from the road.

**The Lower Entrance** is a low crawl into a sizeable chamber which is frequently flooded in winter. The main route is to the right for 290ft (89m) to a sump which must not be free dived as it is over 90ft (27m) long. A difficult 30ft (9m) climb up a rift to the right leads to the Oyster Chamber in the Upper Series (Eyam Passage).

**The Gin Entrance** is the most popular entrance, and is an open rift on a terrace at the base of the cliff. An easy 30ft (9m) scramble down leads to a junction with Eyam Passage. Right is soon blocked, but left leads quickly to Oyster Chamber and the connection with the Lower Series. The main route is ahead: all other passages off are blocked. Three inlet passages enter at roof level in Eyam Passage. The first, 150ft (45m) is very tight.

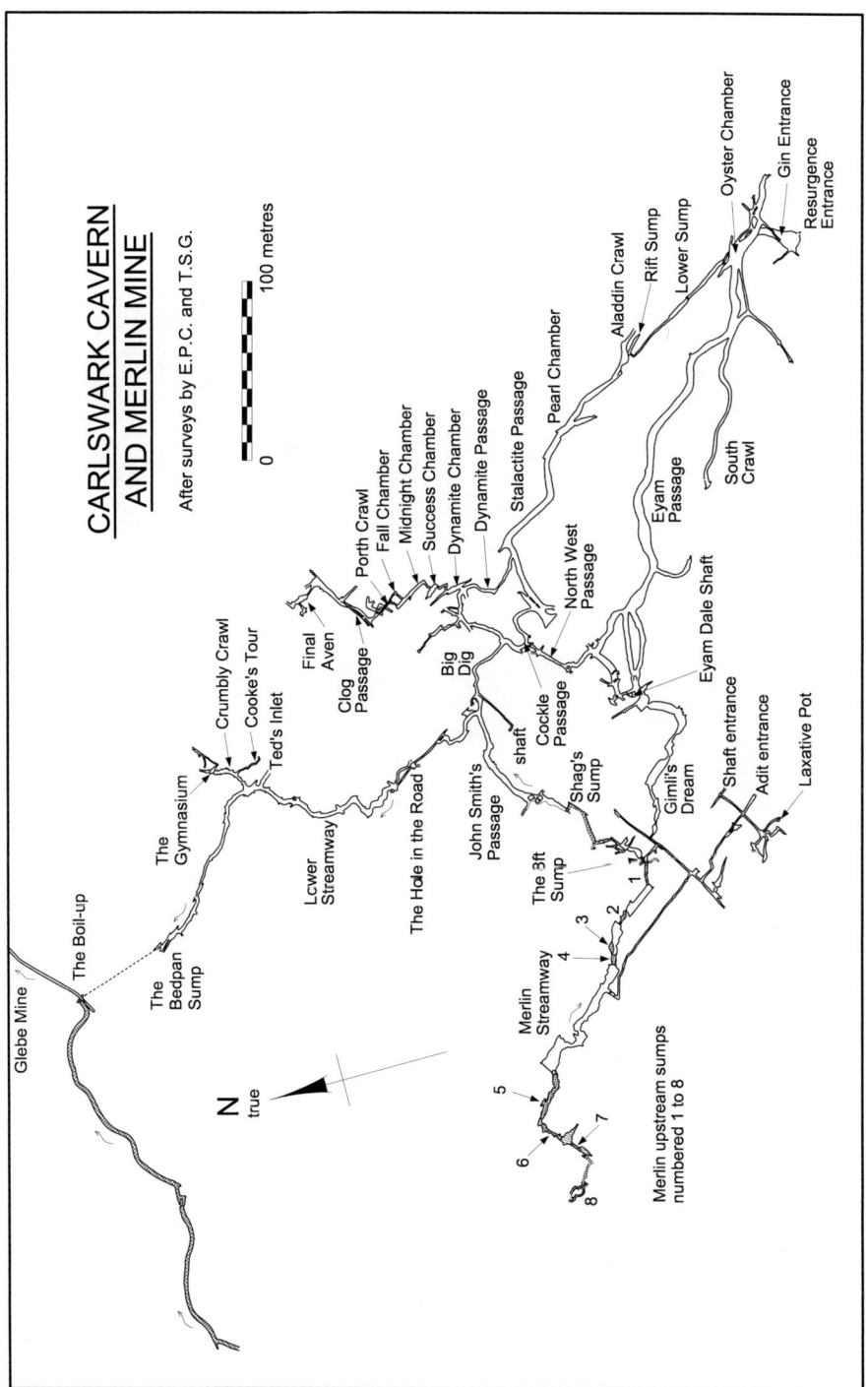

The second, 290ft (89m) is South Crawl and ends at a fall. The third, 99ft (30m) is also tight. Eyam Passage reduces to a crawl between South Crawl and the third inlet, but enlarges again to Noughts and Crosses Chamber, where another fall blocks the way. The way on is to the right of the fall into a low chamber with three ways off. Left is soon blocked by mud, the second is tight at first and leads up close to Eyam Dale Shaft. The main route is right, following a small stream, to a junction with North West Passage. Left leads to Eyam Dale Shaft, 36ft (11m) deep and 1165ft (355m) from the Gin Entrance. A crawl 10ft (3m) up the shaft leads to a chamber where the connection with Gimli's Dream in the Merlin Mine was made (now blocked).

Cockle Passage.
Photo by Rob Eavis

Back at the junction in North West Passage, turning right and following the small stream the size reduces to a crawl, which improves to hands and knees and eventually leads to an awkward squeeze over a boulder and a low junction. Note the way out: many people miss this squeeze on return and end up lost. Left leads to Big Dig, and right leads via Cockle Passage and a duck to a junction with Stalactite Passage. Dynamite Passage soon enters on the left, and can be followed back to Big Dig. The main passage continues to Pearl Chamber, after which the main route ends at a climb down into a rift. In the rift, a mine level on the right leads to the upstream end of the sump in the Lower Entrance passage. The sump has been passed in drought, but is rarely open. The formerly well-decorated Aladdin Crawl is reached by a precarious traverse over the rift.

**The Dynamite Series**, 1065ft (322m) long, is reached by taking the first obvious right turn off Dynamite Passage, a squeeze through boulders. The route consists of a series of joint-oriented chambers connected by mostly tight crawls. The largest is Prospect Chamber, which leads to the very tight Porth Crawl, continuing via a tight ascending rift into Clog Passage. Right ends at a boulder choke, and straight on to Old Man workings, in which the bottoms of run-in shafts can be seen. Natural passage is re-entered beyond, and soon leads to another high aven. A keyhole passage leads to two more avens via tight squeezes, and a passage at floor level (Picnic Passage) can be followed as a very tight crawl for about 250ft (76m). This could still be dug, and may provide a connection with nearby Eyam Dale House Cave. A passage off Prospect Chamber is reached by a short climb. Very tight squeezes lead to Fall Chamber, and climbing into the roof gives access to a passage on the right which leads to the bottom of the Flower Pot Entrance.

**The Big Dig Series** is 1803ft (549m) long. Big Dig is a roomy crawl reached by turning left at the bottom of North West Passage, and again left at a T-junction. 150ft (46m) of crawling, often in water, leads past the blocked route to the deep shaft entrance. This is now partly collapsed and blocked, but consisted of three pitches, total 180ft (55m). The crawl continues through a boulder choke to a T-junction with the streamway, carrying a large stream which dries up in late summer. Left (upstream) is John Smith's Passage, 280ft (85m) of canals, crawls, and a short walking sized stretch to the downstream end of Shag's Sump in the Merlin Mine. Right at the junction, a crawl leads to a rift passage where the stream flows into an impenetrable slot. Follow the rift for 60ft (18m) to a pit (The Hole in the Road). Part of the stream enters at the bottom. Either climb down to a watery crawl, or traverse over to rejoin the stream where the Cowlishaw Vein crosses the cave. 300ft (90m) of stooping passage follows, passing Ted's Inlet (too tight) where most of the stream re-enters. A right hand branch, Crumbly Crawl, is next, and leads to a cross rift after 75ft (23m) with a very tight continuation at roof level. The main streamway continues, soon sumping in wet weather, but penetrable in summer for another 300ft (90m), becoming more and more disagreeable until it is too low.

*Tackle:*

| | |
|---|---|
| *Eyam Dale Shaft:* | *20m rope. Belay to tree with Y hang at head of pitch.* |
| *Flower Pot:* | *5m ladder. Scaffold bar belay.* |

*References: Beck, J.S. 1975. Trans. B.C.R.A. Vol.2. No.1. pp.1-12.*
*Beck, J.S. 1979. T.S.G. N/L No.8. Survey.*
*Beck, J.S. and Christopher, N.J. 1977. Trans. B.C.R.A. Vol.4. No.3. pp.361-365. Survey. Beck, J.S. and Gill, D.W. 1974. D.C.A. N/L No.20 pp.1-2.*
*Buckley, A.L. 1974. D.C.A. N/L No.21.*
*Jefferson, D.P. 1961. Bull. P.D.M.H.S. Vol.1. No.4. pp.37-43.*
*King, B. 1962. Cave Science Vol.4. No.32. pp.377-383. Survey.*
*Mellor, D. 1972. Eldon P.C. Jour. Vol.8. No.1. pp.14-15.*
*Smith, M.E. 1971. Bull. P.D.M.H.S. Vol.4. No.5. pp.370-374. Survey.*

### CAVALIERS' HOLE
NGR 2227 7578　　Grade: 1
Alt. 655ft (199m)
Length: 20ft (6m)

Excavated by John Watts & 44th Colchester Venture Scouts in 1993.
Just to the right of the east entrance of Keyhole Cave.
A low phreatic tube excavated for 20ft (6m).
*References: Descent No. 113. 1993. p.18.*

### CRACKPOT CAVE
(Hardwark)
NGR 2182 7596　　Grade: 1
Alt. 686ft (209m)
Length: 70ft (21m)

Above and to the left of Eyam Dale Shaft entrance to Carlswark. Originally 10ft (3m) long. Dug out for 10ft (3m) through a hole in the calcite roof to 50ft (15m) of well decorated passage ending in a calcite choke. Formations now destroyed by vandals.
*References: Noble, M. 1975. D.C.A. N/L No.24. p.6.*

### CREEP CAVE
NGR 211 757　　Lost
Alt. 800ft (244m)
Length: 110ft (34m)

In Eyam Quarry, below Farnsley Lane, halfway up quarry face. Now thought to be buried.
Phreatic tube 2ft 6in (0.8m) diameter for 70ft (21m) to a small aven. Further 40ft (12m) of passage to a calcite blockage.
*References: Gill, D.W. 1972. British Caver Vol.57. p.102.
Lord, P.J. 1971. Jour. S.U.S.S. Vol.2. No.1. p.26*

### CROCK POT
(Innominate Pot)
NGR 1988 7705　　Grade: 3
Alt. 895ft (273m)
Length: 330ft (100m)
Depth: 25m (82ft)
Status: S.S.S.I.

Found in 1998 when water was seen to have sunk among tree roots to the left of the waterfall in Waterfall Swallet. Excavated to a tight rift which draughted strongly. Entrance enlarged by Masson Caving Group in 1999, and further digging led to a breakthrough into a series of rift passages, one 80ft (25m) long and 50ft (15m) high.
The pot is very tight, awkward and loose in places, and rescue would be extremely difficult. The lower sections flood completely - do not descend if water is backing up in the shakehole.

Excavated entrance in tree roots leads to climb down and series of short tight awkward crawls and climbs dropping into the Miner's Rift. Right here (west) leads to a short hand-picked coffin level (where a bone identified by archaeologists as human was discovered) and left where a climb down leads to the head of Flake Pitch (36ft / 11m). and the tall narrow North Rift (separated 82ft / 25m vertically from Mark and Keith's Bit in Waterfall Hole). Ahead at the Miners Rift is a step up on the right into Stepping Stone Passage which leads via an awkward constricted drop to South Rift and a climb up to the head of Echo Pitch (26ft / 8m). From the bottom of Echo Pitch a steep climb down enters a spacious rift.
*References: Webb, D. 2000. The Derbyshire Caver. 108. pp.1-3. Survey.*

### CROSSLOW CAVERN
NGR 2030 7706　　Lost
Alt. 1000ft (305m)
Length: 300ft (90m)
Depth: 80ft (24m)

Shaft in enclosure in south west corner of field no.281, 200 yards (182m) south west of Black Hole Mine.
A lost cavern listed by Farey, and rediscovered by Peak District Mines Historical Society. On Crosslow Rake. A 60ft (18m) ladder pitch and 20ft (6m) scramble into mine workings. A short passage goes west into natural cavern once used as a washing floor and largely filled with "deads". Drainage towards Waterfall Swallet. The site has been "restored" and the entrance obliterated.
*References: Robey, J. 1964. Bull. P.D.M.H.S. Vol.2. No.3. 151-152. Survey.*

## CUCKLET CHURCH CAVE

NGR 2152 7620  Grade: 1
Alt. 800ft (240m)
Status: S.S.S.I.

High on the west side of Cucklet Delph at the north end.
A series of through arches in a prominent buttress. Used each year for the plague commemoration service.
*References: Pearce, A. 1974. Bull. P.D.M.H.S. Vol.5. No.5.*

## CUCKLET DELPH UPPER CAVE
(Smokey Hole)
NGR 2156 7610  Grade: 1
Alt. 656ft (200m)
Length: 50ft (15m)

Small cave about 6ft (2m) above the stream on the west side of the path.
A short bedding crawl was dug out to 50ft (15m), completely blocked at the end by clay.

## DELPH HOLE

NGR 2165 7595  Grade: 2
Alt. 697ft (212.5m)
Length: 187ft (57m)
Status: S.S.S.I.

High on the east side of Cucklet Delph below Auton Crofts plateau.
Entrance is 6ft (2m) high mine level. After 60ft (18m) from entrance step across a shaft in the floor (with care) to a passage on right. After 25ft (8m) is a natural chamber 30ft (9m) long with a silted passage descending to the left, dug for some distance during 1977. Down the shaft (easy climb 8ft/2.5m) is a mine level which ends at a forefield.
*References: Pearce, A. 1974. Bull.P.D.M.H.S. Vol.5. No.5. pp.243-257. Survey.*
*Pill, A.L. 1950. Cave Science No.15. p.223.*

## DELPH SWALLETS
Digs.
**Delph Top Sink:**
NGR 2157 7618
Alt. 661ft (201m)
Depth: 60ft (18m)

**Delph Bottom Sink:**
NGR 2158 7597
Alt. 626ft (191m)

Top Sink lies close to the brook directly below Cucklet Church.
Delph Bottom Sink by the side of the path up Cucklet Delph 140 yards (128m) north of the main road.
Delph Top Sink.
An obvious sink by the stream can take a large volume of water, which is usually diverted to flow on down the valley. Dug in the early 1980s, a 12ft (4m) oil-drum shaft opened into a large rift dug out to a depth of 60ft (18m). Water backed up to the 50ft (15m) mark and sank in narrow cracks. Water dye tested to Moorwood Sough without passing through the known Carlswark Cavern system. The sink collapsed in 2009 leaving the site as a large open pothole.
Delph Bottom Sink.
Water sinks in the bed of the stream. The sink is soon overpowered and water flows on to join the Dale Brook. Dug in the early 1970's, but no bedrock found. Dye tested to the Merlin Streamway.
*References: Beck, J.S. 1975. Trans B.C.R.A. Vol.2. No.1. pp.1-11.*

### EYAM DALE HOUSE CAVE

**NGR 2196 7626**
Grade: 3
Alt. 760ft (232m)
Length: 1050ft (320m)
Depth: 183ft (56m)
Status: S.S.S.I.

Permission required IN ADVANCE from Eyam Dale House Residential Home for the Elderly.

The shaft entrance lies in the grounds of the house close to the line of the sewer. The manhole cover just off the line of inspection pits is a mineshaft.

60ft (18m) hading entrance shaft discovered by tracing the old sewer (now diverted!) in 1985. Shaft enters natural chamber, with second pitch 35ft (11m) leading only to a further climb down into tight rifts.

From base of entrance shaft pass the second pitch and follow crawls into a parallel rift to the head of a 20ft (6m) pitch which can be free climbed with care. Passage enlarges until the roomy North West Chamber is reached, with various digging possibilities. Back at the base of the 20ft pitch follow a flat-out crawl to the Pearly Gate, a squeeze between stalagmite pillars. Crawl continues well-decorated (care needed to avoid stals) to an 8ft (2.5m) climb down to a bouldery chamber. A fine grotto (The Room with a View) is up the flowstone slope to the left. This looks out along a large rift (The Other Side), 200ft (61m) long and with a vertical range of over 100ft (30m). Climb down boulders and

The Other Side, Eyam Dale House Cave. Photo by Paul Deakin

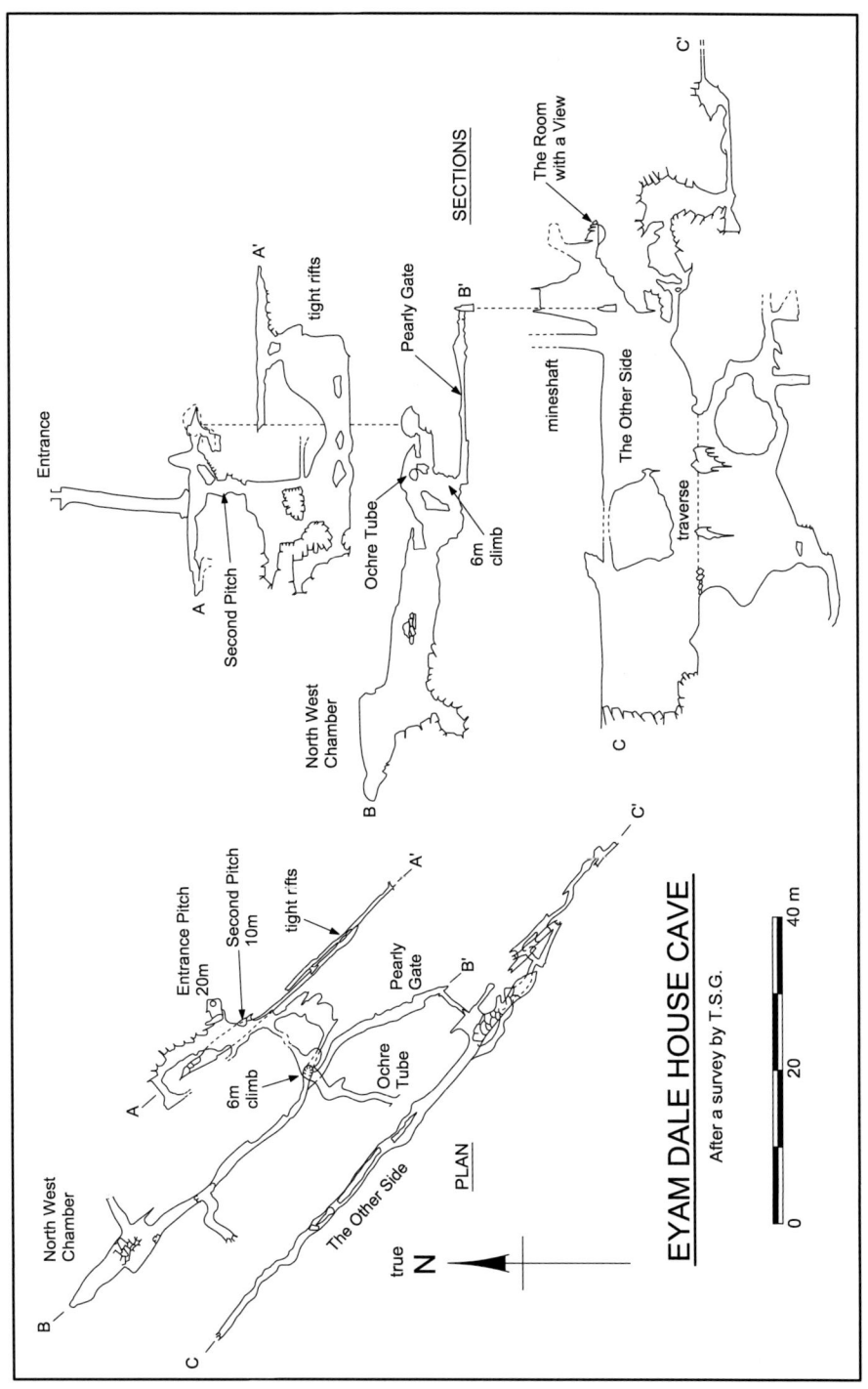

follow rift until the floor drops away and traverse continues. Rift ends at all levels in either boulders or flowstone. Has been climbed to the base of a mineshaft to surface. A series of sharp muddy rifts and crawls leads in the other direction from the climb down boulders to The Other Side. Appears to draught from Dynamite Series in Carlswark Cavern.

*Tackle:*
*Entrance Shaft:*   20m rope. Belay to bar.
*2nd Pitch:*        15m rope  Bolt belays.
*20ft climb:*       6m ladder + lifeline. Natural belays.

*References: Beck, J.S. 1985. T.S.G. Jour. No.12. pp.10-14. Survey.*

### FARNSLEY LANE CAVE
NGR 2102 7571    Grade: 3
Alt. 823ft (251m)
Length: 92ft (28m)
Depth: 23ft (7m)

Discovered 2000 by J.Beck and M.Noble
On the west side of Farnsley Lane above the second right hand bend up from the A623
A tight crawl quickly enlarges and turns right to the head of a 10ft (3m) climb down into a small chamber. A further flat out crawl leads to a second climb, and a crawl at the base develops into a very tight vadose passage which has been pushed to a small chamber with a boulder roof, Farnsley Bitter. A hole through boulders in the floor was shored and a lower aven (about 10ft (3m) high) found. A small passage leads off this for about 30ft (10m) to a mud fill. Work continues. There is a strong draught at times.

*References: Beck, J.S. 2000. Descent 153. pp.10-12*

### FARNSLEY LANE QUARRY CAVES
NGR 211 757    Lost
Alt. 700ft (210m)
Length: 10-50ft (3-15m)

Permission from Wimpey's Quarry at the bottom of Eyam Dale. Not usually granted.
Various caves in the lower bench of what used to be Eyam Quarry, by the sharp bend on the main road.
At present these entrances are buried by "landscaping". One tube 15ft (5m) up the face was about 30ft (9m) long. Directly below Farnsley Lane was a large blind mine level, and to the right of this was a large phreatic tube about 50ft (15m) long ending at a clay choke.

### FARNSLEY LANE SWALLET
NGR 2067 7546    Grade: 3
Alt. 958ft (292m)
Depth: 82ft (25m)

Access strictly through Glebe Mines Ltd. at Cavendish Mill.
Opened up by Laporte Chemicals in 1996 and explored by A.Revell and D.Stables.
On the north side of Farnsley Lane, just below the Cavendish Mill yards.
Most of the cave is in a large boulder choke, and can be descended for 82ft (25m) to a point where the way on is blocked by large dangerous blocks.

*References: Descent No.139. 1998. p.13. Survey.*

### FATIGUE POT
(Colliers Peril Cave)
NGR 2268 7485    Grade: 3
Alt. 600ft (183m)
Length: 620ft (189m)
Depth: 82ft (25m)

No known access restrictions, but please replace cover.
20ft (6m) above the valley floor on the north side of Coombes Dale. Small entrance blocked by removable steel door. Very difficult to find.
Small, muddy, smelly entrance crawl for 30ft (9m) to head of 25ft (8m) pitch. Replacing the cover carefully will help to stop foxes making the crawl worse. Follow the rift down several short

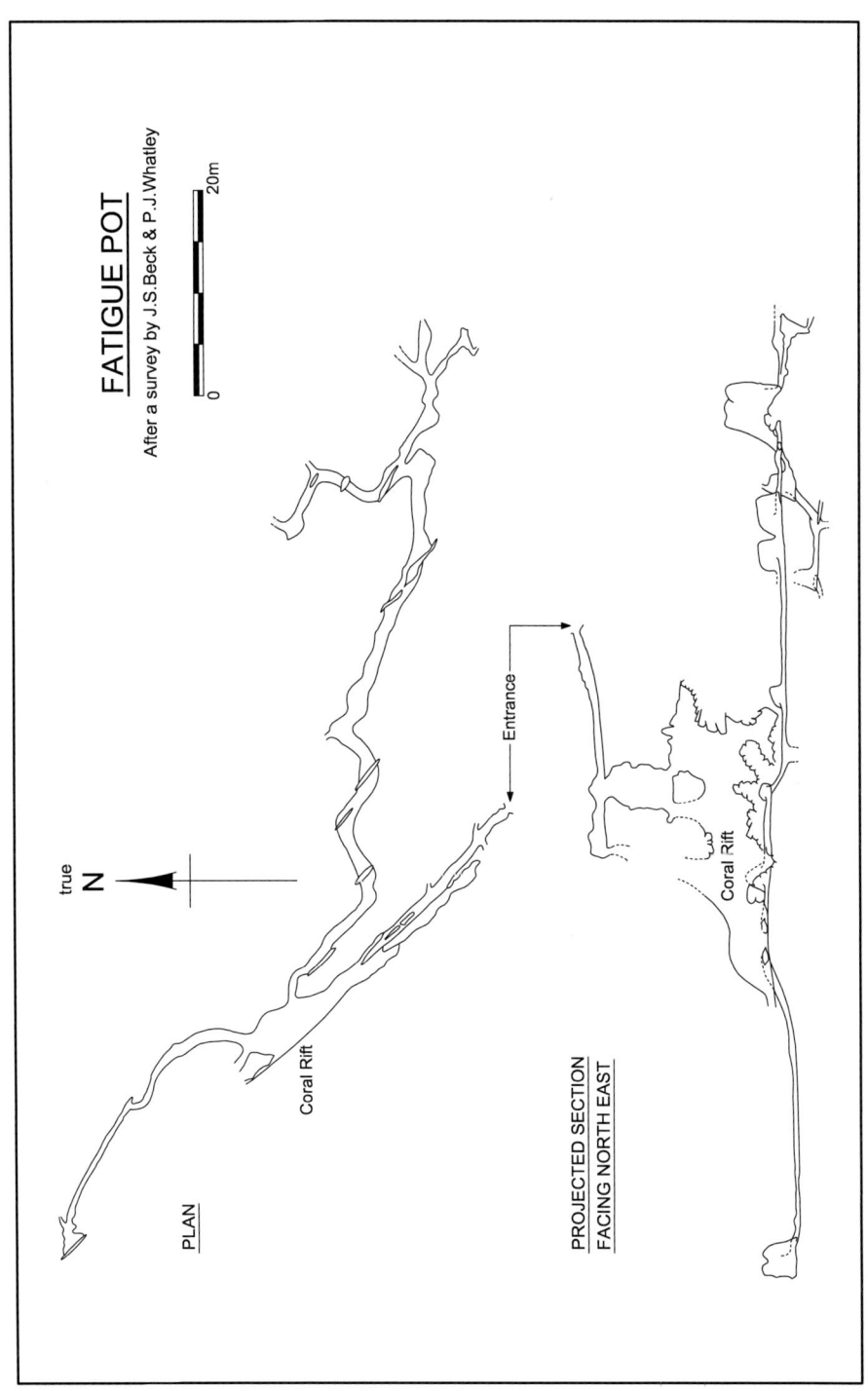

climbs and drop through tight hole in boulders for 15ft (4.5m) into wide rift passage (hand line useful for return). Traverse along the rift above tight holes in the floor for 50ft (15m) approximately. Two crawls on the right. The first leads to 300ft (91m) of low passage with avens at the end, and a strongly draughting continuation which is too tight. The second crawl is very tight for 100ft (30m) with very restricted turning space.

Water could be heard at the lowest point but the cave is badly silted with mining waste and the stream flows on the surface.

*Tackle:*
*8m ladder + lifeline.*
*6m handline useful on short climb.*
References: Beck, J.S. 1979. Jour. Eldon P.C. Vol.9. No.1. pp.1-3. Survey.
Tottle, P. 1954. The Speleologist No.1. pp. 85-91.

### FIRESET SHAFT
NGR 2189 7607   Grade: 2
Alt. 700ft (213.3m)
Length: 154ft (47m)
Depth: 84ft (25.5m)

Shaft excavated in 1982

Shaft on top of the small cliff by the lay-by halfway up Eyam Dale on the west side

50ft (15m) entrance shaft to a short sidestep into a stope which ends at forefields in both directions. Small hole in the floor gives access to a very narrow level with soot-coated walls, which has been driven by the old method of firesetting, ie. without the use of explosives. The level ends at a narrow shaft with further short backfilled fireset workings leading westwards. Draught is thought to come from the Dynamite Series of Carlswark.

*Tackle:    20m rope. Short scaffold bar for belay.*
References: Whitehouse, R.H. 1986. T.S.G. Jour. No.12. pp.6-9. Survey.

### HALE BOPP POT
NGR 2074 7596   Dig
Alt. 755ft (230m) approx.
Depth: 10ft (3m)

Dug by Tom Proctor & Geoff Birtles in the early 1980's. Re-excavated by Pegasus C.C. in 1997 with scaffolding supports, and capped.

Capped entrance below and to the east of Hangover Hole, below Paracetam 'Ole. The rift, approx. 20ft (6m) long has been excavated to varying depths over the years. A very strong outward draught in warm weather.

### HANGING FLAT MINE
NGR 2063 7601   Grade: 2
Alt. 770ft (235m)
Length: 400ft (120m) approx
Depth: 40ft (12m)

Worked for fluorspar in the late 1970s / early 1980s. Entrance collapsed in mid-1990s.

Immediately west of the entrance to Furness (Horseshoe) Quarry, close to the road but hidden in vegetation.

**Warning: Parts of the mine are in an unstable condition.**

A descending crawl leads over the entrance collapse into the adit. This leads shortly to a junction. Left leads to a working face after approx. 330ft (100m), passing slits driven into the vein which are collapsed and should not be entered. The right branch leads to a 40ft (12m) shaft in an unstable area which must be be treated with caution. Workings at the bottom have collapsed.

### HANGOVER HOLE
NGR 2069 7595   Grade: 3
Alt. 787ft (240m)
Length: 230ft (70m)
Depth: 50ft (15m)

Discovered on New Year's Day 1992 by Keyhole Caving Club.

On the south side of Stoney Middleton Dale west of the old explosives store, high above the road.

A descending crawl through large scale breakdown leads to a small chamber. A climb down through the Keyhole Caving Club dig leads to a squeeze into a wide flat-roofed passage. Crawling over breakdown slabs leads into a further area of complex breakdown, and a continuing crawl leads opens into a large chamber, Inferno Chamber, 50ft (15m) by 30ft (9m). Further digging has revealed another larger chamber, Pizzaland, but the area is dangerous and it is unlikely that there is a way forward.

*References: Descent No. 105. 1992. p.14*
*Descent No. 120. 1994. p. 8. Survey.*

---

**HAWKEN EDGE CAVE**
NGR 218 757     Lost
Alt. 650ft (198m)
Length: 52ft (16m)

At the west end of Dalton's (now Wimpey's) Quarry on the south side of the Dale, by the footpath to Lane Head, 50ft (15m) above the road.

A large entrance 15ft (5m) high, which soon closed. Quarrying has now either buried or removed the cave.

---

**HAWKENEDGE WELL**
(Oakenedge Sough)
NGR 2156 7583     Dig
Alt. 600ft (183m)

Small resurgence on the south side of A623 in Middleton Dale, opposite Cucklet Delph.

Discharges a fairly constant flow. Possibly the tail of a sough, though shafts immediately upstream will be under quarry debris.

*References: Kirkham, N. 1967. Bull. P.D.M.H.S. Vol.3. No.4. pp.197-218.*

---

**HOBBIT HOLE**
NGR 2083 7597     Grade: 1
Alt. 715ft (218m)
Length: 35ft (11m)

At road level in the lowest section of Furness (Ben Bennett's) Quarry.

A short unpleasant flat-out crawl to a complete flowstone choke.

---

**HOLE IN THE WALL**
NGR 2096 7604     Grade: 1
Alt. 786ft (240m)
Length: 230ft (70m)
Status: S.S.S.I.

25ft (8m) up the north face in the main part of Furness (Ben Bennett's, or Horseshoe) Quarry, directly opposite the entry point of the track.

An ancient cave passage intersected by the quarry. Entrance about 10ft (3m) high. Dig is about 230ft long. Ends 30ft into a boulder choke.

---

**HUNGERHILL SWALLET**
NGR 2096 7695     Grade: 5
Alt. 920ft (280m)
Length: 1200ft (305m) approx
Depth: 250ft (76m)
Status: S.S.S.I.

Permission from Hungerhill House.

Entrances excavated 1985-1987.

A tree lined shakehole in field west of Hungerhill House, the whitewashed cottage to the north of the road.

**Warning: Some of the squeezes in the cave are very tight and awkward, or through poised boulders. The big pitch (Deep Space) and the streamway (Peristalsis) may quickly become impassable in wet weather.**

Swallet stream captured by shale gate from Little Pasture Mine, seen in a tiny shaft west of the main shakehole, where the stream flows into an impenetrable bedding. The Timbered Shaft Entrance, now run-in but taking road drainage, lay against the south wall of the shakehole. The first shaft, 28ft (8.5m) deep, led to a timbered tunnel to a further rather loose timbered shaft of 15ft (4.5m). The third timbered shaft, 25ft (8m) deep, led to a crawl under loose boulders into a rift passage. A tight descent down a slot in the floor led to the head of a 25ft (8m) pitch into the chamber known as "Happy Breakthrough".

The Mine Level Entrance was re-excavated by CCPC thanks to an Natural England grant in 2005 and a plastic pipe installed. A spanner is needed for access. At the bottom a low and muddy mine

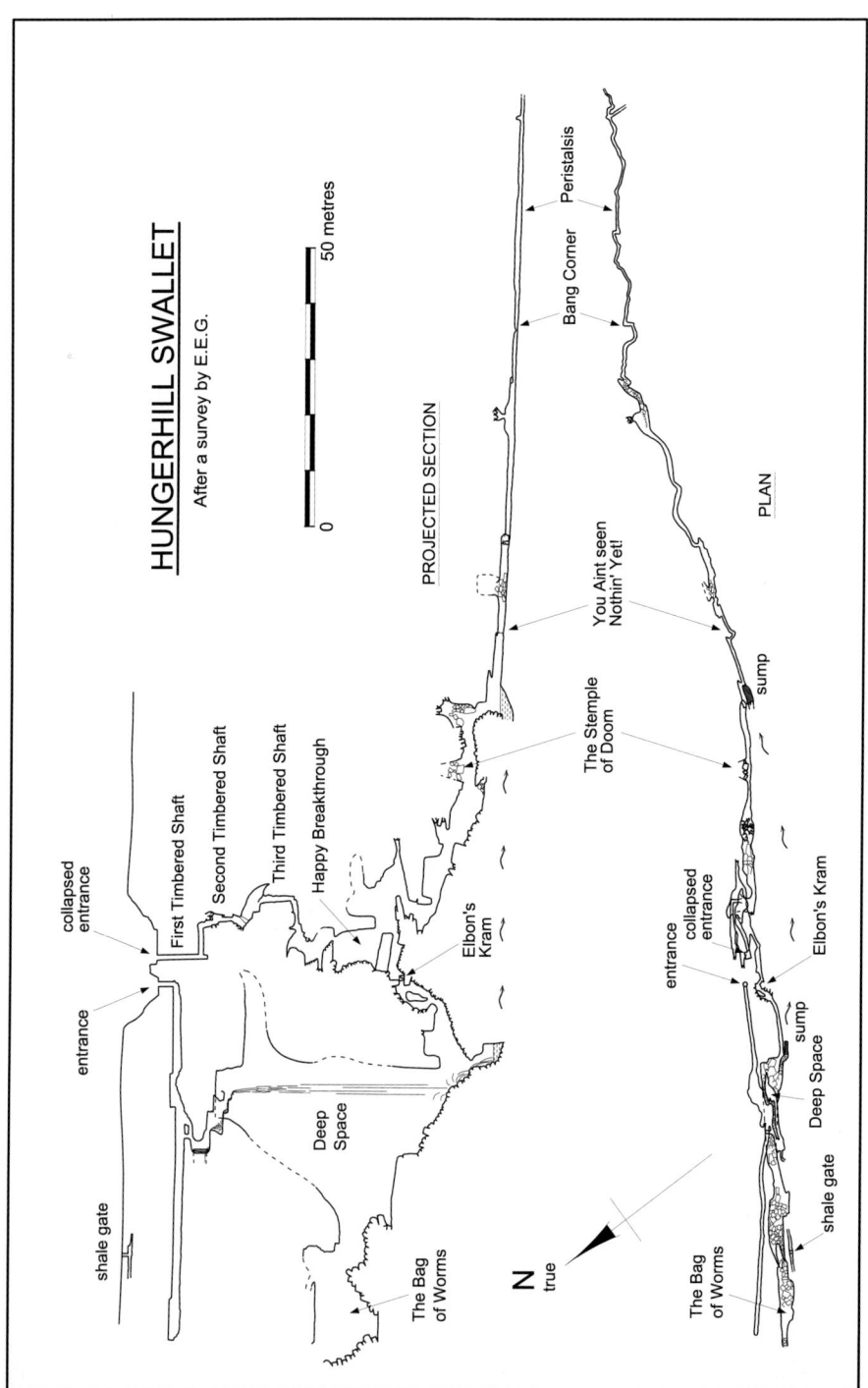

level leads to a chamber. The level, with gours now taped for protection, continues to a forefield, but an obvious crawl in the floor leads to a tight and awkward squeeze, now enlarged, into the Top Streamway. Follow stream in small passage over short cascades to the head of the spectacular 130ft (40m) pitch, "Deep Space". This may become impassable in flood. The pitch begins as a long narrow rift and becomes progressively bigger. The landing is on a boulder slope, down which the stream cascades into a small passage and a choked sump. At the top of the boulder slope a climb and short crawl lead into a breakdown chamber. A further climb and crawl at the far end lead to the head of a flowstoned boulder slope in the "Bag of Worms". The far end of this second chamber consists of a large choke, which has been dug upwards into a small but well decorated chamber 70ft (21m) above the floor. A further dig leads back down into the continuation of the main rift, which continues well decorated until it becomes a wide flat-roofed passage which ends at silt chokes.

A climb above the sump (beware of dangerous boulders) leads via a narrow rift to the bottom of "Elbon's Kram", a strenuous climb up a tight rift to a very awkward squeeze. Collapsed boulders now block this route. Two further squeezes led through to the Happy Breakthrough chamber below the old timbered shafts. Climb down slabs and double back to scramble into a parallel rift. A short crawl leads to a further breakdown chamber. Small stream sinks at the far end, but follow a crawl just above (beware of the dangerously balanced "Stemple of Doom" just beyond). The route continues under more loose boulders to a climb down into a sump pool where the stream from Deep Space emerges.

The Bag of Worms. Photo by Paul Deakin

A narrow stream passage continues along the joint, and turns right into a very tight section, "You Ain't Seen Nothin' Yet!". 150ft (46m) of crawling leads to a small chamber where miners' deads are seen. The miner's way down is blocked with large boulders in the roof. A tight squeeze through boulders leads to 40ft (12m) of frustrating crawling in the stream to Bang Corner. Bang Corner looks passable at roof level, but it is only passable in dry weather by lying in the stream. The next 120ft (37m), "Peristalsis", necessitates wriggling in the stream in a passage about a foot wide, round some very sharp bends. It is sumped in all but dry weather. A tiny cross rift is reached. A short distance beyond, progress in the stream becomes impossible. Wet weather overflow water leaves to the right via the cross rift, which is an unpromising, remote, horrible dig.

**Tackle:**
**Deep Space: 50m rope. Belay to bolts with natural backup. Beware loose rock on opposite wall. 1 rebelay.**
References: Beck, J.S. 1988. Jour. T.S.G. No.13. pp.26-33. Survey.
Webb, D. 2005. Derbyshire Caver No.123. pp 8-10.

### IVY GREEN CAVE
NGR 2224 7580    Grade: 2
Alt. 655ft (199m)
Length: 740ft (225m)
Status: S.S.S.I.

High in the cliff, just east of the terrace, west of Cliff Stile Vein. Awkward climb to the entrance.

Rift-like entrance soon becomes a phreatic tube. Right branch after 90ft (27m) was dug for over 100ft (30m) to a choke in Cliff Stile Vein. Main passage continues through some tight squeezes to a final calcite choke. There is no draught at the end but small silted passages on the left appear to draught from Middleton Dale Mine Level No.5.

References: Beck, J.S. 1975. Trans.B.C.R.A. Vol.2. No.1. pp.1-11.
Noble, M. 1975. D.C.A. N/L No.24. p.7.
Smith, M.E. 1969. S.U.S.S. Jour. Vol.1. No.5. pp.208-210. Survey.

### KEYHOLE CAVE
NGR 2226 7578   Grade: 1
Alt. 655ft (199m)
Length: 50ft (15m)
Status: S.S.S.I.

Immediately east of Cliff Stile vein and east of the terrace.

The obvious downstream continuation of Ivy Green Cave before quarrying intersected the passage. A large passage with a pebbly fill has been partly dug out, and leads right through the buttress with a window in the cliff face halfway through.

### LAY-BY POT
Grade: 2
Alt. 810ft (247m)
Length: 1215ft (370m)
Depth: 76ft (23m)
Shaft Entrance:
NGR 2035 7599
Oil Drum Entrance:
NGR 2043 7599
Status: S.S.S.I.

Entrance dug out by South West London Caving Club in 1973.

On north side of dale, opposite the second lay-by coming from Wardlow. Behind an earth bank and vegetation.

A short mined passage slopes down to the head of a 46ft (14m) pitch. At base of pitch a crawl to the east leads to the 200ft (61m) long "Old Man's Slabbed Level", a dry-stone level which runs beneath the road and ends at a collapse.

The other direction at the base of the pitch leads after 100ft (30m) natural passage to the Cheese Grater, a 23ft (7m) pitch to a static pool. Passage continues to a collapse and an upward slope to a T-junction. Left is the 80ft (24m) long Calcite Passage, passing Initial Aven, where the date "1818" is scratched in the flowstone. Right at the junction leads after 60ft (18m) to Silhouette Grotto. A crawl at the far end of the chamber leads after 30ft (9m) to another low chamber with avens. A further crawl, wet at first,

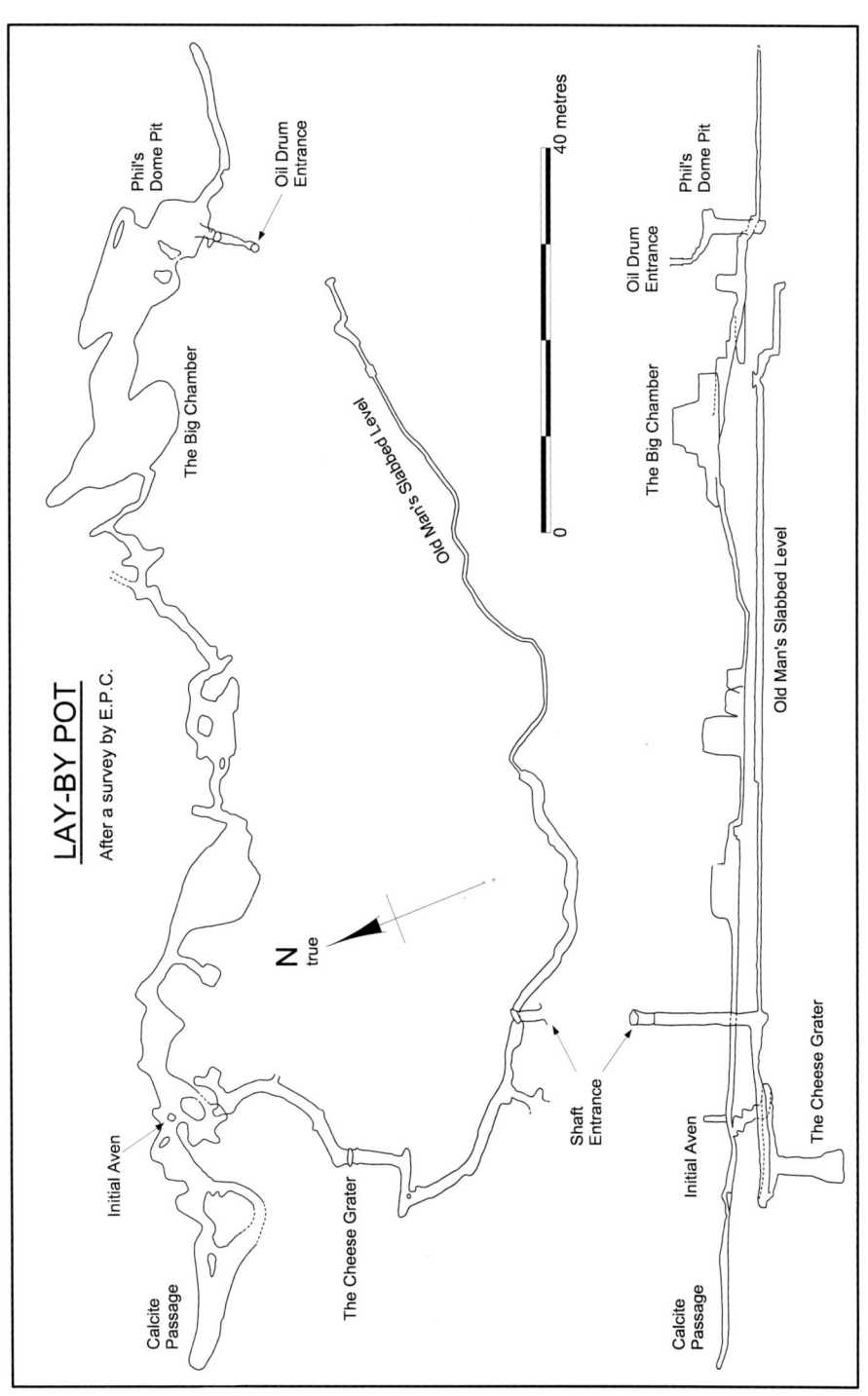

leads after 100ft (31m) to a large chamber about 50ft (15m) long, 20ft (6m) wide, and 25ft (8m) high. A further 60ft (18m) of passage leads to Phil's Dome Pit. The crawl continues beyond this aven, but is soon blocked by clay and breakdown.

Second Entrance: A short drop through an oil drum leads through two tight squeezes to a choice of ways down into Phil's Dome Pit. Either crawl ahead to a 15ft (4.5m) pitch, (beware of the condition of old handlines) or follow very tight squeeze between boulders into a lower passage which emerges over a hole in the floor of the main aven.

Tackle:

Entrance pitch: 25m rope. Belay to tree with rebelay at pitch head.

Second entrance: 5m ladder + lifeline for descent into Phil's Dome Pit.

References: Beck, J.S. & Gill, D.W. 1973. D.C.A. N/L No.18.

Beck, J.S. 1976. E.P.C. Jour. Vol.9. No.1. pp.6-7.

Gill, D.W. 1976. E.P.C. Jour. Vol.9. No.1. pp.4-5.

### LAY-BY SHAFT 2
NGR 2030 7599  Grade: 2
Alt. 805ft (245m)
Depth: 27ft (8m)

Excavated by Chesterfield Caving Club in 1987.
Just west of the Lay-by Pot shaft.
A natural shaft 27ft (8m) deep. Becomes too narrow for progress.

### LAY-BY SHELTER
NGR 2055 7601  Grade: 1
Alt. 770ft (235m)
Length: 20ft (6m)

Immediately west of Hanging Flat Mine, opposite the third lay-by down from Wardlow.
A large entrance visible to westbound traffic. Soon closes to flat out crawls choked with flowstone.

### LINEN DALE CAVE
NGR 1989 7696  Grade: 1
Alt. 950ft (290m)
Length: 45ft (14m)
Depth: 25ft (8m)

At the north end of the valley, south of the Foolow Road, in small walling stone quarry.
A tight dug out crawl to the head of a pot full of mud and boulders. Dug to its present depth by Stockport Caving Group.
References: Beck, J.S. 1975. Trans. B.C.R.A. Vol.2. No.1. p.7.

### LITTLE WATERFALL SWALLET
NGR 2003 7710  Dig
Alt. 870ft (265m)

Permission is unlikely to be granted.
150 yards (137m) north east of Waterfall Swallet.
A large tree-lined shakehole with a stream sinking against the south wall. A dig was begun in the mid 1990s, but was abandoned.
References: Beck, J.S. 1975. Trans B.C.R.A. Vol.2. No.1. p.2.

> **MERLIN'S MINE**
> (Merlin Mine. Merlin's Cavern.
> Merlin's Cave)
> **NGR 2177 7591   Grade: 3**
> **(Mine)**
> **Alt. 686ft (209m)**
> **Length: 3200ft (975m)**
> **Depth: 90ft (27m)**
> 
> Status: S.S.S.I.

Two entrances, of which the lower (adit) entrance is most used. High above Carlswark's Eyam Dale Shaft, but closer to the road junction.

The lower adit entrance is small, but soon opens out to an enlarged natural rift which leads to a crossroads. Right leads to the bottom of the 23ft (7m) upper entrance shaft. Left leads to a natural chamber, with a crawl on the right to a muddy dig, and left to a small passage which ends at the boulder-lined Laxative Pot, 50ft (15m) deep with dig into side passage at bottom. Other small passages soon end. Straight on at the crossroads soon leads to a short climb up into a natural chamber, and the level continues in Merlin Pipe to a T-junction. Left leads to some natural rifts, and right over a collapse to a further junction. To the left is a mine level leading after 276ft (84m) to a blind shaft 33ft (10m) deep on Cowlishaw Vein. Ahead are three shafts in the floor. The first is 18ft (5.5m) deep, with climbs into loose workings. The third is also blind, 20ft (6m) deep.

The second shaft is 26ft (8m) deep to the top of a boulder slope in a stope. A squeeze down in the floor at the bottom of the slope leads to a junction. Left leads to Gimli's Dream, and straight on leads to the Merlin Streamway.

Gimli's Dream: A series of short crawls lead to a series of chambers which were extremely well decorated when first discovered. Further crawls and climbs lead eventually to the original connection with Carlswark, now blocked.

The Merlin Streamway: Turning right after a few yards of mine level leads to Sump Pool Chamber, usually occupied by a fast flowing stream, but dry in dry summers. To the right is a low arch or short sump leading to a bedding cave, and a climb down into a rift leading to the tight Shag's Sump, pumped out and surveyed in drought. The stream reappears in John Smith's Passage in Carlswark Cavern. To the left at Sump Pool Chamber is Sump 1, 60ft (18m) long, constricted at its inner end, and not free-diveable. 66ft (20m) of large passage follows to Sump 2, 30ft (9m) long and emerging in large passage again. Sump 3 lies to the right and is by-passed. Sump 4 is a flat out crawl in water. Merlin 5 is 265ft (80m) of fine large passage up to Sump 5. The first 4 sumps often drop far enough to be passable without diving in late summer. Sump 5, 115ft (35m), was passed in the 1976 drought to an airbell. In the 1990 drought Sump 6, 40ft (12m) was passed to a roomy chamber. Sump 7, 20ft (6m) follows, and a short passage leads to Sump 8. 40ft (12m) into Sump 8 the route forks. Left was baled over dams and continued for 30ft (9m) to become too tight. Right was baled out to give access to a tiny cross rift. A squeeze led into a higher bedding plane continuation which became too low.

*Tackle:*
*Anchors may be in place but should be carefully checked.*
**Cowlishaw Shaft:**   15m rope.
**Laxative Pot:**      20m rope. Boulder belays.
**S1 Shaft:**          6m ladder + lifeline.
**S2 Shaft:**          9m ladder + lifeline.
**S3 Shaft:**          6m ladder + lifeline.

References: Beck, J.S. 1975. Trans. B.C.R.A. Vol.2. No.1. pp.1-11. Area plan.
Beck, J.S. 1976. E.P.C. Jour. Vol.9. No.1. pp.9-11.
Christopher, N.S.J. & Beck, J.S. 1977. Trans. B.C.R.A. Vol.4. No.3. pp.361-365. Survey. Rieuwerts, J. 1960. Bull. P.D.M.H.S. Vol.1. No.3. pp.3-6. Survey.

## MIDDLETON DALE MINE LEVELS
### Grade: 1-2 (Mines).

**LEVEL 1**  NGR 2262 7565
Alt. 590ft (180m)  Length: 150ft (46m) approx.

In garden of first house below the Lovers Leap Garage. A short working in Paul Pipe intersects a level on a north east - south west vein. Two awkward scrambles for 10ft (3m) to a lower level. A tight phreatic tube at the south west end leads to a small solution chamber.

**LEVEL 2**  NGR 2231 7576
Alt. 645ft (196m)  Length: 50ft (18m) approx.

Three trial levels one above the other at the west end of Windy Ledge. A hard climb is necessary to reach the top level, which is about 40ft (12m) long. The lower two close almost immediately.

**LEVEL 3**  NGR 2224 7579
Alt. 650ft (198m)  Length: 20ft (6m) approx.

On Cliffstile Vein between Ivy Green and Keyhole Caves. A large open rift. Until about 1968 a level led out at the back, and ended at a small chamber with a boss of flowstone in the centre after roughly 100ft (30m). The roof was dangerous, and has now collapsed.

**LEVEL 4**  NGR 2212 7581
Alt. 610ft (186m)  Length: 300ft (91m)
(Triple Hole. MKP. The Tuesdig. Lower Bamforth Hole)

At the base of the upper cliff, on the terrace, 180ft (55m) east of Carlswark's rift entrance. A vertical drop of four feet into a partly natural level. This runs north west for 60ft (18m) then turns along a north east vein. After 40ft (12m) a natural passage on the left leads via a muddy chute and short sump to two natural chambers (dug into by TSG 1976/7). Beyond junction main level becomes a dangerous crawl under stacked deads to a blind and unstable shaft after 200ft (61m).

**LEVEL 5**  NGR 2211 7582
Alt. 620ft (189m)  Length: 205ft (62m)
(Fingal's Cave)

Incorrectly referred to as Bamforth Hole. Large rift like entrance above the terrace, 150ft (46m) east of Carlswark's rift entrance. Soon closes down to a small mine level. A short climb up a shaft and along a higher level leads to a natural chamber with phreatic tubes to right and left. Right is soon blocked by flowstone, but there is a strong draught, thought to come from Ivy Green Cave. Passage to left now blocked by collapse of shaft in roof, but was entered by digging and found to be hopelessly blocked by silt and flowstone.

**LEVEL 6**  NGR 2193 7585
Alt. 690ft (210m)  Length: 300ft (91m)

At base of top cliff, 150ft (56m) east of Shining Cliff. Small mine level. Intersects Shining Cliff Scrin after roughly 60ft (18m) and runs northeast. Becomes very loose and ends at a collapsed floor shaft.

**LEVEL 7**  NGR 2165 7586
Alt. 600ft (183m)  Length: 350ft (106m) approx.  Depth: 140ft (43m)

At valley floor level at south east corner of The Delph. Small entrance in narrow vein working leads to level with small solution cavities. A level directly above leads to a shaft to the lower level. The 'Middle Level' is reached through a tight slot on the next rock terrace above, with a fourth entrance dropping 13ft (4m) into it from an open rift just above. Hope Shaft entrance (alt.730ft/222m at 2177 7585) lies at the base of the top cliff in a cleft. A descent of nearly 100ft (30m) lands in the Middle

Level passage. Low narrow passage leads to the Middle entrances, passing a short, natural, silt filled passage in one wall, and a shaft (easily climbed) in the floor to a lower level backfilled in each direction. The other way from the pitch base leads via a crawl to the top of another pitch of 35ft (10.5m) to the bottom level. In one direction is a low, rubble strewn chamber, but in the opposite direction a downhill squeeze leads into a passage with a fine stone-stempled roof, which reaches daylight at the lowest entrance.

*Tackle:*
*Hope Shaft:*     *40m rope. Bolt belays needed.*
*Internal shaft:*     *15m rope. Bolt belays needed.*

## LEVEL 8
Alt. 710ft (216m)      NGR 2137 7598      Length: 100ft (30m)      Depth: 23ft (7m)

In gully between two buttresses of the top cliff, west of The Delph. A tiny shaft 23ft (7m) deep leads to a level. Can be followed north to a solution chamber.

*Tackle:*
*8m ladder + lifeline.*

## LEVEL 9
Alt. 660ft (201m)      NGR 2140 7594      Length: 250ft (76m)      Depth: 80ft (24m)
(Friday Mine. Good Friday Mine)

On hillside west of The Delph, about 40ft (12m) above the road. A blocked adit entrance and 17ft (5m) shaft above. The shaft leads to a level which runs back into the hillside. A 30ft (9m) shaft in the floor leads to a short level, then a short drop into a sump which is blind. Beyond the shaft a short climb up leads to a continuation which soon ends at a forefield.

*Tackle:*
*5m ladder + lifeline.*

## LEVEL 10
Alt. 609ft (185.7m)      NGR 2224 7579      Length: 50ft (15m)

A short roomy pipe working directly below Ivy Green Cave entrance.

## LEVEL 11
Alt. 664ft (202.4m)      NGR 2150 7591      Length: 170ft (52m)      Depth: 70ft (21m)
(Monday Mine)

Narrow descending entrance passage leads to a hole in the floor which can be climbed down to a stope with no way on, and a shaft to surface slabbed over at the top. Straight ahead leads to a second shaft in the floor which can be descended to a static blind sump.

## LEVEL 12
Alt. 725ft (221m)      NGR 2191 7613      Length: 123ft (37.4m)      Depth: 60ft (18m)
(King's Level)

On west side of Eyam Dale at mid-height. A mine level leads to a 60ft (18m) shaft. Flooded level at bottom dived for 10ft (3m) to a blank wall. Entrance blocked at present (2009).

*References:*
*Hope Shaft:*
*Whitehouse, D. 1980. D.C.A. N/L No.46. pp.1-2.*
*Knox C.S. 2001. CCPC Newsletter 70. pp.1-2.*
*Crewe C.P.C. 2005. Peak District Rigging Guide (9th ed.). Sketch survey.*
*Monday Mine:*
*Noble, M. 1985. T.S.G. Jour. No.11. pp.7-8. Survey.*

### MONKEY ROCK CAVE
NGR 2153 7592   Grade: 1
Alt. 725ft (221m)
Length: 32ft (9.7m)
Depth 25ft (8m)

A short solution cave on a major joint in the topmost cliff. A 25ft (8m) shaft in the floor, found by Pegasus C.C. in 1999, capped with boulders, is blind.

*References: Beck, J.S. 1999. Descent No.147, p.11.*

### MRS SMYTHE'S SWALLET
NGR 1879 7738   Dig
Alt. 958ft (292m)

Permission from Swevic House.

In field 590ft (180m) south west of Swevic House.

An active swallet with a fence round it. A small passage, enlarged by cavers, can be followed for a short distance until it becomes too tight. The adjacent shallow shakehole was the site of a dig in which the stream could be heard but was not reached.

*References: Descent no.154, p.17*

### NICKERGROVE MINE
Grade: 2 (Mine)
Length: 1900ft (579m)
Depth: 80ft (24m)

Adit:  NGR 2155 7596
Alt. 675ft (206m)

Palette Shaft:
NGR 2153 7599
Alt. 708ft (216m)

Didsbury Shaft:
NGR 2155 7603
Alt. 662ft (202m)

Status: S.S.S.I.

On the west side of Cucklet Delph. Adit high on the hillside almost directly above end of wall in valley floor. Palette Shaft has a lid and lies north of, and above, the adit entrance. Didsbury Shaft has a lid, and lies north of the Palette Shaft, a short distance above the path.

The obvious adit turns sharp right after 60ft (18m) at a blind hole in the floor. A level on the right after a further 100ft (30m) leads via a very tight squeeze to the bottom of the Palette Shaft. Back in the main level, the main internal shaft is reached after a further 110ft (34m). Cross carefully. The level becomes much smaller, and breaks out into a large rift chamber, the floor of which descends in a series of steps to the continuation of the level. Two more blind shafts were filled in during digging at the final choke in the 1990s. The timbered dig began 790ft (241m) from the entrance, and was 60ft (18m) long. A canal followed, and the level degenerated to a forefield. A climb in the roof at a sharp right bend led to a short natural passage which would still be a good dig if it could be regained.

The main shaft was excavated to a total depth of 80ft (24m) but the bottom 30ft (10m) was backfilled from the Clay Chamber dig. A level to the north east at -25ft (8m) leads via a series of short free climbs to a rift chamber. A further climb down on the far side of the chamber leads to a junction. A level to the north is blind after 130ft (40m), while that to the north east leads into the "Didsbury Shaft" 15ft (5m) from surface. The shaft continues down to 50ft (15m) to short blind levels and a blind sump. At the 50ft (15m) level in the main internal shaft, a short level leads south west to a forefield, and a level with rails in the floor (from the 1984 dig) leads north to the Clay Chamber. A short level continues beyond, and a timbered shaft in the floor led to a short stretch of large stream passage between two sumps. The large upstream sump is the downstream end of Streaks East Sump, and downstream the water is next seen in the Merlin Streamway. The downstream sump was penetrated in the 1990 drought through a very tight squeeze to a roomy chamber. The passage continued for a further 60ft (18m) to a large cross rift beyond which the route sumped.

**Tackle:**   *Main internal shaft:   20m rope. Ring and wire anchor in place for pull-through abseils.*
         *Didsbury Shaft: 5m ladder + lifeline.*

*References: Beck, J.S. & Worley, N.E. 1977. Bull. P.D.M.H.S. Vol.6. No.5. pp.175-179. Survey.*
*Gunn, J. 1975. D.C.A. N/L No.24. p.5.*
*Pearce, A.J. 1974. Bull. P.D.M.H.S. Vol.5. No.5. pp.243-257.*

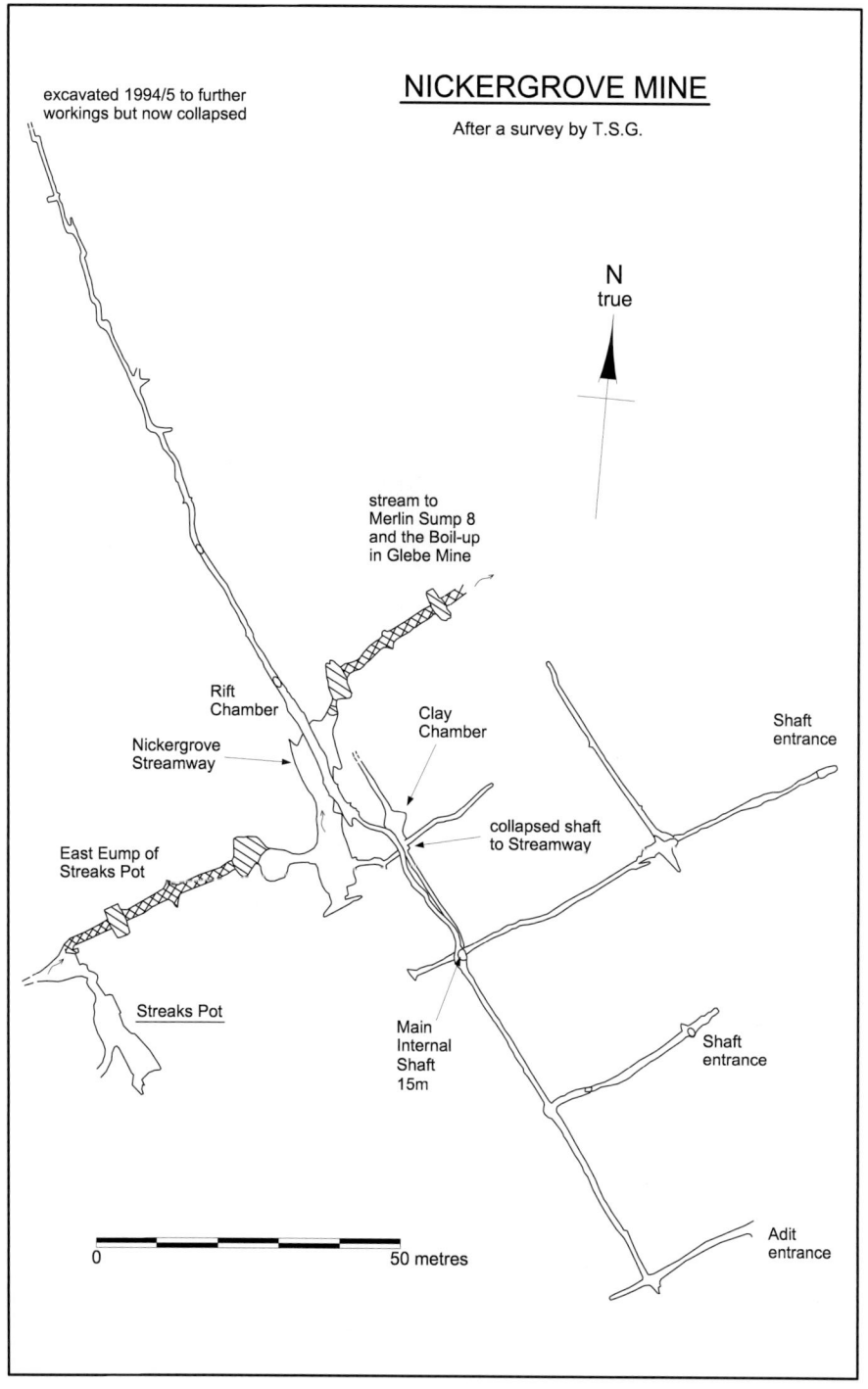

## PARACETAM'OLE

**NGR 2073 7595**  **Grade: 3**
**Alt. 820ft (250m)**
**Length: 385ft (117m)**
**Depth: 45ft (13m)**

No known access restrictions. High on the south side of Middleton Dale east of Hangover Hole.

Discovered 1996 by EEG. Named after the fact that the chamber was larger in area than that in the nearby Hangover Hole (Paracetam 'Ole beats Hangover!)

**Warning: Parts of the cave are dangerously loose, especially the entrance dig.**

A 26ft (8m) climb down through the entrance dig leads to a tight squeeze into a bedding crawl. Further crawls and climbs lead down through breakdown into a larger passage, which emerges into a large chamber 50ft (15m) x 26ft (8m), the Barf Room. A further chamber can be reached via a crawl on the far side, and almost opposite the entry point a short climb up leads to a southward trending passage ending in breakdown. A tight vertical squeeze above the climb leads into a draughting southward trending bedding plane.

*References: Noble, M. 1996. Descent No.131. p.8.*
*Beck, J.S. 2000. Descent No. 152. p.11. Survey.*

Formations in Paracetam 'Ole. Photo by Rob Eavis

### PIECE END SWALLET
**NGR 1904 7728**  **Grade: 2**
**Alt. 945ft (288m)**
**Length: 105ft (32m)**
**Depth: 12ft (4m)**

Excavated in 1998. Permission necessary from Mr Knowles at Crosslow Farm, Eyam.

Capped entrance in field south of the track to Swevic House Farm, Foolow.

Stream sinks into culvert from cattle trough. Entrance is a capped shaft 10ft (3m deep) into the dig, which is through shale. After 20ft (6m) the route forks. Ahead leads to a further fork and cavities in limestone which are too tight. Left leads to the final sink into a 6" (15cm) high bedding in limestone, which draughts.

*References: Descent No. 144. 1998. p.9. Survey.*

### PIPPIN SWALLOW
**NGR 2191 7644**  **Lost**
**Alt. 760ft (232m)**

Under the road in Glebe Park on the site of the Glebe processing plant.

Rediscovered during development of the Glebe Mine site in 2006. The swallow and associated blind valley had been filled with mining waste, then the Glebe processing plant built on top. The developer refilled it with concrete.

A shakehole at the foot of a blind valley which took a large stream when uncovered. The outlet was not found, and short passages were too tight.

*References: Woods, W. 1842. The History and Antiquities of Eyam.*

### ROCK COTTAGE TUBES
**NGR 2273 7570**  **Grade: 1**
**Alt. 580ft (177m)**

In cliff directly above cottage and adjacent garage.

The upper (left hand) tube is a hands and knees crawl for 30ft (10m) to a complete silt choke. A second tube lies below and to the right, and is also hands and knees sized, but only 8ft (2.5m) to a similar complete choke.

*References: Beck, J.S. 1994. Descent No.118. p.9.*

### RUBBLE RIFT
**NGR 2061 7597**  **Grade 2**
**Alt. 788ft (240m)**
**Length: 200ft (60m) approx**
**Depth: 30ft (9m) approx.**

Discovered and excavated by Keyhole Caving Club.

Entrance 80ft (25m) above road level on the South side of Stoney Middleton Dale about 30m East of Layby Shelter. Shored entrance in corner of small rock outcrop.

Entrance rift is 3ft (1m) wide, 15ft (5m) high, and 25ft (8m) long. Climb down into standing rift. This leads to a slippery 4m climb down to a phreatic tube. This is followed for a few metres to a squeeze up over boulders into a chamber, the scene of various digs. A high level rift in the top corner of the chamber leads to a sqeeze into a rift climb back down into the chamber (now blocked by digging spoil). A squeeze down from the chamber leads to a cavity. A pot in the floor (now partly backfilled) led to a low, draughting phreatic tube and squalid dig. A tube opposite the squeeze is a comfortable size phreatic tube leading to the current dig face. A further tube, (again backfilled) led to a small, pretty aven, narrowing to a fissure at its top. A draught is present that appears to come up from the now backfilled pot. The silt filled tube at the bottom of this kept filling with water as the dig progressed, and was abandoned. There is the possibility of a connection to the far Pizzaland chokes in Hangover Hole about 180ft (55m) away.

*References: Descent No. 117. 1994. p.17.*
*Descent No. 135. 1997. p.18.*

### SALLET HOLE CAVE

NGR 2192 7395     Grade: 2
Alt. 900ft (274m)
Length: 75ft (23m)
Depth: 200ft (61m)

High on the west side of a shallow gully above Sallet Hole Mine.

Entrance chamber leads to left passage with 15ft (4.5m) deep pot in the floor, and right passage (partly mined) with 200ft (61m) shaft in the floor. This shaft used to connect with Sallet Hole Mine (no longer worked) but the lower level is now run-in.

### THE SALTPAN

NGR 2158 7636
Alt. 730ft (223m)

At the north end of Cucklet Delph.

A narrow gorge with all the features of a vadose streamway with no roof. Small bedding caves at the lower end are just short oxbows.

### SARAH'S CAVE

NGR 2151 7572     Lost
Alt. c.700ft (213m)

In Hawkenedge Quarry (now Wimpey's Quarry) in a position almost opposite The Delph.

A large well decorated cave discovered during quarrying operations. Part of the cave was certainly destroyed, but some may remain. Fragments of phreatic cave keep appearing in this part of the quarry, but the actual horizon of Sarah's Cave is below the floor of the main bench.

*References: Anon. 1970. D.C.A. N/L No.7. p.8.*
*Gill, D.W. 1976. E.P.C. Jour. Vol.9. No.1. p.2.*
*Lord, P.J. & Wright, A. 1971. S.U.S.S. Jour. Vol.2. No.1. pp.24-25. Survey.*

Sarah's Cave. Photo by Paul Deakin

## STREAKS CAVE
NGR 2121 7590    Grade: 1
Alt. 665ft (202.7m)
Length: 90ft (27m)

## STREAKS POT
(Saturday Pot)
Grade: 4
Length: 2549ft (777m)
Depth: 135ft (41m)
Top Entrance
NGR 2122 7596
Alt. 748ft (228m)
Lower Entrance
NGR 2141 7593
Alt. 636ft (194m)
Status: S.S.S.I.

Above and to the right of Yoga Cave, below Streaks Footpath.

A lower mined entrance leads after 40ft (12m) to a short climb up into a rift chamber which continues for a further 40ft (12m). From the top of the climb, a natural hands and knees crawl leads to an entrance directly above the lower one.

**Upper Entrance:** A small mined entrance at the base of a low cliff, close to the highest cliff line, east of Streaks Footpath.

**Lower Entrance:** Approx.12ft (4m) above the road roughly 200 yards (183m) west of Hawkenedge Well. Entrance via two oil drums, not to be confused with Sunday Mine to the east which was four oil drums deep, but is now largely collapsed.

### Upper Entrance Series

A low mined crawl leads after 15ft (5m) to the head of a 40ft (12m) pitch. Bolt belays available. Possible to traverse over the pitch and free climb down beyond. An opening just above the floor of the pitch leads to a breakdown chamber with a bouldery rift passage in the right hand corner. Scrambling along this through breakdown leads to an aven where an easy climb down a narrow rift (care not to dislodge stacked rocks) leads to a short horizontal section. Enter feet first with care as roof is supported by timbers. An easy 30ft (9m) climb follows (but beware of loose rocks). At the bottom a short muddy tube leads to the stream.

### Lower Entrance Series

Crawl at the bottom of short oil-drum entrance leads to a fork. To the right is a tight crawl to a chamber. Left is main way on, and leads to a T-junction. Right leads to a series of muddy chambers and crawl, and the stream is seen briefly between two sumps. The downstream sump has been followed in drought to within a few metres of the upstream sump in Nickergrove Mine. Left at the T-junction leads through a mined area into Route 66, a spacious sandy crawl which may carry a large stream in wet weather. The crawl reduces to flat-out beyond an area of breakdown.

A crawl on the right soon leads to the stream, with an unpleasant crawl in water for 200ft (61m) to a sump. Beyond the crawl is a small chamber. Low passage on the left leads to a boulder choke, while ahead is a tiny crawl, the Mousehole. After a wet flat out crawl, a tight squeeze into a small breakdown chamber, and a duck, the passage continues past Donkey Dong Inlet on the left, and through a dry stretch to a T-junction with the main stream. Downstream to the right becomes too tight, but upstream becomes more roomy until a crawl round a breakdown pile leads to a short stretch of walking-sized passage.

A window leads to a parallel tube which carries most of the stream. Nervous Breakdown follows - a chaos of boulders in the streamway with crawls in and out of the water. Shortly after the final descent to the stream is a cross rift where the Upper Entrance Series joins the route.

### The Upstream Series

Beyond the bottom of the Upper Entrance Series the stream comes from two tubes. Either route can be a very sporting crawl in the stream. The tubes join, and a T-junction is reached. The stream comes from the left, where a larger passage leads to a small chamber. The stream comes from the Main Stream Inlet, a crawl which becomes too tight. A silted crawl also leads to a rift directly below the floor of the Upper Entrance Series. To the right at the T-junction leads to a rift chamber and crawl that becomes too low. An obscure way ahead at the T-junction leads through boulders into Alexander's Aven, and continues into a roomy crawl. A breakdown chamber is soon reached, and the passage continues, becoming steadily larger to the base of the impressive Telescope Aven. This was climbed for 100ft (30m), but the tubes at the top still await a very thin determined explorer.

Beyond Telescope Aven a left hand branch leads to Lu-Blu Sump, dived inconclusively (Davenport, 1988). The main passage attains a consistent walking size for the first time in the cave, with a vadose trench starting to appear. It ends abruptly at a boulder choke, which draughts strongly.

*Tackle:*
*Upper entrance pitch: 15m rope. Bolt belays.*
*References: Beck, J.S. 1981. T.S.G. N/L No.9. pp. 1-10. Survey.*
*Davenport, J. 1988. C.D.G. N/L No.87. p.19.*

Above Lu Blu Sump. Photo by Robbie Shone

### SUNDAY MINE
NGR 2145 7592   Grade: 2
Alt. 641ft (195.2m)
Length: 200ft (61m) approx.

An oil drum shaft 14ft (4m) deep, now largely collapsed, led via a low crawl to a large natural rift with a small branch mine level. The rift ends at a choke of large boulders. A shaft was sunk from surface (now collapsed) to intersect the continuation, a large natural passage with a silt fill which ended at a scree run. A new entrance (Aaron's Entrance) was constructed here, and lies 115ft (35m) east of Sunday Mine. There is no connection now to the rift.

### SWEVIC HOUSE SWALLET
NGR 1869 7746   Dig
Alt. 975ft (297m)
Length: 20ft (6m)

Digging not allowed.

In the more northerly of two shakeholes in the south east corner of field, 230 yards (210m) west of Swevic House Farm.

At present a 20ft (6m) long crawl in the stream which becomes too low. Has been reported as having been dug for 200ft (61m) to the west in a 3ft (1m) high stream passage.

Other small swallets to the south of Swevic House may represent promising digs.

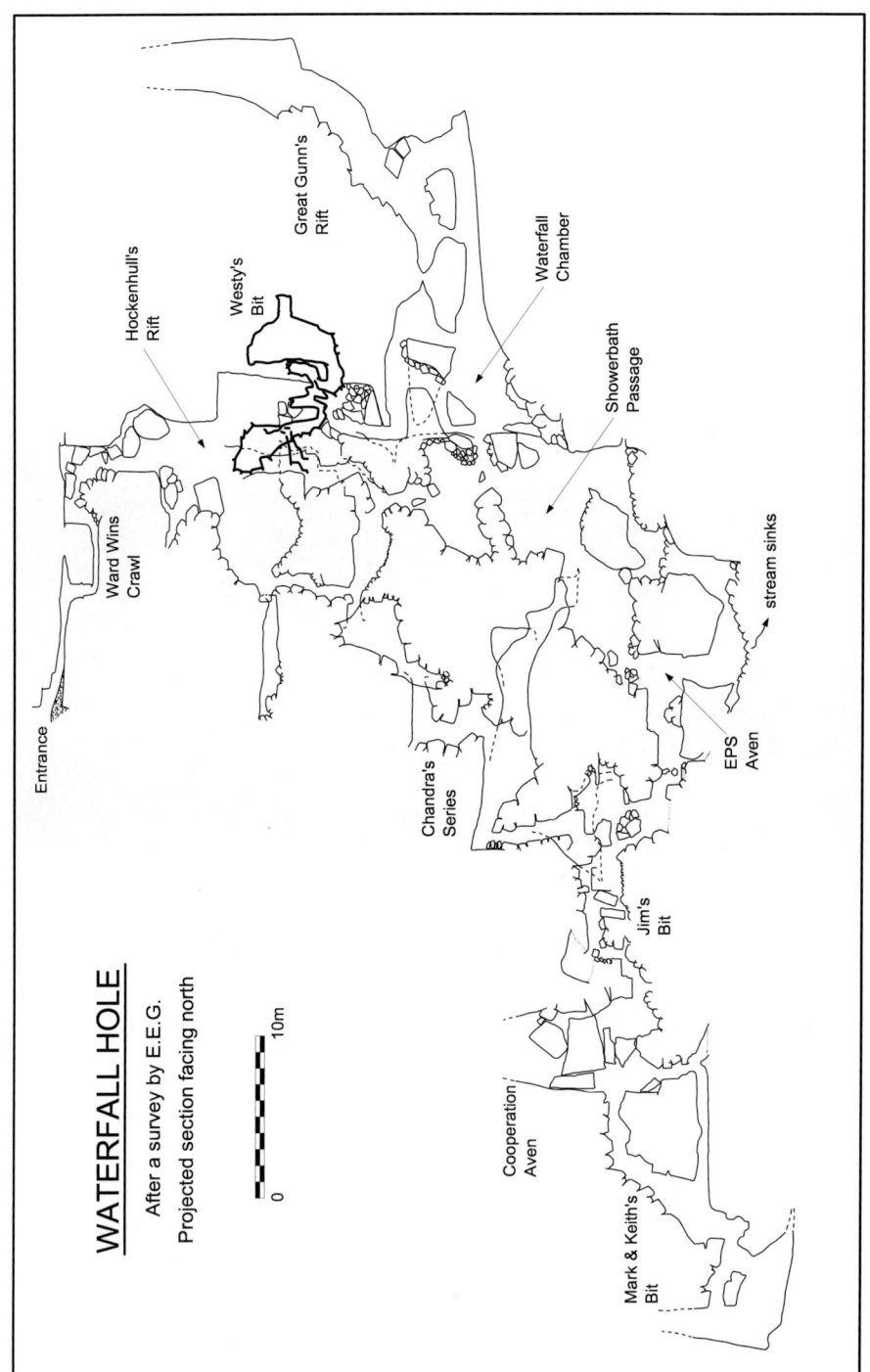

> **WATERFALL HOLE**
> NGR 1988 7705      Grade: 4
> Alt. 896ft (273m)
> Length: 1150ft (350m)
> Depth: 140ft (43m)
> Status: S.S.S.I.

No access restrictions. Landowner asks cavers to park sensibly, not in entrances or on the sharp road bend.

Discovered in 1959 by Eldon Pothole Club after clearing debris.

A large open tree-lined pothole on the north side of the Eyam-Foolow road, with a stream falling into it.

In extreme flood the entrance passage sumps. Do not descend if water is backing up significantly in the shakehole. A very loose cave in places, and rescue would be almost impossible through the tight entrance passages.

An easy walk down into the shakehole on the east side. An entrance to the right of the waterfall is blind, and an entrance to the left of the waterfall (Crock Pot, qv.) was opened by floods in 1998. Stream sinks at four places in the floor, overflowing into a bedding cave on the north east side in flood. A low bedding crawl for 30ft (9m) to a drop of 6ft (2m). Small passage at the bottom, Ward Wins Crawl, leads to a small chamber. Ward Wins Crawl sumps in flood. Scramble through boulders, taking care not to fall down Hockenhull's Rift, 35ft (11m) deep. Belay to boulders above the pitch head. Main Route: Many ways down at bottom of rift. Easiest is a small hole, down which the stream can be heard, close to the pitch landing. Follow the noise of water, and scramble down to the stream. The stream falls over a 20ft (6m) pitch, but step across and down into small chamber. In far corner is another 20ft (6m) drop, and care is needed to enter a bedding 3ft (1m) down, feet first. Turn round and climb down on far side of tiny bedding chamber. Scramble down into Waterfall Chamber. At base of waterfall scramble through boulders to a right turn. Traverse over a 20ft (6m) drop with the stream in the bottom, and enter Showerbath Passage. At extreme end of Showerbath Passage, on the right, a small hole drops into EPS Aven (30ft/9m). Long belay needed to boulder on floor. Stream reappears in the bottom and sinks in a hopeless boulder choke.

### Jim's Bit

Halfway down the EPS Aven pitch step across onto a ledge. A series of muddy passages can be followed through tortuous squeezes and scrambles to a short drop into a narrow rift which opens into Co-operation Aven. The roof is a choke of huge boulders. A further climb down leads into a muddy rift, and a tight crawl was pushed in 1987 to a further series of rifts in which the stream from a new sink directly below the waterfall in the surface shakehole was met. This is the lowest point. Do not have an accident here: rescue would be virtually impossible. The main rift was climbed, but only led to a circular route back to Cooperation Aven.

### Westy's Bit

Follow obvious passage down boulder slope from bottom of Hockenhull's Rift pitch. Climb into flowstoned rift right at the end, and by squeezing to its extreme end, the right wall is found to consist of a flake. A very difficult sideways manoeuvre lies above a drop. Climb down, and a further series of rift passages leads south eastwards under the east end of the shakehole.

### Chandra's Series

Climb down into boulders before the entrance to Westy's Bit. A tiny chamber and a short climb open above a drop which goes right through to the roof of Showerbath Passage. At the top, a right hand passage leads back to the Main Route below Hockenhull's Rift.

The left hand passage is a tight rift leading to a small chamber. Climb boulder slope to squeeze on left. Through squeeze is a climb down into a rift, and a boulder slope leads down to an inlet from the boulder roof. A passage on the right before this leads to an inclined chamber, and further rift passages. Parts of Chandra's Series are very loose.

*Tackle:*
*Hockenhull's Rift:*     *20m rope. Belay to boulders.*
*EPS Aven pitch:*        *10m ladder + lifeline.*

*References:* Beck, J.S. 1975. Trans. B.C.R.A. Vol.2. No.1. pp.1-11.
Beck, J.S. 1985. T.S.G. Jour. No.11. pp.1-4. Full survey.
Gill, D.W. & Lord, P.J. 1970. D.C.A. N/L No.8. pp.5-6.
Gunn, J. 1974. Trans. B.C.R.A. Vol.1. No.3. pp.159-164.
Hatherley, P. S.U.S.S. Jour. Vol.2. No.6. pp.40 & 42. Survey.
Hurt, L. 1968. D.C.A. N/L. No.48. p.21.
King, B. 1962. B.S.A. Cave Science No.32. pp.381-382.
Lord, P.J. 1971. S.U.S.S. Jour. Vol.2. No.1. p.26.
Lord, P.J. & Batey, A. 1970. S.U.S.S. Jour. Vol.1. No.6. p.248.
Yonge, C.J. Undated. S.U.S.S. Jour. Vol.2. No.2. p.31. Survey.

### WATERGROVE SOUGH
NGR Tail: 2107 7582

Shaft: 2091 7592  Grade: 3

Alt. Tail: 640ft (195m)

Well Shaft: 670ft (204m)

Length: 800ft (244m)

The sough tail lies between the sharp bend and the bottom of Farnsley Lane in Stoney Middleton Dale, where the water is piped under the main road. A lidded shaft (Well Shaft) lies north of the road a little further west.

The 30ft (9m) shaft drops directly into the sough, which is accessible downstream for approx. 100ft (30m), and upstream for approx. 700ft (213m). The trip upstream involves several ducks in wet weather, and may become impassable. Some small stopes are passed near the end, and a southward branch leads immediately to the base of a run-in shaft. Progress is halted by large scale collapse.

*Tackle:*
*Entrance shaft: 10m ladder + lifeline.*

Watergrove Sough Shaft. Photo by Rob Eavis

## YOGA CAVE

**Grade: 2**
**Crawl Entrance:**
NGR 2122 7589
Alt. 650ft (198m)
**Rubbish Bag Entrance:**
NGR 2115 7587
Alt. 680ft (207m)
**Length: 600ft (183m)**

Status: S.S.S.I.

On the north side of the road, 15ft (5m) above the road just east of the sharp bend by Eyam Quarry. Rubbish Bag entrance is in the corner of the quarry north of Streaks Footpath, with the shaft entrance on a ledge 20ft (6m) above.

Low crawl excavated in places leads after 150ft (46m) to a 'T' junction. Turning right leads into a chamber which has been entered by miners. A dig terminates at a blockage after 30ft (10m), but is known to connect with the chamber at the end of Latrine Passage (see below). Straight on leads to a second larger chamber with a short passage on the left. A short climb up boulders at the far end leads to a continuation, which soon ends in Streaks Vein, in a dangerous state of run-in.

Left at the first T junction leads to a clay blockage, but a crawl on the right before the blockage leads to a chamber. To the right is a dig, but to the left is a scramble up through very loose boulders into a large natural chamber entered by the miners, "Toad Hall". Various ways off the cavern soon end, except for a passage up a slope to the left, which closes down to a crawl leading to the bottom of the 20ft (6m) deep unstable Shaft Entrance, excavated in 1980. A narrow slot high in one wall of the cavern is Rubbish Bag Entrance, dug by Masson Caving Group in 1989. The cave has been used by foxes and contains many bones.

**Tackle:**　　Shaft entrance:　　　　6m ladder + lifeline.
　　　　　　Rubbish Bag entrance:　5m handline.

*References: Beck, J.S. & Gill, D.W. 1974. D.C.A. N/L No.21. p.2.*
*Chandler, P. 1990. D.C.A. N/L No.73. pp.8-9. Survey.*
*Gill, D.W. 1973. D.C.A. N/L No.18. p.1.*
*Gill, D.W. 1976. E.P.C. Jour. Vol.9. No.1. p.7. Survey*

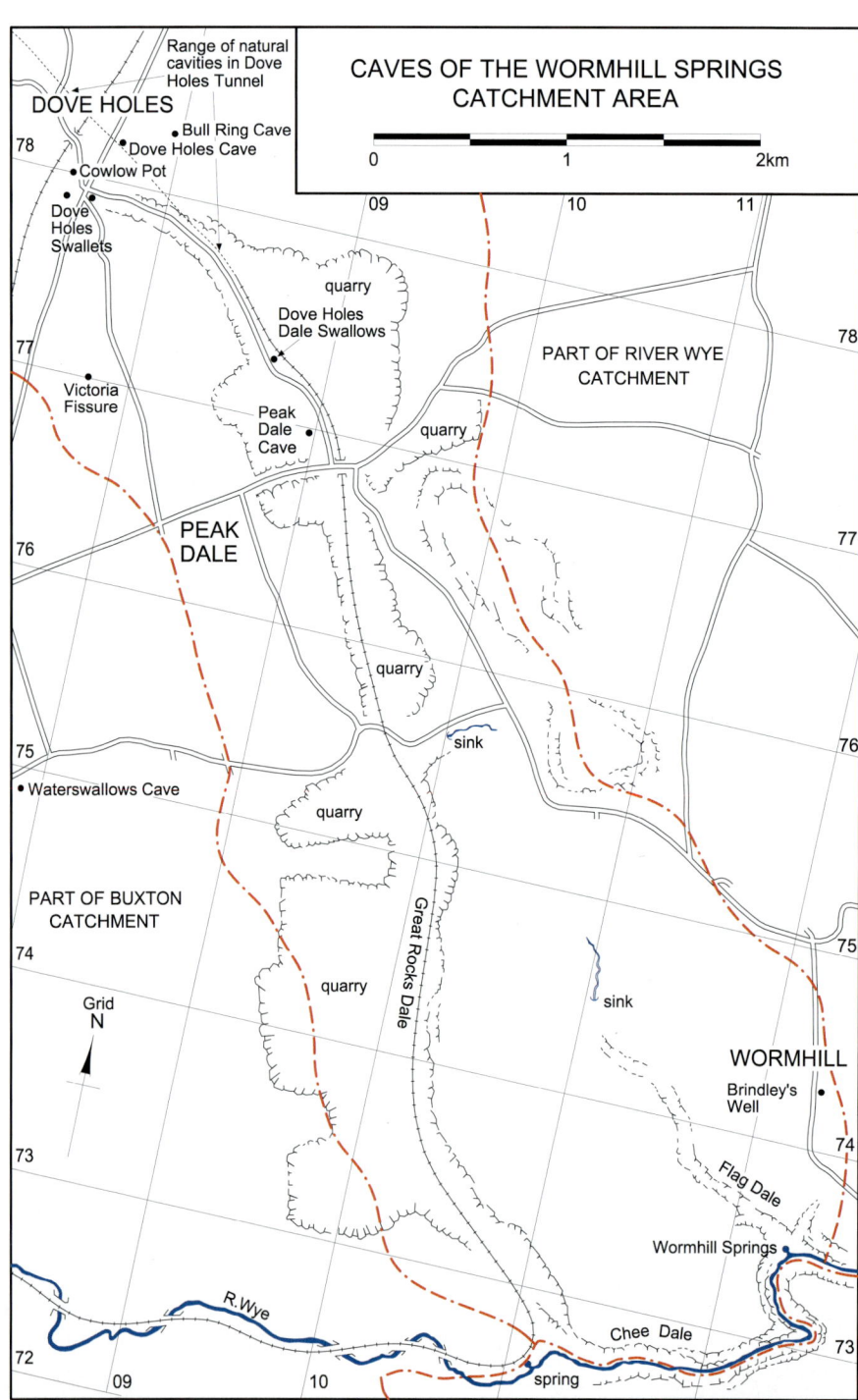

# THE WORMHILL CATCHMENT AREA

Wormhill Springs

Wormhill Springs is one of the largest risings in the limestone area, with an estimated discharge of at least 10 mgd., and the catchment is probably the most promising area in the White Peak for an undiscovered large cave system.

The springs lie to the south of the axis of the Wormhill - Priestcliffe Syncline close to a fault parallel to the axis. To the north west the Upper and Lower Millers Dale Lavas have concentric outcrops, while between Great Rocks Dale and the shale margin extensive faulting gives rise to complex dolerite and lava outcrops. There is little evidence of high level cave development, suggesting that the Great Rocks Dale and Wormhill Springs have been the main outlets for a considerable period. Numerous small dolines exist on the margins of the lava outcrops, but none have been dug.

Apart from Cow Low Pot, the major swallets at Dove Holes have not been extensively dug, but have been dye tested to the impenetrable fissures in the Dove Holes railway tunnel. It has also been claimed (along with some very unlikely claims!) that they were tested many years ago to the Great Rocks Dale risings.

The driving of the railway tunnel effectively captured the drainage, sending it to the Irish Sea via the Mersey instead of to the North Sea via the Trent. The artificial lowering of water levels may have rendered more cave penetrable than would otherwise have been the case. Further digging should bring interesting results.

Wormhill Springs responds fast in flood conditions, and becomes milky in colour, suggesting that the catchment area includes the floors of the quarries in Great Rocks Dale. Rumours of a hole with a large stream flowing in it appearing in the quarry floor have not been substantiated but should not be entirely discounted. The drainage from Dove Holes must pass through faults in the Lower Millers Dale Lava to reach either the springs at Great Rocks Dale or the Wormhill risings. East-west faults may carry water eastwards to Great Rocks Dale, while faults further to the north carry water eastwards to join the Wormhill system.

Perched groundwater rises above the Upper Millers Dale Lava around Bole Hill and Withered Low, flows over both lavas, and sinks again. Digging at these small sinks may well prove worthwhile.

The existence of the flood-prone Wormhill springs, the swallets nearly four miles away at Dove Holes, the many dolines, and the favourable geological structure suggest the existence of a large cave system. The rising itself may be a deep one, but large vadose canyon passages could exist further upstream. Perhaps a JCB at Wormhill Springs could be the answer!

### BRINDLEY'S WELL
NGR 123 743  Spring
Alt. 1050ft (320m)

A small spring which feeds the well in Wormhill village.

### BULL RING CAVE
NGR 079 783  Grade: 1
Alt. 1075ft (327m)
Length: 28ft (8m)

On the west side of the old tramroad cutting.

A 4ft (1.2m) by 3ft (.9m) phreatic tube 28ft (8m) long ends at a clay fill.

### COWLOW POT
NGR 075 780  Grade: 4
Alt. 1075ft (327m)
Length: Approx. 600ft (183m)
Depth: Approx. 50ft (15m)

Permission and the key to the lid must be obtained from Mr Burton, Old House Farm, Back Lane, Dove Holes.

Discovered by members of Disley Underground Group in 1981.

Situated to the south of Station Road, Dove Holes, through ginnel between houses. Entrance is lidded oil drum shaft by wall, above stream sink.

Some sections are tight and awkward, and rescue from beyond would be extremely difficult. The cave floods to the roof in places in wet weather. Danger of infection from broken glass and rubbish in initial stages, also known discharge of sewage into the cave.

Drop down shaft to streamway. In a few feet stream passes under slot. Way on is squeeze through vertical crack above, Surprise Squeeze. The Surprise is an occasional dousing with bathwater from cracked drain above! Forward into small chamber. Stream sinks through choked slot ahead. Way on is left. Drop down and back under into crawl, bearing left then right after several feet. Ahead is wet and muddy tube. Left is upward draughting crawl, Rip-off Gulch. Crawl through muddy tube, Sludge Street, drop and crawl left, then right through confusion of miniature cross rifts to meet small pool with sharp flake of rock. Cross pool and flake, crawl through water, then follow water to short flowing duck. Follow water beyond duck to meet Sump 1. Just before muddy tube, way on is up Rip-off Gulch. Follow this crawl through pool and awkward bends (Magic Roundabout) and drop down to cross rift with small stream and Sump 2. Continue along crawl ahead on opposite side of stream, through tight left and right squeeze (The Chicane) to top of muddy bank (the 1st Pitch). Drop down this (handline useful). Crawl left is Chisel Passage above small stream which sumps below and is seen through slots in floor. Climb up out of Chisel Passage. Right leads to Zigger

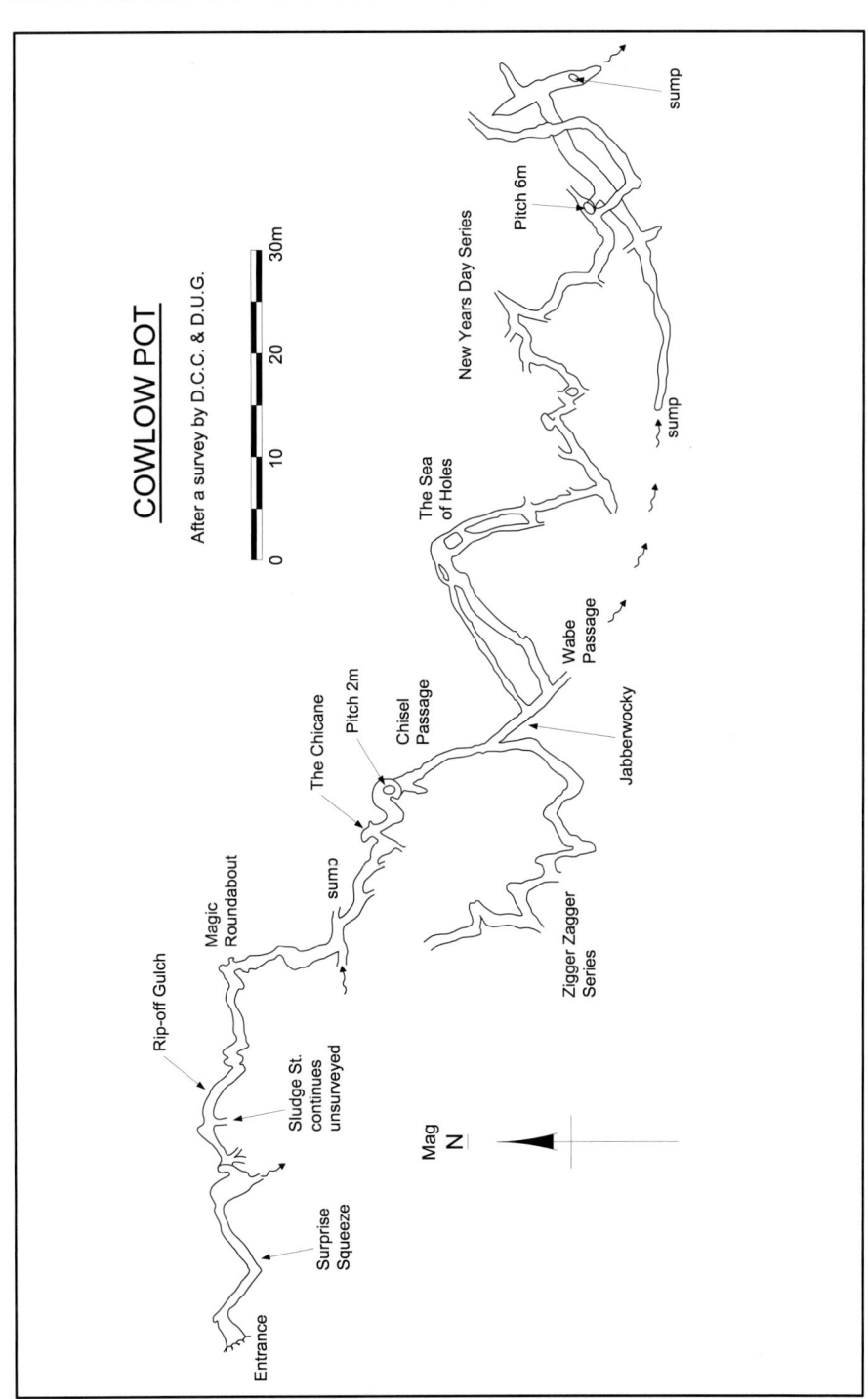

Zagger Series. Tube on right comes to short upward climb. Awkward bend follows with water and small stream. Straight on from Chisel Passage leads to Jabberwocky. Short climb down boulder and partially dug crawl (Wabe Passage) is seen ahead. Way on is left through short upward crawl with pool to emerge into boulder strewn rift, The Sea of Holes. Left leads through muddy crawl to hole in floor through which Jabberwocky can be seen and entered once more. Two routes to the right in the Sea of Holes eventually unite in a narrow rift. The area is confusing. The narrow rift becomes a crawl to a right hand bend followed by an awkward squeeze up by a large boulder (take care). This is the start of the New Year Series. Meandering passage eventually leads to a low too-tight bedding crawl, with too-tight branches. Two thirds of the way along New Year Series is a slot. This is the head of the 2nd Pitch, 20ft (6m) deep to a longish passage with a stream. Short upstream section leads nowhere. Downstream leads to too-tight streamway and gravel filled muddy tube. Dye tested to inlets on the left hand wall of the Dove Holes railway tunnel.

**Tackle:**
**First Pitch:**     *10m handline useful.*
**Second Pitch:**   *8m ladder + lifeline.*

### DOVE HOLES CAVE
NGR 077 782    Grade: 1
Alt. 1075ft (327m)
Length: 10ft (3m)

Discovered in 1962 by Eldon Pothole Club after clearing rubbish.
Near the recreation ground, behind Marchington's lorry park.
The entrance is 3ft (0.9m) wide and 1ft (0.3m) high. Leads into 10ft (3m) square chamber. Possible dig.

### DOVE HOLES DALE SWALLOWS
NGR 086 778, 087 773, 089 772
Digs
Alt. c.1000ft (305m)

In the floor of Dove Holes Dale.
Three abortive digs in small swallows.
*References: Frost, R.V. 1954. The Speleologist, Vol.1. No.3. p.95.*

### DOVE HOLES SWALLET 1
NGR 075 779    Dig
Alt. c.1065ft (325m)

In garden of house on west side of A6.
The main sink, which takes a very large volume of water in wet weather.

### DOVE HOLES SWALLET 2
NGR 076 779    Dig
Alt. c.1060ft (323m)
Length: 20ft (6m)

Access not normally granted.
Opposite the Queens Hotel on the south east corner of the crossroads.
A small stream sinks, but the swallet takes a large volume of flood water. Three possible digs in the same artificially deepened shakehole. The first is too tight. The second is a tight crawl for roughly 30ft (10m) blocked with mud. Could be a good dig. The third consists of tight possibilities in large boulders.
*References: Eldon Pothole Club Newsletter Vol.2. No.12.*

## DOVE HOLES TUNNEL CAVES
NGR 083 778 to 074 784
Grade: 1
Alt. c.940ft (287m)

A number of inlets were encountered during the construction of the Dove Holes railway tunnel. All are close to the limestone/shale boundary, and still give a large quantity of water which is culverted under the lines to the north end of the tunnel, thus diverting the water from the North Sea to the Irish Sea! All the inlets soon become impenetrable. No access is allowed.

1) Two small inlets on the west wall. Impenetrable.
2) Walled off inlet. Discharges a small stream.
3) Three inlets close together. The first two are too tight, but the third is a large inlet 13ft (4m) long to a climb up of 13ft (4m). Water emerges from impenetrable bedding plane.
4) At mark 46 on the east wall is an inlet rift blocked with boulders.
5) Just beyond No.4 is a 23ft (7m) climb against the tunnel lining, tight at the top, emerging in a chamber approx. 20ft x 20ft (6m x 6m), approx 10ft (3m) high, with an inlet in the roof which is too tight. Dye tested from Cowlow Pot and Dove Holes Swallet 1.

## GREAT ROCKS DALE SPRING
NGR 1114 7266    Spring
Alt. 740ft (225m)

A large spring on the west side of the junction of Great Rocks Dale and the Wye Valley. A possible destination of water from the Water Swallows area.

## PEAK DALE CAVE
NGR 090 770    Lost
Alt. 1000ft (305m)
Length: 90ft (27m)

South of road, opposite signal box, in quarry entrance which has been bridged over.

A low entrance into a passage 5ft (1.5m) high and 2.5ft (76cm) wide, with 2ft (61cm) of water. Ended in a fine grotto which has been largely destroyed in attempts to push further. Water has been pumped out and a crack leads to a narrow pitch. The cave is below a waste lime tip and the water is mildly caustic. A calcite film soon forms on the water if left undisturbed. Now completely buried by "landscaping".

References: Gill, D.W. 1973. The Burial of Peak Dale Cave. D.C.A. N/L No.17. p.3.

## VICTORY QUARRY FISSURE
NGR 075 770    Lost

A unique fissure containing Pliocene (pre-Ice Age) mammal remains. Now quarried away. Others may be awaiting discovery. Animal remains include "sabre toothed tiger". Remains now in Buxton and Manchester Museums, and in the Natural History Museum, London.

References: Dawkins, W.B. 1903. Quart. Jour. Geol. Soc. Vol.59. pp.105-129.
Spencer, H.E. & Melville, R.V. 1974. Bull. Geological Survey of Great Britain. No.48. pp.43-53.

## WORMHILL SPRINGS
NGR 123 735    Dig
Alt. 700ft (213m)

On the north bank of the River Wye where Flag Dale meets Cheedale.

A series of large springs, the most westerly of which yields an impressive amount of water, and is presumed to have its farthest source at Dove Holes. The springs turn milky in wet weather as a result of runoff from the Great Rocks Dale quarries. The large pit immediately upstream from the main rising was dug by the Derbyshire Pennine Club around 1936. The ring bolt embedded in a tree is their work.

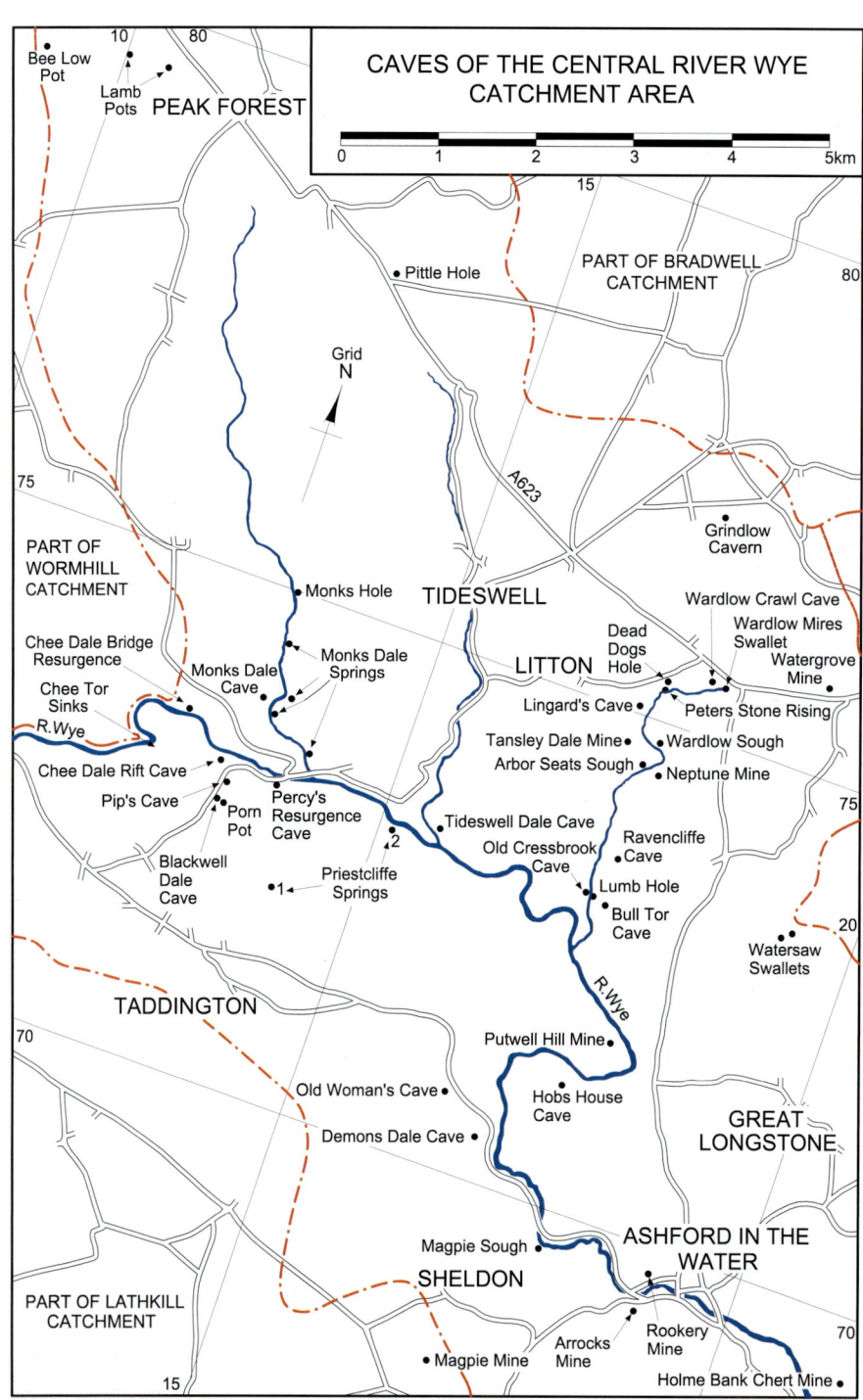

# THE RIVER WYE CATCHMENT AREA

Wardlow Mires and Peter's Stone

The catchment of the central River Wye, covering an area of almost 100 square kilometres, represents the largest area of limestone in the Peak District, but contains few caves of any significance.

The River Wye is the largest of the two permanent rivers on the limestone. The river crosses several lavas in its course across the central limestone area, and these are a major factor in the river's surface course throughout. The flow is increased by numerous springs on both banks, but to date all have proved to be impenetrable. The increase in volume between Buxton and Bakewell is more than can be accounted for by the known springs, and it is likely that a lot of water rises from undetected risings in the river bed. The largest input below Buxton, Wormhill Springs, is treated as a separate catchment area.

The tributary valleys are normally dry, but Monks Dale, Tideswell Dale, Cressbrook Dale and Deep Dale carry surface streams except in very dry conditions. These are generally fed by risings close to the valley floors which carry local perched groundwater.

The area contains many dolines, although many have been filled in by farmers or modified by surface and underground mineral workings along the rakes. Few have been dug. There are no major allogenic sinks, but the lack of surface streams and the high rainfall suggest that extensive underground systems may exist. The catchment area boundary reflects the surface topography, and underground drainage does not necessarily coincide with this. Thus the only major sink at Wardlow Mires, which is a resurgence in flood, probably drains eastwards via the Watergrove Sough to Stoney Middleton in normal conditions.

The major rising at Lumb Hole, in Cressbrook Dale, was extended considerably during the 1990s, making it the longest known cave in the catchment. It is thought to drain the western end of Longstone Edge, and it is a dramatic rising during floods.

A further possibility exists in the large risings at the foot of Taddington Dale, although here it is less clear where a worthwhile dig could be started.

The complex geology and mineralisation of the area gives rise to a complex and little understood hydrology. The reader is referred to the cited references for detailed information.

**ARBOR SEATS SOUGH**
NGR 1746 7461
Grade: 1 (Mine)
Alt. 750ft (228m)
Length: 300ft (91m)

Adit on west side of Cressbrook Dale, in line with shafts on hillside above and with Neptune Mine opposite.

Small entrance leads to an adit, with roof sections of stacked deads. Some run-ins have been dug through and a draught blows through the present limit of exploration. Furthest shaft at 850ft (259m) and 173 746 is into impressive hading stope over 60ft (18m) high.

*References: Beck, J.S. 1978. Bull P.D.M.H.S. Vol.7. No.2. pp.107-115.*
*Conde, N. 2002. C.C.P.C. N/L No.75b. pp.1-2.*

**ARROCKS BLACK MARBLE MINE**
NGR 191 694
Grade: 1-2 (Mine)
Alt. 436ft (133m)
Length: 700ft (213m)

Gated. Contact Peak District Mining Museum, Matlock Bath (01629 583834)

Two entrances in old quarry on left side of Ashford - Sheldon road. Only lower entrance accessible.

**Warning: Mine contains collapsed areas, rotten timber supports etc.**

Inside entrance is short roomy passage to left. Main passage continues to collapsed area, but partway along is short low crawl on right leading to main part of mine. Crawl emerges in large inclined passage. To right uphill leads to grilled second entrance. To left downhill the roof lowers, turns to the right and passage soon ends. Straight on at junction is large passage which soon ends. Two branch passages: a short branch to the left drops steeply to a working face, but longer passage on right leads through collapsed area, passing short passage on right to end at a roomy working face. Black Marble is seen here but is not pure. Shortly before the end is a passage on the left which slopes down to a final working area with timber supports and a voice and light connection to a lower passage.

*References: Ford, T.D. 1964. Bull. P.D.M.H.S. Vol.2. No.4. pp.179-188. Survey.*
*Tomlinson, J.M. 1996. Derbyshire Black Marble. P.D.M.H.S. Special Publication No.4. Survey.*

**ASHFORD BLACK MARBLE MINE**
(Rookery Mine)
NGR 191 697   Grade: 1 (Mine)
Alt. 550ft (168m)
Length: 1/2 mile (800m) approx.

Entrance in small quarry at top of Rookery Wood beside Ashford Road off A6. Gated: contact DCA for access.

An intriguing network of roomy walking passages and mined out flat-roofed cavities, popular with novice cavers, and an impressive example of former pillar and stall mining of black marble.

*References: Ford, T.D. 1964. Bull. P.D.M.H.S. Vol.2. No.4. pp.179-188. Survey.*
*Tomlinson, J.M. 1996. Derbyshire Black Marble. P.D.M.H.S. Special Publication No.4. Survey.*

**BEE LOW POT**
NGR 092 793
Dig
Alt. 1325ft (403m)

Near a group of boulders behind Bee Low Quarry.

A heavily fluted shaft ends in a tight fissure. Entrance is now blocked.

Crushed timber in Arrocks Mine.
Photo by Paul Chandler.

### BLACKWELL DALE CAVE
**NGR 1327 7271**
**Grade: 2**
**Alt. 825ft (251m)**
**Length: 355ft (108m)**

Status: R.I.G.S. (Blackwell Dale)

Access to the final chamber is controlled by the Orpheus Caving Club.

Opens from the east side of the main Millers Dale - Taddington road in Blackwell Dale.

Stooping for the first 25ft (8m), then opens into a chamber 15ft (5m) high. Continues through pools and crawls for 160ft (49m) to an excavated crawl through a choke (fitted with a gate) to a decorated chamber with the choked passage continuing beyond. A crawl on the left (facing into the cave) is wet and muddy, and after 110ft (34m) emerges in the valley side on a ledge. A tight crawl on the right at the entrance is soon choked.
*References:* Turner, D. 1951. S.T.P.C.Jour. Vol.1. No.1. p.13.

### BLEAKLOW CAVE
**NGR 233 735**  **Grade: 2**
**Alt. 690ft (210m) approx.**
**Length: 350ft (106m)**

Access not generally allowed.

Discovered by Derek "Teapot" Stables May 1995. In the north face of Bleaklow Quarry between Calver and Hassop.

A small phreatic passage zig zags along joints until it meets a fluorspar vein. Thrutching along a narrow rift leads to a climb up into a chamber 30ft (9m) long on the vein. Continuing rifts all end at clay chokes. A climb in the roof leads up into a mine level, and the bottom of a run-in shaft.

*References: Beck, J.S. 1995. Descent No. 125. p.12. Survey.*

### BULL TOR CAVE
(Good Friday Cave)
**NGR 1742 7313**  **Grade: 1**
**Alt. 1000ft (305m)**

High on the side of Cressbrook Dale, to the south of Ravencliffe Cave.

Entrance about 6ft (1.8m) wide into a long crawl with a badger lair.

### CHEE DALE BRIDGE RESURGENCE
**NGR 127 735**
**Dig**
**Alt. 655ft (200m)**

A short distance upstream from the footbridge on the north bank of the River Wye.

A large volume of water rises from scree. Possibly controlled by the intersection of the outcrop of the Lower Millers Dale Lava with the valley floor.

*References: Christopher, N.S.J. Unpublished PhD Thesis. University of Leicester.*

### CHEE DALE RIFT CAVE
**NGR 132 732**  **Grade: 1**
**Alt. 660ft (201m)**
**Length: 160ft (48m)**
**Depth: 40ft (12m)**

Discovered Eldon P.C. 1968.

On the south bank of the River Wye, 120ft (36m) above river level.

Entrance drops steeply to a 10ft (3m) pitch. A high rift 5ft (1.5m) wide can be followed for 40ft (12m) narrowing down to a crack. A 20ft (6m) climb up in the roof leads to a short high level continuation. At the base of the 10ft climb the north west continuation of the rift can be followed for 50ft (15m) before it becomes too narrow. 12ft (4m) down the entrance slope a small passage on the right can be followed to a junction. Right soon ends at an earth fill while left arrives at a further junction. Right is blocked, while left rises up a climb to the top of the 10ft pitch. 300 yards (274m) down dale on same side (1325 7319) is a small unnamed cave near river level, blocked with mud after 12ft (4m).

*References: Bridger, R. 1975. D.C.A. N/L No.25.*

### CHEE TOR SINKS
**NGR 1256 7309**
**Dig**
**Alt. 700ft (213m)**

Upstream of the footbridge at the sharp bend in the River Wye on the right bank.

Water sinks into the base of the scree, and in flood into a 10ft (3m) diameter depression on the marshy bank. At the base of the adjacent cliff a rubble slope partially obscures a constricted passage along an undercut, said to take a large amount of water in extreme flood. The water may emerge downstream of the footbridge at a small rising, but the undercut can emit a strong draught.

*Reference: Beck, J.S. 2008. Descent No.201. p.15.*

| **CHELMORTON CAVERN** Lost | Listed in Caves of Derbyshire 1984. Probably does not exist, as the cave referred to by Farey was first described by Pilkington, and is almost certainly Thirst House Cave. |

| **DEAD DOGS' HOLE**<br>NGR 1725 7538   Grade: 1<br>Alt. 900ft (270m)<br>Length: 50ft (15m) approx. | High in the crags opposite Peter's Stone. On Natural England land.<br>A winding tube dug out by TSG.<br>*References: Beck, J.S. 1978. Bull. P.D.M.H.S. Vol.7. No. 2. p.110.* |

| **DEMONS DALE CAVE**<br>(Taddington Dale Resurgence Cave)<br>NGR 1689 7045<br>Grade: 1 (Arch)<br>Alt. 650ft (198m)<br>Length: 35ft (11m) | On the right of the path from the car park into Deep Dale.<br>A large rock shelter archaeologically excavated for 15ft (5m) being 5ft (1.5m) high ending in large scale breakdown. At rear of shelter is a tight bedding which has been forced for a further 6m and may be pushed further by a thin man. A large volume of water resurges in flood. Neolithic and Roman remains found.<br>*References: Armstrong, A.L. 1948. Archaeological Newsletter p.5.*<br>*Orpheus Caving Club Newsletter 1974. Vol.10. No.3.* |

| **GRINDLOW CAVERN**<br>NGR 1725 7713<br>Grade: 2<br>Alt. 975ft (292m)<br>Length: about 100ft (30m)<br>Depth: 40ft (12m) | Owner is Mr P. Furness, Cartledge Farm, Great Hucklow.<br>30 yards south of a small walled quarry in field, 50 yards east of the Grindlow-Tideswell road.<br>The 25ft (8m) entrance shaft has a steel lid. Shaft drops into a bedding cave which extends for 50ft (15m) to the west. Squeezes and climbs down between boulders lead to a short lower level, with crawls in a decorated extension to the north which becomes too tight. A short crawl to the east of the shaft was dug in 1991 to give access to a chamber, with further crawls leading off. All leads closed down.<br>Tackle: 8m ladder + lifeline. Scaffold pole for belay.<br>*References: Lord P.J. & Smith, M.E. 1969. Jour. S.U.S.S. Vol.1. No.6. pp.234-5. Survey.* |

| **HOB'S HOUSE CAVE**<br>(Hob Thirst Hole, Hob Hurst House, Hob's Hurst Cave, Monsal Dale Cave)<br>NGR 176 712  Grade: 1 (Arch)<br>Alt. 800ft (240m)<br>Length: 80ft (24m) | At the back of the landslips on the north side of Fin Cop.<br>A narrow descending fissure. A human skeleton of early British date was found among the debris at the bottom. No attempt at further excavation is recorded. Has been confused with Thirst House in Deepdale.<br>*References: Fox, W. Storrs. 1913. Derbys. Arch. Jour. No.35. pp.99-102.* |

## HOLME BANK CHERT MINE

**NGR 213 694  Grade: 2 (Mine)**
**Alt. 590ft (180m)**
**Length: 2.2 miles (3500m) approx.**

Permission from J.Oldfield, Tel: 01629 813301. Insurance is needed for permission to be granted.

Entrance 1 lies on right of track, below crane. 2 & 3 in old quarry above the crane. 4 to right of track just before gate. 6 & 8 are in the quarry on the hill top. 1 & 8 were the main entrances. 5 & 7 are now sealed. Very complex, with over 70 junctions. From entrance 8, facing an old hut, the mine starts as an unstable passage about 8ft (2.5m) square. A passage immediately on the left eventually leads to entrances 1,2, & 3. Main passage continues to the right and links eventually to entrance 4. Branch passages on the right leads to entrances 5,6, & 7 in the quarry. Another passage on the right leads to New Year Chamber, with New Year Pot, natural pot 10ft (3m) deep to a silted bedding plane. Several passages on the left link with the main passages to entrances 1,2,& 3.

Passage on left inside entrance 8 heads north east with several branches on the right, then a sharp bend and a drop into another passage. Turn right and then left to a chamber. Right here leads to a passage with more branches to the right. Second, third, fourth and fifth branches lead to entrance 3. Sixth, seventh and eighth branches lead to entrances 1 & 2. Main passage continues ahead to the flooded sections, popular with the Cave Diving Group due to the clear water. The amount of accessible passage varies according to water levels.

*References: Critchley, M.F. & Wilson, P.J. 1975. Bull. P.D.M.H.S. Vol.6. No.1. pp.1-5. Survey.*

Diving in Holme Bank Chert Mine.
Photo by John Cordingley.

## LAMB POTS

**NGR 100 795 to 104 795**
**Grade: 1 (Digs)**
**Alt. 1150-1200ft (285-300m)**
**Depth: 30-60ft (9-18m)**

On hillside 1/4 mile (0.4km) west of Chambers Farm, west of Peak Forest.

A series of 7 open natural shafts, choked at depths of 30-60ft (9-18m) with boulders. Other pots on the same hillside choked to surface.

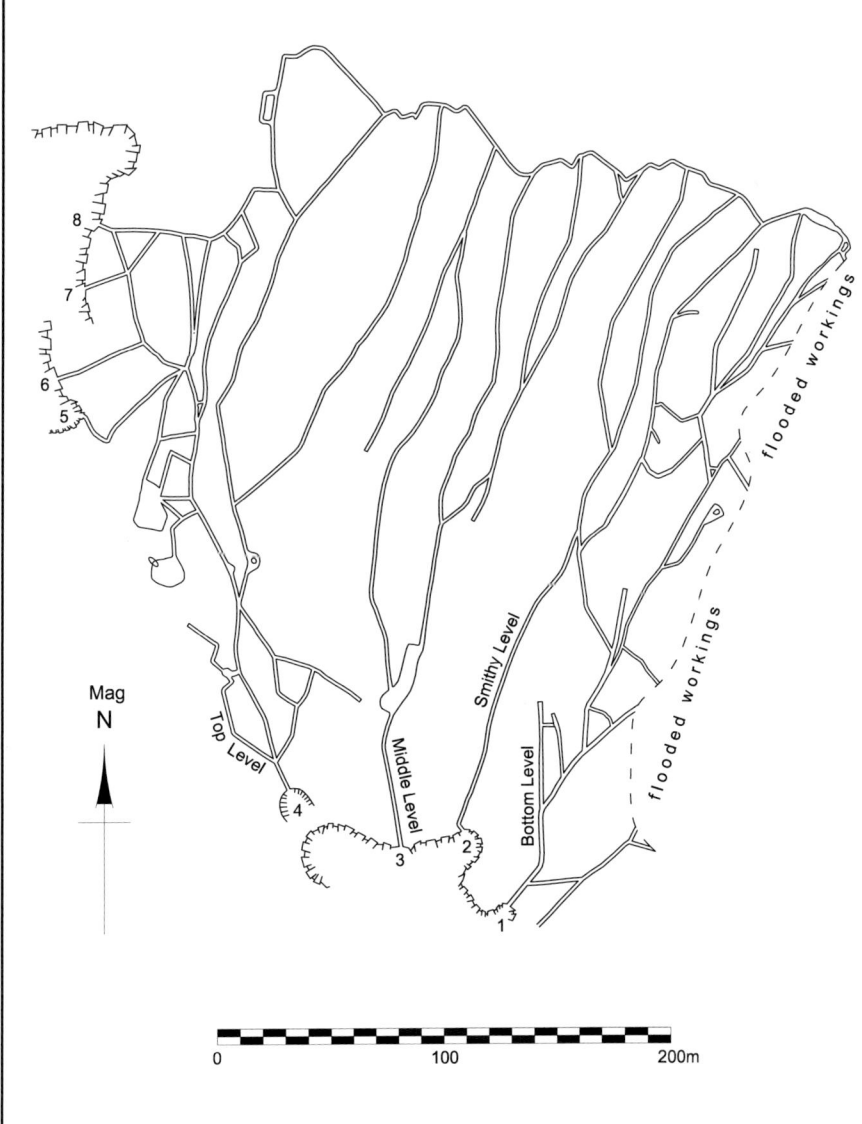

### LINGARD'S CAVE
**NGR 1706 7506**
Grade: 1
Alt. 900ft (274m)
Length: 60ft (18m)

On west side of Cressbrook Dale 150ft (46m) above the valley floor on the north side of small depression, hidden by a bush.

A short passage to a chamber, rather smelly and used by badgers. A second chamber follows with a drop through boulders to a crawl and possible dig. On the left side of the entrance chamber climb down short pitch to mined workings. The cave is named after the last man to be publicly gibbeted at Wardlow Mires, executed for the murder of the toll keeper's wife.

*References: Beck, J.S. 1975. Trans. B.C.R.S. Vol.2. No.1. p.8.*
*Beck, J.S. 1978. Bull. P.D.M.H.S. Vol.7. No.2. p.110.*
*Gill, D.W. 1973. British Caver No.60. p.66.*

### LITTLE MONKS HOLE
**NGR 1325 7525**
Length: 7ft (2m)

Uphill, and about 30 metres to the right (south) of Monks Hole. A low arched opening has been fully excavated to reveal a short passage which closes completely.

### LUMB HOLE
(Cressbrookdale Resurgence)
**NGR 1725 7313**
Grade: 3
Alt. 630ft (192m)
Length: 460ft (140m)
Depth: 100ft (30m)

Dug extensively by CCPC 1987 to 1995. Main extensions 1993-95.

Large entrance on the east side of the Cressbrook Dale gorge.

**Warning: sections of cave beyond junction with roof chamber passage flood to roof in wet weather. Speed of flooding not known but suspected to be very rapid.**

Large entrance to the left of the stream resurgence soon reduces to flat out crawl just beyond small low blasted chamber. Flat out / low crawl for 10m to junction. Left is short passage to roof chamber, a large low bedding with straws. Straight on is flat out descending crawl to squeeze, just beyond hanging boulder in roof - care! In winter this section and beyond is usually submerged.

Just beyond squeeze, short flat crawl enters larger passage at junction, where it is possible to sit up. Ahead, up through boulders is silty crawl over more boulders to a low junction with silted up passages to left and right.

Back at last junction right leads down three steeply descending hands and knees crawls, with connection with bouldery crawl entering on left. At bottom, passage levels out and bears left to flat out crawl through boulders to emerge in phreatic tube. Walk/stooping for 10m to sump. Dived by TSG 1995 to constriction 15m from base, at -2m. Sump could be seen to continue beyond constriction. The sump level at the time was some 30m below river level.

*References: Beck, J.S. 1975. Trans. B.C.R.A. Vol.2. No.1. p.8.*
*Beck, J.S. 1978. Bull. P.D.M.H.S. Vol.7. No.2. p.110.*
*Conde D. 2000. CCPC N/L No. 64. p.6.*
*Frost, R.V. 1956. The Speleologist Vol.1. No.4.*
*Kealy L. & Reynolds T. 1995. CCPC N/L. Survey.*

Lumb Hole resurgence.
Photo, Bill Whitehouse

### MAGPIE MINE
**Grade: 2 (Mine)**
**Shaft: NGR 172 682**
**Alt. 1100ft (330m)**
**Sough Tail: NGR 179 696**
**Alt. 480ft (144m)**
**Length: 1 mile (1.5km) approx.**
**Depth: 600ft (180m) approx.**

No access allowed at present.

Shaft amongst the mine buildings of Magpie Mine, near Sheldon. Sough tail on south bank of River Wye, opposite Black Rock Corner. Gated.

Engine shaft covered. Nearly 600ft (180m) deep. The sough is over a mile long, mostly waist deep or deeper, with interesting lock-gates and water feeders in cross veins. Blende Vein, 600 yards north of the shaft, has a series of calcite lined pipe-vein cavities which have been pirated by a solution channel in places. Can be followed for about 100 yards and could perhaps be dug further. Extensive workings in vein under shaft no longer accessible owing to partial collapse. "Chatsworth Cavern" was a large vein cavity now submerged, which may have been re-entered by divers at 150ft (46m) depth.

*References:* Butcher, N.J.D. 1975. Bull. P.D.M.H.S. Vol.6. No.2. pp.65-70. Survey.
Willies, L.M., Roche, V.S., Worley, N.E., & Ford, T.D. 1971. P.D.M.H.S. Special Publication No.3.
Worley, N.E. 1975. Bull. P.D.M.H.S. Vol.6. No.1. pp.28-32. Survey.

### MONKS DALE CAVE
NGR 134 739   Grade: 1
Alt. 900ft (270m)
Depth: 30ft (9m)

Natural England land. Permission required from Natural England.

On the west side of the dale, 200ft (61m) above the valley floor, at the base of a small cliff.

First entered and dug by Eldon P.C. 10ft (3m) climb down entrance rift. Two ways on at the bottom. Left leads to 20ft (6m) descent with small wet weather stream sinking in the bottom. Right leads after a few feet to a small wet weather inlet sinking down a 6 inch (15cm) rift. Presumed to resurge directly below the cave in the valley floor at 135 738.
*References: Gill, D.W. 1973. British Caver No.60. p.67.*

### MONKS DALE SPRINGS
Digs
Alt. 665 - 690ft (203 - 210m)

1: On the east bank at 140 735.
2: Three springs on the west bank and one on the east bank close to 136 740.
3: Spring at 135 738.

4: Large rising at 135 745 on the east bank. Nos. 1 & 2 are relatively small springs. No. 3. is presumed to be the resurgence of the stream seen in Monks Dale Cave. No. 4. is a large rising on the east bank, and could be a good dig.
*References: Gill, D.W. 1973. British Caver No.60. p.67.*

### MONKS HOLE
NGR 134 750   Grade: 1
Alt. 875ft (262m)
Length: 25ft (8m)

Dug out by Oldham Hydrological Group in 1955.

On east side of Monksdale 100ft (30m) above the valley floor at the base of a cliff.

A 25ft (8m) crawl leading to a short blind pot.

### NEPTUNE MINE
(Ney Green Mine)
NGR 175 745   Grade: 2 (Mine)
Alt. 875ft (267m)
Length: 1142ft (348m)
Depth: 92ft (28m)

On the east side of Cressbrook Dale, 150 yards (46m) south of Wardlow Sough.

The plastic pipe entrance (installed by CCPC 2005) leads into the adit, which is 650ft (198m) long, with shafts in the floor flooded to varying depths. The first is the main shaft, 60ft (18m) from the surface to the level (shaft capped), with an ancient timber bridge. A traverse line is needed to cross. First level on right is 125ft (38m) long. The second right is 213ft (65m) to a backfilled natural rift which could be a good dig. The only level on the left is 50ft (15m) long.
*References: Beck, J.S. 1978. Bull. P.D.M.H.S. Vol.7. No.2. pp.113-115.*

### OLD CRESSBROOK CAVE
NGR 1723 7312   Grade: 1
Alt. 660ft (201m)
Length: 50ft (15m)

Directly opposite Lumb Hole.

A large cave entrance diminishes in size after 30ft (9m) and a muddy crawl continues to a small chamber.
*References: Beck, J.S. 1975. Trans. B.C.R.A. Vol.2. No.1. p.8.*
*Beck, J.S. 1978. Bull. P.D.M.H.S. Vol.7. No. 2. p.110.*

### OLD WOMAN'S CAVE
NGR 1641 7119
Grade: 1 (Arch)
Alt. 700ft (210m)
Length: 44ft (13m)
Depth: 20ft (6m)

100ft (30m) above the road south side of Taddington Dale above crags.

Difficult to find in broken ground and undergrowth. An easy climb down 15ft (5m) into chamber, with small passages leading off. Iron Age pottery in British Museum, London.
*References: Brailsford, J.W. 1959. Derbys. Arch. Jour. No.77. p.56.*
*Fox, W. Storrs. 1911. Derbys. Arch. Jour. No.33. pp.115-126.*
*Smith, P. & Frost, E.G. 1997. Derbys. Arch. Jour No.117. pp. 54-55.*

## PERCY'S RESURGENCE CAVE
NGR 138 732    Dig
Alt. 575ft (175m)

Above the road on the south side of the bridge at Millers Dale. A small resurgence cave which issues a small amount of water. Used to supply the Dale Hotel with water. Has since been dug inconclusively.

## PETER'S STONE RISING
NGR 175 753    Dig
Alt. 775ft (236m)

On the hillside opposite Peter's Stone, about 20ft (6m) above the valley floor.
A small choked cave entrance which discharges a considerable stream in very wet weather.
*References: Beck, J.S. 1978. P.D.M.H.S. Bull. Vol.7. No.2. p.107.*

## PIPS CAVE
NGR 133 730    Grade: 1
Alt. 800ft (244m)
Length: 25ft (8m)

On the east side of the dale above the road, near a small crag. Well hidden.
A 25ft (8m) long crawl blocked with calcite. Inhabited by badgers.
*References: Gill, D.W. 1975. D.C.A. N/L. No.26. p.7.*

## PITTLE HOLE
(Pittle Mere Pot)
NGR 133 783
Grade: 1. (Dig.)
Alt. 1170ft (357m)
Depth: 45ft (14m)

Permission from landowner (first farm on right descending into Peak Forest). 100 yards (91m) north of the main A623 road, immediately west of the minor road from Pittle Mere to Little Hucklow.
At the foot of a dry valley on the edge of a dolerite outcrop. A timbered shaft was excavated for 10ft to enter several open joints. Main joint, heavily fluted, descended for 10ft to tight squeeze into tiny chamber with washed out wayboard penetrable for 20ft. Further drop down parallel rift for 25ft via enlarged squeeze until too tight. Slight outward draught. Site now covered with boulders.
*References: Beck, J.S. 1978. TSG N/L No.4. p.2.*

## PORN POT
NGR 133 728    Dig
Alt. 825ft (251m)
Length:
Depth: 12ft (4m)

Directly above Blackwell Dale Cave.
A 12ft (4m) deep fissure blocked with earth.
*References: Gill, D.W. 1975. D.C.A. N/L No.26. p.7.*

## PRETORIA MINE
NGR 211 681

On the west side of the Monyash road out of Bakewell.
Contact the Mining Museum, Matlock Bath. Do not disturb the riding stables.
Access is down a 6m steel ladder in a shaft built to intersect the head of the incline when the quarry was backfilled. A complex of chert workings running down dip. A crawl connects to further workings referred to as Greenfields Mine, which ends at a large scale collapse covered with a thick flowstone cascade.
*References: Bowering, G. & Flindall, R. 1998. Bull. PDMHS Vol 13. No.5. pp.24-25.*

### PRIESTCLIFFE SPRING 1
NGR 141 721  Dig
Alt. 1000ft (305m)

Near Priestcliffe village.
Water issues from a bedding plane. Source unknown but old mine workings above.

### PRIESTCLIFFE SPRING 2
NGR 151 731  Dig
Alt. 625ft (190m)

On the south bank of the River Wye.
A strong spring, possibly a sough. It is thought that it was blocked when the railway was built over its course.

### PUTWELL HILL MINE
NGR 1775 7165
Grade: 2 (Mine)
Alt. 670ft (204m)
Length: c.300ft (c.90m)

Entrance by the old railway track sealed, but other entrances on the hillside above.
Permission needed from Chatsworth Estate.
A short distance up the ravine a flat-out crawl under the right wall soon leads into an easier crawl along a narrow passage with stacked 'deads'. After 15 metres the top of a 7 metre deep shaft is reached, with workings continuing beyond. The loose pitch lands in a large, forked passage with rubble everywhere, and a short level in the wall above. The passages all end in blind faces, but close to the junction an awkward climb down between fallen boulders leads to the top of an impressive slope between the vertical walls of a huge rift. The loose slope should be treated as a pitch, and ends at the lip of the true second pitch, which is free hanging. A 35 metre rope is adequate to rig both. The impressive rift below contains areas of unstable debris, and progress is eventually halted by a major collapse.

Back at the top of the slope, a low, gritty crawl leads to the top of a second, steep slope in the opposite direction, leading down into the main working of the mine. The route, with several short climbs, passes around the base of a large diameter engine shaft, and passes a deep hole, to arrive at a pile of decaying tree-trunks below the concrete capping which now covers the original open rift. Just beyond, is the climb (now blocked) which once led out to the railway.

References: Bird, R. 1972. Bull. P.D.M.H.S. Vol.5. No.1. pp.54-60. Survey.
Knox, C.S. 2001. C.C.P.C. N/L No.69. pp.4-7.
Shaw, R.P. 1980. Bull. P.D.M.H.S. Vol.7. No.6. pp.342-344. Survey.
Thompson, S. 1971. Bull. P.D.M.H.S. Vol.4. No.6. pp.413-416.

### RAVENCLIFFE CAVE
NGR 1739 7356
Grade: 1 (Arch)
Alt. 1000ft (305m)
Length: 25ft (8m)

In cliffs high on the east side of Cressbrook Dale. West of Hay Tor.
On land owned by Chatsworth Estate.
A single large chamber with a crawl at the back. Archaeologically excavated.
References: Beck, J.S. 1975. Trans. B.C.R.A. Vol.2. No.1. p.8.
Brailsford, J.W. 1957. Derbys. Arch. Jour. No.77. pp.55-56.
Bramwell, D. 1974. Archaeology in the Peak District. pp.12 & 62.
Fox, W.S. 1910. Derbys. Arch. Jour. No.32. p.141-146.
Read, C.H. 1910. Derbys. Arch. Jour. No.32. pp.147-151.

## SHELOB'S LAIR
NGR 134 741  Grade: 1
Alt. 900ft (274m)
Length: 20ft (6m)
Depth: 25ft (8m)

High on the west side of Monks Dale, north of Monksdale Cave. A small entrance opens directly into the top of a rift approximately 25ft (8m) deep, floored with boulders. The rumble of a stream can be heard some way down. Digging is awkward. The cave is a prolific breeding ground for large spiders.

## TADDINGTON DALE GROTTO
Lost.

The exact location is unknown, but it is most likely to lie in one of the road cuttings on the Taddington by-pass, now grassed over.

Several photographs and vague articles about this cave, apparently very well decorated, appeared in the press in about 1936 during the construction of the Taddington by-pass.

## TANSLEY DALE MINE
NGR 171 747
Grade: 3 (Mine)
Alt. 850ft (259m)
Length: 200ft (61m)
Depth: 120ft (37m)

Mine entrance on the south side of the dale floor.

Small crawl entrance enlarges to walking sized level. A shaft in the roof at a kink in the level is slabbed over at surface. The level continues to a shaft in the floor, 120ft (36m) deep to some very unstable workings. The entrance has now been filled.

*References: Beck, J.S. 1978. Bull. P.D.M.H.S. Vol.7. No.2. pp.113-114. Gill, D.W. 1973. British Caver No.60. p.67.*

## TIDESWELL DALE CAVE
NGR 1555 7319  Grade: 1
Alt. 700ft (213m)
Length: 100ft (30m)

About 200 yards (183m) upstream from the junction of Tideswell Dale and Millers Dale, on the east side of the footpath.

A small bedding cave enlarged by mining. Ends at a small chamber on a mineral vein. Continuation is too tight. Acts as a resurgence in wet weather.

*References: Gill, D.W. 1974. British Caver Vol.62. p.48.*

## WARDLOW CRAWL CAVE
NGR 178 755  Grade: 1
Alt. 810ft (247m)
Length: 10ft (3m)

Situated on the right hand corner of a small terrace just above dale floor level, 410ft (125m) down dale from Wardlow Mires Swallet, on the north west side.

Dug out entrance to 10ft (3m) long flat out crawl blocked by stalagmite. Water can be heard flowing beyond in wet weather when the nearby swallets become resurgences.

*References: Bridger, R. 1978. D.C.A. N/L No.38.*

## WARDLOW MIRES SWALLET
NGR 1791 7557  Dig
Alt. 775ft (236m)

A few yards south of the A623 Peak Forest to Stoney Middleton road, in the valley floor at the head of Cressbrook Dale.

A stream flowing from the shales is culverted under the road, and sinks in an obvious depression. In wet weather, the swallet continues to take water until the water table rises above the valley floor, and the swallet and nearby depressions become powerful resurgences. In flood conditions the volume of water rising here and at several places along the north west bank further down the valley may be very large. The water sinking in dry weather is thought to flow to Watergrove Mine. Several depressions have been dug in the past, but have become too tight so far.

*References: Beck, J.S. 1978. Bull. P.D.M.H.S. Vol.7. No.2. pp.106-115.*

## WARDLOW SOUGH
NGR 174 748
Grade: 3 (Mine)
Alt. 720ft (219m)
Length: 1200ft (366m)

On the east side of Cressbrook Dale at the base of a line of shaft hillocks running diagonally up the hillside.

A timbered passage (now collapsed) under a shaft mound (now partly backfilled for safety) led into the sough, which could be followed past two filled shafts to surface, and a large shaft which was climbed for approx. 130ft (40m) to a level through toadstone and some small natural cavities. The sough continued to a complete collapse 950ft (290m) from the tail. A large volume of water issues in wet weather.

*References: Beck, J.S. 1978. Bull. P.D.M.H.S. Vol.7. No.2. pp.113-114.*

## WATERGROVE MINE
NGR 189 759
Grade: Mine
Alt. 800ft (240m)
Depth: 350ft (107m)

A group of shafts on the east side of the Wardlow Basin around Housley.

The Fairburn Engine Shaft is 350ft (107m) deep, with the sough crosscut at 150ft (46m). The crosscut leads to the Forefield Shaft, from where the Watergrove Pipe was explored for some 300ft (91m) in the 1976 drought. The sough is accessible for some distance in dry weather, passing various other shafts. Other workings have been entered in dry weather, but the whole complex is normally submerged. The workings are used as a water supply to Cavendish fluorspar mill, pumping taking place from the Fairburn Engine Shaft. The sough tail lies west of the sharp bend in Stoney Middleton Dale, and is described in the Stoney Middleton chapter.

*References: Beck, J.S. 1975. Trans. B.C.R.A. Vol.2. No.1. p.8.*
*Beck, J.S. 1978. Bull. P.D.M.H.S. Vol.7. No.2. pp. 106-115.*

## WATERSAW SWALLETS
NGR 1925 7337 & 1928 7338
Lost
Alt. 1100ft (335m)
Depth: 12ft (4m)

In shallow valley north of the opencast workings on Watersaw Rake.

Two sinkholes which took water from the peat cover were excavated to a depth of 12ft (4m). They were obliterated when the adit to Watersaw Mine was driven.

*References: Beck, J.S. 1975. Trans B.C.R.A. Vol.2. No.1. p.8.*

## Features listed as potential archaeological sites

1: NGR 1244 7307   Alt: 203m   A large, long, high rock shelter along Chee Dale.
2: NGR 1237 7335   Alt: 225m   A very long, high rock shelter in Chee Dale.
3: NGR 1229 7327   Alt: 221m   A cave formed by collapse.
4: NGR 1224 7334   Alt: 220m   Long, deep rock shelter.
5: NGR 1209 7361   Alt: 206m   A small cave in a secluded dale. A low crawl entrance goes back 2.10m.
6: NGR 1199 7364   Alt: 235m   An open fissure not visible from the path with a cave dropping away to the back. Used by Badgers.
7: NGR 1411 7341   Alt: 215m   A collapsed rock shelter.
8: NGR 1373 7356   Alt: 230m   An obvious rock shelter high in Monks Dale.
9: NGR 1378 7361   Alt: 246m   A small rock shelter.
10: NGR 1336 7507  Alt: 264m   A low bedding cave used by badgers.
11: NGR 1340 7506  Alt: 252m   A low cave used by badgers.
12: NGR 1736 7381  Alt: 285m   A deep rock arch.
13: NGR 1325 7271  Alt: 257m   Large rock shelter above Blackwell Dale Road.

# GLOSSARY

**ADIT.** A level or sloping entrance to a mine, sometimes used for drainage.

**ANASTOMOSIS.** A random distribution of tubular channels of various sizes in bedding planes, also called spongework.

**ARAGONITE.** An unusual crystalline form of calcium carbonate.

**AVEN.** A vertical extension up from a passage, not breaking through to the surface, but sometimes leading to passages at higher levels.

**BEDDING PLANE.** The parting between two beds of rock, often enlarged to give a wide low cave penetrable by flat-out crawling.

**BELAY.** Point used for anchoring a ladder or rope, or a lifeline operator. **TO BELAY**: to attach the rope or ladder. **BELAY ROPE**: a short length used for anchoring.

**BOULDER CHOKE.** A mass of boulders blocking progress in a passage.

**CALCITE.** The commonest crystalline form of calcium carbonate; the chief constituent of limestone and stalactites.

**CAVE.** A natural underground cavity or passage. The term is often restricted to those cavities not requiring tackle for exploration.

**CAVE PEARLS.** Small unattached concretions of stalactitic calcite usually formed in pools round nuclei of rock. Clusters of pearls in a pool are often called "nests".

**CAVERN.** Usually restricted to large chambers in caves or to large cave systems.

**CHAMBER.** A relatively large part of a cave.

**CHERT.** A cryptocrystalline form of silica found as nodules, etc., in limestones and often weathered out as projections from walls or forming pebbles on the floors of caves.

**CHIMNEY.** An ascending or descending shaft which is climbable by back and knee method.

**COFFIN LEVEL.** A horizontal passage in a mine with a cross-section like a coffin and usually dating from before explosives were widely used.

**CRAWL.** Any passage which has to be traversed on hands and knees or lower, i.e., lying flat out. Often necessary to reverse out, a very tiring procedure.

**CURTAIN.** Either a rock barrier nearly to the floor of a passage necessitating crawling OR a thin elongated dripstone (stalactite) formation on walls or roof.

**DEADS.** Stacked boulders, usually mine debris, at the side of a passage. Often "supported" by wood of unknown age and dangerously unstable.

**DOG TOOTH SPAR.** A pointed form of calcite crystals.

**DOLOMITE.** A mineral composed of carbonate of calcium and magnesium. Or a rock chiefly composed of that material.

**DRIPSTONE.** A general term to cover formations deposited by dripping water, i.e. stalactites and stalagmites, etc.

**DUCK.** A short water-filled passage necessitating complete immersion. Usually restricted to those with a little air-space.

**EFFLUENT CAVE.** A cave from which water flows out.

**ERRATICS.** Boulders transported by ice action.

**FAULT.** A fracture in rocks causing relative displacement of the two sides either vertically or horizontally. Fault-surfaces are often marked by grooving known as "slickensides".

**FISSURE.** A natural narrow but relatively high passage, often in a joint or fault, but the term does not necessarily signify displacement.

**FLOWSTONE.** Stalactite or stalagmite formation deposited as a sheet on walls or floors, usually from a film of gently moving water.

**FORMATION.** Either a group of strata bearing a name, OR any kind of mineral deposit in a cave, such as stalactites, gypsum, clay, etc.

**GINGING.** The "dry" stone walling supporting the loose ground round the top of a mine shaft. Often unstable and best avoided.

**GOUR** A pool rimmed by deposited calcite, usually in association with stalagmites. Also called a "rimstone pool".

**GROTTO.** A cave or chamber well-decorated with stalactites.

**HELICTITE.** A stalactitic formation of calcite, aragonite, or gypsum, which does not grow vertically, and which may branch. Often wrongly known as "erratics" (qv).

**JOINT.** Natural fractures of rock strata without displacement. Often perpendicular to bedding.

**KARABINER.** A metal snap-link used for attachment to a rope, ladder or belay.

**LEVEL.** A horizontal passage in a mine, sometimes the entrance.

**LIFELINE.** A strong safety rope attached to anyone negotiating difficult obstacles or climbing ladders, etc., paid out and kept taut by a lifeliner.

**LIMESTONE.** A rock composed of more than 50 per cent calcium carbonate, the remainder being sand, clay, shale, dolomite, chert, etc., etc. Dolomised limestone has been altered by the introduction of magnesium after deposition. Reef limestones differ in bedding and jointing characters from most other limestones, and there is some evidence in Derbyshire that they contain more caves.

**MASTER-CAVE.** A rather hypothetical concept of a "main drain" cave of large proportions which takes all the drainage from an area via many tributaries. Only the Peak - Speedwell Cavern system approaches this concept in Derbyshire.

**MOON-MILK.** A colloidal form of calcium carbonate, believed to be deposited by bacterial action and usually found near entrances.

**OX-BOW.** An abandoned stream meander passage, sometimes providing a dry by-pass to a wet section.

**PHREATIC.** Used to describe a cave or a feature in a cave formed by solution below the water-table, usually characterised by a lack of small scallops indicating the direction of flow.

**PIPE-VEIN.** A mineral vein elongated along the bedding.

**PITCH.** A vertical or near vertical-descent usually requiring tackle.

**PITON.** A metal spike or peg driven into the rock for a belay.

**POT.** A vertical natural shaft entered at the top (the same shaft could be an aven entered from below).

**POTHOLE.** A vertical pitch open to the surface, or a cave system dominated by vertical descents requiring tackle, OR a hollow in a stream bed worn out by stones swirling in the water, also called a "rock mill".

**RAKE.** A large mineral vein whose workings can often be traced across country for a mile or more. Usually near vertical.

**RESURGENCE.** The re-appearance of an underground stream at the surface whose source is known.

**RISING.** The appearance of a stream on the surface whose source is unknown.

**RIFT.** Strictly should apply only to chambers opened by faulting but often applied to any large chamber elongated in the vertical plane.

**RIMSTONE.** Calcite deposited round the edge of a pool.

**RUCKLE.** A jumble of large boulders, sometimes large enough to be penetrated by crawling between them.

**SCALLOPS.** Current-marking or faceting of rock due to turbulent water flow.

**SHAFT.** A vertical entrance or extension to mine, sometimes used for mine-like pots in caves.

**SHACK, SHAKE** or **SHAKEHOLE.** A depression in the ground surface due to the collapse of a cave beneath.

**SINK** or **SINKHOLE.** Any place where water disappears underground or has done so in the past.

**SIPHON.** A term often used incorrectly for a trap or sump, but which should strictly apply only to those with siphon action as evidenced by ebbing and flowing.

**SLICKENSIDES.** Polished, striated or grooved surface of a fault plane.

**SOUGH.** A mine drainage level, sometimes providing the entrance to a mine or cave.

**SPELEOLOGY.** The scientific study of caves.

**SQUEEZE.** A narrow part of a cave passable only with effort. Careful consideration of the return is often necessary.

**STALACTITE.** A cave formation, usually of calcite, hanging from the roof.

**STRAW-STALACTITE.** A stalactite of straw-like dimensions, and hollow.

**STALAGMITE.** A cave formation building up from the floor, usually calcite. Other forms must be specified.

**STEMPLE.** A wooden bar set between notches in the rock walls for miners' climbing purposes, often one of a series forming a ladder. Sometimes later used as a support for stacked deads. Usually rotten and not to be trusted.

**SUMP** or **TRAP.** A submerged passage, sometimes passable by diving. A "sump" in a mine may refer to any short underground shaft.

**SWALLET** or **SWALLOW.** Any hole taking a stream underground from the surface, or in a mine a natural hole draining the workings.

**TACKLE.** Equipment needed for descending a cave or pothole, i.e., ladders, ropes etc.

**TETHER.** A belay, or to belay.

**TRAP.** A short sump which can be passed by diving.

**TRAVERSE.** A climb along ledges, etc., above the floor of a passage or pothole.

**TUBE.** A small passage of nearly circular cross-section. A roof-tube is the upper half of a tube left by downward erosion of the floor.

**VADOSE.** Used to describe a cave or part of a cave formed by freely running water above or at the water-table.

**WATER-TABLE.** The surface of the zone of permanent saturation. It may fluctuate with weather and seasons. A perched water-table is held above the usual height by a local barrier to downward percolation.

**WAYBOARD.** A thin clay occupying a bedding plane in the limestone sequence. Often forms a barrier to downward percolation of water, and often contains iron pyrites, which decomposes to acid, thus contributing to enlargement of the cave below the wayboard.

Exploring Bagshawe Cavern; from a late 19th Century print

*Caves of the Peak District*
ISBN: 978-0-9563473-2-9
Compiled by Iain Barker and John Beck
Derbyshire Caving Association

Design, Layout and Artwork by
Peter J Miles
Hucklow Publishing
Ash House, Great Hucklow
Derbyshire SK17 8RF

Printed by
Northend Creative Print Solutions
Clyde Road
Sheffield S8 0TZ